RATIONAL ANCESTORS

Scientific Rationality
and
African Indigenous Religions

by

James L Cox

Including field descriptions of
Zimbabwean myths and rituals
by University of Zimbabwe Students

REFERENCE

Religions of Africa
a series of the
African Association for the Study of Religions

Editors
Jacob K. Olupona and David Westerlund

Editorial Advisory Board
Ulrich Berner, Louis Brenner, Rosalind Hackett,
Jocelyn Hellig, Isaria Kimambo, Penda Mbow, V. Y. Mudimbe,
Jan Platvoet, Martin Prozesky and Benjamin Ray

1. Jan Platvoet, James Cox and Jacob Olupona (eds), *The Study of Religions in Africa: Past, Present and Prospects*. Cambridge: Roots and Branches, 1996.

2. Simeon O. Ilesanmi, *Religious Pluralism and the Nigerian State*. Athens, Ohio: Ohio University Press, 1997.

3. James Cox, *Rational Ancestors: Scientific Rationality and African Indigenous Religions*. Cardiff: Cardiff Academic Press, 1998.

Religions of Africa covers all forms of religion found in Africa. Works on religions of African origin in other parts of the world may also be included. The series is open not only to scholars of religion but also to other academics who write on African religions. For further information, please contact Professor Jacob K. Olupona, African American and African Studies Program, University of California, Davis, CA 95616, USA or Associate Professor David Westerlund, History of Religions, Faculty of Theology, Uppsala University, Box 1604, S-75146 Uppsala, Sweden.

ISSN 1026-9355

To Chief Miclot Chingoma
in appreciation

Cardiff Academic Press
St Fagans Road, Fairwater, Cardiff CF5 3AE

British Library Cataloguing in Publication Data

A catalogue record for this book is available from
the British Library.

ISBN 1899025-081

Printed & Bound in Great Britain by
Antony Rowe Ltd.

Cover design by Mike White

Typeset by Pagecraft, Cardiff

Published in Great Britain by
Cardiff Academic Press
St Fagans Road, Fairwater, Cardiff CF5 3AE
1998

TABLE OF CONTENTS

PART TWO

THE MYTHOLOGUMENA

Stories of Origins

1. Mountains, Rain and the World As We Know It

2. Settling of a People in a Land

3. Totems and Animals

4. Death

Socio-Moral Stories

Stories of Mysterious Occurrences

PART THREE

THE RITUALS

Rituals Honouring Ancestors

Rituals of Communication with the Ancestors

Rites of Passage

A Special Ritual of Protection

Acknowledgements

I wish to express my deepest gratitude to the students within the Department of Religious Studies, Classics and Philosophy in the University of Zimbabwe who conducted a good portion of the field research on which much of the theory and method expressed in this book are based. These students, mainly from my Phenomenology of Religion courses in 1991 and 1992, have now completed their first degrees and most of them are employed in various jobs throughout Zimbabwe, many of them teaching in rural areas. I hope that this book will reward their hard research work and their patience in waiting for its publication. I am profoundly grateful to the students for giving me permission to use and to edit their original essays.

I am also deeply indebted to Chief Chingoma for his support in enabling my personal research to go forward in the Mberengwa Region of southcentral Zimbabwe. The Chief assisted me in attending rituals and obtaining interviews in 1992 and 1995. I am also grateful to the chief's son, Douglas Dziva, for accompanying me on my research trips, acting as my interpreter, and engaging me in meaningful discussion as I sought to understand both my ritual observations and my interview responses.

I have edited the field material comprising Parts Two and Three of this book for English usage and clarity of expression. However, wherever possible, I have attempted to retain the original language of each student. I acknowledge with thanks the assistance of Douglas Dziva and Dr. Tabona Shoko, lecturer in African Traditional Religions in the University of Zimbabwe, who reviewed and corrected the Shona and Ndebele portions of the texts. Dr. Shoko also translated some Shona verses quoted in the stories and made helpful comments on the organisation of the oral literature.

My appreciation is also due to the Department of Religious Studies, Classics and Philosophy in the University of Zimbabwe for its encouragement in this research and to the Centre for the Study of Christianity in the Non-Western World in the University of Edinburgh and its former and current Directors, Prof A. F. Walls and Prof. David Kerr, who gave me permission and time to pursue further research in

Zimbabwe and to complete the manuscript in 1995 and 1996. I acknowledge with gratitude the African Christianity Project within the Centre in Edinburgh, funded by the Pew Charitable Trusts, which facilitated me, as Coordinator of the Project, to spend time in southern Africa combining research with my other administrative and teaching duties.

I wish to thank the African Association for the Study of Religions and its editors, David Westerlund and Jacob Olupona, for reviewing the text and making helpful suggestions to improve its presentation. With the kind cooperation of Mr R. G. Drake, Managing Editor of the Cardiff Academic Press, I am pleased that this work forms a part of the 'Religions of Africa' Series.

Finally, I want to thank Mike White for designing the cover of this book.

Edinburgh
1998

Preface

When I originally conceived this book, I envisaged that it would comprise almost entirely a collection of selected myths and rituals provided by my Phenomenology of Religion students in the University of Zimbabwe. I understood my role primarily as one who would edit, organise and facilitate the distribution of the field material. I intended to write a short introduction explaining the context, background and setting for the contents of the book.

I also believed originally that this book would serve as a companion to my *Expressing the Sacred: An Introduction to the Phenomenology of Religion*, first published in 1992 by the University of Zimbabwe and now in its second printing. My aim was to provide subsequent students not only with an introductory text on the phenomenological method, achieved by *Expressing the Sacred*, but with a collection of data which could be used in the classroom for the application of the method.

These original objectives still obtain, but as I reviewed the literature in this field, I began to feel strongly that a deeper and more thorough exploration of methodological issues was required than could be done in an introductory book limited largely to explaining and interpreting somewhat strictly the phenomenological method in the study of religions. Specifically, I saw a need to focus on three main areas.

First, the whole field of myth and ritual theory needed a fuller explanation than I could provide in an introductory textbook. I thus have pursued in this work, not only a review of interpretations of myth and ritual in religious studies literature, but a critical analysis leading to my own suggestions for a reinterpretation of the relationships between these two identifiable, but in my current thinking, independent religious typologies.

Second, I needed to focus the discussion directly on Africa. In this regard, I have examined myth and ritual theory in Africa and then based my own analyses largely, although not exclusively, on the material provided by my students. From these investigations, I have suggested a theory of myth and ritual aimed at enhancing our capacity to understand indigenous religious expressions in Africa.

Third, I have become increasingly aware of the problems entailed in classical phenomenological approaches to the study of religions. For this reason, after analysing myth and ritual theory, I construct a scientific methodology which in my view goes beyond, without contradicting, the phenomenological categories of *epoché* and empathetic interpolation to achieve a more advanced type of understanding of African indigenous religions than is implied solely by the phenomenologist's eidetic intuition.

My theoretical discussions in this book will demonstrate, I believe, that religious studies scholarship now commonly acknowledges the inherent limitations within the phenomenological method. Nevertheless, I contend that we can still use phenomenology to deepen our awareness of the problems entailed in achieving an understanding of religious traditions of which we are not a part without at the same time necessarily accepting all of its conclusions. My proposals in this book regarding theory and method in the study of African indigenous religions represent my effort at taking the next steps beyond classical phenomenology.

Following my theoretical and methodological investigations in part one of this volume, I have compiled and edited the stories and ritual observations produced in 1991 and 1992 by my Phenomenology of Religion students. These appear in parts two and three under the headings, 'The Mythologumena' and 'The Rituals'. I explain the background to this research in chapter one. I simply want to note here that I have obtained the permission from the students to use these materials in such a publication and I list the name of each student researcher whenever his or her work is cited. Wherever possible, I have also noted the region in Zimbabwe from which the data was obtained.

Parts two and three, therefore, are very much in line with my original aim of providing a rich descriptive source for the oral traditions and ritual practices found within the indigenous religions of Zimbabwe. I hope, however, that I have served through this writing the further critical functions of clarifying and advancing the discussions surrounding theoretical problems relevant to methods in religious studies research in Africa.

Part One

THEORY AND METHOD

Chapter One

SETTING THE SCENE

This book is divided into three parts. Part one contains my own analyses and application of theories relevant to the study of religions based largely on field data obtained by my Phenomenology of Religion students in the University of Zimbabwe. Parts two and three are comprised of my edited versions of the students' descriptions. My own contribution demonstrates a primary concern with methodology, defined by David Krieger (1991, 2-3) from its original Greek usage as a 'pursuit' of knowledge. In contemporary philosophy, Krieger notes, the term has come to designate 'a systematic procedure, technique, or mode of inquiry'. A method thus clearly and precisely illuminates a pathway for understanding in a scientific manner. This means that it can be applied by anyone following the stages outlined and its effectiveness can be tested empirically.

In part one of this book, I am seeking to identify a methodology aimed at producing an understanding of specific religious communities. My main focus is on the indigenous religions of Zimbabwe and how they can be understood using the methodology I eventually outline and exemplify. In many instances, my discussions are applicable more broadly to indigenous religions in Africa, such as in my analyses of oral literature and ritual re-enactments. In the end, because I am developing a methodology, my systematic approach should pertain to the study of religious communities generally.

I have selected issues in this book which have presented particular problems in the understanding of indigenous religions in Africa. I begin in chapter two by posing the preliminary, but critical, problem of terminology. I contend that the underlying presuppositions which scholars have employed generally when classifying the religions of indigenous peoples around the world tend to distort the capacity for researchers to understand them scientifically.

I then move in chapters three and four to raise the specific problems found throughout much of Africa related to theories of myths and rituals. I endeavour to show how the definitions of myths and rituals obtained largely from archaic religions or from secondary and frequently elicited sources lack support not only in the field material I

1

have utilised but in the findings of many scholars studying African religions. When data contradict accepted theories, explanations are required and, at times, new theories need to be developed. This is what I have proposed in the light of the apparent deficiencies in the interpretations commonly offered about myths and their ritual re-enactments in Africa.

My revised theory of myth and ritual, as outlined in chapter six, is particularly important for delineating a methodology for understanding because I continue to maintain that myths, which following Raimundo Panikkar (1979, 101) I rename mythologumena, and rituals provide the primary sources for seeing into the meaning of any religion. Prior to offering my own approach for reinterpreting myth and ritual, therefore, I examine in chapter five what it means to understand a religion. This requires me to enter into the current debate in religious studies concerning understanding from the inside, the autonomy of religion, and the irreducibility of religious understanding to other interpretive approaches.

I have written in other places (1993, 1994) about the methodology I describe, which again following Panikkar (1979, 9-10), is termed diatopical hermeneutics or, in the words of David Krieger (1991, 51-54), a methodological conversion. I have never attempted, however, to put the methodology into practice. In chapter seven, therefore, I engage my own confession, faith in the autonomy of reason, in diatopical hermeneutics with the faith of the indigenous Zimbabwean described earlier as focused mainly on ancestors. Through this systematic process, I endeavour to elucidate a new horizon of understanding based on an interaction between reason and the indigenous religions of Zimbabwe. I contend, moreover, that this method can be applied in other settings to attain a scientific understanding of any religion, the implications of which I explore in chapter eight.

Obtaining the Field Data

As I noted above, the myths and rituals which comprise most of the field material for my analyses in part one of this book, and which are presented in parts two and three, were obtained by Phenomenology of Religion students in their first year at the University of Zimbabwe, with the exception of two rituals provided by third and fourth year students in the Studies in World Religions course. The myths were obtained entirely by students enrolled in the 1992 first year course, whereas the ritual descriptions were undertaken by students in June and July of 1991.

Prior to engaging in their fieldwork assignments, the students had received a term of lectures and readings on the history and implementation of the phenomenological method in the study of religion. They had been introduced also to phenomenological typologies and in particular to the principal theories of myths and rituals as I describe them in the first parts of chapters three and four of this book.

Those whose assignment was to obtain myths were instructed to obtain permission to interview one of the oldest people in their home villages. After explaining the purpose of the interview, they were to ask the person to recount a traditional story that he or she remembered hearing as a child. The elders were not told what type of story to select,

2

but they were asked to try to remember one which they regarded as representing their cultural traditions.

Those who observed rituals were given a somewhat different assignment. They were instructed to observe a traditional African ritual of their choice using the phenomenological method. They were to take particular care to suspend their personal judgements, to write descriptions of the rituals as objectively as possible, and then to record the feelings they experienced during the ritual.

The main purpose of this assignment was to give the students practical experience by helping them understand the importance of seeking, and yet the extreme difficulty in producing, value-free descriptions of religious phenomena. Many of the students found it extremely perplexing to try to separate their roles as observers and participants in the rituals. In itself, this proved to be an important learning experience for them. Moreover, it was clear from their introduction to the descriptions that for many students this was the first traditional African ritual they had ever observed.

Except in a few cases where I think it would interfere with the integrity of the descriptions, I have removed the personal comments of students from the ritual accounts in this book. Although these are interesting in themselves, often they are of a confidential nature and, for the purposes of this book, they would divert me from my principal aim of using the material as a descriptive base on which to build my analyses. That the students were particularly alert to their own feelings, potential biases and use of descriptive terminology, however, in my view, has made their accounts more reliable than they might otherwise have been.

For the convenience of the reader, I have grouped the field descriptions in parts two and three into categories based on their main content or intention. I have clustered what I call the 'mythologumena' (the telling of the myths) into stories of origins, socio-moral stories, and tales of mysterious occurrences. I have classified the rituals as those which honour ancestors, those which effect communication with ancestors, those largely falling into what generally are labelled rites of passage, and one which I call a special ritual to protect the family from an avenging spirit.

These classifications are based loosely on my discussions of myths and rituals in chapters three and four, but they should not be regarded as rigidly delineating the stories or rituals within fixed boundaries. For example, many socio-moral stories can be related to origins of certain norms, beliefs or quasi-historical accounts and most origin stories contain moral implications and may refer to mysterious occurrences. In the case of rituals, it is clear, for example, that ceremonies honouring ancestors frequently include spirit possession and thus initiate communication with the ancestors.

The reader will note also that certain stories carry quite similar themes, such as those describing the origin of death or those referring to a foolish woman. I deliberately have included a number of versions of the same story in order that the different accounts can be compared for content and in the light of the diverse locations from which they were derived.

The same rationale applies to ritual descriptions. By far, the ritual that was most commonly observed by my students describes the ceremony, called *kurova guva* among many Shona speaking peoples of Zimbabwe, which brings the spirit of the deceased back to the homestead about one year after the death to be made an ancestor with the responsibilities of protecting and guarding the family. I have selected a number of these descriptions to show both differences and similarities in their practice but particularly to demonstrate the variations which occur within different regions of Zimbabwe.

Other references to field data to which I refer in part one were obtained by me on two trips to Chief Chingoma's area near Mberengwa in southcentral Zimbabwe, the first in March 1992 and the second in August 1995. On both occasions, I was assisted by the Chief's son, Douglas Dziva, who in 1992 was my MA student in the University of Zimbabwe and by 1995 was a PhD student in the Department of Religious Studies in the University of Natal, Pietermaritzburg, South Africa. Mr. Dziva and the Chief facilitated my observations of several rituals featuring spirit possession and assisted me in obtaining numerous interviews with mediums, elders, headmen and religious specialists. I refer to these principally in chapters five and eight and also in many of the examples I use below when I explain the stages in the phenomenological method.

A Summary of the Stages in the Phenomenological Method
I devoted the first term of both my Phenomenology of Religion and Studies in World Religions courses to methodological issues. All of the students were instructed in a systematic organisation of the phenomenological method as outlined in my book *Expressing the Sacred: An Introduction to the Phenomenology of Religion* (1996). I have summarised these steps briefly below to clarify the background to the students' descriptions, but for a fuller outline of each stage, I refer the reader to my text.

The students were informed that in my summary of the stages I did not follow a historical approach outlining developments in the method. For this they were advised to consult Eric Sharpe's *Comparative Religion: A History* (1986). I chose rather to present the method in a step-by-step format based on the writings of some leading twentieth-century phenomenologists.

The students were warned, moreover, against regarding the stages as defining how every phenomenologist would choose to employ the method. As such, they do not constitute *the* steps in the phenomenological method in any absolute sense. I presented the components of the method in lectures in this format to assist students in applying the method practically and in understanding it systematically. I issue the same warning in this chapter asking the reader to note that I have sought to describe accurately the key concepts employed by phenomenologists of religion, but my summary should be taken as explaining the background to the students' research rather than as prescribing without qualification how religious studies research ought to be undertaken.

Stage 1. Performing *epoché*. The first step in the phenomenological method adopts a term from philosophical phenomenology called *epoché*.

4

Literally, it means to hold back judgements or to suspend one's own personal convictions or ideas about any field of investigation. The philosopher Jean-Francois Lyotard (1991, 47) refers to this as observers putting their assumptions about the external world, including its existence, 'out of play, out of circulation, between parentheses'. This is done in order that the phenomena which strike one's consciousness may be experienced in ways which are liberated from prejudgements about their essential form or character.

Students of religions employ the method to rid themselves of obvious biases concerning the truth or the value of the practices they are observing. For example, when I observed a *mutoro* ritual (one of the Shona words referring to a ritual appeal to the ancestors for rain) in the Mberengwa region during the latter part of the drought of 1992, I sought to put aside my own Western scientific presuppositions as to how rain is produced in order that I could discern the views of the participants. As a believer in scientific rationality, I am convinced that rain occurs strictly as a result of atmospheric conditions which cannot be influenced by petitions to supernatural forces. According to the phenomenological method, however, if I am to achieve understanding of what religious people believe and do, I must bracket out my own viewpoint about how rain is produced and seek to perceive the world as the religious adherents do. When applied to religious research, therefore, *epoché* means that subjective observers suspend temporarily their own personal or academic presuppositions about the nature of reality in order that they can appreciate the perspectives of the people they are observing.

Stage 2. Performing empathetic interpolation. Once *epoché* has been accomplished, observers seek to enter empathetically into the religious experience of the adherents they are studying. They cultivate a feeling for what is occurring no matter how strange, bizarre, or alien it may seem. Empathy thus requires that observers endeavour to understand what it would be to experience the world the way the religious practitioners do. In this sense, *epoché* and empathy are closely related: the suspension of personal judgements is undertaken in order that an empathetic attitude may be employed.

Because empathy can never be achieved completely if one is not actually a believer, interpolation is required. This means that what seems strange or foreign needs to be inserted or fit into one's own experience in order to achieve understanding of it. For example, in a scientific age, I consider the widespread Shona belief that some people are able to learn and practise a mysterious craft in order to inflict illness, misfortune and death on innocent people, not only strange or bizarre, but inimical to my own humanistic values. Those who practise this craft are called *varoyi* in Shona or witches in English. Because I hold strong attitudes against this belief, I find it extremely difficult to suspend my judgements about it and regard it empathetically. I can overcome this difficulty in part only if I interpolate the phenomenon of so-called witchcraft into my own experience. I do this by admitting that in my own efforts to understand life I seek an explanation for the existence of injustice in the world. How can I, for example, explain the atrocities of Hitler against the Jewish people from 1939 to 1945 or comprehend that the United States government ordered the killing and maiming of thousands of innocent people in Japan by dropping the atomic bomb on Hiroshima and Nagasaki? When I am faced with the appalling behaviour of one group of people against another, I seek explanations, such as, because humans are free (a desirable condition), they possess the capacity to inflict harm as well as benefit to other humans. Or, to make the issue more personal, my immediate reaction when a member of my own family becomes ill is to ask, 'Why did this have to happen to one I love so much?' I might even ask, 'What have I or my loved one done to deserve this?'

When I look for explanations for what I regard as examples of genuinely evil behaviour in the world or when I appeal against the injustice of innocent suffering, I am acting similarly to indigenous Africans when they seek to explain illness, drought, or injustice by referring to those who possess dangerous powers to inflict evil. This recognition, accompanied by *epoché*, enables me to interpolate into my own experience what otherwise might seem incomprehensible.

The purpose of *epoché* and empathetic interpolation is to provide researchers with a clear method for entering into the religious experience of those they are seeking to understand. By bracketing out their own assumptions about reality and adopting an empathetic approach to the religion they are studying, scholars are able to achieve an 'inside' perspective on a religion, without which they would always remain 'outside' and hence prove incapable of understanding the object of their study in a genuinely scientific sense, i.e. as the religion is in itself.

Stage 3. Maintaining epoché. To attain empathy for a religious tradition other than one's own, according to the method, is not equivalent to converting to the religion under study. Although observers seek to enter into the experiences of believers, they do not adopt (other than in a methodological sense) the actual beliefs of the adherents. Observers continue to suspend judgements about the truth or reality of what is actually occurring in the experiences of religious people.

If they do not do this, they cease to describe the activities of a religious community and produce instead expressions of theological opinion. From the phenomenological point of view, this blocks understanding of the meaning of the phenomena. For example, if I become a believer in the power of *varoyi*, I will no longer understand it as part of a universal effort to explain the existence of evil and misfortune in life. Instead, I will begin to take measures to protect myself against the devious plots of those I regard as threats to my personal welfare. I will become so absorbed in the experience that I will not understand what the experience is about. For this reason, observers must maintain *epoché* not only by suspending their own judgements but also by bracketing out the truth claims of the communities they are endeavouring to study.

Stage 4. Describing the Phenomena. The first three stages in the method might be called necessary preliminary steps to describing accurately the religious behaviour of believing communities. In fact, the first three stages are attitudinal positions adopted by the phenomenologist who tries to eliminate his or her own biases by entering into the perspectives of the believers without actually affirming the truth (or the falsehood) of those perspectives. Descriptions can then follow which try to see what is occurring from the inside and which help those who are on the outside to understand.

In the first instance, therefore, descriptions must be filled with details which are capable of being affirmed by the adherents themselves. For example, terms such as 'worshipping' or 'appeasing' the ancestors might distort the phenomena for the practitioner of African indigenous rituals because this is not what the adherent actually thinks is occurring. A ritual of respect or honour to the ancestors, however, may more accurately portray what a believer thinks is happening when, for example, beer is brewed and poured on the ground while certain appeals are made to the ancestors for protection or an alleviation of misfortune.

Descriptions also must present for a reader a picture of what is happening including words spoken, actions taken, gestures used, utensils employed, the environment in which the action occurs, colours and designs on garments or utensils, and music and dance conducted. In other words, descriptions must be overloaded with details which in themselves portray what is happening without distorting the phenomena from the believer's point of view. This is why this stage in the method endeavours to avoid explanations of meanings of the activities and concentrates on descriptive language.

Stage 5. Naming the Phenomena. After describing what actually is observed in detail, the phenomenologist provides names for the activities of the adherents. These names are given in order to facilitate communication and to help build understandings of various types of phenomena. Selecting the names, however, can be risky since what we label an activity might distort what actually is happening or how it is experienced from a believer's perspective.

Words which commonly have been used to describe religious activities and which tend to misconstrue the phenomena are, for example, magic and superstition. To label a practice such as setting pegs around a homestead to ward off witches a magical practice steeped in superstition is to impose biases from the observer's own worldview and thus misses what an adherent thinks is happening. It would be better to call this a ritual with mythic origins and thereby introduce ritual and myth as two essential names under which religious phenomena can be grouped. Other words to avoid are animism, appeasement, ancestor worship, and even witchcraft since these carry connotations which in the end may prove offensive to believers and hence violate the stage of empathetic interpolation.

Following Hall, Pilgrim and Cavanagh (1986), I have suggested that religious phenomena can be named under the classifications of myths, rituals, sacred practitioners, scripture, art, morality, and belief. I have argued that beliefs form a special case since they are found in the other phenomena and thus forge a link between a people and the sacred (1996, 119-33). The point to note in this context, however, is that the words used to name or to group the phenomena of religion should be chosen carefully to avoid prejudicial language so as not to impede the observer's capacity to apprehend the phenomena as they appear.

Stage 6. Describing Interrelationships and Processes. The phenomena which have been classified at stage 5 are all interrelated. Students need to be aware of this in their descriptions of these relationships. Moreover, the phenomena undergo various processes as they interact with historical developments, intellectual advancements, social changes, and other dynamic factors governing a people's environment.

If we take the classification of sacred practitioner as an example, we can see clearly how the phenomenological categories are interrelated. A sacred practitioner often functions in a ritual as a mediator of the transcendent reality and thus forms a central place in ritual activity. The practitioner, moreover, may use symbols which possess mythic origins and which are conveyed in artistic expressions such as dancing or painting. The practitioner may communicate messages which are intended to re-enforce moral values and thus form a part of the ongoing oral tradition. A description of a sacred practitioner, therefore, almost immediately requires the observer to include the categories of ritual, myth, art, morality and scripture. Overarching the whole will be beliefs about the nature of the sacred, the human situation, and ways to resolve problems encountered in the human situation.[1]

What an observer describes, moreover, will always be linked to historical processes and to current social circumstances. For example, when I interviewed the medium who had become possessed during the *mutoro* ritual referred to above, I learned that part of her message related to the traditional role of chiefs in Zimbabwe and how that had been gradually eroding as decision-making had been transferred to Village Councils frequently comprised of political appointees. These changes had occurred since Independence in 1980 resulting in some cases in an erosion of traditional sources of authority. The medium I interviewed believed that the consequences of such changes meant that the ancestors guarding the land had not been honoured sufficiently nor consulted on important matters. The failure to honour and consult the ancestors had produced the drought. It would be impossible to comprehend such an interpretation of current circumstances without understanding how religious beliefs and practices interact dynamically with historical, social, political, and economic processes.

Stage 7. Constructing the Paradigmatic Model. Thus far a student using the phenomenological method would have concentrated on descriptions derived from one tradition. By understanding the categories of the phenomena, however, the observer is able to construct a model which can be used to analyse any religious tradition. Comparisons can be made, for example, between the role and functioning of socio-moral myths in Karanga religion, which is primarily oral, with cosmogonic myths in Vaishnavite Hinduism, which relies on the written Vedic literature. Such comparisons help to build an understanding of the nature of myth in various traditions. The same can be done with any of the categories of the phenomena.

The paradigm, moreover, enables the student to relate various categories of the phenomena with other categories in a comparative way

---

1. One of the best examples of how the phenomena of religion are interrelated in complex ways is found in Pamela and Thomas Blakely's recent descriptions of oratory and song-dance in funeral performances among the BaHemba of eastern Zaire (Blakely and Blakely, 1994, 399-442).

across religious traditions. How myths correlate to rituals in one tradition may be compared with their functioning in other traditions helping to build up a larger picture of these relationships in religion in general. Processes can also be studied such as, for example, the impact of American missionary education on the indigenous Inuit religion of Alaska or the influence of colonial structures on the traditional practices of the Korekore in northern Zimbabwe. In this way, a basic formal structure is developed for the understanding of religious phenomena, although the content of the components of that structure will vary.

The paradigmatic model provides, therefore, a common framework for the study of any one particular religion or aspects of it and for the comparison of religions or aspects of them. The paradigm is based on descriptions, utilises the classifications of the phenomena, and identifies various interrelationships and processes thus leading to an understanding of any specific phenomenon or many phenomena within particular traditions or more generally across a variety of traditions.

Stage 8. The eidetic intuition. By using the paradigmatic model to understand many religious traditions, the phenomenologist endeavours to see into (intuit) the meaning of religion in general. This stage thus aims at discovering the essence (*eidos*) of human religious experience. It uses every prior step in the method to attain the intuition thus employing both attitudinal and descriptive techniques. This implies that the essential meaning proposed must be capable of being affirmed by believers, and at the same time be demonstrated to have resulted from phenomenological descriptions.

Like *epoché*, the concept of the eidetic intuition is rooted in philosophical phenomenology. It was developed early in the twentieth century by the German philosopher Edmund Husserl (1931) as a reaction against the tendency of the empirical science of his day to limit knowledge to that which can be verified strictly by observation and experimentation. Husserl believed that underlying themes can be discerned beneath the facts of experience. By developing an 'eidetic science', or the forms which guide all empirical knowledge, he contended that he had reintroduced the basis for a genuinely scientific method into contemporary science, which in the words of Lyotard had fallen prey to a 'blind concern for experimentation' (1991, 41). This method, according to M. J. Inwood (1995, 384), means that 'the phenomenologist is not concerned...with particular acts of sense-perception, but with the essential features common to all such acts'.

Discerning philosophical essences, nevertheless, must occur at the end of any study thus ensuring a close connection between experimentation and theory. The study of religion also follows this principle. Identifying the essence of religion results from a comprehensive knowledge of the wide variety of human religious experiences among both living and archaic religions. Moreover, since religious experience is dynamic, the eidetic intuition is never final or static. It remains open to change, criticism, adjustment, and re-evaluation as further studies are undertaken and as new events occur. The eidetic intuition in both philosophy and religion, therefore, represents a formal structure for understanding. It is derived from and accountable to the observed facts, but is not comprised strictly of those facts.

9

An example of an eidetic intuition as a formal structure can be found in the writings of Mircea Eliade who identified the meaning of religion with the human preoccupation to apprehend and be near the unknown and unknowable sacred. In his many studies of the world's archaic and living religions, Eliade discovered a common pattern running through them all. In *The Sacred and the Profane* (1959) he notes that for religious people space and time are made sacred by hierophanies, manifestations of the sacred in an otherwise homogeneous (profane) spatial and temporal environment. The intrusion of the sacred into undifferentiated space and time creates centres around which ritual activity occurs and mythical stories are related.

The centre is variously symbolised in the religions, but the hierophanies always provide points of orientation which define cosmic foci for religious communities. An example is the *kaaba* in Mecca, which for Muslims provides not only a spatial orientation for prayer and pilgrimage, but actually represents the *axis mundi*, the centre of the cosmos, above which Allah resides in the highest heaven.

Eliade argued that his description of the structure of religion was applicable universally. He did not thereby create an essential, unchanging and eternal definition of religion removed from empirical investigation, but he provided a formal pattern which helps to interpret all human religious activity. The adequacy of Eliade's interpretation of religion depends on its faithfulness to the data from which the essence is derived and on its confirmation by testing in a variety of settings. This accountability to the data means that Eliade's model not only is capable of scientific verification or falsification, but it ensures that his eidetic intuition will always remain subject to modification (something I try to demonstrate later in my discussion of his theory of myths and rituals).

Stage 9. Testing the intuition. As I have implied in my reference above to Eliade, any statement of the meaning of religion must be capable of being verified or falsified by testing it against the phenomena themselves. The final stage in the phenomenological method, therefore, involves a moving back along the steps toward descriptions of human religious behaviour. It is in the light of the specific descriptions of the phenomena that any observer's statement of the essence can be evaluated.

I will try to show later that when studies from specific religious traditions do not conform to an interpretive model, such as Eliade's, the model itself must be revised, modified or abandoned as inadequate. If a model cannot be tested in this manner, it is not scientific, but metaphysical or theological. The value of phenomenology as a science of religion resides in its ongoing accountability to empirical investigations without reducing meaning to mere facts.

A part of the phenomenological testing process also includes ascertaining the perspectives of believers. As I noted above, even if certain statements could be verified by examining the data, if they could not be affirmed by believers, they cannot provide understanding of the meaning of religion. An obvious example of this is the claim earlier in the twentieth century by the psychoanalyst Sigmund Freud (1961, 19) that religion is an infantile neurosis whereby adults respond to the dangers of human existence in childlike ways by projecting the solution to those dangers onto a divine parent. Even if Freud's theory is supported by field research, his conclusion could never find support from believers and hence would miss the essence of religion itself.

This does not mean that phenomenology utilises the language of believers, nor that it merely reproduces the thoughts and ideas of religious communities. If it did, it could be classified as theology rather than as a science of religion. If we return to Eliade, this will be clear.

No religious community that I know of would describe its religion literally as the manifestation of the sacred into homogeneous space and time creating cosmic symbols, points of orientation and ritual re-enactments of myths. Eliade contends nonetheless that this precisely describes 'the structure of the religious consciousness' (1969, Preface). Therefore, if Eliade's essence of religion were understood by believers, unlike Freud's, it would not be offensive to them, and quite likely, could be affirmed as representing accurately the meaning of their various symbols and actions.

The nine steps described above form a composite picture of the phenomenological approach to the study of religion as it has been developed during this century. Although various scholars have tended to emphasise one aspect of the method over others, my own review (as shown in *Expressing the Sacred*) demonstrates that the components listed above emerge as the most crucial. Taken together, the nine stages not only summarise, incorporate, and interpret the positions of leading phenomenologists but they also present them in a way which can be applied practically within actual field studies.

Limitations to the Method

The stages listed above were presented as a teaching tool to the students prior to their engaging in the field assignments. Students were also instructed in the limitations of the method generally, such as its reliance on particular epistemological assumptions which can be challenged, its tendency to create religious typologies without due consideration to historical, cultural and social influences, and its development historically as a reaction to what it regarded as the tendency within the social sciences to explain religion in ways which disregarded the views of believers (social scientific reductionism).

Moreover, the students were cautioned against taking any specific stage in the method uncritically. They were told that *epoché* represents a fundamental attitude but that researchers cannot fully rid themselves of their scholarly precommitments. Many of our presuppositions are so much a part of our way of thinking that we are not even aware of them. Moreover, the students were urged to acknowledge the limitations of empathy and to note that interpolation itself might encourage distortions of the phenomena. Maintaining *epoché* itself is problematic since many traditions would be offended by a refusal to make a commitment to its truth claims thereby introducing a self-contradiction into a method which seeks understanding from the perspectives of believers.

The students were also told that descriptions can never be truly objective. What is included or excluded, emphasised or minimised, results largely from the discretion of the observer. The active role of the researcher in the descriptions thus must be acknowledged. This is true perhaps even more vividly when one moves toward the stages of creating classifications and noting interrelationships and processes.

Finally, students were made aware that at the levels of the paradigmatic model and the eidetic intuition serious pitfalls are likely to be encountered. Comparative studies can be too loosely undertaken and superficially presented. The eidetic intuition resulting from such studies can degenerate into philosophical essentialism less related to field observations than to the researcher's own ideological perspective.

These warnings were given to students not to discredit the methodology but to emphasise its limitations. Within such restraints, the positive value of endeavouring to employ the attitudinal stages prior to providing descriptions and interpretations of meaning was affirmed.

Positive Results obtained from the Student Field Research

The assignment undertaken by the students obtaining myths and recording ritual observations, in my view, has produced three clearly identifiable benefits. Initially, the accounts of myths and rituals offer a potentially valuable written record for analysing Zimbabwean religious beliefs and practices, as I have sought to do in part one of this book. In so far as the students were able to provide descriptions free from their own value-judgements, the material recorded can be regarded as an accurate account of the indigenous religious practices as they occur in many areas of contemporary Zimbabwe.

A second positive result of these descriptions is methodological. By studying the accounts provided, the student of religion is able to evaluate the phenomenological method by identifying its strengths and weaknesses and noting why qualifications must be placed at each stage in the method. For example, it is clear from the descriptions not only that *epoché* can never be performed completely but that in fact it was not performed perfectly. Separating one's own values from what is actually occurring is not fully possible. Moreover, as I noted above, the accounts demonstrate that phenomena never just 'appear' but must be selected by the observer. This introduces the subjective element into what initially was an effort to describe exactly what was occurring objectively. These factors suggest that the descriptions themselves can help to sharpen and enhance the debate surrounding methodologies in the study of African religions, aspects of which I address in this book.

A third positive result from this exercise is historical. In a day when modernisation is advancing within Zimbabwe and when Western education has been adopted at every level of the society, it is possible that many of the stories told and the rituals described in the near future may cease to constitute a central place in the lives of Zimbabwean citizens. This process of cultural change with its inherent difficulties is explored helpfully in a recent book by the Zimbabwean sociologist, M.F.C. Bourdillon (1993). The possibility of losing knowledge of old traditions is also confirmed by the students themselves, many of whom had never heard the stories related to them before nor witnessed traditional rituals. Many students held strong objections to both, particularly the rituals, on the basis of their Christian faith.

Limitations to My Own Analysis

In chapter seven, as I suggested above, I endeavour to apply the method of diatopical hermeneutics by disclosing my own confession of faith and

12

by entering into the faith of an African indigenous believer. In one sense, this dialogue is artificial because it is based on my own interpretation of the meaning of the African field material rather than from an actual encounter. In another sense, however, this is inevitable methodologically, since the scientific analysis of religious data must be undertaken by the researcher and cannot be expected from the adherents.

Nevertheless, I must admit that the process of obtaining the actual field data either by students or in my own case was not conducted strictly by first disclosing our academic presuppositions to the indigenous Africans and then securing a contract for undertaking the field investigations. The students who acquired the myths were instructed to explain the purpose of the interview and honestly told the elders that by recording their stories the oral traditions of their community could be preserved in part.

The students who recorded the rituals participated in them and thus required permission from the elders prior to doing so. In some cases, the students were considered quite young and were allowed to take part because they explained they were undertaking a project as a component of their course at the University of Zimbabwe. Some students reported that they were allowed to attend the rituals on the condition that they did not speak during them nor interfere in any way.

In my own research in the Mberengwa region, I did explain to the Chief and one of the headmen under him my purposes in wishing to attend the rituals and conduct interviews. By obtaining the assistance of the Chief, doors were opened for me that I believe would otherwise have remained closed. My position in the University of Zimbabwe and the fact that in 1992 I was supervising the MA thesis of the Chief's son also aided me, but I cannot determine to what degree this facilitated an understanding from the leaders of the community of my own research agenda.

In the cases of the students' research and of my own, this lack of precise clarity about forming a mutual contract with the believers in indigenous religions who told the stories or permitted ritual observations represents one of the limitations of this book. I do not think this in any way invalidates the data used for my analyses. It does suggest, however, that further studies in this field need to experiment with an approach that begins with a disclosure by scholars of their own academic assumptions, their scholarly faith, followed by securing a clear understanding and negotiable contract between the parties seeking understanding (the researcher and the community being researched). The aim of this is to produce what Panikkar (1979, 243) calls a 'dialogical dialogue', which he defines as an approach advancing 'along the way to truth by relying on the subjective consistency of the dialogical partners'.

To test the interpretation of meaning I provide in chapter seven, therefore, I would propose that a further mutual, relational stage is needed. I would argue, nevertheless, that although the practical testing of my argument still remains unfinished, the new horizon of understanding I endeavour to disclose based on the field data contained in this book, and the many new horizons which may result from the application of the method I advocate, promise to open the way for developing radically different methodologies in religious studies with results which could alter our understanding of what a scientific approach to the study of religion entails.

References

Blakely, P. A. R. and Blakely, T. D. 1994. 'Ancestors, "witchcraft", and foregrounding the poetic: Men's oratory and women's song-dance in Hemba funerary performance,' in T.D. Blakely, W.E.A. van Beek, and D.L. Thomson (eds.), *Religion in Africa*. London: James Currey and Portsmouth, New Hampshire: Heinemann, 399-442.

Bourdillon, M. F. C. 1993. *Where are the ancestors? Changing culture in Zimbabwe*. Harare: University of Zimbabwe Publications.

Cox, J. L. 1996 2nd ed. *Expressing the sacred: An introduction to the phenomenology of religion*. Harare: University of Zimbabwe Publications.

1993. 'Not a new Bible but a new hermeneutics: An approach from within the science of religion,' in I. Mukonyora, J. L. Cox, and F. J. Verstraelen (eds.), *'Re-writing' the Bible: The real issues*. Gweru: Mambo Press, 103-123.

1994. 'Religious studies by the religious: A discussion of the relationship between theology and the science of religion,' *Journal for the Study of Religion* 7(2), 3-31.

Eliade, M. 1959. *The Sacred and the profane*, Trans. W. Trask. New York: Harcourt, Brace.

1969. *The Quest: History and meaning in religion*. Chicago: University of Chicago Press.

Freud, S. 1961. 'The future of an illusion,' in *The Standard Edition of the Complete Psychological Works of Sigmund Freud: Volume XXI*, Trans. J. Strachey. London: Hogarth, 5-56.

Hall, T., Pilgrim, R. B. and Cavanagh, R. R. 1986. *Religion: An introduction*. San Francisco: Harper and Row.

Husserl, E. 1931. *Ideas: General introduction to pure phenomenology*, Trans. W. R. Boyce Gibson. London: Allen and Unwin.

Inwood, M. J. 1995. 'Husserl, Edmund,' in T. Honderich (ed.), *The Oxford companion to philosophy*. Oxford: Oxford University Press, 382-84.

Krieger, D. 1991. *The new universalism: Foundations for a global theology*. Maryknoll, New York: Orbis Books.

Lyotard, J. F. 1991. *Phenomenology*, Trans. B. Beakley. Albany: State University of New York Press.

Panikkar, R. 1979. *Myth, faith and hermeneutics*. New York: Paulist Press.

Prozesky, M. 1985. *Religion and ultimate well being*. London: Macmillan.

Sharpe, E. 1986. *Comparative religion: a history*. London: Duckworth.

Chapter Two

THE CLASSIFICATION 'PRIMAL RELIGIONS' AS A NON-EMPIRICAL CHRISTIAN THEOLOGICAL CONSTRUCT[1]

Before I discuss myths and rituals and my interpretation of them for achieving an understanding of African religions, I address the preliminary problem of how to classify the religious expressions I am studying. This entails more than the difficulty of settling on an appropriate nomenclature. It introduces a central methodological issue. The terms we use to describe religious phenomena disclose the presuppositions we bring to our research and, in part, help to shape our results.

In this chapter, I will try to show that academic approaches to the study of indigenous religions around the world have sought artificially to identify unifying factors within them under a variety of names. One of the most methodologically ominous of these has been the classification 'primal religions', not only because it portrays indigenous religions as a unit, but because it betrays a Christian evangelistic motive. At the conclusion of this chapter, I will offer my own limited suggestion for how classifications of indigenous religions can be made both realistic and accurate.

Development of the Term 'Primal Religions'

The term 'primal religions' was introduced as an alternative to the classification 'primitive' which was used widely in the academic study of religion through the middle part of this century to describe the religions of peoples with relatively simple subsistence economies, basic technologies, and localised political structures. The concept of a 'primal vision', which was suggested by John V. Taylor as early as 1963 (Taylor, 1963), influenced the development of courses on 'primal religions' in Britain such as those begun by Harold Turner in Aberdeen in the 1970s. In an early publication on this topic, Turner noted that it is important to avoid the expression 'primitive' or 'to replace it by the rather different term "primal"' (Turner, 1971, 7). John B. Taylor, formerly of the World

---

1. This chapter represents a slightly revised form of an article of the same title appearing in *Studies in World Christianity* 2 (1), 1996, 35-56. It is used here with permission of the editors of the journal.

15

Council of Churches, explained that 'primal' had become the preferred term by the mid-1970s within the WCC's Dialogue Unit to 'a whole series of other terms, each of which is unacceptable today: e.g. pre-literate, primitive, pagan, animistic, primordial, native, ethnic, tribal and traditional' (Taylor, 1976, 3-4).

Although the classification 'primal' is commonly used now in teaching and in textbooks on religion in Britain and the United States, some academics still prefer other terms such as pre-literate or non-literate, basic, indigenous, folk, or traditional. Most scholars acknowledge the limitations within any terminology, but in general they accept that if the religious expressions of indigenous peoples are to be discussed academically alongside the 'world' religions such as Hinduism, Buddhism, Taoism, Christianity, Judaism, and Islam, some scheme for classifying them, however inadequate, must be adopted.[2]

As we have just noted in the citations of Turner and Taylor, the choice of the term in this case was motivated in part by the desire to avoid injecting pejorative attitudes into the study of certain types of religious phenomena, thereby overcoming descriptive biases. 'Primitive' generally has been rejected because it carries with it negative connotations concerning the mentality and stage of development of indigenous peoples. On this point, Harold Turner observed, 'It is a great mistake to think that because a tribal society is primitive or poor in scientific knowledge, tools or agricultural methods, it must also be primitive mentally and in its thinking about human life' (Turner, 1971, 7).

In his introduction to primal religions, John Ferguson stated his preference for 'tribal' as a descriptive category because it stresses the local nature of such religions, but he deferred to wider opinion that to speak of 'tribal religions' is 'patronising' (Ferguson, 1982, vii). Andrew Walls, who has headed the department in Aberdeen where primal religions was endorsed as a scientific classification of religious phenomena and who has influenced its use now in the University of Edinburgh,[3] argues that 'primal' has been used 'in the absence of any term which would be more widely acceptable when treating a worldwide phenomenon, not confined to any one region of the world.' He then asks, 'How else are we to bring together the religions of circumpolar peoples, of various peoples of Africa, the Indian sub-continent, South East Asia, North and South America, Australia and the Pacific?' The choice of 'primal religions', moreover, is defended by Walls as avoiding the bias of the term 'primitive' and as overcoming the tendency of Western scientific classifications to employ 'evolutionistic undertones' (Walls, 1987, 252).

Despite Walls' defence of 'primal' as scientific, the term has been criticised by scholars such as Rosalind Shaw as a non-empirical invention of Western academics. As we will see shortly, Shaw rejects the claim made by Walls that primal religions represent a 'worldwide phenomenon' and, in the process, she poses a challenge more broadly to

2. For example, as editor of an introductory text on religion, Robert F. Weir states that the chapter on African religions is about 'African religious traditions, with a focus on common patterns. In view of the diversity of cultures and peoples in Africa, these patterns can only illustrate selected aspects of some religions' (Weir, 1982, 8).

3. James Mackey, Professor of Theology in New College at the University of Edinburgh, has incorporated the term into the title of his article on Celtic religions (Mackey, 1992, 66-84).

the academic community's assumptions concerning the unifying factors inherent among the religious phenomena of indigenous peoples (Shaw, 1990, 339-53).

Beyond the question of the empirical validation of such a term, however, looms a further issue surrounding 'primal' religions. This points toward a theological agenda behind the term. The rejection of 'primitive' as containing an evolutionary bias in favour of Western civilisation and the label 'tribal' as 'patronising' are now well understood. Even the classification 'traditional', which is common in African universities, is recognised by scholars as limited because it implies that the religious practices of indigenous peoples are static, rooted in the past, and thus only historically relevant.

The term 'primal', however, appears to be used not only as a scientific classification but also as a construct employed in Christian theologies of contextualisation. If this use means that it is actually a theological category rather than a scientific one, the term should be removed from the academic study of religion and placed within theology or, at least, acknowledged as an empirically questionable classification which is valuable for theology. Such an admission would prevent an incursion of theology into the science of religion and thereby avoid justifying, in this case, charges levelled by advocates of reductionism such as Robert Segal, Donald Wiebe and Ivan Strenski that the science of religion in its phenomenological form represents a crypto-theology (Segal, 1983, 97-124; Wiebe, 1984, 78-95; Strenski, 1993), an issue to which I will return in chapter five.

Definitions and Characteristics of Primal Religions

The term 'primal religions' is generally defined, in the words of John B. Taylor, as referring to that which is 'basic' or 'fundamental' to all religions and which is observable among 'those forms of society or religion...which are associated with what are commonly called tribal peoples or cultures'. Taylor explains that the term does not suggest that 'these are more...authentic or "true" than other religious systems, but simply that in historical fact they have been widely distributed across all continents' (Taylor, 1976, 3). In his textbook on what he calls African 'Primal' Religions, Robert Cameron Mitchell defines the word 'primal' as connoting 'something basic, fundamental, prior' and adds that the primal religions are 'nonuniversal' and the religions of 'preliterate peoples' (Mitchell, 1977, 98).

Harold Turner, who has played a key role in promoting the use of the term in Britain, defines primal religions as the 'most basic or fundamental religious forms in the overall history of mankind.' Such forms, he argues, 'have preceded and contributed to the other great religious systems.' As such, they are 'both primary and prior; they represent a common religious heritage of humanity' (cited by Shaw, 1990, 341). In line with Turner, Andrew Walls explains that 'primal religions underlie all the other faiths, and often exist in symbiosis with them, continuing (sometimes more, sometimes less transformed) to have an active life within and around cultures and communities influenced by those faiths' (Walls, 1987, 250). This means that such religions possess 'historical anteriority' and that they represent a 'basic, elemental status in human experience' (Walls, 1987, 252).

Philippa Baylis, who has drawn much of the material for her *Introduction to Primal Religions* from the works of Harold Turner, identifies six basic characteristics of primal religions:

1) They cannot be separated from society as a whole. 'Practically every activity, both individual and communal, within a primal society has religious significance'.

2) Each primal religion possesses its own local and hence unique characteristics.

3) Primal religions are tolerant of the religions of other peoples and often borrow and incorporate aspects of them into their own beliefs and practices.

4) In contrast to world religions, which are universal in intent, primal religions are 'ethnocentric and non-missionary by nature'.

5) Primal religions possess no written sources and thus are marked by oral traditions, usually mythical, which are passed on from generation to generation.

6) No creeds or organised statements of belief are found in primal religions (Baylis, 1988, 3).

In his discussion of the primal elements in North American Indian religions, Joseph Eppes Brown adds to Baylis' list two further components: primal religions utilise symbols as conveyors of power and they understand time as cyclical. Brown notes that for primal peoples symbols obtain a special potency through speech or sounds and, particularly in the case of North American Indians, through arts and crafts. Moreover, the primal world view, according to Brown, understands the cyclical nature of time as dynamic, conceived as a process of infinite repeatability, in direct contrast to the Western linear experience of time (Brown, 1984, 394).

Roger Schmidt, who has written an introductory textbook on religion for university students in the United States, includes the same characteristics of primal religions as identified by Baylis and Brown. He specifically emphasises the following points: 1) to be born into primal societies means 'to practice religion' since 'all aspects of existence possess religious significance'; 2) such societies are non-literate thus making the sacred power known through oral traditions 'embodied in aphorisms, poems, and stories' which are 'ritually acted out in dance and song'; 3) because primal religions are so rooted in the kinship and lineage of a particular people, 'they cannot easily be extended beyond the tribal circle'; 4) the local nature of such societies means they do not seek religious converts (Schmidt, 1988, 45-8).

The British missiologist and Christian evangelist David Burnett adds some variations to the characteristics of primal religions noted by Baylis, Brown and Schmidt.

1) Primal religions make no distinction between the natural and the supernatural so that so-called 'natural' objects like trees, stones and mountains may be seen to possess 'supernatural' power.

2) The material world is influenced by immaterial forces conceived of as gods and spirits.

3) Primal world views assume that events in life can be manipulated and controlled by 'signs and rituals'.

4) Humanity is a part of the universe as a whole defining what people do in life in terms of either adding to or detracting from the harmony of the social and natural environment (which are perceived largely as one) (Burnett, 1988, 19-21).

It is clear that Burnett is influenced by early anthropological theories including ideas of 'animism' as presented by E.B. Tylor, 'magic' in J.G. Frazer, and 'taboos' in E. Durkheim. Nevertheless, his emphases on the unity of religion with society, the fundamental role of oral traditions, the central place of rituals, and identification of power as a key element in the cosmic order are consistent with other writers who have characterised the nature of primal religions.

The above definitions and characteristics generally identify what proponents of the study of primal religions regard as the unifying features within culturally, historically, and geographically diverse traditions. No contradiction is seen, as noted in Baylis' list, between the unique content of each local expression of the primal world view and the unifying factors. Baylis argues that 'there are as many primal religions as there are primal societies, each with its own unique history and development.' Such religions are found 'scattered all over the world from the Arctic tundra to the Equatorial rain forest.' Baylis admits that 'ideally each primal religion should be studied in its entirety in terms of its social context'. Nevertheless, as her list of characteristics suggests and in agreement with a long Western academic tradition, she concludes that 'there are sufficient similarities between them to make some valid generalisations possible' (Baylis, 1988, 2).

An Evaluation of the Concept on Empirical Grounds

As I noted above, Rosalind Shaw has criticised not only the concept of 'primal religions' but the widespread acceptance by Western scholars that the religions of indigenous peoples can be treated as a unity. She objects that Western academics have expressed a bias toward religions with written scriptures, organised structures, and identifiable doctrines. This bias, she contends, has created problems for classifying religions which are primarily oral, without central organisations, and with little or no articulated beliefs. In order to accommodate the wide range of religious phenomena which do not fit these formulae, Western academics have invented an artificial structure, usually called traditional religions, which conforms to their own predetermined prescription of the nature of religion (Shaw, 1990, 340-41).

If Shaw is correct, the characteristics cited above by scholars employing the term 'primal religions' have also been invented by Western academics. In the context of her larger critique of the term 'traditional', Shaw, therefore, attacks the assumptions underlying the unifying components in primal religions.

One of the key factors put forward by most academics, including Turner and Baylis, as a criterion for identifying primal religions is that they are non-universal, local religious expressions which possess no missionary or proselytising intent. The first four of Baylis' six characteristics refer to this central trait.

Shaw challenges this criterion by asking what is to be included or excluded when classifying a religion either as 'universal' or 'local'. She responds by citing exceptions to universality in the so-called 'world' religions such as the ethnicity of Judaism after the Christianising of the Roman Empire (Shaw, 1990, 340). One could add to this the case of Hinduism, which most scholars admit cannot be discussed as a unified religion apart from its expression in Indian culture and social structures (Hinnells and Sharpe, 1972: 2). Questions could be put also about the universality of classical Chinese religions such as Taoism or Confucianism, if one standard for universality includes overt missionary strategies to spread a religion's teachings throughout the world (Smart, 1984, 216-18).

Universality could also imply that a 'world' religion has what Shaw calls 'an all-encompassing cosmology' making it, potentially at least, capable of being applied anywhere in the world. Shaw responds that much of Christianity or Hinduism as it is actually practised could not fit into such a definition of universality (Shaw, 1990, 340). For example, the concept of salvation in Christ alone has caused great difficulty for many Christians who struggle with a religiously plural world, a struggle which Frank Whaling suggests has 'imprisoned' Christian theology 'within the thought-world of the West' (Whaling, 1986, 140). Or, the Hindu caste system, tied to the concepts of *dharma* and the karmic law, hardly represents an 'all-encompassing cosmology'.[5]

Moreover, exceptions to the ethnic or local nature of primal religions can be found, for example, in the consultations with Mwari in southern Africa, a practice which encompasses at least the Karanga, Ndau, Venda and Ndebele in Zimbabwe and the Kalanga in Botswana. M. L. Daneel in Zimbabwe and Richard Werbner in Botswana have studied this religious expression and have argued, each in his own way, that Mwari points toward a macrocosm which can be directly related to the more localised territorial ritual centres and then to a microcosm of family ancestors (Werbner, 1989, 245-98; Daneel, 1970, 56-7).

The concept of an 'all-encompassing cosmology', nevertheless, can be applied to the religious expressions of indigenous peoples if a scholar identifies common themes or typologies throughout religious experience. In this sense myths, rituals, scriptures (including, and oftentimes primarily, oral traditions), and symbols found across all religions can be interpreted as addressing 'universal' human problems such as the cause of and resolution to suffering (Cox, 1996, 132-3). Scholars, such as Joseph Campbell, have argued that all religions address such universal concerns but they do so in particular ways (Campbell, 1970, 461-2). To conclude in the case of African religions, for example, that because a particular ancestor is addressed in a ritual that it is therefore local and ethnic is to miss the central relationship in all religions between specific symbolic apprehensions of the universal and the universal itself.

The very idea of universality, however, which requires us to catalogue religions according to such criteria as a lack of ethnicity or the presence of an existent or potential world cosmology, presupposes criteria which have been important in the West but which have no necessary or

---

5. Although *dharma* is conceived of in cosmological terms, it is very much connected with the order of Indian society. Younger and Younger (1978, 79), for example, define *dharma* as referring to 'the proper order which supports the cosmos or society. An individual supports this order by doing his "duty" or by living righteously'.

inherent connection to religious phenomena themselves. This is what Shaw means by 'inventing' a classificatory scheme which predisposes us 'to look for common features in the diverse religious ideas and practices' which our classifications then 'try to encompass'. She explains,

If we examine those traditions usually selected as "world religions", we find that even if they have little else in common, they have written texts, explicit doctrines and a centre or centres of authority, all of which have characterized those religious forms which have been dominant in the West (Shaw, 1990, 340).

Another central characteristic of primal religions cited by Baylis and Turner refers to their reliance on oral or nonliterary forms of communication. On this theory, myths, the primary medium for conveying the oral traditions, portray symbolic meanings through rituals which carry a cyclical understanding of time. Because primal religions are identified by the nonliterary transmission of sacred stories, they lack coherent or codified statements of belief.

Classifying primal religions as non or preliterate, however, leaves unexplained the actual content of the classification. Oral traditions vary just as much as written scriptures do. That certain religious communities lack organised creeds or statements of beliefs is equally void of content. What people believe has no relationship to whether or not they have systematised their beliefs.

Most so-called world religions, as Harold Coward has demonstrated, give priority to the spoken over the written word (Coward, 1988, x). This is true even in a religion like Islam which emphasises the revelation as it is recorded in written form. The written form, however, represents what Muhammad heard and was ordered to 'recite'. Faithful Muslims ever since have put the words of the *Qur'an* to memory so they can speak the holy word (Graham, 1981, 593). The primacy of the oral in religions does not represent an early, preliterate phase in the development of the universal religions. Emphasis on the spoken word remains crucial for meditative, ritual, or communicative purposes. Written sources emerged historically largely for practical reasons where certain traditions emphasised absolute accuracy, guarded against wrong beliefs, and sought authoritative accounts of their central stories of faith (Coward, 1988, 173-4).

It is not irrelevant to understanding the specific nature of religions, however, that some developed written scriptures and some remained oral. In the next chapter, I will try to demonstrate the particular problems inherent in understanding oral literature in Africa in the light of typological definitions of myths. I am opposing, however, the contention that written scriptures somehow imply a 'higher form' of religion than those which are exclusively oral in character.

Myths, therefore, whether primarily preserved in written form or told and re-told in various oral contexts, are neither more nor less central for the so-called primal religions than they are for the universal religions. All religions live within a mythical framework, tell sacred stories and express aspects or meanings of the myth in rituals (Smart, 1973, 79-120). Although the understanding of how the myth relates to the rituals in space and time differs among the religions, this is unrelated to what have been called either primal or world perspectives. Religions like Judaism or Christianity, for example, which regard history as linear, re-enact their stories in liturgical time (Eliade, 1959, 111).

When exposed to close analysis, therefore, the classification primal religions is seen as an non-empirical construct which seeks to consolidate a vast amount of religious data according to criteria which tell us very little about the content of the data itself. The characteristics cited, moreover, provide no evidence that they belong to a unique classification since those same characteristics are displayed prominently in all religions.

Additional Problems with the Term 'Primal'

We can see that the objections applicable to the term 'primal' obtain equally to all expressions (such as traditional or pre-literate) which distinguish between the 'world' religions and the religions of indigenous peoples and make broad generalisations about myth and ritual on the basis of this distinction. The term 'primal', however, adds the further complicating concept to the discussion that the religions of indigenous peoples not only share common characteristics but that those characteristics are somehow basic to all religions and thus underlie them all. In the words of Andrew Walls, 'All other believers [other than primalists themselves], and for that matter non-believers, are primalists underneath' (Walls, 1987, 252).

If we can reject the term 'primal' as a non-empirical construction of Western scholars, can we equally challenge the claim on empirical grounds that all religions are somehow descended from or closely related to the religions of indigenous peoples? Clearly, we can. If the unifying factors defining primal religions are discounted as inventions, logically they cannot exist as a common source for the world religions. This does not deny that interaction takes place between and among various religious communities in the way W.C. Smith speaks of 'cumulative traditions' (Smith, 1978, 170-9), but it does challenge the claim that we are justified in speaking as if the religions of indigenous peoples around the world reflected a collective world view which could be deciphered in the universal religions.

The theory of a basic, foundational religion, however, is regarded by its proponents as necessary to explain the development of what Turner calls the 'great historic religions', to define how (again following Turner) 'tribal societies' have interacted with the great religions, and to show how such societies have been transformed by the historical interaction (Turner, 1971, 7). But why is it necessary to posit the existence of a unified tradition as an antecedent to the world religions in order to describe the interaction, for example, between Christianity and the indigenous religious practices of the Karanga of Zimbabwe?

It is here precisely that the non-empirical nature of the concept becomes evident. We have seen already that the unifying factors are based on tenuous empirical data. But the scientific claim for the existence of primal religions is constructed on an even further ideological convention which is now widely discounted, what Shaw calls 'the evolutionary theories of the nineteenth century ethnologists, via the dualistic comparisons of "primitive" and "modern" modes of thought by early twentieth century anthropological theorists.' This 'binary opposition' between the primal and the world religions merely extends the assumptions commonly held earlier in this century that 'the great historical religions' were superior to the religions of 'primitive societies' (Shaw, 1990, 341-42).

The term 'primal religions' can be seen, therefore, not only as a non-empirical construct which exaggerates the similarities between historically and culturally divergent peoples but as doing so for the sake of explaining what is seen as the increasing transformation of the religions of indigenous peoples by the world religions. Although the stated aim of the primal religions theory is to demonstrate historical and scientific realities, for ideological reasons, primal religions are always portrayed, in Shaw's words, as 'essentially inferior to' world religions, especially to Christianity (Shaw, 1990, 341-42). Such a presentation, I would argue, implies that the term should be dropped as a scientific classification for religious phenomena. It may belong quite appropriately, however, in theology.

Primal Religions as a Useful Theological Concept: A.F. Walls
In her discussion of the sources for the study of primal religions, Philippa Baylis commends the research of recent field workers who spend many years living among and learning the languages of a particular people. Such workers, who provide a basic source of information about primal peoples, she says, usually are professional anthropologists or missionaries. She adds, perhaps unwittingly, that these workers (she makes no distinction between anthropologists and missionaries) 'today are increasingly sensitive to and interested in the primal religions they are *seeking to replace*' (emphasis mine) (Baylis, 1988, 3). Baylis may be assuming that anthropologists study primal religions to replace them with Western perspectives, but clearly she infers that missionaries study them to replace primal religions with Christianity.

The scientific study of religions, however, rejects any missionary motive beneath its research methods. Any classification or typology must be descriptively demonstrable and thus be verifiable or falsifiable. In other words, its use must be scientific and not theological. To determine if a theological construct is suggested by the term primal, I want first to examine some of the relevant writings of Andrew Walls, a leading and respected Christian historian of religions who, as we have noted, is closely associated with the development and wide acceptance of the term and then analyse some recent writings of the Ghanaian theologian, Kwame Bediako.

In his contribution to Whaling's *Religion in Today's World*, Walls argues that the forces of modernity characterised by Western political, economic, educational, and religious structures have posed 'certain threats to primal religions'. Chiefly, they threaten traditional values of worth, obligation, patterns of permission and prohibition and they disturb traditional hierarchical patterns evidenced in the changing understandings of the role of ancestors, gender relations, and power status. Such changes, Walls contends, have created what he calls 'disturbances of *focus*' manifested by the necessity of traditional societies to see beyond local concerns in order to account for the reality that they now form a 'part of a total world of events' (Walls, 1987, 266-67).

According to Walls, primal religions have responded to the sources of change in eight ways: recession, absorption, restatement, reduction, invention, adjustment, revitalisation and appropriation. In each of his categories, Walls describes primal religions as being overtaken by events so that what we see in today's world is either some form of incorporation into the universal religions or a restatement in a way which radically alters the original primal world view.

Under the response 'recession', Walls contends that the primal religions, largely because of their local character, have receded and been replaced by the universal religions which are geared to relate 'to the wider universe demanded by modernization.' This trend has been going on throughout this century and before, but, particularly since 1945, large numbers of primalists have embraced either Christianity or Islam (Walls, 1987, 267). The reason for this 'marked' trend relates again to the issue of a local as opposed to a universal focus.

> Christianity and Islam, with their capacity to link into a wider universe, their provision of alternative codes of behaviour and their demand for symbolic change requiring some sort of act of decision, continue to provide keys to meaning and a means of adjustment to new conditions when a people's traditional lore is no longer able to do so (Walls, 1987, 269).

The recession of primal religions as world religions grow needs to be seen alongside a process of 'absorption' whereby 'much of the configuration of primal religions' has been assimilated 'into Christian and Islamic communities'. The process of absorption is identified by 'overlapping worlds of spiritual perception'. In one sense, Walls admits, this means that primal religions continue to have a life of their own within the universal religions, but it is more correct to state that 'the primal chapter of religious history has closed in such cases' (Walls, 1987, 269-70).

The presence of the world religions among primal societies has forced in some instances what Walls calls a 'restatement' of the traditional faith. This means that where primal religions persist in their own right, the content of their faith has been remoulded by the universal religions. This can be observed in the various names ascribed to the Supreme Being among primalists, names which in many Christian contexts have been taken over into regular rituals as a vernacular name for God, but which at the same time have been transformed by the Christian understanding of God. Such a transformation of the traditional words for the deity into the universal faith has resulted in a restatement of the original meaning into one which incorporates the new intention brought in from the outside. This is a process which Walls contends renders the 'academic discussion about the characteristics of the Supreme Being and his place in worship in the pre-contact period of a particular people...rather secondary' (Walls, 1987, 271).

A primal religion may also respond by 'reduction', that is, by reducing its scope with the result that it will cease to affect seriously the complex situations defined by modern societies. In this case, traditional institutions, which once influenced 'the whole of life', no longer make a significant impact on daily living (Walls, 1987, 271).

The first four of Walls' responses of primal religions to modernity clearly are marked by fundamental changes in the impact or integrity of the traditional ways of belief and practice. He then cites what might be called a renewal of primal religions as evidenced by 'invention' and 'adjustment'. Invention is marked by 'bursts of new creative activity'. This usually, however, represents an endeavour to universalise the local character of the primal religion so that it can be regarded by believers as an alternative to the world faiths (Walls, 1987, 272-73). The same is true of 'adjustment', which Walls identifies as an attempt 'to adjust and expand world views to take account of new phenomena'. This generally is distinguished by an expansion of scale whereby, as exemplified in new religious movements in the Pacific, old ethnic divisions are overcome (Walls, 1987, 274).

Walls' final two categories, 'Revitalisation' and 'Appropriation', can be classified better as reactions to the process of change than as responses, because, perhaps more than the others, they are defined in terms of the outside forces. Revitalisation represents a reaction by defenders of African culture to the message of cultural superiority which historically characterised much of Christian and Islamic missionary activity. Africans, particularly academics, says Walls, 'are rediscovering and reaffirming African cultural heritage' (Walls, 1987, 274-75). 'Appropriation' is also a reaction, but in a reverse direction. Many people in the West are beginning to affirm elements of the primal religions which promise an alternative to Western dualistic thinking, such as the merging of the sacred with the profane in primal societies. Reactions, however, are just that and do not define primal religions in their own terms (Walls, 1987, 276-77).

The assumptions regarding the nature of primal religions I discussed above underlie Walls' entire analysis. That primal religions chiefly are characterised as local or ethnic makes them unable to respond to the forces of historical change demanded by the modern world. This, in Walls' view, creates a distortion of focus among primal peoples who no longer believe in the ability of their traditional ways to resolve problems in the wider world. When presented with an alternative to their dissatisfying world view, therefore, they turn in large numbers to religions which more adequately cope with the redefined problems of modern societies or they transform their original world view irretrievably in content, scope, or impact.

Such an interpretation outlining the history of the interpenetration between the world and primal religions appears scientific. But, as Walls' other writings demonstrate, it is just this interpretation which he requires for his theology of Christian mission. This can be seen clearly in his discussion of conversion from primal religions to Christianity.

Walls contends that conversion probably never occurs from one religion to another directly. Something intervenes which exposes the old religion as having failed, thus inducing agnosticism (Walls, 1980, 148). Nevertheless, across the agnosticism separating the old from the new some common assumptions are shared. Walls holds in the case of conversion to Christianity, primalists share with Christians belief in transcendent power. As a result, many missionaries used the 'power encounter' to demonstrate the superior authority of the Christian God over the deities of primal peoples. What had happened in the meantime, Walls notes, is that the traditional powers had in some way failed to meet the needs of the people, for example, in providing rain or a good harvest. Prayers to the Christian God, however, were perceived as effective. Before the adherents to the primal religion could embrace Christianity, therefore, they had experienced a failure of faith in their original religion. Their conversion, nevertheless, was based on their original belief in transcendence; conversion 'translated' that belief (Walls, 1980, 147-48).

Walls uses the word 'translation' in a quite literal sense. When translating a text from one language to another, he notes, the meaning of the source language must be conveyed 'within the working system of the receptor language'. This implies that although something new is introduced into the receptor language, 'that new element can only be comprehended by means of and in terms of the pre-existing language and its conventions.' Both the source language and the receptor language are affected as a result of the translation. That language into which the text has been translated is expanded by the translation, but the receptor language itself has had a transformative effect on the text. 'The receptor language has a dynamic of its own and takes the new material to realms it never touched in the source language' (Walls, 1990, 25).

Translation implies the capacity to carry over ideas, concepts and symbols from one language to the other. Without the translation, however, the ideas, concepts and symbols would be incomprehensible. Translation, nevertheless, assumes some formal correlation between the capacity to express the idea in the original language and its corresponding expression in the receptor language. A gap between the two exists until the translation occurs. Thus, if Christianity is seen as the language to be translated, we can return to Walls' example of the 'power encounter'. Certain 'shared assumptions' between the primal religion and Christianity were necessary if the evidence of the greater transcendent power in Christianity were to prove meaningful (Walls, 1980, 148).

Conversion thus directly parallels the process of translation. The original religious expressions, what Walls calls in this case the 'existing structures', correspond to the receptor language. The structures are already in place; in conversion, they are turned in 'new directions' and assume new 'standards'. 'It is not about substitution, the replacement of something old by something new, but about transformation; the turning of the already existing to new account' (Walls, 1990, 25-6).

In Christian theology, according to Walls, the Incarnation is a translatable event. To follow the linguistic analogy, Christ was 'taken into the functional system of the language'. He was God in human form, the Word literally made flesh. This was a type of divine translation whereby the receptor cultures took over the humanity of God and made this act meaningful in their own contexts. This taking over involves conversion which invokes 'countless retranslations into the thought forms and cultures of the different societies into which Christ is brought' (Walls, 1990, 26).

If we return to the definition of primal religions as that which is fundamental, basic, and antecedent to the world religions, and if we add Walls' analysis of conversion in the light of his description of primal religions in today's world, a missionary theology appears to emerge.

Primal religions represent the base language, the already existing, into which the translation of the incarnate Christ occurs. The primal religions will be transformed by the process, but they will not simply substitute the new for the old. They will continue to live in the new but in such a changed condition that to speak of them as primal any longer is really inappropriate. They are Christians who have used the primal religions as a kind of receptor language into which the translation of the message has been received.

This is a universal phenomenon, according to Walls, and explains why Christianity historically has had its greatest success among primal peoples. Since conversion is preceded by an agnostic phase, the impact of modernisation on primal societies illustrates why Christianity has grown so rapidly, particularly in Africa, since 1945. It also provides a conceptual framework for the processes of conversion to Christianity and the contextualisation of its message in a variety of ways among indigenous peoples. The history of this religious phenomenon as outlined in many of Walls' writings, therefore, when placed in the light of his theology of conversion and translation, shows how the concept 'primal religions' has at the very least proved useful for theology.

Primal Religions as a Necessary Theological Construct: Kwame Bediako

Despite the way in which he seems to have mixed theology with historical descriptions, it must be admitted that Walls has given a convincing account of the interaction between Christianity and primal religions, if one accepts that primal legitimately expresses a scientific category. That a scientific category proves useful for theology does not establish that it is therefore unscientific and an invention of theologians. Moreover, the criticism of the term primal as an empirical classification applies equally to other generalisations concerning the religions of indigenous peoples. The evidence offered thus far that primal is theological rather than an attempt to provide a descriptive account of a type of religious phenomena rests on the additional meaning of primal as fundamental or basic to all religions and how that proves useful for theologies of contextualisation. Further evidence that the term is chiefly theological, however, is provided by Kwame Bediako of Ghana, a former student at Aberdeen and now a leading evangelical Christian theologian.

In a paper originally presented in 1993 at the Seminar Series of the Centre for the Study of Christianity in the Non-Western World in the University of Edinburgh and subsequently published in a revised form in the first issue of *Studies in World Christianity*, Bediako sets out what he calls a 'manifesto' leading toward an 'understanding of Christianity's significance in Africa'. The manifesto is built around five theses, each of which rests on the assumption of a vital relationship between Christianity and primal religions.

Thesis one, that 'African Christianity must be distinguished from the literature on African Christianity', differentiates between the 'living experiences of Christians' and African theology. Bediako argues that an academic theology in which contextualisation occurs emerges only from 'a substratum of vital Christian experience and consciousness'. In Africa, that substratum exists at a level which requires us to speak of

Christianity as *'Africa's "new" religion'* and the primal religions as the continent's *"'old" religions'* (Bediako, 1995, 52-3) (emphasis his).

The African 'genius in religion' is displayed not so much in its 'capacity for adapting and developing indigenous forms of Christianity' but 'in the nature of Christian faith itself' (p.53). Following Walls' lead on the model of linguistic translation, Bediako notes that when missionaries translated the Bible into African languages, they made the fundamental theological assumption that the biblical God had already been at work among Africans before the missionaries arrived. Concepts central to Christian theology, such as a transcendent God, sacrifice, and the creation of the world, already existed in the language of the 'receptor culture'; otherwise, translation into local equivalents could not have occurred.

> For the centrality of Scripture translation points to the significance of African pre-Christian religious cultures, not only as a "valid carriage for the divine revelation", but also as providing the idiom for Christian apprehension (p. 54).

The local equivalents were embedded in 'African traditional religious terminology and ideas' thereby forming the base for the world faith which would come later (p. 54). Theologically, this can be viewed as a divinely planted preparation in the primal religions for the subsequent transmission of the missionary message among indigenous African cultures.

Bediako's second thesis that 'the scholarly penetration of African Christianity, working from the most helpful perspectives, will constitute one of the most important tasks of the future' also relies heavily on the primal religions theory. The scholarly penetration Bediako intends refers precisely to unearthing the historical and theological meaning contained 'in the continent's Primal Religions' and their 'fulfilment in the apprehension of Jesus Christ in African experience' (p. 57). The scholarship called for focuses on an examination of the meaning of an African Christian faith which, Bediako argues, bears 'the marks of the continuing impact of the world view of Primal Religions' (p. 57).

Research will confirm further that the African case is not unique. 'The Primal Religions of the world have provided the religious background of the faith of the majority of Christians everywhere in Christian history to the present' (p. 57). For Bediako, Jesus Christ, who is translatable into every culture, has been anticipated in the primal religions throughout the world and contextualised into them. The African experience, where the primal religions have been shown so clearly and unmistakably to have provided the base for African theology, therefore, furnishes an academic model for understanding the formation of theology in other parts of the world.

Bediako's third thesis, which contends that 'the aim of seeking interpretative depth of African Christianity will require that due stress be placed on the observation and study of the actual life of African Christian communities', extends his argument to the practical level. He urges scholars to develop theologies based on an observation in Africa of the way Christianity is practised and how this reflects a connection with primal religions.

28

For example, what use is made of the Scriptures in resolving problems in daily life? Does the use of the Scriptures relate to the well-known general African inclination towards seeking guidance for living and making decisions? What is the place and role of the pastor or minister, or other "religious specialists" in African communities? Are their roles related to what is known from the expectations and the practice in the Primal Religions? How far does Christian theological formation prepare Christian ministers for such roles? If there are relations between the two, might it be justified to speak of African patterns, or even "traditions" of Christian ministry? (p. 58)

Such observations will lead to new interpretative theologies where certain connections between Christian and primal concepts can be made. This is evident in emerging African christologies where Christ is described as a traditional healer, a master of ceremonies in ritual initiations, or as an ancestor. All of these, Bediako argues, 'are derived directly from the world-view and from the apprehension of reality and the Transcendent within African primal religions' (p.59).

Thesis four holds that 'an understanding of the African accession to Christianity helps towards an understanding of the recession from the Christian faith in the modern West'. This is based on the idea that the centre of gravity for the Christian faith has shifted in this century from the north to the south, a claim based in part on the rapid growth of Christianity in Africa. This fact of modern history implies that it is now possible to 'explore how far the accession to Christianity in the predominantly religious world of Africa has also coincided with the erosion of a religious outlook in the West, particularly in Europe' (p. 59-60).

Bediako contends that the current African accession to Christianity can be instructive for Christian evangelism in the West precisely because 'Europe shares with Africa an identical pre-Christian heritage in the primal religious traditions of the world'. Since scholarship on Africa has brought to the forefront the overall significance of the primal religions in Christian history, African Christianity can play a critical role in an eventual resurgence of Christianity in the West as theology 'seeks to be communicative, evangelistic and missionary in its own context' (p. 60).

This follows because the 'African vindication of the theological significance of African Primal Religions' may also 'affirm that the European primal heritage was not illusory'. The implications for the continuing relevance of the conversion of the modern West are clear:

A serious Christian theological interest in the European primal traditions and the early Christianity amid those traditions, could provide a fresh approach to understanding Christian identity in Europe too, as well as opening new possibilities for Christian theological endeavour today (p. 60-1).

Bediako's final thesis that 'the study of Christianity in Africa in its total religious and socio-political context will help point the way for the church to exist in a post-Christendom era' provides a kind of overarching conclusion to his four previous theses. The close connection between Christianity in Africa and the primal religions points toward the possibility of affirming 'that Jesus is Lord in the midst of other claims to lordship'. The 'normal' African experience is one of religious pluralism as evidenced, for example, in the widespread African belief in 'other spiritual presences' (p. 61-2).

The primal religions and Christianity, as Walls noted earlier, both share, in Bediako's words, 'the general capacity to expect to experience transcendence in the context of the modern conditions of life' (p. 62). The West, which lives in a post-Christendom and a 'World Christianity' era, can learn from the study of African Christianity that 'secularity as an ideological posture is "abnormal" and need not be accepted as a necessary accompaniment of modernity' (p. 62).

Why is secularity 'abnormal'? Although Bediako does not explicitly state it, we may presume this is because the primal world view, as the fundamental and basic human apprehension of reality, historically defines what is ideologically 'normal'. Modern secularism with its denial of transcendent power thus reflects a human deviation away from the primal apprehension which under the impact of modernisation finds its natural response not in denial of divine power but by converting to Christianity which as a universal religion is capable of maintaining faith in the widened context of global awareness. Africa can thus become the 'Christian laboratory' for the world demonstrating that '"Christian uniqueness" or distinctiveness need not be lost in the midst of pluralism' (p. 62).

From the above accounts, it is clear that Bediako's five theses cannot stand apart from the concept of primal religions as forming the basic or fundamental world view within every culture and as a forerunner to the universal religions. This concept provides the necessary ingredient for his interpretation not only of an African theology but also of the significance of such a theology in the modern world. In Bediako, therefore, we see how an empirically questionable classification has been embraced as a scientific and historical fact which then is interpreted as providing theological evidence that God has prepared historically distinct and varied cultures to receive the Christian faith through his work among their primal religions.

The Need for an Appropriate Descriptive Terminology

A theology of contextualisation, as exemplified by Kwame Bediako's 'manifesto', can be traced to a series of ideological developments beginning with Harold Turner's use of primal as a scientific classification for a type of religious phenomena to the assumption of Andrew Walls that because the primal religions are restricted by definition to local concerns they are being overtaken by the universal religions. Bediako's theses, moreover, depend on Walls' incarnational analogy of linguistic translation into primal cultures but expands it beyond its mere usefulness for theology into an indispensable theological construct.

If my analysis is correct, primal religions should be removed as a classification within religious studies. It is not merely a substitute for other unsatisfactory words like 'primitive', 'preliterate' or 'traditional'; it conveys a theological meaning which if used more persistently, widely and uncritically within religious studies will implant a theological agenda into what otherwise endeavours to be an empirical science.

The question of how religious studies should address the problem of classifying the religions of indigenous peoples is not answered by the removal of primal from the scientific approach to religion. I personally believe that the clue to this lies in the direction suggested by Wilfred Cantwell Smith over thirty years ago that all terms for classifying any cluster of religious phenomena such as 'Hinduism', 'Buddhism', 'Christianity' and so on are suspect since they are inadequate in themselves, misleading, and subject to innumerable qualifications (Smith, 1964). Smith preferred the term 'cumulative traditions' because he wanted to stress that traditions are never static but develop dynamically in response to various internal and external factors.

Throughout this chapter, I have been referring to the religions of *indigenous* peoples. I prefer to keep this nomenclature but would add, where appropriate, geographical, ethnic and linguistic qualifiers. For example, when discussing the religion of the indigenous people of Zimbabwe, I would include specific limitations such as the Shona-speaking Karanga peoples of the southcentral region of the country.

This scheme for classifying religions, because it stresses particular expressions, does not prevent the scholar from identifying universal themes which exist within them nor prohibit the study of religious typologies characteristic, for example, of oral traditions.[6] When generalisations are made about similarities among indigenous religions, however, we should take extreme care by referring back to the specific practices upon which such generalisations are based and at the same time note both the dynamic nature and the context of such practices. This will overcome the tendency to impose an artificial unity on indigenous religions.

---

6. A similar point has been made by Thomas Blakely and Walter van Beek (1994, 3) in their introduction to the multi-authored volume, *Religion in Africa*. They note, 'Today's students of religion focus on particular forms of religious expression and try to point out the consonances with other cultural and historical processes, while still trying to preserve the integrity of the religious experience-*cum*-expression'.

References

Baylis, P. 1988. *An introduction to Primal Religions.* Edinburgh: Traditional Cosmology Society.

Bediako, K. 1995. 'The significance of modern African Christianity – a manifesto', *Studies in world Christianity* 1 (1), 51-67.

Beek, W. E. A. van and Blakely, T. D 1994. 'Introduction', in T.D. Blakely, W. E. A. van Beek and D. L. Thomson (eds.), *Religion in Africa.* London: James Currey and Portsmouth, New Hampshire: Heinemann, 3-20.

Brown, J. E. 1984. 'Religion in primal societies; North American Indian Religions', in J. Hinnells (ed.), *A handbook of living religions.* Harmondsworth: Penguin Books, 392-412.

Burnett, D. 1988. *Unearthly powers. A Christian perspective on Primal and Folk Religions.* Eastbourne: MARC.

Campbell, J. 1970. *The masks of God: Primitive mythology.* New York: The Viking Press.

Coward, H. 1988. *Sacred word and sacred text.* Maryknoll: Orbis.

Cox, J. L. 1996, 2nd ed. *Expressing the sacred. An introduction to the phenomenology of religion.* Harare: University of Zimbabwe Publications.

Daneel, M. L. 1970. *The God of the Matopos Hills.* The Hague: Mouton.

Eliade, M. 1959. *The sacred and the profane.* New York: Harcourt, Brace.

Ferguson, J. 1982. *Gods many and lords many. A study in Primal Religions.* Guildford: Lutterworth Educational.

Graham, W. A. 1981. 'Qur'an', in K. Crim (general ed.), *Abingdon Dictionary of Living Religions.* Nashville: Abingdon, 592-94.

Hinnells, J. and Sharpe, E. (eds.) 1972. *Hinduism.* Newcastle upon Tyne: Oriel Press.

Hopfe, L. 1983. *Religions of the world.* New York: Macmillan.

Mackey, J. 1992. 'Magic and Celtic Primal Religions', *Zeitschrift fur Celtische Philology* 45, 66-84.

Mitchell, R. C. 1977. *African Primal Religions.* Niles, Illinois: Argus Communications.

Parrinder, E. G. 1981, 3rd ed. *African Traditional Religion.* London: Sheldon Press.

Schmidt, R. 1988. *Exploring religion.* Belmont, California: Wadsworth Publishing Company.

Segal, R. 1983. 'In defense of reductionism', *Journal of the American Academy of Religion* 51 (1), 97-124.

Shaw, R. 1990. 'The invention of African Traditional Religion', *Religion* 20, 339-53.

Smart, N. 1973. *The phenomenon of religion.* New York: The Seabury Press.

1984. *The religious experience of mankind.* Glasgow: Collins Fount Paperbacks.

1989. *The world's religions. Old traditions and modern transformations.* Cambridge: Cambridge University Press.

Smith, W. C. 1964 and 1978. *The meaning and end of religion.* New York: New American Library (1st ed.). San Francisco: Harper and Row (Torchback ed.).

Strenski, I. 1993. *Religion in relation: Method, application and moral location.* London: Macmillan.

Taylor, J. B. (ed.) 1976. *Primal world views: Christian dialogue with Traditional thought forms.* Ibadan, Nigeria: Daystar Press.

Taylor, J. V. 1963. *The primal vision: Christian presence amid African Religion.* London: SCM Press.

Turner, H. W. 1971. *Living tribal religions.* London: Ward Lock Educational.

Walls, A. F. 1980. 'Ruminations on rainmaking: the transmission and receipt of religious expertise in Africa', in J. C. Stone (ed.), *Experts in Africa.* Aberdeen: University of Aberdeen African Studies Group, 146-51.

1987. 'Primal religious traditions in today's world,' in F. Whaling (ed.), *Religion in today's world.* Edinburgh: T. and T. Clark, 250-78.

1990. 'The translation principle in Christian history', in P. Stint (ed.), *Bible translation and the spread of the church.* Leiden: E. J. Brill, 24-39.

Weir, R. (ed.) 1982. *The religious world: Communities of faith.* New York: Macmillan.

Werbner, R. 1989. *Ritual passage. Sacred journey.* Washington: Smithsonian Institution Press and Manchester: Manchester University Press.

Whaling, F. 1986. *Christian theology and world religions: A global perspective.* Basingstoke: Marshall Pickering.

Wiebe, D. 1985. 'A positive episteme for the study of religion', *Scottish Journal of Religious Studies* 6 (1), 78-95.

Younger, P. and Younger, S. O. 1978. *Hinduism.* Niles, Illinois: Argus Communications.

Chapter Three
MYTH AND THE PROBLEM POSED BY
AFRICAN ORAL LITERATURE

Most books on religions include myths as a category or type of religious phenomena. In my introduction to the phenomenology of religion, I include myths as one of the interrelated expressions of religious communities (Cox, 1996, 83-95). In his textbook on the world religions, Ninian Smart (1984, 18) refers to this as 'the mythological dimension' of human religious experience.

In this chapter, I develop a definition of myth as a classification of religious phenomena as it has been approached by numerous scholars. This will lead me toward a summary of the essential characteristics of myths as derived from the basic definitions noted. After defining the term and providing some examples, I will examine problems of the definition in an African context. This will set the background in the next chapter for the discussion of ritual and the myth-ritual theory in Africa.

The Question of Truth

An initial problem whenever the term 'myth' is used as a classification of religious phenomena relates to the connotation of the term in general usage as that which is fictitious or untrue. By using the term 'myth' some would argue that the scholar has utilised a pejorative expression much in line with one of the definitions in the *Concise Oxford Dictionary* as 'a widely held but false notion' (see Schmidt, 1988, 184). Most academics, however, would agree with Ninian Smart who contends that the term 'myth' is neutral concerning the actual truth or falsehood of the story being told. What is important in order to achieve understanding of any community's myths is not whether they are true or false but to describe accurately 'what is believed' (Smart, 1984, 18). Leo Schneiderman agrees adding that scholars need not regard myths as 'a defective system of communication' but 'as a code for conveying shared feelings, images, memories, and desires' (1981, 2).

This neutral or objective approach to any community's mythic world raises methodological issues in the study of religion to which I will refer in later chapters. At this point, I want only to emphasise that the term myth is being used in this context as a story which for believers is true because they experience the world just as it is told in the myth. This does not mean that the myth is always believed to be historically or scientifically true. But, for religious communities, myths always recount what is ultimately real.

Toward a Preliminary Definition of Myth

The characteristics of myths have been outlined variously by scholars. The Finnish historian of religions, Lauri Honko (1984, 49), identifies four basic components of a myth:

1) It is a story of the gods. This suggests that the major characters of a myth are divinities, deities, or beings with some supernatural characteristics.

2) It is a religious account of the beginning of the world. Honko identifies the gods with religion and suggests that a myth relates how the gods brought the world into being.

3) It tells of the exemplary deeds of the gods as a result of which the world, nature and culture are related together. A myth thus points not only to supernatural beings and their creative activities, but it explains how the gods interact with humans. The stories of the divinities become a paradigm for all human activities and bind the people together into a culturally cohesive unit. The natural order also obtains its place in the cosmic structure according to the mythic account.

4) It expresses and confirms society's religious values and norms. The moral injunctions of society are given a sacred origin through the myth and thus achieve an authoritative status.

Dorothy Rowe adds a psychological dimension to myths which Honko seems to have omitted and which is emphasised in the school of mythological theory largely exemplified by C. G. Jung. Rowe, who is herself a psychologist and writing in the context of the causes of psychological depression, states that myths help people answer life questions such as 'Who am I?' 'How was I created?' 'Is there any reason for my existence?' (1988, 39).

Jung believed that myths represent a 'collective unconscious' shared by all persons in every society. He determined this through extensive dream analysis which he thought had its parallel in human mythology. Embedded in myths and their symbols such as the flood, the resurrected hero, or the child-god are universal 'archetypes' or similar images. The images are encountered in myths; the capacity to form the images is inherited. Recognition of the mythic archetypes, for Jung, leads to positive psychological states characterised by integrated personalities and maturity. Myths thus possess a meaning-giving function for individuals and cultures (Ruthven, 1976, 20).

Myths not only provide a basis for meaning, they also point toward a mysterious element in human existence. The anthropologist Edmund Leach defines myth primarily as 'a formulation of religious mystery'. This mystery, which is unobservable, is expressed mythologically in terms of 'observable phenomena'. That, he says, explains why the best definition of a myth is simply to call it a 'sacred tale' (Leach, 1970, 54).

For some scholars, like Mircea Eliade, Honko's emphasis on the beginnings of the world delineates the most important feature of myths. Eliade says that a myth recounts an event that took place *in illo tempore*, in the time of the beginnings, and therefore constitutes a pattern for all significant events in life (1958, 430). Because the myth transports believers back into the moment of creation, it is told repeatedly, and as we shall see, for Eliade, forms the basis for ritual re-enactments.

Eliade's theory of myth is based on what he perceives as the structure of the religious consciousness, which he claims is characterised by the religious person's longing to be as near the sacred as possible (1969, Preface; see also, Cox, 1996, 144-47). The religious person is informed about the beginnings of things through myth which tells how the original homogeneity of space and time was broken by sacred intrusions or manifestations called hierophanies. The sacred thus introduces order out of chaos by creating centres of orientation around mundane objects like trees, rivers, mountains, stones, animals, or even people. Once they become the avenue for the sacred manifestation, however, ordinary objects of this world are transformed into symbols which mediate the sacred for the religious community (1959, 26).

Alan Dundes (1984, 1) agrees with Eliade noting that 'a myth is a sacred narrative explaining how the world and man came to be in their present form'. Although it provided one of the components of myth in Honko's list, for Eliade and Dundes, myths are preeminently *cosmogonic*, telling of the origin of the world as it is experienced by various cultures.[1] For them, other aspects of myths, such as their socio-moral characteristics, can be traced back to and ultimately are derived from the cosmogonic stories.

In his book on Middle Eastern mythology, S.H. Hooke (1966, 14-15) identifies two further types of myths: the *prestige* myth and the *eschatological* myth. A prestige myth refers to stories of culture heroes who are surrounded 'with an aura of mystery and wonder'. He cites the Hebrew account of Moses being hidden amongst the bulrushes in the Nile River as an example of this. Other examples include Cyrus in the Persian context and Romulus and Remus of ancient Roman mythology.

An eschatological myth points toward a catastrophic end of the present world-order and is prominent in Zoroastrian, Jewish, Christian, and Islamic literature. The prophets of Israel, for example, believed that history must have its consummation in a final, decisive act involving a supernatural intervention.

William Bascom (1984, 5-29) includes myth as a distinct form of verbal art he calls *prose narratives*. The other forms are legends and folktales. Prose narratives are to be distinguished structurally from other types of verbal expression such as proverbs, riddles, ballads, poems and tongue twisters. Bascom defines myths as 'prose narratives which, in the society in which they are told are considered to be truthful accounts of what happened in the remote past' (p. 7). He adds that they are usually sacred with the main characters comprised of deities, culture heroes or animals with human attributes. Myths are set in a different time and place from the present and 'account for the origin of the world, of mankind, of death, or for the characteristics of birds, animals, geographical features, and the phenomena of nature' (p. 9).

---

1. Eliade says, 'From one point of view, every myth is "cosmogonic" because every myth expresses the appearance of a new cosmic "situation" or primeval event which becomes, simply by being thus expressed, a paradigm for all time to come' (1958, 416).

Legends, he says, are 'prose narratives which are regarded as true by the society but are set in a period less remote when the world was much as it is today'(p. 9). Hence, they are more often secular than sacred. The principal characters of legends are human and are of a historical or quasi-historical character recounting 'migrations, wars and victories, deeds of past heroes, chiefs, and kings, and succession in ruling dynasties' (p. 9-10).

Folktales are prose narratives regarded as fiction. Although they are often told for entertainment, they usually carry a moral and may be set in any time or place. Unlike myths, they do not form what Bascom calls the basis of dogma and thus frequently are not taken seriously. The principal characters generally are not deities or culture heroes, but consist of humans or animals. European 'fairy tales' fall under this category (p. 8).

Bascom's delineation of types of prose narratives is based on the anthropologist Bronislaw Malinowski's earlier distinctions between 'fairy tales', legends and myths. For Malinowski, fairy tales can be privately owned and dramatically told whereas legends are believed to be true and convey important factual information. They are not private nor are they told in what Malinowski calls a 'stereotyped way' with 'magical' effect. Myths are regarded not simply as true but as 'venerable and sacred' (Malinowski, 1948, 101-07).

The above definitions of myths and their distinguishing characteristics from legends and folktales comprise the primary components necessary for a comprehensive definition of the term.

1) Myths, which are prose narratives, are true for believers.
2) Since myths are sacred stories, the principal characters described in them are deities, supernatural beings, or culture heroes.
3) The primary concern of myths is to explain the origin of the world.
4) Socio-moral, prestige or eschatological myths, although not present in every society, are derived from cosmogonic myths.
5) Myths make the mysterious comprehensible by using language and speaking of the sacred through descriptions of events and objects projected out of common human experiences or concepts.
6) Myths provide a paradigm of meaning for nature, culture, society, and the individual.
7) Because they are preeminently cosmogonic, unlike legends and folktales, myths take place in a world which is different from the present world but they explain how and why the world came to be as it is now constituted.

Some Examples from Varying Traditions

In order to illustrate the typological characteristics of myths, I have chosen two examples from different traditions, eras, and geographical regions. The first is the *enuma elish* myth of ancient Babylonia as recounted by S. H. Hooke. The second tells of the birth of the Buddha in a story recorded in approximately the 3rd century BCE. Although they come from distinct traditions and vary dramatically in content, each example demonstrates at least some of the components of myth noted in the seven points above.

The ancient Mesopotamian myth, the *enuma elish*, has been dated to the 2nd millennium BCE. In the Babylonian version, the primeval scene consists of a universe in which nothing existed but Apsu, the sweet-water ocean, and Tiamat, the salt water ocean. From the union of these two, the gods were brought into existence including Lahmu and Lahamu who in turn gave birth to Anshar and Kishar. Anshar and Kishar produced Anu, the sky, and Ea, the earth. Ea, who is regarded as the god of wisdom, gave birth to Marduk who became the hero of later Babylonian myths.

In the story as summarised by Hooke, before Marduk is born, the first warfare among the primeval gods occurs. Tiamat and Apsu are disturbed by the noisy behaviour of their children and are persuaded by Mummu, Apsu's adviser, to destroy the younger gods. Tiamat is reluctant to carry out the plan, but Apsu and Mummu proceed anyway. The gods discover the plan, but are saved by the intervention of Ea who slays Apsu while he is sleeping and binds Mummu with a cord.

Other gods, however, criticise Tiamat for allowing Apsu to be destroyed. She recognises her error and sets about to kill Anu by making Kingu (her firstborn) the leader of the attack. She then gives birth to monsters like the scorpion man and the centaur. Kingu is thus set to lead in the effort to gain revenge for Apsu's death.

In order to deal with this attack, after a long series of deliberations, the assembly of the gods eventually appoints Marduk, Ea's son, to stop Tiamat's threat. As the battle ensues, Marduk fills his body with flame creating seven hurricanes. He mounts the storm chariot and advances against Tiamat and her warriors. Marduk casts a net over Tiamat and when she opens her mouth to swallow him, he blows the mighty hurricanes into her body so that she swells up like a balloon. Marduk then shoots his arrow through her heart splitting her in half. Marduk places Tiamat's top half above the earth as the sky (Hooke, 1966, 42-4).

Although this represents just a portion of the story which culminates with the creation of humanity through the sacrificial death of Kingu, it illustrates how a myth portrays the drama of the gods living and acting in a time and space distinctly different from our current world but whose activities bring the world into being. The story, moreover, conveys the mystery of how the cosmos came to be by describing the gods with humanlike characteristics and feelings. The inexplicable can thereby be comprehended without losing its extramundane character. As the gods acted, however, patterns for all human activity emerge, thus forming the basis for social and moral norms.

A different type of myth is portrayed in a Buddhist context where the birth of Siddhartha Gautama is described as a miraculous event.[2] The version of the story of Siddhartha's birth recounted below developed several hundred years after his death and is paraphrased by the Buddhist scholar Maurice Percheron (1982, 18-21).

According to Percheron's account, the Buddha, who had been born into the world already five hundred times in previous lives, once again enters the world to lead humanity in the pathway of salvation. The story

---

2. Richard Gard explains that in the course of time 'the veneration of the Buddha led to a Buddha-cult which fostered new conceptions of the Buddha: he was idealized in superhuman terms, conceived in metaphysical forms, and symbolized through the cultural arts' (Gard, 1961, 76).

begins by describing how an archangel resident in the highest heaven becomes concerned about the persistent suffering of humanity. He thus sends his 'earthly reflection' into the womb of queen Maya, wife of King Suddhodana, who, although married to the king for thirty-two months, has never consummated her marriage. She then has a strange dream in which she is taken up to heaven on a cloud, transported to a beautiful palace, and is impregnated by a white elephant. The elephant painlessly pierces Maya's side with one of his six tusks thereby inserting the future Buddha into Maya's body. When the birth takes place, blossoms fall from the sky, heavenly music is sounded, and parasols appear in the air. The infant emerges from Queen Maya's side in a pure state already filled with wisdom and knowledge of his previous lives.

The new Buddha is laid on a white lotus flower by his mother. He surveys space 'with a lion's glance' and then takes seven steps toward each of the four cardinal points, the cosmic east, west, north and south. He then raises his finger towards the place where the cardinal points converge and declares, 'I shall watch over all living beings'. Queen Maya, who after the birth of the Buddha is too holy to ever give birth to any other child, is taken back up to the paradise she had visited in her dreamlike state.

The story of the birth of Siddhartha Gautama, although not cosmogonic in the strict sense of describing the origin of the world, represents rebirth and thus possesses the elements of a creation story. The abode of the gods is quite different from that of the earth which is caught in a cycle of suffering. The mysterious freedom from the world which Maya experiences is symbolised through a vision of paradise, blossoms, music and parasols. The birth of the Buddha is effected through the action of the pure white elephant who impregnates Maya nonsexually and painlessly (without defilement and free from suffering). The transcendent is thereby manifested in earthly symbols so that those on the earth can comprehend its mystery. That suffering characterises the dominant mode of existence in this world and that the Buddha has led the way out of suffering are confirmed in experience and in this way demonstrate that the myth is true.

Much deeper analysis than I have provided is needed to draw out the meanings contained within the two myths cited. This, however, is not my purpose here. I have sought through these brief examples to demonstrate how myths from quite different traditions can be made to conform to the typological characteristics found in the various definitions noted above.

Problems in Common Examples of Cosmogonic Myths in Africa

If the idea of a phenomenological religious typology is to work, it must conform not simply to selected myths, such as the two just cited, but it must incorporate findings from a broad cross-section of religious traditions. I will try to show in the remainder of this chapter that the cosmogonic components of myths, although present in African societies, play a much less significant role than either historical legends or stories reenforcing socio-moral values.

Many Western and African Christian scholars writing on indigenous African religions, nevertheless, emphasise the importance of cosmogonic myths. A typical example is related by Noel King in his *African Cosmos* where he introduces a discussion of the Yoruba people of Nigeria by referring to the Supreme Being called Olorun or Olodumare. King then summarises one form of a Yoruba myth of creation.

When Olodumare and certain divinities resided in the heavens above, the earth was like a marsh and wasteland. Heaven and earth were not far apart, and the inhabitants of the above came at times to earth to take their pastimes and hunting herein. When Olodumare made the decision to cause firm land to appear, he called Orisa-nla (Great-divinity) and commanded him to carry out this design. He provided him with some soil, a hen with five toes, and a pigeon. Orisa-nla came to earth, threw down the soil, and released the birds. The hen spread the soil, the waters were driven back, dry land appeared. When the land was wide and firm enough, Olodumare sent Orisa-nla to place trees upon the earth. The first trees were the palm and three others that provide food, drink, shade, and shelter. Olodumare then breathed life into sixteen human beings and sent them to earth. He taught Orisa-nla how to make the forms of human beings, after which Olodumare himself would give them life (King, 1986, 8).

King does not indicate from which source he obtained the story. Nor does he offer any explanation of the setting in which the story is told. That this points toward a potential difficulty is clear when he admits shortly after recounting the story that 'no myth can be fully understood outside of its context in ritual and sacred space' (p. 8).[3]

A cosmogonic myth is commonly cited also in Zimbabwe where the word for the Supreme Being usually is translated as Mwari. A typical account of the Mwari creation story is cited by C. S. Banana in his introduction to Christian theology. Sections of Banana's account are as follows:

In the beginning Mwari (God) created the first man, Mwedzi, whom he placed in a pool. He asked to be released into the world for the pool life was boring. He was given a go-ahead after a bitter debate with Mwari. Mwari had insisted that Mwedzi would regret it since the earth was a lonely and desolate place. After a few days of wandering Mwedzi came back to Mwari and complained that he wanted a partner to stay with. He was given Massasi (Nyamasase = the evening star). The two departed to the earth. In the evening they made a fire to warm their bodies. Mwedzi had a medicine horn. He grabbed it and rubbed its oil on his index finger. Suddenly he jumped to the side where Massasi was after

---

3. A quite similar story is related in Ulli Beier's collection of Yoruba myths under the heading 'Obatala and Oduduwa' (1980, 9-10). Beier, like King, provides little information on the context in which the story has been told, nor does he inform the reader how his material has been obtained. Wande Abimbola (1994, 101-2), former head of the Department of African Languages at Obafemi Awolowu University in Ile-Ife, Nigeria, attributes the story to *Ifa*, what he calls 'a literary and divination system' found among many groups in West Africa. Abimbola notes that this form of oral literature, if translated into written form, would result in hundreds of books. It should be noted that in his discussion of *Ifa*, however, Abimbola is concerned to delineate a cosmological structure within West African religious systems in order, in his own words, 'to demonstrate that *Ifa* is a coherent, self-consistent system of belief par excellence'. Van Beek and Blakely (1994, 5) observe that Abimbola's intention 'implicity uses an Anglo-Christian grid as a comparative frame of reference for his data'.

41

having remarked that he was capable of jumping to the other side of the furnace. He touched Massasi. She became pregnant. Massasi bore trees, grass, cattle and goats and also the herbivores of the forest (abyss). After two years Mwari took Massasi back to the pools leaving Mwedzi lonely. Mwedzi petitioned for another wife. He was given Murombo, the morning star. Mwedzi repeated the same act and Murombo conceived. She gave birth to the first boys and girls, wild carnivores such as the lion and its kind, the civet cat and the snake (Banana, 1991, 44-5).

Banana, who derives this story from George Kahari's *Aspects of the Shona Novel* (1992, 116-24), argues that it is a 'representative item of traditional Shona Creation-mythology' (p. 45). Kahari's interpretation of the story, however, is quite different from Banana's. As an expert in Shona literature, Kahari is looking for 'techniques and methods used by the modern narrators as compared to those used by the traditionalists' (p. 116). By contrast, Banana is seeking to establish a theological point that the Shona, prior to Christian influence, believed in a Creator God. For Banana, the story can even function as a pre-Christian form of divine revelation.

Kahari, on the other hand, identifies the 'genesis and roots' of the story in the 'annual harvesting-threshing beer party and in the ceremonial father-in-law burial rites' (p. 120), suggesting that the story conveys meanings for the natural order and the structure of traditional society. He also suggests that the story, which he labels under the genre of the 'fantastic', 'is used to deal with issues that are embarrassing under normal circumstances', such as the act of procreation (p. 122). Although Kahari admits that the story tells of the creation of the world, what seems most important is that it establishes the VaUngwe people 'and possibly other adjacent people' in a particular region.

It should be noted that neither Kahari nor Banana have derived the Mwedzi story from direct field research. Kahari cites his source as the German ethnologist Leo Frobenius (p. 119). Neither Kahari nor Banana refer to any living sources for the myth. During my phenomenology of religion classes in the University of Zimbabwe, I asked if any of the students knew of this myth. Although many had read it in various books, none of them had actually heard the myth recited nor told in any context. My own investigations also failed to discover any knowledge of the myth among the elders in southcentral Zimbabwe. This does not invalidate either Kahari's or Banana's interpretations of the story, but, it calls into question its importance in contemporary Shona society, and casts suspicion on the theological significance Banana places on it.

Geoffrey Parrinder is another scholar in Africa who has recorded accounts of cosmogonic myths. He refers, for example, to the myth of the Margi of Nigeria which explains why the Supreme Being is not involved in day to day living.

In the past the sky could be touched and there was no need to work...God filled men's calabashes without them working; but a woman put out a dirty calabash and infected the finger of one of the sky children, and God retired in anger to his present distance (Parrinder, 1981, 40).

Parrinder goes on to recount how the Ngombe of the Congo say that humans in the past lived in the sky, but one woman became such a nuisance that God lowered her down from heaven in a basket. From then on, people no longer lived with God (p. 41). These stories, Parrinder argues, typically represent African myths explaining the remoteness of God and demonstrate that the Supreme Being is a *deus otiosus*.

Other myths, Parrinder says, such as those of the Mende of Sierra Leone, tell how things went wrong between humans and God and how even the animals 'sinned'. Other stories, such as the well known myth of the chameleon told widely throughout southern Africa, explain the origin of death (p. 41). Still others, such as the Kono of Sierra Leone, refer to a snake who becomes the symbol of ancestral reincarnation (p. 42).

The many African myths, accompanied by prayers and an analysis for the names of God, according to Parrinder, 'clearly show that nearly all Africans, "untutored" though some may be, do conceive of God'. God is the creator of all things, but has withdrawn to the sky leaving to ancestors and lesser divinities the control of ordinary living. He is like 'the most mighty of kings', only rarely approached (p. 42).

The stories cited by King, Banana, and Parrinder, although apparently containing most of the components defined within the typology of myths, actually create difficulties for those who wish to use them to confirm that African myths are primarily cosmogonic. Each account relies on secondary sources and each begins with the assumption that the Supreme Being is the most important element in understanding the African cosmological scheme. This seems to reflect a largely Western academic or Christian bias toward theistic forms of religion and justifies at the very least a scholarly attitude of suspicion regarding the general typological classification of myths in Africa.[4]

Ruth Finnegan: The Nature of Oral Literature in Africa

The shared academic view expressed by King, Banana and Parrinder that cosmogonic myths form a central part of African oral literature much in line with the overall definitions of myth noted earlier is challenged by Ruth Finnegan, who conducted extensive research among the Limba of Sierra Leone. She claims that in oral societies, the telling of stories fundamentally depends on the storyteller. 'Oral literature is by definition dependent on a performer who formulates it in words on a specific occasion' (1970, 2). For this reason, what are called myths in Africa are less like stories recorded in books than like music or dance. They are performative.

Whenever a performance take place, the interaction between the performer and the audience affects the outcome. Finnegan argues that this means that no 'authorised' version of the story exists. Extemporaneous presentations or elaborations often occur depending

---

4. For my discussion of how Christian concepts of God have influenced interpretations of the sacred in Africa both by African theologians and by Western sociologists and anthropologists, see, J. L. Cox, 'Ancestors, the Sacred and God: Reflections on the meaning of the sacred in Zimbabwean death rituals', *Religion* 25 (4), 1995, 339-55.

on the storyteller and the audience. She concludes, 'There is no escape for the oral artist from a face-to-face confrontation with his audience, and this is something he can exploit as well as be influenced by' (p. 10).

Since African stories are always related orally, they will differ with each telling, not only in content but also in their context. The storyteller may be different, the audience may be diverse, or the purpose for its telling may vary. As a result, African stories are not handed down verbatim from generation to generation (p. 319).

Finnegan contrasts this to the general classification of myth as it is understood in Western literature. She notes that most scholars in the West distinguish between myths and folktales, i.e. between prose narratives believed to be true and concerned with the origin of things and those prose narratives taken much less seriously and regarded as fictional. As we have seen, this is a distinction employed by Bascom and earlier by Malinowski.

Finnegan argues, however, that in Africa this distinction is not generally observed. Many African peoples, she says, 'regard both as belonging in the same general genre of oral literature.' Some differences may be noted by scholars who write down and classify African stories, but 'the people themselves are not conscious of it'. Often, however, the basis for the differentiation itself is missing and 'it is not possible to find any local or empirical distinction between different groups of narratives' (pp. 327-8).[5]

Myths as they are generally defined, Finnegan asserts, 'are by no means common in African oral literature'. She contends this to be the case 'in spite of the narratives presented as myths in many popular collections'. Although African stories often tell of beginnings, refer to supernatural beings, and may be concerned with events set in the remote past, they do not possess an 'authoritative nature', are not necessarily accepted as truthful accounts, and, most importantly, seldom depict 'the activities of deities or other supernatural beings alone or even as the central subject' (p. 362).

Other important factors should be noted in the discussion. It is significant, Finnegan argues, that generally no term in vernacular languages corresponds to 'myth'. This suggests that in local usage, no distinctions among types of stories are made (p. 363). Where any differences are devised among the people between myth or myth-legend and folktale, she adds, they depend less on the content of the story than on the context. Among the Ashanti of Ghana, for example, what Westerners call myths 'are told within circumscribed groups or are limited to a select group of elders who guard them with care' (p. 365).

Finnegan concludes, therefore, that books on African oral literature in which myths are cited as evidence of religious phenomena appear to be 'elicited narratives'. 'It is not clear that they would have been expressed in narrative and literary form were it not for the request of the

---

5. This point is confirmed by the stories presented in part two of this book. I have created the distinctions between stories of origin, socio-moral myths, and tales of mysterious occurrences based on my reading of their general content. There is no evidence, however, that the informants made any such distinction in type or classification. I have organised the material in this way for the sake of academic analyses and to assist the reader by providing a coherent structure within the collection.

collector.' It should be noted in support of this contention, Finnegan adds, that 'among collectors who have had the closest knowledge of the peoples they are writing about...we find a telling absence of any reference to or inclusion of religious narratives'. As a result, it is fair to conclude that 'there is an absence of any solid evidence for myth as a developed literary form in most areas of Africa' (pp. 366-7).[6]

What then comprises the nature of African stories? Finnegan notes that there is far more interest in what she calls 'historical narrative', 'the deeds of historical heroes in the not so remote past', than in myths in the sense of the actions of deities in the furthest past of cosmological speculations (p. 369).

Narratives purporting to recount, for instance, how the ancestors of the present ruling houses first came to the area as saviours, or first settlers, or even victorious conquerors (all common themes) provide a justification for the continued position and power of these houses in the present. The 'mythical charter' thus given by the stories can be an important support for the existing distribution of political power, and it is not surprising that in these conditions there is a marked emphasis on history (p. 372).[7]

Finnegan thus seems to be suggesting that most stories told in Africa fall closest to Bascom's definition of a legend or what Hooke calls a prestige myth.[8] The central characteristic that myths tell of the beginnings of the world in a remote time and space with the chief players being gods, divinities or superheroes seems to be missing.[9] Whether or not they can be classified as sacred stories is a question to which I will return later. It is clear, however, that if Finnegan is correct, the myths which have been passed on by scholars on African religions as cosmogonic have been elicited for the purposes of collection, taken out of context, and perhaps given a place of importance based largely on

6. This same criticism can be levelled against the collection of oral literature which is presented in part two of this book. The students were instructed to ask elders to relate a story they remembered being told long ago, and thus the students did not observe the telling of the stories as drama. This represents one of the limitations of the field material in part two. However, the students also reported that opportunities to observe storytelling as performances were rare, whereas possibilities for participating in rituals were abundant. Rather inadvertently, this may confirm Finnegan's contention that myth is not a developed literary genre in Africa.

7. Luc de Heusch (1994), who has done extensive research in central Africa, supports Finnegan's contention that Bantu stories, what he calls epics, 'lay the foundations for sacred kingship' and 'legitimate this key institution in the social and cosmic order' (p. 229). Nevertheless, he argues that such stories need to be regarded as myths for the purposes of literary analysis. This means that epics cannot be reduced to a poor accounting of history, what de Heusch calls 'the wreck of memories about history' because they give 'real or imaginary history a poetic depth and density' (p. 238), a point I take up in chapter seven where I redefine the meaning of myth.

8. In his introduction to *African Folklore*, Richard Dorson devotes many pages to an analysis of Finnegan's thesis. Although he criticises many of her points, he concludes that her book is 'good enough to crystallize misconceptions about the relationship of oral literature to folklore'. He also notes that Finnegan's rejection of Bascom's categories of prose narratives is justified since Bascom's examples do not fit well in non-literate societies (Dorson, 1973, 10-17).

9. In his analysis of heroic poetry in southern Africa, Daniel Kunene confirms Finnegan's emphasis on the historical myth in Africa. He says, 'The heroes are not superior beings except in so far as their earthly deeds make them so; least of all are they gods or descendants of gods. They do not possess supernatural powers, nor do they pit their strength against supernatural beings... In short, they are ordinary human beings engaged in ordinary human activities' (1971, xvi).

Western theistic assumptions concerning what should be central within religious phenomena.[10]

The Findings of Herbert Aschwanden[11]

Herbert Aschwanden, a Swiss medical doctor working in Zimbabwe, has compiled myths obtained from the Karanga in southcentral Zimbabwe. Most of his research was conducted in the 1960s and carried out by African nursing sisters of the Musiso Hospital near Saka, approximately eighty kilometres southeast of Masvingo. In his book under the title *Karanga Mythology: An Analysis of the Consciousness of the Karanga of Zimbabwe* (1989), Aschwanden begins with eight cosmogonic myths. On the surface, this would seem to contradict my argument, supported by Finnegan's analysis, that cosmogonic myths are given a primary position among many Western academics because they have been influenced by Christian understandings of the importance of God in religious typologies.

Aschwanden's case, however, is no different from that of King, Banana or Parrinder in that he attributes cosmic significance to myths because he claims they tell how God created the world. His telling of the myth of the 'creation of water' (pp. 11-12), paraphrased below, provides a good example.

A man called Mudzanapabwe came long ago from a foreign land carrying bow and arrows as well as a red needle. Before he started on his journey to a new land, his father warned him, 'You will probably suffer, but you will find happiness eventually'. His father told him that his name meant that he had great strength and promised him that he would become a king.

When he arrived in the new land, Mudzanapabwe stood on a rock and stamped his foot causing a large dust-cloud to rise in the sky. As he looked upward Mudzanapabwe saw huge rocks forming out of the dust-cloud which he shot with an arrow making a great noise and turning the rocks black. Soon, it started to rain without ceasing until the whole country was flooded. Mudzanapabwe then shot another arrow into the sky separating earth and heaven. The rain stopped and vegetation appeared on the earth. After this, Mudzanapabwe praised his father for faithfully fulfilling all that he had promised. After honouring his father in this way, Mudzanapabwe stamped his foot on the ground again, inducing rocks to fly into the sky which he then shot with his arrow causing the rain to fall once more.

Although this abbreviated form of Aschwanden's account tells of the beginning of the world as the Karanga now experience it, it primarily

---

10. Ulli Beier says that Yoruba myths are multi-functional in nature. Some convey religious ideas thus exposing the worldview of the people. Others can be classified better as folklore or as historical legends. These classifications, however, cannot be regarded as anything more than guidelines for understanding the Yoruba oral literature because 'the categories overlap'. In a point similar to Finnegan's, Beier emphasises the importance of the particular function intended by the storyteller in relating the story. 'Religious myths are often told in sparse language... The less serious myths, the folkloristic themes, are often more playful and elaborate in their language' (Beier, 1980, xiv).

11. I discuss Aschwanden and the myth of Mudzanapabwe in the context of understanding the sacred in Zimbabwe in 'Ancestors, the sacred and God: Reflections on the meaning of the sacred in Zimbabwean death rituals', *Religion* 25 (4), 1995, 339-55.

offers a story about rain and the abundance produced by rain through one who is perceived as the first king of the region. If God plays a role in this story at all, it is as the great father, the one who commissioned Mudzanapabwe to go into another country.

Mudzanapabwe's father, however, is not conceived as God in the Christian meaning but as the great ancestor, the ultimate progenitor of the Karanga people. In this sense, no break between the role of ancestors and the one who makes the conditions necessary for rain to occur is noted. To call this God without noting its clear distinctions from a Christian concept of the supreme being is quite misleading.

The role of the original ancestor may conform to many roles assigned by Christians to God since both cause all things good to happen and maintain a beneficent role so long as they are acknowledged and thanked. But the Karanga are descendants of the father of Mudzanapabwe who takes on the characteristics of a quasi-historical figure establishing the people in their present land, lending confirmation more to Finnegan's interpretation than Aschwanden's.

Aschwanden's account nevertheless helps us understand the way the world is perceived and experienced by the Karanga. The problem which seems apparent to me in the early section of his book and in his later discussion of myths about God (pp. 200-221) is that he does not relate his interpretation stressing the importance of God to the context or religious practices of the Karanga, particularly in rituals. This points to a larger problem with his collection as a whole. Almost no space is given to the conditions under which the stories were obtained, how they were elicited, in what context they were told, and how widely they are known in the region.

Such information would have been helpful, but it does not discredit the importance of Aschwanden's accounts which, in my view, largely confirm my contention, which I try to support in chapter four, that rituals demonstrate the central preoccupation in Zimbabwean religions with the ancestors. Aschwanden's story of Mudzanapabwe, and his other creation stories, in my view, suggest this conclusion. It is certainly clear from the myth of Mudzanapabwe that stories of beginnings are not perceived as occurring in a remote time and space but form a continuous line relevant to the people's everyday concerns with health, abundance of the land, prosperity and proper relationships with one's neighbours. This implies a fundamental distinction from what normally are defined as cosmogonic myths.

A Story from Fieldwork in Zimbabwe

Among the stories collected by my phenomenology of religion students in the University of Zimbabwe in 1992, an excellent example of a quasi-historical story is provided by Eresina Hwede under the title, 'The Founding of Gazaland'. The version which follows was obtained by the student from a spirit medium of the present chief in Gazaland, a region in southeastern Zimbabwe now comprising the Chimanimani and Chipinge Districts.

In the story, we see precisely what Finnegan has called narratives recounting how the ancestors first came to an area. The time is not the remote past and historical factors are present, but certain supernatural or at least mysterious characteristics are evident.[12] I will relate the story in edited version below and then provide an interpretive analysis in the light of the myth theories and the related African problem noted above.

The Founding of Gazaland

A man called Gaza travelled from South Africa with his family into Zimbabwe. He settled in Gazaland and he had one son called Chamusa. These became known as the Gaza people and their language was Tshangani, probably a Nguni dialect. They knew nothing about *midzimu* (ancestral spirits) and possession. They lived a simple life without religion or sacredness. When Chamusa's father (Gaza) died, his son called Nguvoyame became possessed by Gaza. By then Nguvoyame was seven years old. There was a severe drought in Gazaland and Chamusa and his family were starving.

One night, Nguvoyame's father had decided to move away with his family in search of water. When they woke their little son Nguvoyame to start their journey, he refused and he told his father to go and look for water at the pool which was near the hill where his grandfather Gaza was buried.

Chamusa argued with his son for a time refusing to go and later Nguvoyame started to speak in his grandfather's voice commanding Chamusa to go and fetch water at the pool. By then Nguvoyame was no longer calling Chamusa father but 'my son' implying that he was possessed by Gaza, Chamusa's late father.

When Chamusa went to the pool, he found it full of fresh water and he told his wife and children to fetch water. Nguvoyame told them to use the water for whatever purpose, even to water their gardens because the pool was never to dry up.

Nguvoyame built his fireplace near the pool. He became known as the *svikiro* (a possessed person), usually one who is possessed by the great ancestors or founder of a tribe or a family. They also named him *Goko rama Changani* which means that he was the offspring of the founder of the nation or tribe. His existence resembled the existence of Gaza. Therefore, from the age of seven Nguvoyame acted as a *svikiro*. He intervened between Gaza and the people. He also became a king and after his death one member of the family became possessed by the same spirit and therefore became a king.

Analysis of the Founding of Gazaland

This story tells of the founding of a people in a particular region. The world is much as it is today except that the people have no knowledge of their ancestral spirits and are ignorant of the fact that the spirits can communicate through chosen mediums. Nor are they aware that ancestor spirits provide for and respond to the needs of their children.

---

12. Beach says that the Gaza state was established in the south-eastern highlands in the middle of the nineteenth century as a part of the larger invasions among the Shona by the Nguni speaking peoples. The other great incursion occurred in the west by the Ndebele speaking groups (Beach, 1980, 282; Beach, 1984, 52-59).

The story relates how the first ancestor, Gaza, came to the region and how, after the people began to suffer due to drought, he chose a young boy to be his medium. This provides a particularly stark contrast to the normal position of a young boy in relation to elders. When told by his father to depart from the land struck by drought, the boy refuses. He then becomes transformed into the wise elder who directs his father to a life-giving source of water. The young boy, Nguvoyame, becomes a mediator between the people and the original ancestor so much so that he adopts his voice and mannerisms and even appears to resemble him. Eventually, Nguvoyame becomes a king in succession to his grandfather.

That the story conveys what forms the essential beliefs of the people is clear, but it does not seem to fall within the classification of myth as it has been described earlier in this chapter. The characters in this story are not divinities and do not operate in a world different from the present one. Gaza has died, but retains his original role as leader and protector of the people. He is known by name, as are his descendants.

Yet the story is not actually historical in content or intention. It provides an idealised account meant to confirm and explain the present life, order, and rituals of a people. It thus fits into Finnegan's classification as oral literature told on various occasions in specific contexts to the current generation. Its historical account differs greatly from how an academic historian would describe the migrations of peoples into the region.

Nguvoyame could be called a culture hero, but no great achievements or grand acts are attributed to him other than his becoming a model for all subsequent acts of spirit mediumship. The story thereby provides a paradigm for how the people are to relate to one another in society through respect for elders and ancestors, but, in contrast to the definition of myth given above, it does not derive from a cosmogonic myth. Under Bascom's categories, therefore, it would be called a historical legend.

A Wider Application of the Historical Legend

I believe that the story of the founding of Gazaland is typical of African stories of origin. It is not the only type of story told, as we shall see shortly, but it represents what I would call an African story of beginnings. The origin spoken of is not the cosmos but of a people and how the structure of their society and its relation to the spiritual world has come to be. That this type of story is typical for Zimbabwean religions is confirmed in the MA thesis of the late T. Chiura who wrote on a sacred tree called the Mutiusinazita Tree (a tree without a name) near the present day Marondera in central Zimbabwe. Chiura indicates that in his field research almost all of his informants referred to a story relating how a voice emanating from rocks or trees led the people from their land of origin to a new land now designated Mashonaland. While the voice was in this area, it spoke from the nameless tree.

Chiura's account of the story is similar to that reported in the works of A. S. Chigwedere (1980) who has written about the traditional stories of migration to Zimbabwe. Chiura, however, relates it as it was told by his own informant named M. E. Mushangwe, the chief leader and spirit medium at the time of the interviews around the Mutiusinazita cult.

Since Mushangwe's version is so similar to that found in Chigwedere, Chiura admits that he is unsure if Chigwedere had used the same sources as he or if the informant himself was familiar with Chigwedere's account.

As the story was told to Chiura, Mambiri, also known as Munembire, was the first ancestor of the Mbire people while they were in Tanzania. Mambiri had a son named Tovera whose own son was named Murenga. The latter was the father of Chaminuka who led the people southward at the leading of the voice. Through many hardships, Chaminuka brought the people as far south as what is now Malawi. Chaminuka died and became the chief ancestral spirit remembered in later events, but his son Kutamadzoka continued to lead the people southward until they crossed the Zambezi River. Kutamadzoka became the highest chief in the hierarchy and assumed the name Mutapa. He finally reached what is now Marondera and called the area Mbire in honour of the first ancestor. There, amongst a rocky outcropping, stood a tree the people had never seen before, a tree without a name. Kutamadzoka was attracted by the tree and built his court around it.

D. N. Beach takes great care to outline how such a story lacks historical credibility. In his book *Zimbabwe before 1900* (1984), he limits his discussion of migrations 'to reality not to myth'. He notes that the longest migrations were 'less than 500 kilometres long, or about a month's walk for a fit traveller'. Most were much shorter (1984, 6). In his earlier more extensive book outlining the history of the Shona between 900 and 1850, moreover, he notes that 'there is considerable doubt that there ever was a "Mutapa Munembire"' (1980, 121).

The Zimbabwean historian Stanlake Samkange (1968, 3) refers to the oral traditions of the Shona peoples in which their ancestors were said to have migrated from a place in the north consisting of tall grass (*Guruwuskwa*). Associated with this oral tradition, as shown in Chiura's account, is the development of the Mwari (High God) cults at Great Zimbabwe which after the fall of the Rozvi Empire in the mid-nineteenth century seemingly moved to the regions of the Matopos Hills in the western areas. These oracular centres would have added to the tradition of the voice of Mwari leading the great ancestors in their migrations southward. What actually happened is much more complex and inconclusive as noted recently by M. Daneel (1998, 95) who observed, 'With oral tradition, conclusive proof is elusive'.

What is significant in Chiura's account is that actual historical developments are mixed, just as in the Gaza story, with an idealised version of a people's movement into an area. In both stories, a first ancestor is described as leading a movement of his people into another region. The subsequent descendants continue to follow the directions of the ancestors. In Chiura's narrative, the mysterious voice is purported to have led the people, although it is not clear from his informant whether this is conceived of as the High God or as an even earlier ancestor. The central point both in Chiura's account and in the Gazaland story, however, is to establish how a people came to a region and how certain symbols (in the case of the Mbire migrations, the Mutiusinazita tree, and in the case of Gazaland, the spirit medium) represent the continued care and presence of the ancestors.

Socio-Moral Myths

Another type of myth which seems prevalent in Africa is what I call the socio-moral myth. This is a story which is told chiefly for the purpose of reenforcing the norms of the society. Some scholars, such as the French sociologist Emile Durkheim and the anthropologist Bronislaw Malinowski, have understood the primary characteristic of all myths in this way. Malinowski followed Durkheim by suggesting that myths express in words the mores of a society just as rituals act them out (Shinn, 1981, 516).

As I indicated above, however, those who follow the Eliade theory of myth and ritual view socio-moral myths as derived from cosmogonic myths. Although they play an important role by expressing and authorising social values, myths are not seen primarily as social in origin and function but as religious accounts of how the sacred established the world by interrupting the homogeneity of space and time. In the African case, however, if Ruth Finnegan and I are correct, socio-moral stories are not derivative from cosmogonic myths because the latter are largely absent from African oral literature.

Finnegan, however, also rejects the social functionalist interpretation of African myths. Although she acknowledges the widespread use of such stories, she denies that they constitute the primary form of African oral literature. She admits that 'some stories do end with a moral or a proverb' and that 'stories are sometimes told to educate or admonish children'. There may even be a term in some languages for this type of oral literature. Nevertheless, she contends, 'there is no evidence at all to suggest that this is the only or the primary aim of stories – and plenty of evidence that many African tales contain neither direct nor indirect moralizing' (p. 377-78).

The socio-moral stories of African oral literature, therefore, need to be seen as a common type set alongside the historical category of narrative. Neither can be reduced simply to social functions, although both influence the people's understanding of what constitutes proper moral behaviour and the correct political structure. The widespread knowledge of socio-moral stories in Africa, however, underscores the point I have just made about historical legends, namely, that the classical definitions of myth as cosmogonic and set in a remote space and time seem inapplicable to many parts of Africa.

Among the thirty-seven stories I collected and edited from my students in the University of Zimbabwe and which appear in part two of this book, I have classified sixteen as socio-moral. I have selected one here to demonstrate how this type fails to meet the criteria for myths as I have derived them from the scholars noted above. The version I have chosen here was supplied by Timothy Sango who obtained it from his grandfather who at the time of the telling was the oldest man in his village located in the Honde Valley of Eastern Zimbabwe.

The Story of the Foolish Wife

In the village of Mr. Sadunhu, lived Mr. Rema with his wife Revesai and their three sons. Mr. Rema's wife was the most foolish woman ever found in the village and even beyond. She neither respected any man nor the spirits. It happened one year that there was a terrible drought that had threatened both human and animal lives. One day, Mr. Rema's wife went to a nearby river and began plucking a certain plant that was growing by the river banks. Among the villagers, such a plant was known to be inedible. Anyone who eats of that plant will die or have a terrible illness and only survive by the grace of the ancestors. After filling her basket, Revesai went home. Early in the evening, she began preparing the supper. After the food was ready, she called her family and they began eating.

As they were eating, one of the sons choked on the plant. Mr. Rema and his wife tried all means to help the child but to no avail and eventually he passed away. The next day, Mr. Rema, his wife and their remaining two sons began suffering from a terrible illness from which it took them three weeks to recover with the help of a *n'anga* (traditional healer) named Godobare.[13] They were told by the *n'anga* that tradition forbade eating of that particular plant.

Some months passed and Revesai brought home a bunch of firewood. Among the firewood was some of the wood that is not supposed to be used as firewood. She placed the forbidden wood in the hearth to make some fire, but it would not light. She applied all different methods but it did not materialise. She even went to fetch some burning charcoal from a nearby woman, but the charcoal was extinguished when it came into contact with the wood. She later called her neighbour and explained to her what was happening. Her neighbour discovered that at the fire hearth there was some of the firewood that was not supposed to be used. She pulled the wood out and the fire started. When Mr. Rema heard this, he was almost boiling with rage. He almost divorced his wife, but the village elders told him not to do so.

Then one day during the summer season in the afternoon Revesai went to the village well to fetch water. When she arrived at the well, she saw a big frog in the well busy swimming. This frustrated her. She pulled the frog out of the well and in a rage crushed it with a big stone. As soon as the frog died, the water in the well disappeared and the well was left dry. The woman was not worried and she took her empty bucket and headed homeward. On the way home, Revesai met the chief's wife and explained to her what had happened at the well. The chief's wife told her that she had committed a great offence to the ancestor spirits who would need to be reconciled to the community for the water to come back.

When Mr. Rema heard about this issue, he almost axed Revesai but once again the village elders comforted him. Mr. Rema was then told by the spirit medium that he should pay a black bull and a black cock to the ancestors, otherwise the spirits would destroy the whole family. Fortunately, Mr. Rema had the required things and he paid causing the water to return and fill the

---

13. In Shona, Godobari refers to a very skilled *n'anga*.

well as before. The chief told Revesai not to repeat the same mistake, otherwise she would be victimised by being a prey to the *Mhondoro* (lion, representing the senior ancestor spirits). On top of that, she was ordered to brew beer to the spirits in order to cool down their anger and ask for forgiveness.

Days, months and years passed without anything happening to the wife of Mr. Rema so that everybody in the village thought she had reformed. Even her husband was pleased with her and promised her a present for the good way in which she was controlling herself.

However, it happened one day in the summer season that the women in the village, including Revesai, went to a nearby forest to fetch some mushrooms. As the women were scattered in the forest, Revesai came across some mushrooms which were inedible and she began to despise them and shouted out that they were poisonous. Suddenly, she began wandering about in the forest aimlessly and became lost. When the other women realised that she was missing, they were shocked. They began calling her name and looking for her, but they could not find her. They went home and told her husband and the chief. The next day the villagers searched for her, but they never found her. After a week, they went to consult the *n'anga* Godobare who instructed them to brew beer for the ancestors in order that Revesai might return home. When the beer was brewed and appeals were made to the ancestors, she returned home and immediately was divorced by her husband who was given her young sister for a replacement.

This story demonstrates the close connection between nature, the ancestors, and acceptable moral behaviour in society by reenforcing respect for the environment and for the ancestor spirits. It falls into what I would call a socio-moral myth because the primary purpose of the myth seems to be to exemplify the disastrous social effects of failing to follow the rules of respect known widely within the village.

Although this story points toward the fundamental beliefs of the people, just as the historical narratives do, it does not fit easily into the characteristics of myths noted earlier in this chapter. In a similar way to the historical type of stories, the socio-moral myths lack cosmogonic elements, are not set in a time and space different from the present world, do not feature divinities or culture heroes as the chief characters, and do not establish a paradigmatic model for all essential human activities.

The story told above resembles what Bascom would call a folktale. It certainly would be entertaining when recited and at the same time underscores a moral lesson. Nevertheless, if Finnegan is correct, Bascom's distinctions would be unknown to the people and irrelevant to their understanding of sacred realities.

The Essential Problem
The Zimbabwean examples obtained largely from student fieldwork cited above and the other scripts of the stories which are presented in part two of this book, appear to confirm what Finnegan has contended to be the case for most of Africa. Myths, in the classical sense, are largely

absent from direct fieldwork recounting oral literature in Africa. What Bascom calls historical legends telling of the founding of a people and folktales with social and moral intentions, however, are common.

As the stories recounted in part two demonstrate, failure to find myths as I defined them earlier does not mean that none of the stories relate to origins. Indeed, I have classified sixteen of the Zimbabwean stories as dealing with the origin of various natural, social and personal experiences, such as the formation of sacred and mysterious mountains, the establishment of a people in the land, the source of totems and other stories dealing with animals, and stories explaining how death entered the world.

Only one story, 'Nyatene's Body and the Origins of the World' (as related by A. B. Bonzo), can be called cosmogonic in the sense of telling how the world began in a remote space and time and referring to a central character whose name can be translated as 'Supreme Being'. In Bonzo's account, Nyatene is called 'a person' who 'is believed to have been complex in nature'. 'Everything we see today was once fused together in the complex body of Nyatene'. The story tells how over time Nyatene became so huge that he had to shake his body and eventually separate himself from all living beings and natural objects. A struggle for supremacy among humans, the sun, moon, clouds and the other objects of the world ensued. Eventually, the conflicts became so great that Nyatene became angry and 'could not easily be placated'. Thus, the world as it now is with its various threats to well-being came into existence.

Although this account may appear to conform to the broad classification of cosmogonic myths as related earlier in this chapter and thus prove an exception to my general argument, a close reading demonstrates that the purpose of the story is not primarily to relate events in a time of beginnings, nor to explain the nature of the Supreme Being, but to legitimate the place and function of ancestors and to explain why rituals of honour need to be offered regularly to them. The conclusion of the story confirms this:

> The ancestors would then act as protectors of their children against all evil forces. The living would brew beer and sacrifice to their ancestors so that they would remain pleased and avoid causing any more havoc amongst the people.

Unlike the narrative of Nyatene, the great majority of the stories recounted in part two feature humans or animals as the chief actors. Where God is referred to at all, as in the stories of death, the central figures still remain the animal or human characters and not a Supreme Being or a divinity of some sort.

The interconnected worlds of spirits and humans, nevertheless, are implied within all of the stories. In both the historical and socio-moral myths recounted above, the ancestors communicate through a medium conveying information necessary for the people's well-being. The medium varies from a family member possessed by the ancestor spirit to a *n'anga* who uses special techniques to ascertain the necessary information (such as casting divining sticks or spirit possession) or, as in the case of the widely known story of the Mbire migration, a voice leads the people on their southward journeys. Even in the story of Nyatene, the central purpose of its telling seems to justify the authority of the ancestor spirits and the rituals connected to them.

This problem of the failure to find evidence for myth in the typical sense in Africa despite the references to spiritual beings in the narratives leads me to raise some critical questions regarding myths in Africa. Do Africans actually lack myths or are the components in the definition lacking?" If it is the former, does this mean that in Africa what otherwise appears to be a universal religious typology is fundamentally deficient? And does this make analysis of religion in Africa at once more difficult than other traditions and at the same time less rich? Finally, can this explain why it is a particularly perplexing task to systematise African world views?

I shall endeavour to answer these questions later by reformulating a theory of myth in chapter six. The spiritual backdrop for the African stories suggests that such a reformulation is necessary since the telling of the stories mediates sacred realities for the adherents. In the next chapter, I seek to demonstrate further how complicating the essential problem of the African oral tradition becomes in the light of theories of ritual and in particular the hypothesis that rituals primarily re-enact cosmogonic myths.

---

14. G. S. Kirk would hold that the essential problem is not confined to African myths at all since myths are not properly defined as related exclusively to the actions of gods and the origins of the world. In his influential book, *Myth: Its Meaning and Functions in Ancient and Other Cultures* (1970), he argues that 'many myths embody a belief in the supernatural, and for most cultures that will involve polytheist religion; but many other myths, or what seem like myths, do not'. Kirk concludes that many stories both from classical Greek mythology and from what he calls 'savage societies' 'have no serious religious component whatsoever' (p. 11).

References

Abimbola, W. 1994. '*Ifa*: A West African cosmological system' in T. D. Blakely, W. E. A. van Beek and D. L. Thompson (eds.), *Religion in Africa*. London: James Currey and Portsmouth, New Hampshire: Heinemann, 101-31.

Aschwanden, H. 1989. *Karanga mythology: An analysis of the consciousness of the Karanga in Zimbabwe*. Gweru: Mambo Press.

Banana, C. S. 1991. *Come and share: An introduction to Christian theology*. Gweru: Mambo Press.

Bascom, W. 1984. 'The forms of folklore: Prose narratives', in A. Dundes (ed.), *Sacred narrative. Readings in the theory of myth*. Berkeley: University of California Press, 5-29.

Beach, D. N. 1980. *The Shona and Zimbabwe 900-1850*. London: Heinemann.

1984. *Zimbabwe before 1900*. Gweru: Mambo Press.

Beek, W. E. A. van and Blakely, T. D. 1994. 'Introduction', in T. D. Blakely, W. E. A. van Beek and D.L. Thomson (eds.), *Religion in Africa*. London: James Currey and Portsmouth, New Hampshire: Heinemann, 3-20.

Beier, U. 1980. *Yoruba myths*. Cambridge: Cambridge University Press.

Chigwedere, A. S. 1980. *From Mutapa to Rhodes 1000-1890 A.D.* London: Macmillan.

Chiura, T. 1991. *Mutiusinazita religious cult in Marondera District, Zimbabwe*. Unpublished MA Thesis, University of Zimbabwe.

Cox, J. L. 1995. 'Ancestors, the sacred and God: Reflections on the meaning of the sacred in Zimbabwean death rituals. *Religion* 25 (4), 339-55.

1996 2nd ed. *Expressing the sacred: An introduction to the phenomenology of religion*. Harare: University of Zimbabwe Publications.

Daneel, M. L. 1998. 'Mwari the liberator: Oracular intervention in Zimbabwe's quest for the "Lost Lands"', in J. L. Cox (ed.), *Rites of passage in contemporary Africa*. Cardiff: Cardiff Academic Press, 97-125.

Dorson, R. D. 1973 2nd ed. 'Africa and the folklorist', in R.D. Dorson (ed.), *African folklore*. Bloomington: Indiana University Press, 3-67.

Dundes, A. 1984. 'Introduction', in A. Dundes (ed.), *Sacred narrative. Readings in the theory of myth*. Berkeley: University of California Press.

Eliade, M. 1958. *Patterns in comparative religion*. London: Sheed and Ward.

1959. *The Sacred and the profane*, Trans. W.R. Trask. New York: Harcourt, Brace and World.

1969. *The quest: History and meaning in religion*. Chicago and London: University of Chicago Press.

Finnegan, R. 1970. *Oral literature in Africa*. Oxford: The Clarendon Press.

Gard, R. (ed.) 1962. *Buddhism*. New York: George Braziller.

Heusch, L. de 1994. 'Myth and epic in Central Africa', in W. E. A. van Beek, T. D. Blakely and D. L. Thomson (eds.), *Religion in Africa*. London: James Currey and Portsmouth, New Hampshire: Heinemann, 229-38.

Honko, L. 1984. 'The problem of defining myth,' in A Dundes (ed.), *Sacred narrative: Readings in the theory of myth*. Berkeley: University of California Press, 41-52.

Hooke, S. H. 1966. *Middle Eastern mythology*. Harmondsworth: Penguin Books.

Kahari, G. 1992 2nd ed. *Aspects of the Shona novel*. Gweru: Mambo Press.

Kirk, G. S. 1970. *Myth: Its meaning and functions in ancient and other cultures*. Cambridge: Cambridge University Press.

King, N. G. 1986. *African cosmos: An introduction to religion in Africa*. Belmont, California: Wadsworth Publishing Company.

Kunene, D. P. 1971. *The heroic poetry of the Basotho*. Oxford: The Clarendon Press.

Kup, A. P. 1961. *A history of Sierra Leone: 1400-1787* Cambridge, Cambridge University Press.

Leach, E. 1970. *Levi-Strauss*. Glasgow: Fontana Collins.

Malinowski, B. 1948. *Magic, science and religion and other essays*. Boston: Beacon Press.

Parrinder, E. G. 1981 3rd ed. *African Traditional Religion*. London: Sheldon Press.

Percheron, M. 1982. *Buddha and Buddhism*. Woodstock, New York: Overlook Press.

Rowe, D. 1988. *Choosing not losing. The experience of depression*. London: Fontana Paperbacks.

Ruthven, K. K. 1976. *Myth*. London: Methuen and Company.

Samkange, S. 1968. *Origins of Rhodesia*. London: Heinemann.

Schmidt, R. 1988. *Exploring religion*. Belmont: California, Wadsworth Publishing Company.

Schneiderman, L. 1981. *The psychology of myth, folklore, and religion*. Chicago: Nelson-Hall.

Shinn, L. D. 1981. 'Myth', in K. Crim (General ed.), *Abingdon Dictionary of Living Religions*. Nashville: Abingdon, 514-517.

Smart, N. 1984. *The religious experience of mankind*. Glasgow: Collins Fount Paperbacks.

Chapter Four

RITUAL AND THE PROBLEM OF THE
RITUAL RE-ENACTMENT THEORY IN AFRICA

In this chapter, I pursue further problems related to the study of myth in Africa by focusing on the ritual re-enactment theory. I will suggest that not only do we fail to find support for the classical definition of myths in Africa, as noted in the previous chapter, but myths appear not to be re-enacted in rituals as the myth-ritual hypothesis would expect.

In order to explore this theme, I want first to discuss the nature of ritual in general. I will then define the ritual re-enactment theory as it has been explained largely by those influenced by Mircea Eliade. I follow this with an analysis of recent theories that ritual possesses its own intrinsic meaning and cannot be explained in terms of myth. I have selected a case study from Zimbabwean field material to demonstrate how the ritual re-enactment theory lacks support in the description cited.

A Working Definition of Ritual

Just as we saw with the classification 'myth', ritual has been defined variously and widely in literature on religious studies. In his contribution to the *Abingdon Dictionary of Living Religions*, F. W. Clothey (1981, 624-28) claims that ritual is so important for understanding religion that it functions as 'a paradigm and dramatization of the intent of religion itself'. It does this, he adds, by the use of symbols, both visual and aural, which 'along with intellectual and sensual images' provide the participant with a sense of identity. The paradigmatic element of rituals is seen in that during their performance they transform the participant 'into a new mode of being'.

Roger Schmidt (1988, 392) refers to 'holy rites' as 'formalized and symbolic actions' which direct people toward an experience of the sacred. He adds that rituals do this whether or not the sacred is conceived of as a personal being (or beings) or as an impersonal 'creative process'. The term 'sacred' is used by Schmidt interchangeably with the 'holy' and refers to that which for believers is 'ultimate', 'nonordinary' and represents 'awesome' or 'majestic power' (pp. 62-73).

In his book examining sacred space and ritual action, J. Z. Smith (1987) notes that initially ritual is 'a mode of paying attention' (p. 103).

Space directs or focuses the attention. Sacred places, therefore, represent the 'extraordinary setting' wherein 'quite ordinary activities' take place (p. 109). This setting provides ritual with its power and makes clear the contrast between the way things are and the way things ought to be. Rituals perform or act out how the religious person perceives the ideal.

In his discussion of rituals and religious pluralism, J. G. Platvoet (1995, 6) argues that ritual refers to 'any sequence of customary symbolic actions' which are standardised 'through repetition in social interaction'. Rituals utilise symbols to express and convey meanings and thus at their core always entail modes of communication, both verbal and non-verbal. This definition of ritual can be applied to any form of customary, standardised and symbolic social communication and is not restricted to religious rituals. The importance of such a definition for our purposes results from its stress on fixed behaviour as a means for communicating meanings within any society.

In my own discussion of this subject (Cox, 1996, 89-90), I also emphasise that rituals are repeatable according to established patterns. As such, there are correct and incorrect ways of performing rituals which determine their efficacy as sources of transformative power. Actions within the rituals are employed prescriptively in ways known to the participants.

The key terms which appear in the above definitions help us arrive at some general characterisations of rituals.

1) Rituals point toward the sacred through dramatic actions and symbols.

2) They are repeated according to a fixed pattern.

3) Although ritual actions form a part of the ordinary world, they take place in an extraordinary setting.

4) Rituals provide a shared identity for participants thereby creating a sense of community.

5) Rituals operate as symbolic modes of communication.

6) Ritual performances possess a transformative power for participants by overcoming the contrast between what is and what ought to be.

A general definition of ritual based on the six characteristics above is as follows:

A ritual is a repeated and symbolic dramatisation that directs attention to a place where the sacred enters life thereby granting identity to participants in the drama, transforming them into a new state of being, communicating social meaning verbally and non-verbally, and offering a paradigm for how the world ought to be.

Types of Rituals

Rituals can be subdivided according to the function they perform for the believing community. Each type, however, shares the characteristics noted in the definition above. Generally, the subclassifications include: 1) life cycle rituals; 2) crisis rituals; and 3) calendrical rituals. The term 'Rites of Passage' has been employed widely since the publication of the book of the same title in 1908 by the French anthropologist Arnold van Gennep to refer to a ritual process shared by the first and third types.

60

The British anthropologist Victor Turner (1969) later incorporated what he called 'rituals of affliction', referred to here as crisis rituals, into the rites of passage.

Life cycle rituals. According to C. R. Taber (1981, 426), the related concepts of social status within a community and liminality form the basis for understanding life cycle rituals. Communities are comprised of social systems with clearly defined properties, rights and obligations for their members. Individuals in societies pass through transitional phases which reenforce their roles in the community and which are marked by the rites of passage. During the moments of transition, individuals possess no clearly defined role in the community. They are in the state of liminality (from the Latin *'limin'* meaning threshold), at the point of passage – neither in the previous state nor yet in the new one. People in the state of liminality often are considered dangerous and are in danger themselves. Hence, the rites of passage are designed to ensure that the person in transition neither acts in a harmful way nor becomes a victim of dangerous forces during the passage.

At each transition, Taber notes, life cycle observances 'typically include rites of separation, to ensure proper departure out of the prior status; rites of transition, to ensure safety during the hazardous liminal period; and rites of incorporation, to ensure proper identification with and recognition in the new status' (p. 426). The various stages may not always be distinguished sharply in the minds of those undergoing the rituals. One ritual, for example, may contain the separation, transition and incorporation phases, but the trained observer can identify how each is formalised throughout aspects of the ritual.

M. F. C. Bourdillon (1990, 45) adds that although members of a particular society may regard the rituals as having 'the effect of moving them from the status of one grade to another', in practice social change is more complex. Frequently, shifts in status are gradual, informal and correspond to physical age. Nevertheless, members of a society need mental constructs around which they can organise their perceptions of the social order. 'A system of rites of passage allows us to create that kind of order.'

Turner has explored the concept of liminality in depth basing his analysis in part on his work among the Ndembu of Zambia. In an article appearing in the Victor Turner commemorative issue of *Religion* (1985, 205-217), he explains that liminality literally divides two spaces or two times from one another just as a threshold separates the space demarcated by a closed from an open door or divides two times such as work time from leisure time. Cultures thus use the idea of a threshold as a crossing point in space and time such as, Turner notes, when a bride is carried across the threshold of a home symbolising 'vital sociocultural changes from unweddedness to weddedness' (p. 205).

In rituals this is seen as the movement from one state of being to another, as in the case of initiation rituals where a person is transformed from the state of being a child to that of an adult. This is true also in death rituals where through an often prolonged series of rituals a person is delivered safely into the world of the dead so that, depending on the understanding of the religious community, the person may assume the roles assigned to the deceased.

All societies have different age-linked rituals, and mark the passage from one to another, but not all have the same rituals, either in number or in kind. Following van Gennep, Turner lists the following as typical:

1) prenatal (e.g. rituals to confirm pregnancy, for fetal growth and for safe delivery);
2) naming rituals;
3) pre-pubertal and pubertal initiation rituals for the entrance into adulthood;
4) betrothal and marriage;
5) initiation into prestige bestowing adult associations;
6) rituals elevating individuals to high office or to priestly functions;
7) funeral (p. 206).

Turner suggested that the entire ritual process from separation through transition to incorporation is liminal because each phase occurs in a time between times and in a space that is 'set apart' from other places (p. 209). This means that the liminal contradicts normal social experience as, for example in many initiation rites, where the participants are taken to a place away from the village centre, a so-called 'bush school', and exposed to a world which is 'dark, dangerous, unpredictable, personified often by witches, demons, ghosts, ... and portrayed by masks and other disguises worn by elders'(p. 210).

The rite of incorporation will have been anticipated during the 'bush school' where instruction in the mores, customs, stories, patterns of behaviour, and sex education are given. Incorporation is consummated when the candidates are presented to society in their new status, in Taber's words 'often complete with a new name, new clothes, hairdo, and/or adornment, sometimes new place of residence, and of course new rights and duties' (p. 428). This represents the conclusion of the ritual where the initiate has assumed his newly defined role in the society. The entire ritual process thus binds the community together creating what Turner calls *communitas* (Schmidt, 1988, 408).

Asmarom Legesse (1994, 318-19) explains that *communitas* 'is the social dimension of liminality'. In normal social life, people relate to one another in segmented, functionally differentiated roles. In the state of liminality, because the participants are in a stage between defined social roles, according to Legesse, they form a group 'without social structure that is powerfully held together by factors other than kinship and the division of labor'. The solidarity that forms in the liminal state creates social cohesion once the participants are reincorporated into the larger community. However, Legesse argues that it is precisely through the *communitas* created in the state of liminality that the forces for social change are found, a factor he claims Turner did not explore fully. The end result of the process, nevertheless, is the same: in Bourdillon's words, 'to strengthen the moral values of the society when the period of sacred time is over' (1990, 318).

The processes involved in life cycle rites, as delineated particularly by van Gennep and Turner, clearly display the characteristics of rituals noted in the definition above. In each instance, the rites employ symbols in repeated patterns to effect transformations in the lives of the participants. Place, as demonstrated by Smith, is central and, when seen in the processes of preparation, separation and incorporation demarcates the boundary situations constituting the social and cosmic paradigms dramatised by the rituals.

Crisis rituals. As previously noted, Turner referred to crisis rituals as rituals of affliction. He also called them 'drums of affliction', according to John Janzen (1994, 162), in order to reflect 'the significance of drumming and rhythmic song-dancing' which frequently accompany such rituals. Affliction rituals aim at rectifying misfortunes in life as diverse as illness, barrenness, drought and war. Bourdillon claims that in African societies illness provides the most common cause for conducting the rituals (1990, 315).

When misfortune occurs, generally the causes are determined by a religious practitioner or diviner who uses a variety of means such as spirit possession, dreams, animals or mechanical devices (such as specially marked sticks) to explain why the affliction has occurred. He may then prescribe a particular ritual to perform which will alleviate the affliction. Walter van Beek (1994, 197) describes one such situation among the Kapsiki of northern Cameroon and northeastern Nigeria, where a diviner was consulted to explain why a woman had remained barren for ten years. The diviner placed a crabfish in a pot and discerned that the cause of the woman's inability to conceive children was her 'personal god' who required a ritual sacrifice to restore her fertility.

Turner argues that in 'pre-industrial societies' crises are regarded as 'a consequence of the transgression of moral norms and/or magical taboos established by deities or ancestral spirits' (1985, 208). Rituals, from a believer's perspective, are intended to restore harmony to a cosmic and social order which in some manner has been disrupted. The crisis provides the evidence for such disruptions. The ultimate causes of the crises are spiritual, but usually the spiritual causes are not seen in the believer's mind as distinct from the social and communal concerns. Turner goes so far as to argue that rites of affliction 'relate directly or indirectly to the current state of inter-personal and inter-group conflicts in a demarcated field of on-going social relations' (p. 208).

Crisis rituals, unlike life cycle rites, occur only when things go wrong in individual, familial, or communal life. They are therefore irregular and depend on circumstances peculiar to individuals or specific communities. However, because many of the crises, such as illness, occur frequently, in many societies, crisis rituals are commonly observed. Rituals aimed at alleviating crises utilise symbols in a fixed and repetitive pattern with the aim of transforming the participants from the state of abnormality by presenting an ideal picture of what the world ought to be. The place of the ritual is important since it is in the sacred space that the ideal can be realised during the ritual drama.

Calendrical rituals. Van Gennep included seasonal rituals as a part of communal rites of passage. They refer to rituals which occur at set times according to the seasonal or liturgical calendar. Examples include new year's festivals, planting and harvesting rituals, thanksgiving ceremonies, annual or regular rituals honouring the ancestors, preparations for hunting, and, in the case of liturgical religions, festivals which re-enact regularly the key stories of the faith such as Christmas and Easter for Christians and the Passover for the Jewish community.

This type of ritual is significant for the identity of religious communities. For example, new year festivals display the stages of separation, transition and incorporation in that as the old year draws to an end, the society enters a period of liminality where it is neither in the old nor yet in the new. This in-between stage frequently is marked by a breakdown in the order of the society reflected by a retreat into original chaos. During this period, the normal moral codes of the society no longer apply. It is as if the world has reverted back to its original state before the sacred formed it and made it what it is. As the ritual proceeds, order is reestablished and the community is incorporated into the new year in which the dangers of chaos so evident between the years is overcome.

An example of this is cited by V. Lanternari (1988, 847) in his discussion of Melanesian religions. Lanternari argues that the New Year feast of the Melanesians is rooted in the sense of the community that unless annual rituals are held in honour of the ancestors, when the ground is tilled during the next agricultural season, an offence is being committed against the ancestors who are buried in the soil. During the time between the years, the liminal period, the normal rules of society are suspended and a kind of primordial chaos prevails before the community is reincorporated into another agricultural cycle. Lanternari explains:

> The final feasting, the joyful and frantic indulging in eating and dancing and in the sexual orgy after the expiatory role of the previous rites and after the expulsion of the spirits, play the complementary role of clearing the way for the community to proceed trustfully and joyfully towards the new cycle of life and of agricultural activity.

Other calendrical rituals are important for community well-being as, for example, regular rain rituals in traditional agricultural societies during which appeals are made to the ancestors for good rains to ensure the productivity of the land. The rain ritual, however, provides more than an appeal for rain; it acknowledges the close relationship between the ancestors and the land and establishes the importance of respect for elders. This applies also to regular rituals honouring the ancestors, which may be observed by different families at regular calendrical intervals.

Religions which base their rituals on liturgical seasons tend to hold a linear view of history and repeat rituals as the historical events of the community are retold and re-enacted. This is true for the Jewish, Christian and Islamic faiths. In Islam, the pilgrimage to Mecca is marked each year by established rituals recounting significant events in the Muslim story. For example, the day after having stood before Allah from noon to sunset at Arafat begging for forgiveness, the pilgrim goes back along the road to Mecca collecting stones en route to throw at three specially demarcated pillars. This act represents the pilgrim's anger at the devil who, according to Islamic tradition, tempted Abraham to disobey God by urging him to sacrifice his son Ishmael at the sites symbolised by the pillars (Partin, 1981, 291). In Judaism, the annual observance of the Passover festival or in Christianity Holy Week recounting the events leading up to the crucifixion and resurrection of Jesus also exemplify liturgical re-enactments.

Calendrical rituals, whether cyclical or historical-liturgical, repeat events crucial to the life and identity of the community. They represent a movement through a process whereby what Turner calls 'liminal systems' can be seen at work. A threshold is passed through regularly and repeatedly so that the ritual transformation can be accomplished and the ritual paradigm of the ideal world maintained and ensured.

The Ritual Re-enactment Theory

The subclassifications of rituals noted above have been suggested largely by anthropologists who were describing the social function of rituals. Although no inherent contradiction exists between the social and religious analyses of rituals, the ritual re-enactment theory has endeavoured to elucidate what the rituals mean from the perspective of believers and hence seeks to decipher the essential religious structure of myths and rituals. An early exponent of the myth-ritual theory was S. H. Hooke, who up until the mid 1950s was Professor of Old Testament Studies in the University of London. In his book on *Middle Eastern Mythology*, to which I referred in the previous chapter, Hooke (1966) outlines clearly the meaning of the ritual re-enactment hypothesis.

Hooke defines ritual as 'a system of actions performed in a fixed way, at regular times, by authorized persons who possessed the specialized knowledge of the correct way in which these actions should be carried out.' The purpose of the actions in the ancient civilisations of Egypt and Mesopotamia was 'to secure the well-being of the community by controlling the incalculable forces by which man found himself surrounded' (p. 12).

Hooke notes, however, that ancient rituals were not comprised simply of actions but were accompanied by 'spoken words, chants, and incantations'. The spoken part was called by the Greeks *muthos* or myth.

In the ritual the myth told the story of what was being enacted; it described a situation; but the story was not told to amuse an audience; it was a word of power. The repetition of the magic words had power to bring about or recreate, the situation which they described (p. 12).

Hooke, just as Mircea Eliade (1959, 77-80) had done earlier, exemplified the ritual re-enactment of rituals by relating the story of the Babylonian New Year Festival. During each festival, the priests would recite the chant called *Enuma Elish*, which, as we have seen, recounted the Babylonian cosmogonic myth. Hooke says that the 'recitation *did* something; it brought about a change in the situation which the ritual was enacting' (p. 12). The function of the myth, as an essential part of ritual, according to Hooke, 'was to secure those conditions upon which the life of the community depended' (p. 13).

The ritual re-enactment theory holds, therefore, as Lauri Honko (1984, 51) explains, that 'the *context* of myth is, in normal cases, *ritual*'. This is because myths tell of the beginnings of time in the far off past. In order for them to come alive with meaning, they must operate through the transformative power of ritual by repeating the myths 'here and now, in the present'. According to Honko, this provides ritual precisely with its content and brings the believer into the ideal world as it was at the creation. 'What was once possible and operative in the beginning of time becomes possible once more and can exert its influence anew'.

Eric Lott (1988, 126) sees religious symbols as closely tied to myth and ritual, both of which, he says, 'function as a kind of elaborated expression of symbols'. Because ritual is performative, it makes the activities recounted in myths and the sacred beings related in them real in the lives of ritual participants.

By dramatically depicting the character of sacred beings, and their earth-relationship, ritual action is stimulated, whether this is in the form of the worship of such beings, or the means for ensuring their blessings, or acts for warding off evil.

Ritual activity, therefore, in Lott's view, essentially re-enacts 'ultimately significant events in the relationship between the sacred and mortal worlds'.

Ninian Smart (1973, 83) notes that it should not be surprising that myth and ritual go together since the gods which populate myths define the object of a religious community's worship. He concludes that 'the matter of myths has to do with Foci of ritual'. Time and space thus gain their transformative significance when ritual re-enacts myth. Again, according to Smart, 'In re-enacting the myth…one time is represented in another' and one place 'is present in another'.

The theory that rituals re-enact myths formed the cornerstone for Mircea Eliade's analysis of religious symbols. For Eliade, the history of religions can be understood as a series of hierophanies, sacred irruptions into the otherwise homogeneity of space and time. The hierophanies are recounted in myths and re-enacted in rituals which are centred around the symbols expressed in the myths. Eliade distinguished between the primitive mind and the modern understanding of the world. The former represents the exemplary religious person, the *homo religiosus*, who longs to be as near the sacred as possible (1959, 202). Rituals, during which space and time revert back to their mythic origins, transport the religious person into the presence of the sacred. Symbols orientate the religious person in space by creating sacred centres founded by the original hierophanies. Rituals orientate the religious person in time by punctuating otherwise undifferentiated moments with sacred meaning. The modern person lacks these significant points of orientation in space and time because the myths and their ritual re-enactments have been overtaken by the process of secularisation, a process nevertheless which has not erased religious sentiments altogether since 'profane man is the descendant of *homo religiosus*' (1959, 209).

Homo religiosus understands history as coincident with myth. Eliade explains that 'every *event* (every occurrence with any meaning), simply by being *effected in time*, represents a break in profane time and an irruption of the Great Time'. As such, 'every event, simply by happening, by taking place in time, is a hierophany' (1958, 396).

Myths operate not only in rituals, periodic re-enactments of the hierophanies, but as exemplary models for all human activities – work, eating, play, sexual activity and so on. 'Every idea of renewal, of beginning again, of restoring what once was, at whatever level it appears, can be traced back to the notion of "birth" and that, in its turn, to the notion of "the creation of the cosmos"' (1958, 412). Rituals form a part of the entire mythic consciousness of the religious person who, in Eliade's words, 'must do what the gods did in the beginning' (1958, 417). Because the religious person longs to be near the sacred in every aspect of life, rituals reproduce events which took place in the times of the beginnings by repeating 'a mythical archetype'. Through such repetitions, rituals abolish profane space and time by placing the religious person in 'the "eternal now" of mythical time'. Eliade concludes, 'Anyone who performs any rite transcends profane time and space' and 'is taken out of profane "becoming", and returns to the Great Time' (1958, 430).

In his discussion of Eliade's concept of the 'religious man', John Saliba (1976) confirms this interpretation of Eliade's theory of myth and ritual noting that for Eliade freedom from profane (meaningless and homogeneous) time occurs 'by a ritual repetition of the sacred action outlined in the myth itself' (p. 53). Saliba underscores Eliade's contention that rituals transport humans into a time and place marked by a sacred timelessness and symbolising the centre of the world. He concludes, 'Myth and rite are thus an effort on man's part to return to his blissful origins, the primordial, paradisial life before he was burdened by historical time and circumstances' (p. 54).

From the above brief review of scholars who have addressed the subject, we can see that although variations occur in the ritual re-enactment hypothesis, it can be summarised as the theory that myths and rituals participate in the same process of making space and time sacred. The analysis of myths and rituals as separate entities for academic purposes elucidates the meaning of each classification, but for the religious practitioner they operate together. In one sense, the telling of a myth constitutes a ritual; ritual activity is mythical.

Critique of the Theory I: Contesting the Idea of Cosmological Centres

Eliade's theory has been criticised by J. Z. Smith, his colleague at the University of Chicago. In an article appearing in *History of Religions* in 1980, Smith anticipated his more complete discussion on the theory of ritual which he elaborated in his later book entitled *To Take Place* (1987). In his article, Smith claims that sacred space serves as a 'focusing lens, marking and revealing significance'(1980, 113). In places like temples, churches, or other demarcated sacred spaces, the focusing lens operates as a point of clarification where communication between humans and the gods occurs. The means for achieving the communication, Smith says, is through ritual redundancy comprised of 'repetition and routinization' (1980, 114).

Sacredness does not result from a cosmological mythical event symbolised by various objects, but it occurs simply by having 'attention directed' in a special way. Ordinary objects become sacred by virtue of 'being there' or 'because they are used in a sacred place.' Hence, sacredness is a situational or relational category rather than possessing substantive characteristics. 'There is nothing that is in-itself sacred, only things sacred-in-relation-to' (1980, 115). Ritual pertains to the space where the communication between humans and the deities occurs by creating what Smith calls a 'controlled environment'. Ordinary life is comprised of variables which by their accidental quality make the outcomes quite uncertain. Ritual takes away the accidents of ordinary life by always successfully 'performing the way things ought to be'. This underscores a tension between ritual perfection and ordinary life because what occurs in ritual can never be realised in reality. Nevertheless, in the ordinary, uncontrolled course of events, the ritual is recollected or remembered displaying in principle what is 'possible for every occurrence' (1980, 124-5).

Ritual, therefore, represents the human capacity for 'reflection and rationalization'. Humans know the difference between what is and what ought to be and thus they rationalise the tension through ritual. In this sense, ritual cannot be understood in terms of or, to use Smith's term, as congruent with something else. It certainly cannot be reduced to 'a dramatization of a text', as the ritual re-enactment theory holds. In fact, according to Smith, 'ritual gains its force where incongruency is perceived' (1980, 125).

To exemplify the meaning of incongruency, Smith refers to the bear festival of northern (Siberian, North American Arctic and Scandinavian) traditional hunters. What the hunter in actual experience remembers is that he is in a reciprocal relationship with the animal. He knows that, according to ritual, he must invite the bear to offer itself for the kill by asking it to turn around. He then submits words of thanksgiving for the offering and kills by avoiding excessive spilling of blood (for example, by not shooting it in the eye). After the kill, he treats the body of the bear with respect. What actually happens is quite different. A hunter faced with a life-threatening situation or with the prospect of losing the kill will not undergo such formalised rituals. Nor will the bear respond to the hunter's words by turning around and sacrificing itself to the hunter's arrow.

In the ritual of the bear festival, however, a bear is taken into captivity and led through the idealised hunt. Smith explains:

> All the variables have been controlled. The animal has played its part. The bear was treated correctly as a guest. It has been compelled to rejoice in its fate, to walk to its death rather than run away, to assume the correct posture for its slaughter, to have the proper words addressed to it before it is shot, and to be killed in the proper, all-but-bloodless manner (1980, 126).

Smith assumes that a hunter in a real situation will remember the ritualised killing and reflect on the discrepancy between the actual world and the perfection achieved in the ritual performance. In this way, ritual represents incongruency. Ordinary life is marked by 'contingency, variability, and accidentality'. Ritual factors these out and thereby 'provides a focusing lens of the ordinary' allowing 'its full significance to be perceived, a significance which the rules express but are powerless to effectuate' (1980, 127).

In *To Take Place*, Smith elaborates on this theme noting once again the crucial difference between the 'now' of the ordinary world and the 'now of ritual place'. For example,

> Here (in the world) blood is a major source of impurity; there (in ritual space) blood removes impurity. Here (in the world) water is the central agent by which impurity is transmitted; there (in ritual)

washing with water carries away impurities. Neither the blood nor the water has changed; what has changed is their location. This absolute discrepancy invites thought, but cannot be thought away. One is invited to think of the potentialities of the one "now" in terms of the other; but the one cannot become the other (1987, 110).

Ritual focuses on relative differences which can never be overcome, a fact underscored by the distinction, understood clearly by the believer, between ritual space and the ordinary world.

By contrast, myth, according to Smith, achieves a far different purpose and is perceived in a different light from ritual. Myth 'begins with absolute duality', the duality of 'then' and 'now'. Through narration, myth transforms the 'then' into the 'now' (1987, 112). This is precisely what the ritual re-enactment theory says occurs in ritual. By restating the myth ritually, the disparity between the ordinary world and the world of the original creation is overcome. During the sacred time of ritual, which takes place in a sacred space demarcated by symbols, participants experience the transformation from the imperfect to the perfect. Smith's point, however, is that ritual operates simultaneously with the 'now' where incongruency is experienced. It does not achieve a correspondence, as does myth, between the 'then' and the 'now'. The ritual participant knows the difference and experiences the incongruency.

Is there then a way in which myth and ritual can be understood together? Smith seems to suggest there is by referring to myth/ritual in the singular. Myth and ritual combine precisely by transposing the duality of time expressed in myth into spatial locations. Although time is marked by 'then' and 'now', place possesses an almost unlimited potential for sacredness. 'Anything, any place, can potentially become the object of attention; the details of any object of place can be infinitely elaborated in the myth' (1987, 114).

Smith exemplifies this by referring to the myths of the Aranda of Australia who distinguish between Dreamtime and present time. Although Dreamtime seems to reside in the mythic past, through dreams, the ancestor becomes 'emplaced' in another, usually a person, but sometimes an object or a symbol of the clan. In this way, what existed only in the 'then' of myth becomes metamorphosed into that which is permanently accessible, the relative differences of ritual. For Smith, this demonstrates how myth/ritual taken together differs from either myth or ritual considered separately (1987, 112).

Smith's analysis seems to attack the ritual re-enactment theory in at least three ways:

1) Rituals and myths do not correspond in function or in practice. The aim of each is different and hence the way each is experienced varies.

2) The sacred is defined not by hierophanies which create cosmological sacred centres in profane space and time. Rather, what is sacred depends on its relationship to a place which is set apart from other places – the place of the ritual. Nothing, therefore, is intrinsically sacred for believers. The sacred object is sacred only in context: sacred in one place and quite ordinary in another.

3) Ritual needs to be understood as a category of its own and not as a subcategory of myth. This frees ritual from being a conveyor of

mythic elements to a phenomenon in its own right allowing for interpretations, such as Smith's incongruency theory. This does not prevent an analysis of ritual in relationship to other forms of religious phenomena, including myth, but it detaches ritual from its intrinsic connection to myth.

The second point above appears to be open to the charge that Smith has avoided the question of what makes a place sacred. He addresses this by arguing that places achieve sacredness through avenues of power, whether or not they are related to cosmogonies and cosmogonic myths. The ancestral places amongst the nomadic Tjilpa of Australia, for example, are places of ritual remembrance established not by cosmological intrusions but by the travels of the original ancestors. In the context of ancient Near Eastern mythology, centres are 'preeminently political and only secondarily cosmological' (1987, 17). Places are not therefore best understood as hierophanies linking heaven to earth to hell, but as modes of 'archaic ideologies of kingship and the royal function' (1987, 17).

In his review of *To Take Place*, Kess W. Bolle (1990, 204-212) argues that Smith convincingly has replaced Eliade's idea of the sacred centre as a cosmological entity with the concept of the centre as a symbol of power. Bolle agrees with Smith that Eliade's emphasis on the *axis mundi*, cosmic centres of the world symbolised by mountains, trees, poles etc., is derived exclusively from what recent scholarship has shown to be a misreading of ancient Near Eastern documents. By making the cosmic centre into the core of religion, therefore, Eliade has committed, in Bolle's words, a 'sin against sound scholarship by universalizing erroneous principles' (p. 205).

If Eliade's interpretation of sacred cosmological centres is erroneous, his theory that myths tell of original hierophanies which are re-enacted in rituals around the symbols of the centre is also mistaken. Smith's analysis suggests that rituals are better understood as acts of remembering the power of kings, rulers, or ancestors rather than being regarded as re-enactments of sacred cosmological intrusions into space and time. Bolle summarises Smith's position in the following way:

> We should forget altogether about such unilluminating notions as "religious experience" and "the sacred" and instead focus on the undeniable human function of memory with its principal object: the power established in a particular place which in the course of history can become associated with a ruler or dynasty (p. 206).

Critique of the Theory II: Ritual as 'Performative Utterances'

In the late 1960s, Ruth Finnegan (1969, 537-52), whom we noted had been critical of the emphasis in scholarly research on cosmogonic myths by arguing that they were largely inapplicable in Africa, sought to employ the linguistic analysis of the British philosopher J. L. Austin in the study of African rituals. Her position was elaborated shortly afterwards by the scholar of African religions, Benjamin Ray (1973, 16-35). Both Finnegan and Ray concentrate on Austin's use of the 'performative utterance' as a clue to understanding the way language operates in many African rituals. Although their aim was not specifically to refute the ritual re-enactment thesis, their application of Austin's theory to African rituals leads to this conclusion.

From her research in the oral traditions of the Limba of Sierra Leone, Finnegan concluded that the function of language among nonliterate peoples corresponds to its use in literate societies. Rituals, in particular, have suffered under the bias of previous researchers who, according to both Finnegan and Ray, have quite unhelpfully classified the ritual language of oral societies as magically seeking to manipulate forces or spirits for desired ends. It was here that Finnegan and Ray found Austin's linguistic analysis most helpful.

Finnegan distinguishes between 'locutionary' and 'illocutionary' statements. Following Austin, she defines 'locutionary' utterances as 'the "mere" stating of something rather than the performance of an act'. 'Illocutionary' statements, on the other hand, refer to the 'performance of an act in saying something'. They involve a 'doing' in the 'saying'. In our examination of African rituals, therefore, 'we need to be concerned as much with what they *do* as with what they *say*' (1969, 548-9).

In an article inspired by Finnegan's interpretation of Austin, Ray differentiates further between 'perlocutionary' and 'illocutionary' acts of speech. Verbal acts, he explains, fall into two parts: doing something in the act of saying and accomplishing something by the act of saying. For example, if I say 'Close the door', I perform an act by giving an order. The action is contained in the statement and thus is perlocutionary. I may also influence someone actually to close the door by my statement, an illocutionary use of language (1973, 18).

Ray argues that his accounts of sacrificial rituals among the Dinka of southern Sudan demonstrate that the acts of saying and doing 'belong to the same action, not to different types of action'. The perlocutionary and illocutionary aspects of language are combined in the rituals. The participant performs an act in the utterance itself and cannot be regarded as 'magically' voicing words to achieve a result (pp. 23-4). Rituals thus can best be understood by directing attention to their 'internal verbal structure' where the central role of language is shown to be performative (p. 35). This allows African rituals to be understood in the light of universal linguistic categories without restricting them 'to the sphere of the "primitive", the "magical", or the "symbolic"' (p. 17).

Finnegan's study of African myths and rituals, when combined with Ray's examination of ritual language, suggests that although both myths and rituals are performative, they function in quite different contexts. Largely through the use of locutionary language concluding with illocutionary statements intended to influence actions, mythic performances re-enforce values which a society deems necessary for its members to uphold. Rituals may also re-enforce cultural and societal values but, unlike myths, they accomplish this, among other quite important acts such as divining, healing and reconciling ancestors, by combining perlocutionary and illocutionary statements. On the basis of linguistic analysis alone, therefore, the contention that the main purpose for rituals is to transpose a people back to an original time of beginnings by re-enacting cosmogonic myths cannot be maintained.

Critique of the Theory III: The Meaninglessness of Ritual

Like Smith, Frits Staal of the University of California at Berkeley has been developing a theory of ritual over the past twenty years which challenges the ritual re-enactment theory. Staal, who has based his analyses on Vedic sources and the observation in 1975 of the *Agnicayana*, a 3000 year old Vedic ritual, is chiefly known for his argument that ritual is a meaningless, rule-governed activity.

In a landmark article appearing in *Numen* (1979, 2-22), Staal disputes prior theories which characterise ritual as symbolic activity referring to something else such as myth, manipulation of forces for desired ends, or social function. Ritual activity, he argues, is 'self-contained and self-absorbed' and the performers of this activity are 'totally immersed in the proper execution of their complex tasks' (p. 3). Because of its preoccupation with the proper performance of rule-governed activities, ritual cannot be understood in itself as an expression of religion. Ritual is unconcerned with orthodoxy, but obsessed with orthopraxy.

This can be seen clearly when ritual is separated from its purported connection to myth. Staal argues that it has been 'fashionable' for some time to suggest that 'rites re-enact myths', an assumption, he says, 'partly inspired by the Babylonian festival of the New Year, which involves a recital of the myth of creation'. Empirical evidence beyond this one example, however, is difficult to find. Besides, he asks, 'Why should anybody wish to re-enact a myth?' (p. 7).

Other theories emanating from sociology and anthropology equally find little empirical substantiation. For example, the notion that ritual reflects social structure is confronted with the question: 'Why should social structures be represented or enacted ritually, and in a very roundabout manner at that?' (p. 7) Anthropologists have put forward the related theory that rituals, in pre-literate societies at least, 'transmit "cultural and social values" to the younger generation'. Another central question can be raised in this context: Why should the values relating to such things as gods, myths, and kinship systems be transmitted by rituals when this task is accomplished already 'by grandmothers and through language'? To sociologists and anthropologists, Staal retorts, 'The only cultural values rituals transmit are rituals' (pp. 7-8).

In what might be regarded as a criticism of Eliade and of J.Z. Smith's reinterpretation of Eliade, Staal attacks the 'widespread theory that ritual effects a transition from the realm of the profane to that of the sacred'. He notes that the term 'transition' frequently is softened to 'communication', as indeed Smith has done. Both Eliade and Smith distinguish between two types of experience. Eliade refers to the sacred and the profane, Smith to the incongruency between the ritual and ordinary worlds. Staal argues that if the sacred and the profane (the ritual and ordinary worlds) are defined in terms of ritual, it is 'circular and uninformative' to define ritual in terms of the sacred and the profane (p. 8). When extracted from its layers of religious and social referents, therefore, ritual is exposed as having 'no meaning, goal, or aim' (p. 8). Staal does not suggest by this that ritual has no value; what value it possesses, however, is intrinsic to it rather than extrinsically derived from religion or social function.

Staal then leads his reader into an analysis of ritual itself where he reiterates that it consists of 'pure activity'. He notes that the activity 'is all that counts' (p. 10). The study of ritual thus must be very much like the study of language, particularly syntax where 'meanings and sounds are related to each other through a vast and complicated domain of structured rules' (p. 19). The rules of syntax are 'unlogical and inefficient' making 'the transition between sound and meaning...unnecessarily complex, roundabout and mathematically absurd' (p. 19).

The relationship between syntax and ritual is more than an analogy for Staal; a scientific analysis of ritual demonstrates that ritual preceded language in human development. The origin of syntax is ritual. This is explained by human evolution. One of the earliest discoveries of the human was that 'he affected the outside world by engaging in activity,...a pursuit wrought with risk and danger'. In order to cope with a threatening world, humans created an ideal activity, i.e, 'a world of ritual'. Such a world was 'intrinsically successful', free from contingencies, and it 'expressed man's awareness of himself' (p. 14).

The meaninglessness of ritual did not become apparent to the human until much later in the evolutionary process when ritual was contrasted with 'ordinary, everyday activity'. This led to its association with religion because various rationalisations for it were needed. Religion always stands 'in need of the mysterious and unexplained'. In this way, ritual became 'attached to all important events' (p. 14). Ritual as ritual, however, remains a vestigial element of human evolution and needs to be studied in a similar way to syntax. 'No linguist will have failed to observe the similarity of...ritual rules with the rules of syntax'. Since 'syntax is the part of language which stands most in need of explanation' and because ritual precedes language, the study of the structure of ritual forms will need to be delineated scientifically just as the rules of language or mathematics are done (p. 19).

Staal concludes that the theory of the meaninglessness of ritual has three implications for religious studies. Initially, the student of religion should be aware that although ritual is replete with language, very often it is meaningless language. Second, the student of religion should recognise that ritual is comprised in part of a 'pre-linguistic state' demonstrated by recitation, silent meditation, or mantras. Third, in Vedic literature the cosmos was created not only through ritual recitations but also through 'meters and chants' which, like ritual, fail to express meaning. This supports the conclusion that rituals 'reflect syntactic structure in its pure form, hence pure activity' (pp. 20-21).

In 1989, Staal published a book which more fully expounded the ideas expressed in his earlier article, but which did not change them in any significant way. Under the title, *Rules without Meaning: Ritual, Mantras and the Human Sciences*, Staal, however, more clearly underscored his earlier call for ritual studies to comprise a field of its own within the human sciences. Commenting on the contribution of the social scientific studies to an understanding of ritual, Staal (1991, 229-30) noted that, although valuable, such studies throw 'scant light on ritual itself'. Both the social scientific study of ritual *and* ritual studies as a field in itself are needed. Both are 'justified and compatible' but ritual studies comprises a scientific field *sui generis* and thus is not reducible to the social sciences or to religious studies.

Staal's thesis, if correct, effectively destroys the ritual re-enactment theory. Ritual, as ritual, not only must be studied in its own right as a separate classification incapable of being subsumed under myth, but in itself is a meaningless activity. The endeavour of those like Eliade, or even Victor Turner, to attach symbolic meaning to ritual activity, under Staal's theory, cannot be substantiated scientifically. The study of ritual becomes the analysis of the structure and rules of a self-contained, self-absorbed human activity. The attachment of symbolic meanings to ritual by scholars from within the social sciences and religious studies is not derived from the study of ritual but from their own disciplines using their own tools of analysis. There is no intrinsic connection between these disciplines and ritual studies just as there is no intrinsic relationship between medical surgery and geography (Staal, 1991, 230).

Further Criticisms of the Ritual Re-enactment Theory

Further criticisms of the ritual re-enactment theory followed the publication of Staal's book on the meaninglessness of ritual. For example, in a special edition of *Religion* dealing with Staal's thesis, Burton Mack (1991, 213-18) of the Claremont School of Theology in California argued that the ritual re-enactment theory reflects a Western, Christian interpretation of ritual which is not inherent in the phenomenon itself. For Mack, Eliade is the principal culprit who has perpetrated this error. 'Eliade's program is...a theory of religion that celebrates Christianity surreptitiously by translating theological language into (semi-) neutral terminology' (p. 215).

Eliade's theological purpose is most evident, according to Mack, in his theory that 'ritual reenacts the myth'. By stressing the importance of the cosmogonic event, Mack charges that Eliade has placed his own agenda within the study of religion: 'history with purpose, theodicy with grace, and salvation as religious experience and incorporation' (p. 215). That Christian theology emerges unscathed under such an agenda, disguised in the scientific terminology of the history of religions, at the very least issues some warnings for scholars.

By contrast with Eliade, Mack finds much in Staal's thesis that is promising but which, he warns, will disturb those who recoil at the 'demystification of religion'. It is not only Staal's 'insistence on the separation of ritual from myth' which will distress many scholars, but, more significantly, Mack suggests, it is his call for us to abandon the 'quest for meaning' altogether. This reorientation of thinking may cause 'religionists' in the Eliade school to stumble, but, in Mack's view, it is to be commended as a challenge for academics to study ritual activity itself 'as the data to build a rational anthropology' (p. 216).

In his comments on Staal's position, Ivan Strenski (1991, 219-25) of the University of California agrees with Mack's appraisal of the ritual re-enactment theory. Strenski refers to the 'overemphasis on seeing cultural and religious subjects in terms of meaning only' and accuses Eliade's 'creative hermeneutics' of 'the absurdity of compulsive one-for-one correspondence' between cultural data and meaning. Eliade's theories, in Strenski's view, advocate 'a simplistic lock-step one-for-one identification of symbol and referent' which produces a formula 'for meaning madness' (p. 221).

Eliade's analysis, to which I will return in greater detail in chapter five, relates in part to the idea of the autonomy of religion as a discipline distinct from theology and the social sciences. The history of religions, for Eliade, as a scientific discipline interprets the meaning of religious symbols, largely through myths and their ritual re-enactments, to disclose the structure of the religious consciousness (1969, Preface). Strenski calls this a 'methodological fideism' promising an 'illusory' refuge 'from a heartless world where religion was generally disparaged'. This ideological or even theological agenda by 'religionists' such as Eliade prevents a genuinely scientific analysis of rituals. Staal's contribution to ritual studies, therefore, unlike Eliade's, 'focuses the reader's concentration upon just what there is special about rituals' without implying covert theological assumptions (p. 221).

Although Mack and Strenski object at points to Staal's theory of meaninglessness, both find that his approach elucidates many of the methodological issues in ritual studies and exposes meaning-laden theories as biased and confusing. Both also agree that Staal's deconstruction of previous theories permits ritual to be studied as a phenomenon in its own right. What is most significant for our overall discussion, however, is the growing scholarly rejection of the ritual re-enactment theory on scientific grounds as noted by all of the scholars discussed above from J. Z. Smith through Benjamin Ray and Ruth Finnegan to Frits Staal (and his anti-religionist supporters).

In Defence of Meaning

Among the theories noted above, only Staal adopts the radical position that rituals are meaningless, rule-governed activities. Both Mack and Strenski, although endorsing Staal's essential aims, question his methodologies for arriving at his conclusion and at some points even challenge the significance of the conclusion itself. I would argue that even if Staal is correct that ritual originally reflected a pre-syntactic form of expression dictated by senseless rules, it cannot be regarded as such when studied as a part of religious phenomena. At the very least, rituals have obtained meanings and functions through use and hence are not meaningless to those who perform them. This latter point seemingly would be both accepted and discounted by Staal who submits that 'if we want to know the meaning or theory of ritual, we should not confine ourselves to practising ritualists' (1979, 4).

It is significant, moreover, that Staal chose to study mantras, which indeed are repeated according to a prescribed formula often comprised of metric patterns. Such forms fit exceptionally well into Staal's theory, but, many other types, such as most observed in Africa, lack the aspect of structured repetition characteristic of mantras. Staal seems to accept the possibility of this limitation when he admits that the syntactic rules of 'embedding and modification are in fact very basic rules of ritual, *or at least of Vedic ritual*' (emphasis mine) (1979, 19).

If repetitive chants and metric hymns comprise a primitive form of stylised behaviour, I would ask if Staal is interested in ritual practice or primarily in a theory of the origins of ritual. If he is concerned with origins, his hypothesis proves interesting to a wide field of disciplines including religious studies. But the study of religion cannot be narrowed to theories of origins because it primarily is concerned to elucidate the meaning of religion as it is practised by adherents. Theories about the origins of rituals, or any other phenomena, are not irrelevant to an understanding of religion, but at the very least they are of secondary interest to believers. Meaning, however, is essential. Because the reciting of mantras, for example, helps to induce mystic states, what Staal calls 'practising ritualists' would not accept his reduction of them to pre-linguistic, rule-governed and meaningless activities.

Moreover, Staal's delineation of the pattern of rituals according to the syntactic structure of language is of limited assistance to understanding in any other than a technical sense, not only because it ignores the importance of meaning for believers, but because it discounts the primary significance of the fact that the meanings, over time, have become indissolubly attached to the rituals themselves. In Mack's words, 'Meaninglessness is a throwback to an age long since bypassed by the course of evolution' (1991, 223). As such, it cannot constitute the core of ritual as a religious phenomenon because meaninglessness, even if Staal's evolutionary hypothesis is correct, can only be regarded as vestigial.

In my view, the scholar of religion must develop a scientific methodology in order to decipher the structures of meaning embedded within the phenomena of religion. The structures identified will not duplicate the explanations of meaning as a believer would state them, but neither will they be offensive to believers as Staal's conclusions apparently are. I will return to the importance of attaining a scientific understanding of meaning from a believer's perspective in the concluding chapters. It is important to note at this point, however, that although significant differences exist concerning the interpretations of rituals, current scholarly opinion clearly concurs that no inherent relationship exists between myths and rituals.

I want to illustrate this in the concluding section of this chapter by relating and analysing a case example of a crisis ritual obtained from student field research in Zimbabwe. I will endeavour in my analysis to demonstrate how the study of ritual as its own classification apart from myth can be enriched by referring, in overview, to the importance of place, the concept of liminality, the nature of incongruency, and the practice of performative utterances.

An African Example

The ritual which is described below was undertaken because members of an extended family in the Murewa region of Zimbabwe (among the Shona speaking Zezuru people) were experiencing a series of misfortunes, including deaths of family members. Although the stages leading up to the ritual are not recounted below, it would have been typical for family elders to have consulted a religious practitioner, a *n'anga*, to determine the cause of the series of misfortunes afflicting the family.

In this case, the family was informed that an avenging spirit, *ngozi*, was inflicting suffering on the family to seek restitution for a murder of one of its own family members. Michael Gelfand, a medical doctor who conducted extensive research among the Shona during the 1950s and 60s, explains that one of the principal causes of the appearance of an *ngozi* spirit is as a result of murder. 'If a man is murdered, his angry and restless spirit (*ngozi*) seeks revenge among the members of the guilty family, killing one after the other until full recompense has been made' (Gelfand, 1968, 12).

In his discussion of the Shona peoples, M. F. C. Bourdillon (1976) calls the *ngozi* an 'angry spirit' which attacks 'suddenly and very harshly'(p. 270). In addition to reprisal for a murder, Bourdillon explains that the avenging spirit may represent 'an acquaintance or relative who had been angered or wronged during life, such as an ill-treated parent, a neglected spouse [or] creditor' (p. 271). Sometimes, the spirit may attack many years after the grievance has occurred. Bourdillon provides the following example:

The angry spirit of a man murdered some eighty years ago is believed to have caused the deaths of the two brothers who plotted the murder, their father and six of their children, and still claims the occasional victim among their descendants while the surviving relatives are still trying to raise the large fine in cattle necessary to appease the spirit (p. 270).

Bourdillon notes that when a family suspects that the *ngozi* has become active, a type of *n'anga* specialising in avenging spirits is consulted. The *n'anga* will be able to diagnose the problem and suggest what is required to satisfy the angry spirit. Bourdillon explains that 'the full appeasement of the angry spirit involves severe punishment, either in loss of wealth or in extreme humiliation, which further indicates how fearful such a spirit is to the Shona' (p. 272).

The ritual which is described in detail below must be seen in the context of the Shona interpretation of the *ngozi* spirit. The details are described by Nicholas Mukarakate, who participated in the ritual in early July 1991 both as a religious studies student in the University of Zimbabwe and as a member of the afflicted family.

Protecting Clan Members from an Avenging Spirit

On Sunday, 7th July, I observed the traditional African ritual of protecting clan members from the wrath of an avenging spirit of an unrelated person who had been killed by a late member of that clan. The ritual took place in the early hours of the morning, immediately after sunrise on a private place by a riverside in the Murewa communal areas.

The first part of the ritual required ten selected male members of the clan to go to an agreed place by the riverside. This occurred long before the sun rose. They made there a very big fire on which a big drum half filled with water was placed. While the water was being boiled, the men slaughtered a huge black he-goat and skinned it. The liver and the lungs of the goat were taken and thrown into the drum of hot water and left to boil. No salt or cooking oil or any other ingredients were added to the drum. The men were chatting and talking as if nothing serious was happening. A *n'anga*, dressed in a black cloth wound around his waist down to just below the knees and wearing a necklace of black and white beads, watched the whole procedure carefully. His face was expressionless. He held a black tail of a beast in his right hand.

Just as the sun began to rise, the rest of the members of the clan started arriving at the place where the men and the *n'anga* were

77

boiling the meat of the slaughtered goat. They did not all arrive at the same time but in groups of five or six and not more than ten people at a time. They all grouped together in the bushes along the river talking in low and subdued voices, but they were not solemn.

When it seemed that everybody was present, the *n'anga* instructed an elderly member of the clan to tell the people to go and wash in the river in two groups. The males went a little distance down the river while the females went somewhere up the river. Only unperfumed washing soap was used. No lotions were to be applied after washing. The men bathed first and the boys last according to seniority, but all bathed at the same spot. I assume the same thing happened to the women and girls. All the washing was done in silence.

From the point of bathing, the eldest member of the clan led us all in a single file back to the drum of boiled meat where the *n'anga* had remained. The women also came in a single file from the other direction to meet the men at the drum. At the drum, the *n'anga* with the help of two aides gave everybody a very small piece of the liver plus some soup (the water which was tasteless from the drum) using a small cooking lid. It was compulsory to finish all that was in the lid. After everybody had his share, the fathers returned to get some meat and drink for their sons and daughters who were absent. Nobody seemed to be in any mood for conversation at this stage in the ritual. (It should be noted that the fathers went to collect the food for their absent children since the mothers had remained behind because of the fact that they do not have the same totemic symbol with their husbands. Only the people of the heart totem were present at this ritual.)

After this, the *n'anga*'s aides called us all together again and then divided us as in the first time when we went to wash. The males were told to follow the *n'anga*'s male aide to another spot in the river. The aide went into the water and walked to a point where the water level comes just below the waist. Whilst there, the aide waited with a small dishful of reddish water (as if some blood had been added to it), and there was an African body oil container, *chini*, in the dish. Again, from the most senior man of the clan to the youngest boy, everybody took turns getting into the water where the *n'anga*'s aide stood waiting. An expression of seriousness and businessmindedness constituted the features of the aide's face. In the water, everybody was instructed to dip his hands in the dish and rub them on his face and body and to utter the following words:

Please, you vengeant soul of the murder victim, leave us alone. We are mere kids. The evil was done by long-gone elders and we do not know anything about it. Leave us alone. We are innocent.

These words were said after the aide, i.e. we were merely repeating what the aide said.

After this, each participant got out of the water and put on his clothes without drying his body first. But before putting on the clothes, the *n'anga* stamped the person on the chest with a black

78

piece of cooked meat. The women later came to the same place after the men had finished and underwent the same process.

After this procedure, we all grouped together as in the beginning to have some razor blade cuts made twice on the neck, twice on both hands, and twice on both feet. These are called *nyora* in Shona. Then the *n'anga* and his aides rubbed some black powdery medicine on the bleeding places where they had cut us with the razor blades. Then the ritual was over but no one was allowed to go and bathe again that day, to use perfumed soaps, or to apply any lotion.

Analysis of the Ritual

That this description fits my definition of ritual provided earlier in this chapter is clear. The events described follow a prescribed pattern using symbols within a drama to achieve at the riverside a transformation in the life experience of the affected family. No overt reference in the ritual can be found to a specific myth – cosmogonic, historical, or socio-moral. The symbols within the ritual, nevertheless, purify the family in a traditional manner and transform their experience. The only words cited appeal to the avenging spirit to desist by urging the spirit to recognise the lack of culpability for the murder by this generation. Clearly, this ritual does not literally re-enact a myth nor bring the people into a time beyond time, a mythic time. The place, however, is important since, as Smith suggests, it directs attention by operating as a focusing lens on the drama as it unfolds.

Following Victor Turner, it is possible to view the ritual as a process moving from a separation through a liminal to an incorporation phase. Preparation is undertaken initially by the elders, but eventually each family member prepares to separate from ordinary life by washing in the river (a symbol of purification) and by eating the meat from the slaughtered goat and drinking the broth (probably representing the protective power of their own ancestors).

The participants re-enter the water in the liminal state where each recites the words dictated by the *n'anga*'s aide appealing to the *ngozi* spirit to cease his vengeful activities. The participants cover themselves with a bloodlike substance representing the attachment of blame for an ancestral murderer's activity into the present generation. No denial of the ancestor's guilt is attempted. Such contact is risky since the appeal is made for an end to this generation's suffering to the source itself of the family's misfortunes.

The stage of incorporation occurs after all have petitioned the *ngozi* spirit. This includes receiving a mark from a piece of cooked meat on the chest while still in the water, inserting razor cuts in six places on the body, and applying a medicinal powder to the cuts to aid in healing. This process can be understood as a summary of the entire ritual whereby, just as the cuts on the body are healed, death and suffering cease as social and spiritual harmony are restored.

Smith's theory of incongruency can be seen in this account in two ways. First, the use of ordinary objects for quite extraordinary purposes is evident throughout the ritual. The river, for example, which normally is used for bathing and washing clothes, becomes set apart in the ritual for a sacred purpose. Ordinary soap with perfumes cannot be used as would be expected in the usual act of washing, nor are the lotions normally applied following bathing permitted. This is a ritual bath; the river cleanses the family's ancestors from a previous evil act.

The outcome of the ritual, however, is never in doubt leading to a second way incongruency can be understood. The prescribed activities result in a communal purification. The idealised world of the ritual placates the angry spirit and restores order to the ordinary world. Incongruency thus is witnessed between the world as experienced in the ritual and the actual world which is punctuated by misfortune and death. The ritual operates as a transformative paradigm of how restitution should be achieved and how it should influence ordinary life. If Smith is right, the participants are aware of this incongruency. Indeed, after the ritual, as Bourdillon (1976, 272) notes, the family will make recompense to the descendants of the murdered man, sometimes in the form of an oxen and in other circumstances by giving one of its own young women to the offended family. The ideal world of ritual and the ordinary world of social relations are shown by this to be incongruent because, in Smith's words, both, unlike myth, 'operate simultaneously with the "now"' (1987, 110).

The only words recited in the student's account clearly are ritualised, and following Staal, may be called stylised. But they possess meaning. The words which each participant recites after the instructions of the *n'anga*'s aide represent a combination of saying and doing. The ritualised command to the *ngozi* to stop tormenting the family is a performative utterance in the sense of Finnegan and Ray. As such, it is complete in itself and cannot be separated from the results which may occur following the statement. In the ritual utterance, the words do not attain a causal power in an incomprehensible, magical way. The perlocutionary and illocutionary forms of speech are combined: what follows is already contained in what is said. That this is understood in the ritual performance is clear when the appeal to logic is made: 'The evil was done by long-gone elders and we do not know anything about it'.

This brief review of a Zimbabwean case study demonstrates that rituals do not require myths as a context for their performance. The detailed analyses provided in the scholarly literature by Smith, Turner, Finnegan and Ray, as ritual theories in themselves, apply readily to my own interpretation of the *ngozi* ritual. References to cosmic centres symbolising original mythic hierophanies re-enacted in the ritual, however, clearly do not.

Toward a Scientific Methodology

Two essential points emerge decisively from the theoretical discussions of this chapter and from the description and brief interpretation provided of the Zimbabwean case study: 1) rituals cannot be understood religiously apart from the meanings they convey to adherents; 2) the meaning of rituals must be derived from the study of rituals in their own right and not as a subclassification of myths.

The second point underscores the growing scholarly consensus, based on empirical investigations, that the myth-ritual association functions no more universally than the conjunction of ritual with any other phenomena in the complex interweaving of religious expressions. Certainly, in the African context, I believe I have shown in this and in the previous chapter that the ritual re-enactment theory has been discredited. Meaning is not diminished by the separation of myth from ritual, but it implies that a methodological framework, drawn clearly along scientific lines, is required so that the underlying logic inherent in both myths and rituals can be discerned by the scholar. I endeavour to construct such a framework in the next chapter prior to redefining myth in chapter six as an overarching horizon informing what to believers is an oftentimes transparent apprehension of the world.

References

Bolle, K. W. 1990. 'Review of *To Take Place*', *History of Religions* 30 (2), 204-12.

Bourdillon, M. F. C. 1976. *The Shona peoples*. Gweru: Mambo Press.

1990. *Religion and society: A text for Africa*. Gweru: Mambo Press.

Clothey, F. W. 1981. 'Ritual', in K. Crim (General Editor), *Abingdon Dictionary of Living Religions*. Nashville: Abingdon Press, 624-8.

Cox, J. L. 1996, 2nd ed. *Expressing the sacred: An introduction to the phenomenology of Religion*. Harare: University of Zimbabwe Publications.

Eliade, M. 1958. *Patterns in comparative religion*. London: Sheed and Ward.

1959. *The sacred and the profane*. New York: Harcourt, Brace and World.

1969. *The quest. History and meaning in religion*. Chicago and London: The University of Chicago Press.

Finnegan, R. 1969. 'How to do things with words: Performative utterances among the Limba of Sierra Leone', *Man* NS 4 (4), 537-52.

Gelfand, M. 1968. *African crucible. An ethico-religious study with special reference to the Shona-speaking people*. Cape Town: Juta.

Hooke, S. H. 1966. *Middle Eastern mythology*. Harmondsworth: Penguin Books.

Honko, L. 1984. 'The problem of defining myth', in A. Dundes (ed.), *Sacred narrative: Readings in the theory of myth*. Berkeley: University of California Press, 41-52.

Janzen, J. 1994. 'Drums of affliction: Real phenomenon or scholarly chimera?', in T. D. Blakely, Walter E. A. van Beek, and Dennis L Thomson (eds.), *Religion in Africa*. London: James Currey and Portsmouth, NH: Heinemann, 160-81.

Lanternari, V. 1988. 'Melanesian religions', in S. Sutherland, L. Houlden, P. Clarke and F. Hardy (eds.), *The world's religions*. London: Routledge, 843-53.

Legesse, A. 1994. 'Prophetism, democharisma and social change', in T. D. Blakely, W. E. A. van Beek, and D. Thomson (eds.), *Religion in Africa*. London: James Currey and Portsmouth, NH: Heinemann, 314-41.

Lott, E. 1988. *Vision, tradition, interpretation: Theology, religion and the study of religion*. Berlin: Mouton de Gruyter.

Mack, B. 1991. 'Staal's gauntlet and the queen', *Religion* 21, 213-8.

Partin, H. B. 1981. *'Hajj'*, in K. Crim (General Editor), *Abingdon Dictionary of Living Religions*. Nashville: Abingdon Press, 290-92.

Platvoet J. and van der Toorn K. 1995. 'Ritual responses to plurality and pluralism', in J Platvoet and K. Van der Toorn (eds.), *Pluralism and identity: Studies in ritual behaviour*. Leiden: E. J. Brill, 1-21.

Ray, B. 1973. '"Performative utterances" in African rituals', *History of Religions* 13 (1), 16-35.

Saliba, J. A. 1976. *Homo religiosus in Mircea Eliade*. Leiden: E J Brill.

Schmidt, R. 1988. *Exploring religion*. Belmont, California: Wadsworth Publishing Company.

Smart, N. 1973. *The phenomenon of religion*. New York: Seabury.

Smith, J. Z. 1980. 'The bare facts of ritual', *History of Religions* 20 (1 and 2), 112-27.

1987. *To take place: Toward a theory in ritual*. Chicago and London: University of Chicago Press.

Staal, F. 1979. 'The meaninglessness of ritual,' *Numen* 26 (1), 2-22.

1989. *Rules without meaning: Ritual, mantras and the human sciences*. New York: Peter Lang.

1991. 'Within ritual, about ritual, and beyond', *Religion* 21, 227-234.

Strenski, I. 'What's rite? Evolution, exchange and the big picture', *Religion* 21, 219-25.

Taber, C. R. 1981. 'Life Cycle Rites', in K. Crim (General Editor), *Abingdon Dictionary of Living Religions*. Nashville: Abingdon Press, 426-8.

Turner, V. W. 1969. *The ritual process: Structure and anti-structure*. Harmondsworth: Penguin Books.

1985. 'Liminality, kabbalah, and the media', *Religion* 15, 205-17.

Van Beek, W. E. A. 1994. 'The innocent sorcerer: Coping with evil in two African societies (Kapsiki and Dogon),' in T. D. Blakely, W. E. A. van Beek and D. L. Thomson (eds.), *Religion in Africa*. London: James Currey and Portsmouth, New Hampshire: Heinemann, 196-228.

Van Gennep, A. [1908] 1960. *The rites of passage*. London: Routledge and Kegan Paul.

Chapter Five

METHODOLOGICAL CONSIDERATIONS RELEVANT
TO UNDERSTANDING AFRICAN INDIGENOUS RELIGIONS[1]

In this chapter, I discuss methodological issues relevant to achieving an understanding of the indigenous religions of Africa. I am using understanding in the sense suggested by the phenomenological term, the eidetic intuition, which implies a seeing into meaning (Cox, 1996, 37-39). Although toward the conclusion of this chapter I will seek to go beyond the traditional phenomenological interpretation of meaning, I share the basic starting point of most phenomenologists that understanding requires the capacity of the subjective observer, at least in part, to see as a believer sees. This assumption raises important issues which have defined much of the academic debate in recent years over appropriate methodologies in the study of religion.

The Controversy over Reductionism
Over ten years ago, Daniel Pals of the University of Miami contributed an article to the *Journal of Religion* (1986, 18-36) discussing recent attacks on the concept of irreducible religion as it had been espoused earlier in the century by Rudolph Otto and later by Mircea Eliade. Pals contends that reductionism, which he defines as theories which 'are concerned to show that a religious phenomenon...owes its existence to non-religious causes' (p. 18), has undergone a revival not so much from its traditional sources (sociology, psychology, and anthropology) but from those who write from within religious studies itself. One such recent critic Pals identifies is Robert Segal who has attacked Eliade for confusing the study of religion in its own right with religious faith and thus of moving out of science into theology (1983, 97-124).

This debate bears strongly on the study of African indigenous religions partly because of the historical tendency within the social sciences to explain African religions in terms of social functions, but chiefly because it raises the question of true understanding in religion. Segal accuses Eliade of adopting a faith stance through his insistence that the central component in religion is the sacred which believing

---

1. This chapter has appeared largely in its present form in J.G. Platvoet, J.L. Cox, and J. Olupona (eds.) 1996. *From object to subject: the study of religion in Africa*. Cambridge: Roots and Branches, pp. 153-68. It is used with permission.

83

communities apprehend through hierophanies, appearances or manifestations of the sacred in space and time (1959, 11). Eliade argues that the apprehensions of the sacred through hierophanies represent the believers' own view and that if scholars wish to understand a religious tradition scientifically, their accounts must reflect accurately the perspectives of adherents, which reveal the sacred to be a 'structure of consciousness' (1978, xiii).

Segal objects to this arguing that to present accurately the believers' own view not only is to describe it, which does not include understanding, but is to endorse it. According to Segal, Eliade's position forces him to affirm that 'the conscious, irreducibly religious meaning of religion for believers is its true one, which means at once its true one for them and its true one in itself' (p. 101).

Segal bases this analysis on the claim that nonbelievers may 'appreciate' some aspects of believers' points of view, such as 'the serenity or the security religion provides', but they can never appreciate the *reality* of religion for believers (p. 108). But it is just the *reality* which believers place at the centre of their religious affirmations and precisely what observers must appreciate if they are to view the world the way believers view it. This means, according to Segal, not that a nonbeliever cannot appreciate the meaning of religion for a believer, but that one who does not believe cannot 'appreciate its meaning in a believer's own, conscious terms'. Segal explains,

> Take the conventional statement that a nonbeliever can appreciate religion in a believer's own terms. As what can he appreciate it? As a response to the divine? But what can the divine mean to him when he does not accept its reality?...Would not a *believer* say that to appreciate its meaning is to accept it? How then can a nonbeliever profess to be appreciating its reality for a believer without accepting it himself? (p. 110).

Segal's criticism strikes at one of the fundamental assumptions within the phenomenology of religion, of which I count Eliade an exponent, that an observer can enter into the religious experience of believing communities and achieve understanding, initially through the technique of *epoché*, followed by employing empathetic interpolation while maintaining *epoché* concerning the reality of the community's object of faith. The phenomenologist argues that nonbelievers can appreciate the meaning of religion in believers' own terms because they have suspended their own personal or academic presuppositions by temporarily placing them within brackets (*epoché*) thus permitting them to cultivate a feeling for the believer's own faith position (empathy). Where that 'feeling for' involves engaging with what is strange or unusual, observers interpolate it by analogy into their own personal experiences (Smart 1984, 264). This enables observers to see as believers see even if what they perceive is not precisely identical to an adherent's own perspective. Throughout this, however, scholars continue to bracket out their own personal judgements, which permits them to appreciate the meaning for the believer without actually affirming either the reality or the unreality of what the believer calls true.

It is precisely this which Segal says cannot be accomplished.

> Even if the *epoché* were intended to reveal the significance of religion in fact, not just for believers, phenomenologists...invariably

neglect to explain how to practice it. To prescribe the suspension of biases is one thing. To achieve it, is quite another (p.108).

Segal challenges phenomenologists to provide a clear means for suspending judgements claiming that until *epoché* is explained, it 'must remain a forlorn ideal' (p. 108).

In response to Segal's position, Pals endeavours to recover for the phenomenological method the viability of its approach from the inside, but he does so in a way which actually robs it of its ultimate goal of seeing into the meaning or the essence of religion. Phenomenologists, from Kristensen to Bleeker to van der Leeuw (including the Chicago school of Wach, Eliade, Long, and, even to some degree, J. Z. Smith), have sought to discern accurately the meaning of religion (or at least of religious phenomena), sometimes called the eidetic intuition or vision (Sharpe 1986, 224; Cox 1996, 37-39; J. Z. Smith 1987). It is this which Segal says cannot be obtained because 'the secondary objection to the *epoché* proves the primary one here: the absence of a means' (p. 108).

Pals counters this by arguing that the observer does not need to affirm the reality of the object of faith but can remain content to describe what the adherent believes. Phenomenologists, he contends, have opposed reductionism because it violates 'truth' for believers, but this 'truth' refers to 'the claim that such beliefs cannot be reduced to the accidental product of fear or ignorance, of psychic need or social circumstance' (p. 28). This is different from embracing the reality of any community's object of faith.

Pals maintains that this defines the critical error in Segal's argument. 'It does not occur to Segal that this is the chief sense in which advocates of irreducible religion may be said to endorse the beliefs of those whose faith they interpret' (p. 28). In other words, for Pals, it is possible to maintain *epoché* concerning the real or apparent nature of the ultimate precisely because observers initially have performed *epoché* concerning their own personal or intellectual biases.

For example, the phenomenologist will suspend the Freudian claim that religion results from inner psychic needs projected onto an all-powerful parent figure. The truth or falsehood of the Freudian claim from within psychology can be analysed according to the tools of its own discipline. But it cannot yield understanding of religion as religion because it ignores the view of believers who universally would deny that their object of faith has been created by an infantile neurosis. By bracketing out this presupposition, the phenomenologist is able to see into the meaning of the object of faith from a believer's perspective, but, according to Pals, this should not be confused with endorsing the reality of what the adherent believes.

Thus far, Pals seems faithful to the phenomenological method and clearly portrays its opposition to any form of scientific reductionism. But he goes too far when he concludes by way of example that 'we can agree with the Aztec who insists he is not a Freudian neurotic and still deny that Quetzalcoatl exists' (p. 29). At this point, Pals succumbs to Segal's argument. The observer cannot deny that Quetzalcoatl exists without distorting the perspective of the believers. It is not enough simply to oppose explanations of religion in non-religious terms; the meaning of religion arrived at through the method must be capable of being affirmed by believers. If it is not, a fundamental principle of the phenomenologist has been violated, as expressed by W. Brede Kristensen (1960, 13), that historians of religion must 'investigate what religious value the believers...attached to their faith, what religion meant for them'. If Pals' distinction is permitted, therefore, Segal wins the debate by relegating phenomenology to mere descriptions of what religious people believe without finding a category within religion (i.e. the sacred, transcendent, holy, numinous) out of which an understanding of the meaning of religion can emerge.

Pals grants to the observer the right to deny the actual truth of what the believer affirms because he is convinced at this point by Segal's argument that to do otherwise forces the scholar to adopt the opposite position of endorsing the reality of the believer's object of faith. If we cannot somehow weave a way between the dilemma Segal poses that the phenomenologist either merely describes beliefs or actually affirms faith, therefore, the idea of the irreducibility of religion based on the phenomenological categories of *epoché* and the eidetic intuition will be lost.

I have said that this issue is significant for the study of African indigenous religions since for Western observers much of what is described in Africa appears strange, alien, foreign and hence incomprehensible in its own terms. If the techniques of *epoché* and empathetic interpolation mean that the observer must endorse the beliefs of indigenous Africans in order to attain understanding, therefore, such a goal will remain elusive. Even Africans who employ the method of the academic or scientific study of indigenous religions would find such a task difficult since they themselves by virtue of their own academic approaches, educational backgrounds, and Western influences generally cannot embrace the beliefs found within their own traditions.

Whether the difficulty of affirming African beliefs is greater than endorsing the beliefs of any other tradition is not the crucial issue here. The fundamental conclusion to which we are forced by Segal, despite Pals' efforts at refuting him, is that indigenous African religions cannot be understood from within religious studies without subscribing to indigenous beliefs as true in themselves. This would mean affirming not just the reality of the African's world of ancestral, alien, and avenging spirits (including the phenomenon of so-called witchcraft) as real for believers, but as endorsing it as an accurate picture of reality itself. Most observers of African religions cannot do this and thus, if Segal is right, he would limit them either to providing descriptions without understanding or to adopting reductionist interpretations from within various disciplines.

Reductionism as Necessary for a Scientific Methodology
Another important contributor to this debate is Ivan Strenski, who has been a vocal opponent of Eliade's non-reductionist approach to the study of religion. Strenski (1993) suggests that reductionism, which he defines positively as a competition between theories of explanation, forms an essential part of any scientific methodology.

The empirical method, according to Strenski, operates by challenging accepted scientific theories through explanations which overrule or supersede them. When a theory is superseded, the scientist uses reductionism, his own explanation, to account for why the previous theory succeeded so well for a time in explaining events and why eventually it failed (p. 41).

Reductionism in this sense is not a closed system which explains everything in terms of its own presuppositions. Rather, it represents an empirical 'openness to theoretical change' (p. 5). During the development and competition of theories, neutral phases occur until finally theories are expounded which are verified according to scientifically testable principles. Although reductive explanations of facts in the world occur from within many disciplines, none of them claims an absolute privilege in understanding, but operate in mutual systems of relation.

The concept of relation, which Strenski defines as knowledge in context, results in 'good understanding'. For the study of religion, this means that understanding can occur only through genuinely inter-disciplinary studies. 'Real spanning of intellectual fields means satisfying the standards of the sister disciplines of the study of religion, not only those of religious studies' (p. 2).

Strenski argues that Eliade has 'tried to smuggle into his methodological approaches to the study of religion his own religious faith in the transcendental existence of the Sacred'. For this reason, he and those who employ the phenomenological and historical approaches within religious studies, claim a unique privilege in understanding religion. Eliade's approach, Strenski contends, depends on a 'theological programme', because for him 'if the Sacred does not exist, the history of religions...would be impossible' (p. 2). As a result, Eliade and what Strenski calls 'the partisans of absolute autonomy' jealously guard 'the precious epistemological privileges which they awarded themselves and the so-called "History of Religions"' (p. 3).

Strenski's position, in my view, offers only a slight variation from that advanced by Segal, who argues that reductionism provides the only viable *scientific* approach to the study of religion. Phenomenological methods stressing understanding attained from within the religions are condemned as necessarily theological. For those like Segal and Strenski, to portray the significance of what adherents believe – in Eliade's view, the desire to live and be near the sacred – is tantamount to endorsing the believers' perspectives.

Strenski adds that reductive explanations need to be seen as positively reenforcing the scientific method through competitive theories and thus calls for religious studies to enter into such a competition in the 'big, bad world' (p. 1). Those who hold that religion possesses a unique content of its own, disclosed by phenomenology through its methods of *epoché* and empathetic interpolation, for Strenski, are operating in fear of theoretical competition and thus enclosing religious studies within theology rather than opening them to genuine scientific enquiry.

A Description of an African Rain Ritual

In order to understand the impact and seriousness of this debate for the study of African indigenous religions, I want to provide a brief description of a Zimbabwean ritual I observed in March 1992 in Mberengwa, near Gwai School in the District of Chief Chingoma. I stayed at the home of the Chief and was accompanied by his son who was my MA student and who served as my interpreter. This is a Shona speaking area approximately 100 kilometres south of Gweru and around 120 kilometres southwest of Masvingo.

The 1991-92 planting and harvesting season in southern Africa was disrupted by a severe drought which resulted in the failure of crops, the dying of cattle, and the drying up of bore holes. The Mberengwa District was one of the most severely affected areas in Zimbabwe. It is significant, therefore, that the ceremony I observed was a *mutoro* (appeal for rain) ritual. Although it was already late in the year, many expressed hope that rain still could come so that some crops could be salvaged, animals could survive, and the water supplies could be replenished.

On the morning of March 8th 1992, I went to the place of the ritual, which was conducted beneath a large *mukamba* tree. I arrived around 9:00 a.m. to find a group of around 25 men seated on a granite slope around the tree. The Chief was in the midst of the group leading a discussion. To the east of the tree, approximately 10 women were seated in a group on their own. The men's conversation centred on why there had been no rain. The general conclusion was that the traditional ways had been forgotten or ignored largely because the chiefs no longer played a leading role in decision-making at local and regional levels. Particular complaints were made about the Village Development Committees (VIDCO) which they claimed had been filled with political appointees by the ruling party (ZANU-PF) without regard for the authority of the chief. Moreover, the traditional rituals had been abandoned by those in authority at virtually all levels resulting in the drought which had been developing over several years.

After this discussion was completed, Chief Chingoma ordered the women to go to collect the pots of beer which had been prepared during the week and tested earlier that morning. In around 20 to 30 minutes, the women returned carrying pots of traditional beer on their heads. As they approached the tree, they placed the pots one by one beneath the tree as the other women ululated and the men clapped their hands. There were nine pots in all. By the time the women had returned to the tree, the number of people gathered had grown to around 50 participants. After all of the pots had been placed beneath the tree, the group moved more closely around it and passed snuff (*bute*) from person to person. As this was occurring, an old woman came to the tree and dipped a gourd in one of the pots, pulled it out, and began to pour beer on the ground at the base of the tree. As she did this, she said:

Here is your beer we have prepared for you.
Our people are suffering.
Our cattle are dying; the crops are failing;
There is no rain.

During this, the women were ululating and the men clapping. The procedure of pouring beer on the ground with various responses from the people lasted just a minute or two. Then the people moved back from around the tree.

A man who had been charged with distributing the beer called out the names of the headmen. Each headman went forward and took a pot of beer. Groups formed around the various pots and the beer was passed around from person to person in the small groups. People talked, smoked cigarettes, and sniffed *bute* until early afternoon. During this process, a few men and women began to dance in a line to the east of the tree facing the groups of people while others drummed or blew on a horn obtained from an antelope.

Sometime shortly after 2:00 p.m., an old woman wearing a black head scarf joined the dancing. After she had been dancing for awhile, she began to cry and her body started to shake. A man came running to her. He told her not to cry. She said she wanted to put on her clothes and sit on her stool. She was then assisted to put on a headdress comprised mostly of eagle feathers. She wore a black cloth around her right shoulder which was wrapped around her waist. Beneath the cloth were various animal skins forming a skirt. She danced for awhile with a rattle in her right hand and a walking stick in her left. One man in the group leaned over to me and whispered, 'She is now possessed'.

After dancing for some time, the woman moved to the base of the tree which had a protruding trunk forming a natural stool on which she sat. She sat with her legs a bit spread like a man and had the mannerisms and voice of a man. Members of the Chief's family formed a circle beneath her. Each member of this group (around 10) knelt or squatted in front of the woman, shook her hand, and exchanged some words which I could not hear. After this, the woman walked with the Chief's family away from the tree approximately 20 metres to the west at the edge of a fence. The remaining people continued to talk and drink beer around the tree. The woman was with the Chief's family for around 45 minutes.

During this time, I was engaged in a conversation with a man who said he had become possessed by a baboon spirit and had just come out of his possession. He claimed that he could cure illnesses when possessed, and do other things such as fly in the air like a bird, prevent lightning from striking, or even cause it to strike. After this conversation, I looked around but could no longer see the old woman. Members of the Chief's family were returning slowly to the tree. Shortly afterward, I saw the old woman, dressed as she had appeared previously in her normal clothes, assume her place among the other women. From this point onward, the dancing, drumming, drinking and conversation continued until the man who originally had called for the distribution of the beer announced that the beer was finished. The people continued dancing and talking, but slowly, in small groups, they began to disperse until by around 5:00 p.m. no one was left at the tree.

Beyond Descriptions to Understanding

The above account of the *mutoro* ritual in Chief Chingoma's region represents my effort to describe the events which I observed as free as possible from my own presuppositions. From the account itself, moreover, I can derive beliefs which the adherents consciously affirm. These include beliefs that the ancestors can bring rain, that they can communicate to the people through a medium, that certain prescribed ways have been provided for the people to air their grievances to the ancestors, and that the remedies for the problems are delivered in the case of regional disturbances to the Chief and through him to the people.

In subsequent interviews, I confirmed the content of the message from the ancestor and learned of the prescribed methods for dealing with the complex problem of the drought.

The description of the events and the derivation of beliefs from the ritual by themselves, however, do not lead to understanding. To achieve this, interpretation is required, called by Eliade a 'creative hermeneutics' (1969, 61-62) through which the scholar 'unveils significations' and assimilates a 'new interpretation'. Phenomenology thus aims at going beyond descriptions. In this way, according to David Cave (1993, 173), it 'can occupy a middle ground between the social sciences and the normative disciplines'.

If we follow Eliade's efforts to decipher a religious meaning within the descriptions, what I observed in Chief Chingoma's region reveals the distinctive southern African understanding of the sacred and its manifestations while at the same time pointing toward a universal religious experience. For example, the woman under possession became a hierophany. Although she was mediating a message, for the participants in the ritual, she was a genuine incarnation of the ancestral spirit, a manifestation in her own person of the sacred reality. For this reason, we can see that the possession comprised, in Eliade's words, 'the experience of the sacred', and hence implied for believers 'the notions of *being*, of *meaning*, and of *truth*' (1978, xiii).

What I am not content to do, therefore, as one employing a phenomenological method, merely is to describe and leave other disciplines to provide interpretations of the meaning of the descriptions from within their own perspectives. I seek understanding from the viewpoint of believers in order that ultimately I can ascertain the essential characteristics of the religion under study in terms which the adherents can affirm. This is because, as we would confirm from the *mutoro* ritual and many other rituals in the African context, as Eliade argues, religious phenomena possess a *'fundamental unity'* operating within an 'inexhaustible *newness* of their expressions' (1978, xv). Does this mean, as Segal argues, that I must be converted and re-converted repeatedly in order to understand the actual expressions of the many traditions I might observe? For me actually to comprehend the meaning of the *mutoro* ritual, for example, would I have to *endorse* the truth of ancestor spirits, the efficacy of ritual performances, and the reality of spirit possession? Or in Strenski's sense, must I adopt a theological stance in broad terms when I perceive, as a believer does, the truth of the sacred reality in the spirit possession? If I must answer these questions affirmatively, seemingly I would never attain understanding of the African religious experience because I do not believe in the empirical *reality* of the expressions of African faith.

Although I could re-open the discussion about the adequacy of *epoché* and empathetic interpolation to resolve this problem, I want to let this pass for the moment and assume that Segal and Strenski are right. I must believe if I am to understand; I must be converted to see what a believer sees. By accepting this, however, I am not led to the Segal-Strenski conclusion that a nonbeliever cannot understand religion and thus must revert to non-religious interpretations from within various disciplines such as sociology or psychology. I find a way through this by adopting a distinction maintained by Raimundo Panikkar (1984) and later expounded helpfully by David Krieger (1991) between confessional and methodological conversion.

Confessional and Methodological Conversion

Like Eliade, Panikkar contends that for a person to understand any religion other than one's own requires hermeneutics, a clearly delineated interpretive method. This is because the religious symbols which are foreign to or culturally distinct from one's own cannot hold the same meaning as they do for those for whom they are familiar and natural. They must be interpreted if they are to make sense to an outsider.

The type of hermeneutics one exercises, however, is crucial. Panikkar (1979, 9-10) calls for a diatopical hermeneutics where one moves from behind one's own faith into a space between the religions. In other words, one leaves the boundaries of one's own confession and enters a place between the confessions. Panikkar explains, 'Diatopical hermeneutics stands for the thematic consideration of understanding the other without assuming that the other has the same basic self-understanding and understanding as I have'. It is in a place between confessions that genuine dialogue leading to understanding can occur. Interpretation which takes place from behind one's own barriers of faith can produce explanations which make sense alone to those who operate from behind those same confessional boundaries. But an interpretation which is diatopical occurs between the boundaries of religious confessions and leads to authentic inter-religious understanding (Cox 1993, 110-112).

Conversion is necessary for such an understanding to be achieved. Panikkar argues that 'to understand is to be convinced' (cited by Krieger, 51). Krieger adds that such an understanding includes seeing into the meaning of 'the very boundaries of the world' where its meaning *is* its truth' (p. 51). Panikkar concludes, 'To understand something as false is a contradiction in itself' (cited by Krieger, 51).

Thus far, Panikkar and Krieger seem to follow a line of thought consistent with Segal. A nonbeliever cannot understand the experience of a believer because the nonbeliever views the object of the believer's faith as false. Nonbelievers deny the reality of the object of faith within a community of which they are not a part because they uphold a different object of faith defined from behind their own confessional boundaries. Christians, for example, regard Buddhists, Hindus, Muslims and Jews as nonbelievers since adherents within these traditions consider the beliefs of Christian faith to be false, at least in the way Christians understand them (Dinoia 1992, 1-33). For Krieger, however, secular humanists also interpret the world confessionally, the content of which he defines as 'autonomous reason, critical of all faith commitments and convinced of its ability to secure a human future independent of tradition and religious authority' (p.12). Segal, as a secularist whose confession is the scientific method, therefore, is no different from any other nonbeliever in another religion's object of faith.

Any understanding of religious confessions other than our own, therefore, according to Panikkar and Krieger, requires conversion. The conversion they call for, however, is not a confessional one, where one moves from behind one's own boundary to a place behind another boundary, but a methodological one. Confessional conversions are characterised, according to Krieger, by 'a model of *rejection* and acceptance, that is, as a complete rejection of the "old" view and a similarly total and unquestioning acceptance of the "new"' (p. 53). This, in fact, is the way conversion usually is conceived. In its place, Panikkar and Krieger want to substitute the idea of methodological conversion.

To understand this, Panikkar takes us out of the discussion of religion as such and asks us to consider cross-cultural studies. He asks how a person from one culture can understand a person from another. Genuine cross-cultural understanding cannot result, he argues, 'when we mean only the study of another culture different from our own but still with the categories of the latter' (1984, 207-208). The method which yields understanding uses 'categories derived from the two cultures concerned' (p. 208). Applied to religion, this suggests that we cannot understand the religious experiences of people who come from confessions (including the scientific) which are different from our own if we use only the categories of our own tradition.

Panikkar contends further that to achieve understanding of people different from ourselves requires a dialogue among subjects using the tools of language and engaging in discussion about something which, because it is dialogue, cannot merely reflect one's own perspective. Dialogue is not like looking in a mirror in order to see one's own image. It involves 'trusting in the other, considering the other a true source of understanding and knowledge, the listening attitude toward my partner, the common search for truth'. And it is based on the assumption that reality is a 'radical dynamism...not given once and for all, but is real precisely in the fact that it is constantly creating itself' (p. 211).

To accept these premises, which stand beneath diatopical hermeneutics, requires a methodological conversion based on the assumption that the other with whom the dialogue takes place 'is not just an other (*alius*), and much less an object of my knowledge (*aliud*), but another self (*alter*) who is a source of self-understanding, and also of understanding, not necessarily reducible to my own' (p. 213-214). This is methodological since it involves a way, a process, to achieve understanding. It is a conversion because it requires me to step out from behind my own confession and meet the other in a place where my own convictions are suspended.

Krieger defines this as a genuine conversion, not just an analogous effort to understand. It thus gives substance to and goes beyond empathetic interpolation. In Krieger's words, it denotes 'a transformation of one's whole world-view – in its cognitive, affective and social dimensions' (p. 53-54). Methodological conversion thus requires a turning toward 'new possibilities for life and thought' as a 'function of genuine *communication* between religions' (p. 54). It is diatopical since it moves across the topography of belief to a meeting place between the traditions producing a conversion in the fullest sense of the word.

The scientist of religion, in Krieger's accounting, cannot mean by *epoché*, therefore, the denial of the reality of the believer's object of faith (as Pals suggests) since this would preclude understanding. But diatopical hermeneutics, since it involves methodological as opposed to confessional conversion, does not require scientists of religion to endorse the beliefs of the adherents they wish to understand. Scientists must move out from behind their boundary of faith in autonomous reason and its authority over tradition into an openness toward meaning and reality in the faith of the other. The scientist gives up a personal view, genuinely surrenders it, and communicates with the other (*alter*) on a ground between the scientific confession and the confession of the other. It is this ground which defines the object for scientific enquiry and it is here that hermeneutics which leads to understanding occurs.

Methodological Conversion as Scientific Phenomenology

Traditionally, phenomenologists have stressed that for the study of religion to be scientific, observers must bracket out the truth claims of the religious communities they are studying. No comment is made on the apparent or real nature of the object of a community's faith. Understanding is achieved through the process of empathy whereby scientists endeavour to see as a believer sees by temporarily applying *epoché* to their own personal, cultural or academic assumptions. This process must be temporary because observers will return to the assumptions entailed in the scientific method when analysis of the data entailed in a study occurs. The stage of empathy undertaken in the mode of temporary bracketing is intended to ensure that what actually is analysed proceeds from the believers' perspectives and thus is as true as possible to the phenomena of the religious community under study. This process is inexact and imperfect representing in large measure an attitudinal perspective developed historically in reaction to many of the biases practised by late 19th and early 20th century scholars of religion (Cox 1996, 46-57).

The inadequacies of early phenomenologists such as G. van der Leeuw have been addressed by later adherents of the method such as C. J. Bleeker (1963), Ninian Smart (1973), and Harold Turner (1981). Nevertheless, as Segal and Strenski have demonstrated, the dilemma of understanding scientifically through a process of *epoché* and empathetic interpolation persists. Segal contends that phenomenologists must act 'as if' they are believers while actually maintaining the impartiality required by the scientific method. Believers, however, truly are believers who embrace as real the object of their faith. Those who study religion phenomenologically, that is those who seek understanding from a believer's perspective (religion *sui generis*, the so-called autonomy of religion) and not from reductionist assumptions (in Pals' sense of the term), cannot really understand therefore unless they themselves believe. This creates the dilemma. Either phenomenologists surrender the scientific approach to achieve genuine understanding and thus move into theology or they maintain the scientific method and reduce religious phenomena to categories of analysis which strictly are non-religious.

Students of logic are taught that the way to overcome a dilemma is to grab it by its horns and go between the two seemingly antithetical positions. This precisely is what the Panikkar-Krieger argument attempts to do. By admitting one side of the dilemma (one must believe in order to understand) while re-defining the other (all observers embrace a 'faith'), they provide a way through the polarity. We can understand those who are different from ourselves without confessionally endorsing their worldviews. Yet, we do affirm methodologically what they affirm thereby experiencing what they experience.

That this can be done has been demonstrated by Krieger who bases his argument on Wittgenstein's analysis of language as possessing complex uses with rules governing each use. Like games that we play, one can move into and out of various uses of language without contradiction. At the same time, the uses operate according to clearly defined and publicly owned rules. In order to play one game, one must abide by the regulations of that game, but when one plays a different game, the operable rules vary. We cannot apply the rules of one game to another nor arbitrarily change the rules of a game, but we certainly can understand more than one game at once and know how to play many games well (Wittgenstein 1953, 11-13). This employs a methodology for understanding which all of us use every day in many spheres of life.

The precise scientific stages involved in employing methodological conversion based on Krieger's model (1991, 75-76) and as I have presented it in a recent article (1994, 23-24) are clarified when seen in the light of Wittgenstein's language games. The stages are as follows:

1) Scholars begin with a critical analysis of their own scientific tradition employing the insights of various disciplines including philosophy, history, philology, empirical studies, literary and text criticism etc.

2) A similar analysis is applied to the tradition any scholar wishes to understand.

3) The critical appraisal of the other tradition becomes internalised so that it corresponds experientially to step 1 above undertaken within the scholar's own confession and thereby becomes a conversion.

4) The scholar then engages in a personal intra-religious dialogue between the two confessions, which have now become internalised, producing an interpretation of the meaning of each confession individually, taken together and for the understanding of religion in general.

5) Inter-religious dialogue then takes place whereby the scholar seeks to test the conclusions reached at step 4 in the light of believers' own perspectives and thus produce an interpretation based on actual field research.

6) Where the understanding attained in intra-religious dialogue offends or contradicts the believer of the other tradition based on the actual results of inter-religious dialogue, the scholar returns to the beginning and starts the process over again.

Steps one and two in this process must be performed carefully if the scholar is to achieve methodological as opposed to confessional conversion. At step one, the scholar, although admitting to owning a confession, adopts a critical, scientific stance toward the faith in science itself. Segal's nonbelieving social scientist, for example, examines the philosophical assumptions beneath the rational, causal theories of explanation. The scientist also examines cultural presuppositions which undergird the Western understanding of reality and notes how these might inhibit an understanding of alternative explanations of empirical phenomena. In other words, the scientist exposes the scientific method to a critical, analytical examination while still maintaining belief in the method itself.

At step two, the scientist does the same thing with the religious tradition under study. Because at step one the scholar experienced what it means to believe in the scientific worldview critically, it follows that the same approach can be adopted toward the religion under study. Although the process of internalising the beliefs of another religion involves a conversion, the critical, analytical approach prevents the conversion from becoming confessional.

If the scholar is also a believer in a religion in addition to the scientific understanding, the same process is followed. Because the aim of the science of religion is understanding from a scientific point of view, the scholar who believes in a religion still adopts the position of the scientist at stage one affirming critically that rationality defines the essential criterion for knowledge of the world. At stage two, the same critical but faithful approach must be applied to the religion the scholar is studying, whether or not it is the scholar's own.

If this process is to remain scientific, confessional conversion, whereby the scholar uncritically embraces a worldview (either one's own or another's), must be avoided. Confessional conversion surreptitiously moves the study of religion away from science into theology. It is just this danger which Segal and Strenski correctly warn us against.

The stages in employing methodological conversion, however, help us overcome Segal's dialectical approach where what adherents believe is judged by the scientist of religion as true or false, capable of being endorsed or denied. Methodological conversion allows us to suspend the rules of autonomous rationality and abide by the rules of religious faith while at the same time playing by the rules of scientific rationality. This entering into different 'faiths' is like playing different 'games' which in everyday life represent 'both-and' rather than 'either-or' situations producing, in my view, a fuller application of Strenski's 'relation' than he himself attains through reductionism.

The method advanced by Panikkar and Krieger, therefore, offers what I believe is a genuine advancement within the phenomenology of religion. It does require a form of *epoché*, but rather than endeavouring to bracket out all of one's preconceived academic and personal convictions, it suggests that one can hold differing and even contradictory presuppositions at the same time. This is like knowing how to speak more than one language whereby the rules, grammar and syntax of one may be at variance with another, but the speaker may 'know' and 'use' both intimately.

Methodological conversion also embraces a type of empathy since one must affirm that understanding the other as other holds a higher value than an apologetic endeavour to convert others confessionally to one's own faith. A basic presupposition thus undergirds the method, but this is no different from any other academic study of human behaviour which values understanding the human for its own sake. The empathy employed in diatopical hermeneutics, however, avoids the artificial 'as if' of traditional phenomenological approaches.

Finally, interpolation is involved in the Panikkar-Krieger thesis, but it is not one-sided as in prior phenomenological analyses whereby that which is alien is fitted into one's own experience (Smith, 1972). Rather, the phenomenologist who uses methodological conversion holds at least two 'faith' positions at once and understands both. The rules which apply are different in each, but this poses no inherent contradiction since empathy in this case means internalising what at first was outside of personal experience. The study of religion as religion thereby takes on a new depth and authenticity within the overall academic pursuit of understanding.

Implications of the Panikkar-Krieger Thesis

Segal has argued that no means for employing *epoché* has been delineated. In diatopical hermeneutics, with its insistence on methodological conversion, however, we find just such a means. It involves a genuine turning around (*metanoia*) since *epoché* is not an artificial technique but a transformation of one's own worldview through a dialogue with the other. The eidetic intuition which results, therefore, is based not on Segal's 'forlorn ideal', but on a seeing into meaning, a genuine understanding, based on the truth achieved in the encounter.

To return to the African description I have given by way of example, if I am to achieve an understanding of the religious experience of the Karanga people of Chief Chingoma's region, I must myself experience a religious transformation. I must step out from behind my Western scientific perspective of causality (to which I am committed confessionally), and adopt an openness to the reality of ancestor spirits. I do not thereby renounce my previous view and unquestioningly accept the African; I meet on a ground which reveals a new horizon for understanding the African religious experience not in my own terms but in a creative and dynamic exchange.

To refuse to engage in such a dialogue because I do not believe in the existence of ancestor spirits, as Segal's position implies I must do, merely perpetuates the confessional attitude. I would be saying that I cannot understand because my confession prohibits me from leaving my own boundaries and moving into a space between the African's faith and my own. Segal cannot understand any religion from the believer's point of view because he is too much a believer in the authority of his own confession. He thus resorts to a reductionist position claiming interpretive rights alone for the various non-religious disciplines.

I am aware that the argument I am advancing could be interpreted simply as confirming what Segal and Strenski regard as the phenomenologist's motive all along, namely, of endorsing the reality of the sacred and hence of moving into theology out of the sciences. In other words, I could be accused (predictably on the basis of my assumptions) of perpetuating the Otto, Eliade, Cantwell Smith tradition which argues that the irreducible religious element is the numinous or transcendent mystery. Whereas I happily place myself in the general line of such scholars' methodologies, I do not accept the conclusion that their theories represent covert theologies. I do accept, however, that the aim of religious studies is to achieve understanding, a goal which cannot be attained if we ignore or deny the faith perspectives of believers by trying to explain them in terms which are offensive or even incomprehensible to them.

Understanding, moreover, can be achieved, as Panikkar and Krieger argue, only if the scholar is open to the possibility of the sacred as expressed through the symbols of any religious tradition. If, as a scientist of religion, I am to remain genuinely scientific, I am forced to admit that I confront a mystery in the universe, what Panikkar calls the 'dynamic reality'. That the majority of humans have represented this mystery through religious symbols neither prescribes what the mystery actually entails nor limits the possibility of our apprehension of it in a variety of ways, including autonomous rationality.

Diatopical hermeneutics, therefore, offers to the sciences of religion a way of employing *epoché* concerning our own confessions while at the same time granting a deeper significance to empathetic interpolation than can be afforded by analogy alone. And, it enables us to see into the meaning of religious experience by acknowledging the existence of an open universe with multi-dimensional ways of apprehending its reality.

References

Bleeker, C. J. 1963. *The sacred bridge. Researches into the nature and structure of religion.* Leiden: Brill.

Cave, D. 1993. *Mircea Eliade's vision for a new humanism.* New York and Oxford: Oxford University Press.

Cox, J. L. 1993. 'Not a New Bible but a New Hermeneutics: An Approach from within the Science of Religion,' in I. Mukonyora, J. L. Cox, and F. J. Verstraelen (eds.), *'Rewriting' the Bible: The real issues.* Gweru: Mambo Press, 103-23.

1994. 'Religious Studies by the religious: A discussion of the relationship between theology and the science of religion', *Journal for the Study of Religion* 7 (2), 3-31.

1996, 2nd ed. *Expressing the sacred. An introduction to the phenomenology of religion.* Harare: University of Zimbabwe Publications.

Dinoia, J. A. 1992. *The diversity of religions. A Christian perspective.* Washington, D.C: The Catholic University of America Press.

Eliade, M. 1959. *The sacred and the profane.* Translated by Willard Trask. London and New York: Harcourt Brace Jovanovich.

1978. *A history of religious ideas. Volume I. From the Stone Age to the Eleusinian mysteries.* Translated by Willard Trask. Chicago: University of Chicago Press.

Krieger, D. 1991. *The new universalism. Foundations for a global theology.* Maryknoll, New York: Orbis.

Kristensen, W. B. 1960. *The meaning of religion.* Translated by J. B. Carman. The Hague: Martinus Nijhoff.

Pals, D. 1986. 'Reductionism and belief: An appraisal of recent attacks on the doctrine of irreducible religion.' *The Journal of Religion* 66(1), 18-36.

Panikkar, R. 1979. *Myth, faith and hermeneutics.* New York: Paulist Press.

1984. 'The dialogical dialogue,' in F. Whaling (ed.), *The world's religious traditions.* Edinburgh: T. and T. Clark, 201-21.

Segal, R. 1983. 'In defense of reductionism,' *Journal of the American Academy of Religion,* 51 (1), 97-124.

Sharpe, E. J. 1986. *Comparative religion. A history.* London: Duckworth.

Smart, N. 1973. *The phenomenon of religion.* New York: Seabury.

1984. 'Scientific phenomenology and Wilfred Cantwell Smith's misgivings', in F. Whaling (ed.), *The world's religious traditions.* Edinburgh: T. and T. Clark, 257-69.

Smith, J. Z. 1987. *To take place: Toward a theory in ritual.* Chicago and London: University of Chicago Press.

Smith, W. C. 1972. *The faith of other men.* New York: Harper and Row.

Strenski, I. 1993. *Religion in relation: Method, application and moral location.* London: Macmillan.

Wittgenstein, L. 1953. *Philosophical investigations.* Translated by G.E.M. Anscombe. Oxford: Basil Blackwell.

Chapter Six

ELUCIDATING THE MYTH

Thus far in this book, I have endeavoured largely to redefine the theoretical grounds on which much of the study of African religions has been pursued. In chapter two, I tried to show that terminology used in describing African religions has been based both on Western academic generalisations and on missionary theologies which interpret the indigenous religions of Africa as preparations for the reception of Christianity. In chapters three and four I maintained that theories which define myths as primarily cosmogonic are inapplicable in most parts of Africa and that rituals as re-enactments of myths have been discounted both theoretically and practically.

I am now ready to begin a process, which will be observed throughout the remainder of this book, of applying diatopical hermeneutics to attain understanding of the religious practices of a people from the same general area in Zimbabwe. I start in this chapter by reconstructing theories of myth, ritual and beliefs in Africa in order to overcome the difficulties I posed in chapters two through four.

Toward a New Understanding of Myth

Following Raimundo Panikkar (1979), I want to suggest that myth needs to be defined not as a sacred story but as a horizon of understanding involving an entire cultural apprehension of reality which is often transparent to the believing community because in Panikkar's words, 'it is grounded so deeply in my own roots as to be utterly hidden from me' (p. 243). On this definition, myth outlines the expansiveness of any religion's perspectives on reality while at the same time exposing its limitations.

The analogy of the horizon is appropriate in this context. When one is placed on a viewpoint, what one sees depends on the immediate environment. Flat plateaus are different from mountainous landscapes. What one perceives and how far one sees depend on the geographical setting. If one has grown up in flatlands, the horizon will appear wide and far reaching. If one has been raised among mountains, the direction of perception becomes more vertical than horizontal. How one experiences the world is determined by the horizon within which one lives. And the familiar horizon seems normal, as things ought to be.

New horizons never appear to the subjective observer without movement, without a change of position. Often these changes are disconcerting, disorientating. One who has been raised in flatlands may experience mountains as confining. One who has always lived among mountains may see the flatlands as boring, undifferentiated and without appropriate orientation.

New horizons always appear as one moves toward the once distant horizon and thus are never exhausted. One can move out of one horizon into a different landscape, but horizons never end. This does not mean that each new horizon contrasts starkly from all others. Many are very much alike. When one travels over a large area, some horizons look very much like previous ones and one can recognise similarities to one's own in others. Some, however, appear very different from what one is used to seeing and thus often seem strange, threatening and foreboding.

The analogy of horizons has been employed in philosophy since Nietzsche and Husserl, in existential phenomenology by Karl Jaspers (1935) and in religious studies and theology by Panikkar and David Krieger (1991). It has been discussed at length in relation to history by the German philosopher Hans-Georg Gadamer who defines a horizon as 'the range of vision that includes everything that can be seen from a particular vantage point'. (p. 269)

The concept of a horizon is most applicable to religions when they are conceived as inseparable from cultures, social structures, political and economic systems, geographical factors, climatic influences, and prevailing psychological expectations. All of these factors create the horizon within which any one religious community views the world. As such, they define that community's myth. On this definition, myth is not reducible to any one dimension within a horizon, nor can it be expressed adequately in concepts. Myths create people's expectations, definitions of success, attitudes toward the good, fears and hopes – in short, that which constitutes the shared assumptions of socio-religious cultural communities.

Variations of outlook exist within such communities, but so long as the different perspectives originate from within one myth, they are accommodated within a broad cultural setting. For example, extreme behaviours in Western society are branded either as psychopathological and thus in need of psychiatric treatment or as sociopathological requiring confinement. In either case, society accommodates those on the fringes within its overall horizon of understanding. A community's myth is taken for granted; it is accepted as normative and functions at both conscious and subconscious levels. Although frequently myth is not recognised as such, it is right to speak of it as myth because it represents the perspective of one horizon among endless horizons. Communities often do not acknowledge their own myths because their apprehensions of reality have been conditioned by perspectives visible within one horizon alone.

The equating of myth with reality by religious communities is natural and in one sense could not be otherwise since reality cannot be grasped in general terms, but can be understood and assimilated only within particular world perspectives. Myth thus defines the fundamental perspective on reality from within horizons of understanding. It comprises the way things are; it defines truth for believers.

Mythologumena

Within every tradition, the myth is expressed in various ways. The telling of the myth, the stories which elucidate it, are the mythologumena. These comprise the variety of oral and written traditions commonly called myths as discussed in chapter three. They are not the same as the myth, but live and breathe within the horizon of understanding familiar to believers. They give colour and depth to the myth, fllllng out the fabric of what constitutes reality within the horizon. Most academic studies of and theories concerning myths on this definition refer to the mythologumena rather than to myth. Each religion possesses mythologumena which are told and retold on various occasions.

In one of his most recent books on the world's religions (1989, 1992), Ninian Smart reaffirms what he wrote earlier about the 'mythological dimension' of religion (1969). But in his recent accounting he calls this the 'mythic or narrative' dimension, 'the story side of religion' (1992, 15). He notes that the oral stories in some traditions precede written documents and thus become scriptures which are authoritative for these believing communities.

In the early 1980s Smart and Richard Hecht produced an anthology of world scriptures which follows Smart's divisions of religion into various dimensions of human experience. Beginning with ancient religions extending through the world's major world religions to 'small-scale Traditional Religions', new religions, and 'secular religions', Smart and Hecht devote a section to the 'sacred narratives' of each. In the introduction to their anthology, they explain that every religion has a 'vast body of sacred literature'. They admit that the oral traditions are not technically scriptures, 'for they are not written documents', but they are considered the same as scriptures because they reflect 'the spiritual universe of the people who treat them as sacred' (1982, xi).

For our purposes, it is important to note that Smart and Hecht regard the sacred texts, what I am calling the mythologumena, as playing 'a crucial part in the formation of people's perception of reality' (p. xi). In other words, the mythologumena express the myth; they reveal how people perceive reality. In terms of the above discussion, they point toward and elucidate a believing community's horizon of experience.

The study of any tradition's mythologumena, therefore, will enable the scholar to illuminate and clarify the myth of the believing community. As noted above, the myth elucidated may be transparent in many aspects to believers, but it will be present within the sacred narratives by which they live. In relation to Africa in particular, it must be remembered that the meaning of the mythologumena will often differ according to the circumstances, the storyteller, and the purpose in relating the story. This performative side of the mythologumena, especially in oral societies, needs to be taken into account when seeking to understand through it the myth of the believers.

Ritual

In chapter four, I argued that myth and ritual do not always operate together and that theories explaining rituals as re-enactments of myths cannot be maintained, particularly among the indigenous religions of Africa. On this revised definition of myth, however, rituals perform the same function as the mythologumena – they elucidate the myth.

Although African rituals cannot be understood as re-enactments of the mythologumena, they do participate in and reflect in action the myth of the believers. What we hear or read in the mythologumena, therefore, can be seen in rituals. They reveal the myth through repeated performative acts. For this reason, Smart and Hecht include the ritual dimension within their anthology of sacred texts. They justify this by claiming that 'it is by worship, meditation, services, rites, pilgrimages and other such activities that human beings relate themselves to God and the gods, and prepare themselves for redemption and liberation' (p. xv). By observing these expressions of religious faith, the scholar gains a sense of the believers' myth.

Smart and Hecht have selected rituals as they are recounted in the texts of the various religions within their anthology. They do not provide actual observations of rituals in practice. They demonstrate by this that the mythologumena in many traditions, such as the Lord's Supper of the Christian accounts, either describe or prescribe how the ritual is to be performed. Scriptures rarely, however, offer a precise picture of how various groups within the same tradition actually perform their rituals. Islam may provide an exception to this if one includes as sacred text not only the Qur'an, but also the Hadith.

The difficulty of relying on texts for describing rituals is particularly clear in the case of what Smart and Hecht call 'small-scale traditional religions'(1982, 337-369). None selected are from Africa and two of those chosen are what I would call mythologumena whereas one is a description of a North American Indian Sun Dance. Rituals, thus, despite their undoubted relationship to the mythologumena in some traditions, best reveal the myth when they are observed and/or recounted from such observations.

Precisely how the observations are undertaken becomes a technical question. In the case of the rituals recorded in this book from Zimbabwe, each researcher used a participant observation method within the broad stages of the phenomenological method as described in chapter one. That a participant observer will affect the ritual is admitted, but since most of the accounts recorded were from Zimbabwean students in their home areas, in this case, the problem is minimised. The larger methodological issues relating to mutual engagement and methodological conversion, however, remain. I will return to these later in this chapter. At this point, I want to emphasise that rituals point toward the myth, help to clarify it, and make it apparent to the scholar. Just like mythologumena, therefore, rituals illuminate what it means for believers to live within a particular horizon of understanding.

Mythemes

From an analysis of the mythologumena and rituals, the scholar can begin to form concepts, interpretations, and meanings of the myth of a believing community. The academic articulation of the myth, derived from the mythologumena and rituals, is what, following Panikkar (1979, 154-55), I call *mythemes*. As the word implies, certain themes will emerge from the mythologumena and rituals which express cognitively the nature of the myth. A theme is like a motif which helps the scholar construct an overall pattern for comprehending the myth.

Mythemes, just like mythologumena and rituals, elucidate the myth However, because the myth itself cannot be observed, the mythemes must be derived from that which can be seen and studied – principally that which is said and that which is done, the mythologumena and the rituals. The mythemes cannot be equated with the myth. To do so would be to reduce the myth to concepts or academic reconstructions. This point must be remembered and reiterated, partly because the nature of the academic exercise results necessarily in conceptual interpretations of religions and partly because Western scholarship has tended to emphasise the doctrinal side of religions.

Nor should mythemes be confused with the beliefs or the doctrines of a religion, although they will reflect the cognitive dimension of faith. The mythemes are the creation of the scholar who interacts with the mythologumena and the rituals to ascertain themes which yield understanding of a religion's myth. If the mythemes are regarded as a religion's beliefs or doctrines, they will cease to provide the basis for academic understanding and become instead expositions of what a religion teaches. When the mythemes are identified and articulated in a composite form, the scholar can elucidate the myth of any particular religion by offering an interpretation of its meaning. This represents the limit to and the final end of a researcher's work.

The mythemes are elicited from a detailed analysis of the mythologumena and the rituals. By studying closely both of these, the scholar can create the concepts through which the myth of any believing community can be comprehended academically. A diagram of the procedural relationships is shown below.

The identification of mythemes and the subsequent pattern which emerges from them represents the scholar's creative work. It involves a hermeneutical task, what, as we have seen, Eliade calls 'creative hermeneutics' (1969, 61-62) . It corresponds to the phenomenological 'eidetic vision or intuition' (Cox, 1996, 37-39) since the mythemes are

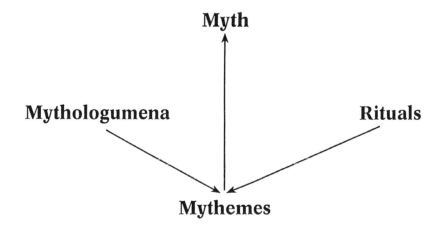

Myth

Mythologumena   **Rituals**

Mythemes

Elucidating the Meaning of the Myth

not mechanically given within the mythologumena and the rituals nor can the interpretation of meaning identified from the mythemes be said to exist inherently within them. They remain a construction of the scientist of religion. Nevertheless, the scholar does not invent the mythemes nor imagine the interpretation of the myth obtained from them. A researcher is accountable to the primary sources, in this case, the mythologumena and the rituals. The validity and the value of interpretations depend in large measure on faithfully relating findings to the field data.

The analysis which follows in the remainder of this chapter endeavours to exemplify the process of identifying mythemes from one mythologumenon and one ritual obtained through student interviews and observations among practitioners of an indigenous religion in broadly the same general area of Zimbabwe. I will then try to elucidate the myth through an examination of the mythemes.

A Mythologumenon: Sacred Mountains, Fire and Rain

The following story was recounted by Needmore Thati, a first year Phenomenology of Religion student in 1992. The story was obtained in an interview with an elderly man in the Muzendo village of the Nhema Area near Shurugwi. This is in a Shona speaking region of Zimbabwe, amongst the Karanga, approximately 50 kilometres south of Gweru and approximately 80 kilometres north of Zvishavane. The edited version of the story follows.

Fire on the Mountains: Needmore Thati

In the beginning a mountain located in the west erupted. This was later called the Shamba Mountain. It became the residence of the major spirit (*mhondoro*) of the whole area. When it was seen that this *mhondoro* needed a partner, a mountain to the east erupted, later called Bongwe Mountain. This became the residence of the *mhondoro's* wife.

When it was discovered that the mountains were only rocks and that it was necessary for them to have life in terms of vegetation, rain fell on the Shamba Mountain. Some of the water accumulated in a very deep pool at the base of the mountain. This pool never dried up.

Because Bongwe Mountain had not received any rains and the wife of the *mhondoro* still lived in a hot and dry area, a fire was lit on Shamba Mountain to signal to the wife that she should come to the side where the rain had fallen. The *mhondoro* and his wife would have a bath in the pool and drink some water to quench their thirst.

The wife responded by also lighting a fire on Bongwe Mountain to signal that she was feeling hot and was surely coming to have a bath and to drink from the pool. These same events occurred every year in the hot season. The *mhondoro* would light the fire first signalling his wife and then she would light her own fire. Then, the rains would fall to ensure that there was plenty of water for their bath and for drinking.

104

Because the rains had fallen first on Shamba Mountain causing vegetation to grow there, when the *mhondoro* lit his fire, it would spread quickly consuming the dry plants and trees. The rain would then fall instantly to avoid the fires causing wide destruction.

And thus the elders say today that when they see the fires burning on the Shamba and Bongwe Mountains they know the rains are about to begin. If in a certain year, the rains do not occur after the fires have been spotted, the elders consult the *mhondoro* to discover what has gone wrong. If someone has breached any of the traditions of the mountains, thunder can be heard expressing the *mhondoro's* anger. Then the elders knew that something had to be done. Usually, beer would be brewed for the ancestor spirits and would be drunk on one of the mountains. After doing this and even before the elders had descended the mountain, they would be soaked by the rain.

I call this a mythologumenon because it relates a story containing mythemes which help to illuminate the myth of the people of the region described. I will list a number of mythemes which seem apparent to me from the story.

Mytheme 1. A region is cared for by territorial ancestor spirits depicted spatially by mountains. The territorial ancestor spirits (*mhondoro*) are regarded as living on the mountains. This creates a perception of reality that everything within the space delineated by the mountains, which are visible to those living between them, falls under the protective care of the territorial ancestor spirits.

Mytheme 2. The care provided by the territorial ancestor spirits affects every family living between the mountains. Principally, this relates to rain which is necessary for the people to survive. Good rains bring abundant crops to everyone in the region; a drought likewise affects everyone. Matters relevant to families, such as illness and death, fall largely to the responsibility of the family ancestors.

Mytheme 3. The *mhondoro* signals his activity for all to see from his mountain. This occurs annually in the hottest season, usually in late October or early November, by fires appearing on the mountains. The people know that when the fires are seen, the rains will begin almost immediately. The mythologumenon explains why it is that the territorial ancestor spirit uses fire. The first part of the explanation is that he communicates with his wife who resides on the western mountain. The fire symbolises his annual invitation for her to join him for a bath and a drink. The other explanation is that the communication by fire threatens the vegetation dried out by the six months since the last rains and thus when the fire appears, the rains must extinguish it immediately to avoid a disaster. The story provides a backdrop for what the people actually see. The fires are attested to by people who live in the region. They understand them as a sign that the rains, the primary indication of ancestral care, are about to commence.

Mytheme 4. If the rains do not come, it means that the territorial ancestor spirits have not performed their responsibility by providing for the people under their care. The explanation of widespread suffering within a region resorts back to the ancestors. No other explanation appears in the story. If the ancestors are fulfilling their role as beneficent providers of rain, the seasons flow according to expected patterns. If the rains do not come at the normal time for planting, it is always understood that the ancestors have withheld their blessings to the people.

Mytheme 5. The story related above offers two explanations as to why the ancestors would not perform their normally beneficent function of providing rain. The first is that some breach of conduct related to the mountain may have occurred. This may have been that people of the region trespassed on the mountain, climbing on it without permission from the chief or from mediators for the ancestors. Some may have climbed on the mountain to eat fruit or other wild foods growing there, food which the ancestors themselves need. Perhaps some sacred places like caves have been invaded without proper ritual preparation. The residence of the *mhondoro* is sacred and cannot be entered without proper permission and preparation. A second explanation implied in the story is that the ancestors have not been properly honoured, remembered, or thanked for their continuing care. For this reason, they have withheld the rains until the people correct this by honouring them properly. In either explanation, this story refers to the anger of the ancestors at either a breach of their sacred space or a lack of respect through a failure to remember them. The anger is symbolised by thunder, which is like the roar of a lion (the actual meaning of the word *mhondoro*).

Mytheme 6. The means of rectifying the offence against the ancestors always involves a ritual. The ritual restores the previous relationship. It must be conducted by the elders of the region and it must take place on the sacred mountain. It involves brewing beer for the ancestors and drinking it on the mountain. That the ritual has restored the broken relationship with the ancestors is confirmed by the rain which usually falls even before the elders return from the mountain.

Ritual: *Bira* (Honouring the Ancestors)

The following ritual account is one of the most complete versions produced by a student. It was reported by Cleophas Gwakwara, a first year phenomenology of religion student in 1991, who at the current writing is pursuing an MA in Religious Studies in the same field. The account describes a ritual honouring family ancestors, and thus helps to complete the overall picture of how people relate to ancestor spirits. In this description, references are made frequently to the *mhondoro* who resides in a mountain visible to the people. This demonstrates that the people do not experience a gap between rituals honouring territorial and family ancestors, although they are aware of the differences, including the personnel who perform them.

Gwakwara's description was obtained in a region not far from the Daramombe mountain range in a village called Gonamombe. It too is among the Shona speaking Karanga people, approximately 20 kilometres west of the main Harare-Masvingo highway and around 180 kilometres south of Harare. The nearest town is Mvuma, approximately 80 kilometres northeast of Gweru. This means that the ritual described took place approximately 130 kilometres by road from Shurugwi, the location of Needmore Thati's mythologumenon outlined above. The differences in world perceptions between the two locations are minimal, and thus for our purposes, Thati's mythologumenon and Gwakwara's ritual description can be regarded as elucidating the same horizon of understanding.

Because Gwakwara's description is so detailed and helpful, I have limited my own editing to some quite minor changes to improve the style of the narration.

Bira Ritual: Cleophas Gwakwara

The *bira* ritual was carried out at a family homestead of the headman. It was carried out for fathers, the elders, the great grandfathers and the mothers of the family who have died. Relatives of the family had already been told long before that the ritual would take place and thus had sent their contributions in the form of rapoko which was used in brewing the beer.

Seven days before the actual day of the ritual, the headman stood in the middle of his homestead, sprinkled some snuff on the ground and said,

To all those who are down, the fathers, the mother and those beyond our reach, your children have thought of giving you a brew…that you may not turn against us saying that we did not inform you.

He then took a cupful of water and poured in a big basket of rapoko. This was when brewing started and those who took part were elderly women, those inactive in sex and no longer bearing children. Nobody tasted the beer until the day of the ritual.

Nobody slept during the night before the ritual since the people were singing and dancing the whole time. The song which was sung repeatedly can be translated thus:

The elders need those who are gathered,
The elders need those of Gonamombe,
The elders love us of one country,
The elders do not live where they are not gathered,
They do not like those who kill each other.

There was one woman who danced all night long and you could hear people say, 'Do not play with Bazvi…'

Early in the morning, people gathered at the cattle kraal. The headman pointed with his walking stick at a big black bull and said,

All those gathered here, this is our uncle, Bazvi, our elder, our leader, for whom we all have gathered here. What is left is for the brothers-in-law to do their duty.

All the people clapped their hands as women danced around the kraal.

Singing continued as people returned to the yard. The headman again stood before the people and sprinkled some snuff on the ground and said, 'To those who are below, your children are gathered here. Lead us as we enter into praising you for keeping us in one good piece'. A clay pot was taken out of the hut. The first calabash of beer was splashed on the ground around the pot. 'This is your beer. No one has ever tasted it before you. Drink this and your children will be happy'. He went on as the people clapped hands.

As this was going on, the bull was being killed by the sons-in-law. They used a knife to strike it because an axe was against their customs. Blood was collected in a clay plate. A woman just dashed from the house and ran to the kraal. One could not help following anxiously the woman's actions. She collected the clay plate full of blood and gulped the whole contents to the point of licking. People clapped their hands as she did so.

Some meat was cooked while the sons-in-law were given a portion of meat and a clay pot of beer to enjoy themselves. The sons-in-law sat together. Fathers-in-law sat in the shade of a mango tree forming their own distinct group. The 'owners of the home' sat in a hut.

Soon after midday, singing resumed, this time tinted with shades of alcohol as we joined in the chorus:

> The bees sting.
> Take my arrow; I want to go.
> They sting. Oh, chief! Oh, chief!
> Gwindingi has a lion that kills.
> I want to go.
> Beware! Gwindingi has a strong lion.

As people sang this song, an old woman pointed to the mountainside that stretched westward. Inquiring later, I was shown where Gwindingi (the popular old hill) was situated.

Another song was:

> You are poor, Oh King.
> Let them build if they so wish.
> Let them build on those who are living.
> One day it shall come back to them.

Pent up emotions began to be aroused by the tune: 'Poverty, oh, mother'.

> We now sacrifice with a goat,
> Poverty, oh, mother.
> The sun is almost setting before we sacrifice,
> The sun comes down before you come.

Singing reached a peak with the song,

> Spirits come back, oh, spirits, come back.
> Greetings to you *sekuru*.
> We receive you happily, old man.

The old woman who had pointed at the Gwindingi Mountain had now become possessed of the family ancestor named Bazvi. She could jump sky-high as if the ground were hot. She would rush as if she wanted to go out or charge backwards before she fell into a squatting position. What did not change was the pointing of her walking stick, three times downwards, once towards Gwindingi

Mountain and once upwards. Her walking stick was black with a carved face of an old man on it.

The woman then fell violently and started weeping and speaking in certain voices which I do not want to believe that I was the only one who could not comprehend. She then began to sing in a very manly voice:

The English took my wife,
Everything is bad.
You are not a relative; why do you fight?
The English took my wife.
Things are bad.

She asked for her clothes and was given a piece of joined black and white cloth which she hung around her shoulders. A baboon skin was placed on her head and she was given a smoking pipe which she put in her mouth. She then requested some water. She gulped a big calabash down without even breathing and asked for more. One old man then said, 'You have come old man. We see you. We are also very happy, but do you not realise that if you drink more, she who is near you will have nowhere to put her beer'?

Bazvi responded: 'You, you want to be too clever. I will cut off your testes!' People gasped in surprise. Bazvi continued, 'Why are you surprised? This is nothing. Anyway, your plea has been heard. Where is my wife?' An old woman came and sat there as they exchanged snuff in a wifely and husbandly manner. 'This is my wife and I love her. Today we are going to sleep together. You understand!' She continued looking at the woman addressed as VaDihori.

During my time, I was very stubborn. I used to have a brown woman and I would beat her at the buttocks. If the woman reported to the fathers-in-law that she was beaten, I would ask, "Where?" Can't you see her face is fine? At that time, I would know that I had finished off with the buttocks and she will never show them.

All the people laughed.

Anyway, my children, I am happy with your gathering and that is why I joke with you. So far no evil has transpired. I will tell Nyakuvamba (he who began creation) that your children still remember you. I am not here for long and am already about to leave.

A clay pot was placed in front of her and one elder said, 'As you said, you are about to leave. Our contribution to you, Bazvi, is this: take this pot and drink with your children'.

Bazvi began sharing the beer with the people, and after a few rounds, gave the responsibility to the old woman VaDihori and just said, 'I am leaving, my children. Thank you'. Bazvi made a violent sneeze, convulsed and then fell down. People clapped hands as this happened. A little later the old woman who had been possessed of Bazvi was asking what was happening, but no one dared to tell her. They only gave her some beer. Singing continued late into the night. The old woman drank, danced and joked with others as if nothing had happened. She danced late into the night.

The following morning, a beer pot 'chiparadza' (the last pot) was brought out and rapoko sadza was eaten with intestines without salt. A clay pot of beer and meat was put on the outskirts of the homestead for those who are not related to the family to eat and drink. No salt was provided. It was also directed to the spirits that move around the air. It was only after this that people began to disperse. Nobody was allowed to take any meat or beer home. If one did that, one would meet a lion or some misfortune, they said.

Mythemes

This excellent description provides the basis for identifying numerous mythemes. After doing this, I shall endeavour to utilise these alongside the mythemes I derived from the mythologumenon above in order to offer an interpretation of the meaning of the myth they elucidate.

Mytheme 1. Rituals of honour are undertaken for the family ancestors regularly and not necessarily when a crisis has occurred. Preparations include informing not only the members of the extended family, but also the ancestors themselves. The purpose of conducting the ritual when there is no crisis is preventative, to ensure that the ancestors continue to perform their protective and beneficent roles.

Mytheme 2. A reciprocal relationship between the ancestors and the people is acknowledged in the ritual. Not only do the people need the protection and blessings of the ancestors, the ancestors also need their children to remember them, honour them, and communicate with them.

Mytheme 3. Symbols play a fundamental role in assisting the communion between the people and the ancestors. Beer is always used. Snuff (*bute*) provides another device used when communicating with the ancestors. The elder ancestor of the extended family is represented by a bull who is dedicated to him. When a medium is involved, a costume is worn which almost always employs a black and white cloth. Such symbols acknowledge that when the ritual commences and communication with the ancestors is established, a different state of affairs exists from normal life.

Mytheme 4. The roles of ritual participants are clearly understood and enforced. The beer is brewed by women beyond childbearing age, presumed no longer active in sex. The chief elder announces the ritual to the ancestors. The bull is killed by the sons-in-law. Fathers-in-law sit in one location while the 'owners' of the land sit in one of the family huts. The spirit medium becomes possessed to form a channel for communication. Those who are not a part of the family and spirits who relate to other families are given a portion of the beer and meat at the outskirts of the homestead.

Mytheme 5. The rules of the ritual are precise and must not be abrogated. Examples include the necessity of removing one's shoes and of eating the meat from the ritual without any salt.

Mytheme 6. The senior family ancestor is seen as conveying the message that the family has rightly honoured the ancestors by performing the ritual to the one who started it all, the originator of creation. This suggests that the one who created is precisely the first ancestor and represents the lineage of ancestors extending through those who are no longer remembered by name.

Mytheme 7. Among the ancestors known by name, the *mhondoro* are more distant than family ancestors and hence have a place of respect tinged with both power and fear. The territorial ancestor spirits live on the mountain. They are symbolised by the lion who can kill. The relationship between the *mhondoro* and the family ancestors, however, is clearly understood and acknowledged. The mountain can be seen, is pointed to, and in a large measure oversees what goes on in the entire region.

Mytheme 8. The family ancestor spirit is familiar with its own family members. He jokes, refers to incidents in life, and refers to human acts like drinking and sexual intercourse. The family ancestor spirit reflects an extension of life displaying a continuity between the living and the dead.

Mytheme 9. Communication between the ancestors and the people and between the people and the ancestors is essential if the world is to function as it ought. If communication is broken in any way, the people have no means to offer their concerns and complaints to the ancestors and the ancestors cannot explain their grievances to the people. Without communication, every aspect of life becomes threatened and enveloped by danger and ultimate chaos.

Mytheme 10. Although various modes of communication exist, the role of a spirit medium seems central. The medium directly relates the words, thoughts, feelings, concerns, and instructions of the ancestor. In one sense, in the hierarchy of modes of communication, to use Eliade's terminology, the medium becomes the supreme hierophany.

Analysis of the Mythemes: Elucidating the Myth

The mythemes elicited from the mythologumenon and the ritual account of this chapter suggest what it is like to live within the horizon of understanding experienced by the believers in the indigenous religion of the Karanga of central and southcentral Zimbabwe. Each region is presided over by a chief and is delineated geographically, usually demarcated by mountains. The mountains represent a constant reminder of the territorial ancestor spirits who reside there and who care for all of the people within the region.

It is clear from both the mythologumenon and the ritual that the people perceive every significant aspect of life as being in relationship to ancestors. Their myth thus is permeated through and through with thoughts, feelings, and actions informed by and in constant communication with the ancestors. The family ancestors are closest and most intimate in this relationship since they are responsible directly for family concerns. The *mhondoro* are more remote, less familiar, more powerful, potentially dangerous if angered, but still form a continuous relationship with family ancestors by adopting a fundamentally beneficent role. The *mhondoro* must concern themselves with issues, threats, and problems relevant to the whole community and thus are not concerned directly with problems peculiar to particular families.

111

The overall myth provides a fundamental sense of security for the people. They know the source of their well being. It also constructs a system for explaining and rectifying failures in maintaining their well being. It describes a horizon in which everything makes sense because events relating to the care and abundance of the land all fall under the provision of the territorial ancestor spirits who established the people in the region in the first place and whose ultimate interest is to ensure that the people prosper through good crops and sufficient cattle, just as it was when they were alive and as it is with the chiefs and elders who have succeeded them. Meanwhile, family ancestor spirits ensure the health, success, and prosperity of members of their own extended families.

The world of the ancestors corresponds to or mirrors proper relationships and responsibilities between members of society. In both the spiritual and social worlds, well being is conditional on living within properly defined relationships. Respect for authority, compliance with well understood rules of obligation, and basic courtesy for others produce a life of harmony. When these fundamental values are contravened either in the social or spiritual realms, disorder, suffering and even the threat to livelihood results.

Although the myth does not discriminate between social and spiritual orders, I point to the correspondence between the two to demonstrate their fundamental interpenetration. I do not believe that participants are unaware, however, that they are entering a different mode of experience from everyday life when ritual activities commence. Otherwise, symbols of the ancestors would be unnecessary. But I am convinced that ancestral and social relationships correspond in structure and in intention.

When a breach of the spiritual/social order occurs, prescribed ways exist to reestablish damaged relationships. The ancestors, although capable of anger, quickly respond when rituals of respect are re-enacted. They seem not to hold a grudge or demand more than a restoration of proper relationships between themselves, the elders, and the people living in their region. That this is accomplished through rituals seems obvious to the believers. It is part of their myth, unquestioned and transparent to them.

Although no direct mention of social ills resulting from rivalry between families in the same region is directly mentioned in either the mythologumenon or ritual, both imply that the family ancestor spirits must relate harmoniously with other spirits, just as families must live with other families in society. For this reason, in the *bira* ritual a portion of the meat and beer is left at the edge of the homestead for other families and their ancestor spirits. One of the songs sung at the *bira* affirms that the 'elders love us of one country' and they 'do not like those who kill each other'. Spiritual and social harmony coincide.

The situation is complicated, of course, because ritual reality does not correspond to the ideal world, as we noted earlier in J. Z. Smith's account of the bear killing ritual. Injustice in the forms of unequal opportunity, ill-gained advantage, and malicious jealousy thus are attributed to various forces of evil. In such cases, the family ancestor spirits can sometimes be convinced to withhold their protection and open the way for witches, sorcerers, and alien spirits which can bring death or illness to family members just as territorial ancestor spirits can withhold rain. In such times of distress, families must determine what has caused their misfortune and ascertain what must be done to rectify the wrong. In almost every case, some form of reinstituting proper relations with their family ancestors will be required. If wrongs committed against other families have been identified as the cause of the misfortune, as was the case of the diagnosis of an *ngozi* spirit described in chapter four, recompense to the injured party may need to be made along with a ritual to the family ancestors before life can return to a state of harmony.

The myth suggested by the mythemes thus points toward a fundamental concern among the Karanga with spiritual and social harmony ensured by communication between ancestor spirits at the family and territorial levels. The horizon of understanding appears to be delimited by ancestor spirits, just as the literal horizon is bounded by the mountains on which the *mhondoro* dwell. When communication with the ancestors is severed, every effort by the ancestors and the people will be made to restore it. Only by an intimate communication between ancestors and the people can the ideal harmony be approximated. Without such communication, the world of the Karanga disintegrates into chaos marked by disorientation and disorder. The myth of the ancestors constitutes the shared reality for this socio-religious cultural community.

Resolving the Problems of Myth, Ritual, the Sacred and Comparative Studies as Outlined in Chapters Two through Four

From the above elucidation of the myth as derived from the mythemes, I have attempted to provide an interpretive key for understanding a particular religious community. I have endeavoured principally to illustrate how the elucidation occurs by identifying mythemes based on mythologumena and rituals. In this way, I believe I have overcome the problems identified in chapters two, three and four of this book.

In chapter two, I pursue the argument that both Western academics and Christian theologians have sought to use classifications for the purposes of either consolidating all indigenous expressions of religion into one homogeneous entity or, and more dangerously, to justify Christian evangelistic motives. The term Primal Religions demonstrates both tendencies clearly. I argue at the end that we are better to accept the narrow limitations of geography, ethnic identity and language rather than creating common classifications based on largely superficial criteria.

In this sense, a basis for comparative studies among African religions is opened by the analysis of this chapter. Prior to recounting the descriptions above, I identified the region from which the accounts were obtained, their ethnic identity and the language spoken. I tried to show that they were near enough geographically to treat as one religion, the indigenous religious expressions of the Shona speaking Karanga of central and southcentral Zimbabwe. From the accounts, I endeavoured to derive mythemes which elucidate the myth by which the people of this African region live. Of course, the accuracy of my interpretation depends on its faithfulness to field data. However, assuming that I have

113

succeeded in deciphering the myth based on mythemes, rituals and mythologumena, it would be possible to look for variations and similarities in other regions of Zimbabwe, southern Africa, other parts of Africa, and in other indigenous religions.

The results of such a comparative approach should then be based on the *content* of the various religions and not on imposed academic classifications. Where shared myths among indigenous religions seem to be found, these can be noted and tested back through the mythemes, rituals and mythologumena. Perhaps of more interest, however, will be where variations occur since these will help demonstrate the distinctiveness of indigenous religious practices. Nevertheless, the framework I have constructed is intended to provide the basis for careful comparative work among indigenous religions and thus speaks to the problems posed in chapter two.

The problem of chapter three that African oral literature seems devoid of myths as defined primarily in cosmogonic terms is resolved. Mythologumena certainly are not always cosmogonic. The argument which makes them refer primarily to origins of the world and only secondarily to social and moral concerns results from the need to attach cosmic significance to them. By introducing myth as the horizon of understanding this problem is overcome. Mythologumena, of whatever type or nature, will always elucidate the myth and mythemes will always be capable of being derived from them.

On this structure, moreover, the mythologumena can be regarded as performative utterances which provide clues to the myth of believers. They do not need to be restricted to written narratives nor removed artificially from their contexts. In so far as they illuminate the myth of the storyteller and his or her audience, they fall within the framework for understanding I have outlined.

The primary problem of chapter four, that rituals do not seem explicitly to re-enact myths in Africa, is also resolved by this analysis. Myths (now redefined as mythologumena), always participate in and reflect a religious community's myth (defined as a horizon of understanding). In this sense, efforts to fit rituals into a narrow theory of re-enactments has been shown to be unnecessary. In some traditions and in certain rituals, such as the Christian Eucharist or the Jewish Passover, the mythologumena are literally re-enacted. In the Zimbabwean rituals I have collected, this never occurs explicitly. But in every case and in every religion, rituals point toward and clarify the myth whether or not they bear a direct correlation to the mythologumena of the tradition.

Under this structure for interpreting religious data, it is even possible to incorporate into it Frits Staal's theory of the meaninglessness of ritual. The meaning for believers ultimately does not reside either in rituals or mythologumena, but in the myth. Even if rituals are rule-regulated and meaningless in themselves, believers see the myth through them. I do not think that Staal is arguing that rituals perform no function, any more than he would suggest that grammar performs no function for language. The choice of behaviours in rituals may be arbitrary, but the function is to elucidate the myth. I would argue, therefore, that the distinction between myth, mythologumena, rituals and mythemes is able to accommodate even the most radical interpretation of rituals.

Potentially, however, the most difficult methodological issues raised in this book remain. Following Panikkar and Krieger, I am challenged to utilise my elucidation of the myth of the Karanga through a process of dialogue between it and my own myth rooted in the autonomy of reason. In theory, this is accomplished by stepping out onto a ground between the myths of either in order to reveal a new horizon of understanding. I endeavour to apply and analyse this critical methodological stage in my final two chapters.

References

Cox, J. L. 1996, 2nd ed. *Expressing the sacred: An introduction to the phenomenology of religion.* Harare: University of Zimbabwe Publications.

Eliade, M. 1969. *The quest: history and meaning in religion.* Chicago and London: University of Chicago Press.

Gadamer, H.G. 1980. *Truth and method.* London: Sheed and Ward.

Krieger, D. J. 1991. *The new universalism. Foundations for a global theology.* Maryknoll: Orbis Books.

Panikkar, R. 1979. *Myth, faith and hermeneutics.* New York: Paulist Press.

Smart, N. and Hecht, R. 1982. *Sacred texts of the world: A universal anthology.* London: Macmillan Reference Books.

Chapter Seven

TOWARD A NEW HORIZON OF UNDERSTANDING: THE MEETING OF AFRICAN INDIGENOUS AND WESTERN SCIENTIFIC MYTHS

I would characterise the myth by which I live as the Western faith in the autonomy of reason. Although my myth may be regarded as transparent to me (because it defines my horizon of understanding), following Panikkar, in this chapter I will attempt to relate a mythologumenon which clarifies it and a ritual which demonstrates it in action. From these I should be able to derive the mythemes implicit within them in order to elucidate the myth of reason. In this sense, I am contending that the faith in reason embodies a religious perspective similar in kind to that upheld by any traditionally constituted religious community.

Following Krieger's stages in methodological conversion, I endeavour later in this chapter to step outside of my myth into a place between confessions by interacting with the African myth as derived from the mythemes of the last chapter. In the end, I hope to elucidate a new horizon of understanding

Western Mythologumenon

I find a good example of the telling of the story surrounding faith in the autonomy of reason in Karl Jaspers' series of lectures presented in Heidelberg University and first published in 1952 as *Reason and Anti-Reason in Our Time* (1971). Jaspers sets out to show how the scientific method provides an indispensable component of reason before moving on to explain the nature of reason and to define its struggle with forces (called anti-reason) which would seek to defeat it.

For Jaspers, the scientific method proceeds on the basis of a proper philosophical understanding of the relationship between the subject and the object. The primary purpose of science, he argues, is to elaborate a 'methodological system' which shows the subject 'what processes' and 'what means' are encountered in the apprehension of particular objects (p. 29).

Jaspers describes the scientific attitude as involving experimentation, methodical intercourse with things themselves, and a methodological consciousness (p. 38). Experimentation is aimed at testing hypotheses, to confirm or deny theories of causality or to modify various explanations. This testing follows clearly defined stages which must be observed in intricate detail if verification or falsification is to be reliable.

The methodological clarity obtained by science ensures that the subject recognises the difference between what can and what cannot be known. It is this which leads Jaspers to confess 'an unconditional belief in modern science as the way to truth' (p. 31). Science, however, is not self-sufficient. Even what it elects to research is not derived from itself but from choices and criteria which fundamentally are philosophical. This means that science alone can never attain a comprehensive knowledge of the world but only an infinite progression of facts.

What science cannot satisfy, philosophical methods can. This brings us back to the subject-object dichotomy which philosophical reason elucidates. The subject refers to 'existence', 'consciousness', or 'the possibility of existence'. Objects are the things themselves which form the content of consciousness. Hence, any endeavour to understand what we know and how we know centres around the question 'With what subject are we relating ourselves to which object?' (p. 35).

It is the subject, utilising reason, who perceives causal connections and relationships between objects. This is why, although providing the way to truth, science is 'not adequate to embrace Truth' (p. 38). Reason provides this additional component, that which is 'more than science'.

But what is reason? Reason is characterised by the critical attitude. It moves to one position, but then proceeds to criticise the position attained. Reason thus always involves further thought. It rejects 'irrevocably fixed ideas'. Because reason seeks a unity, that is 'the real and only unity', it never stops at half-truths or prematurely embraces partial unity in place of a complete understanding. This is why, for Jaspers, reason is best characterised as 'a boundless openness' (p. 39).

It is here that the mythologumenon is related clearly and thus is articulated best in Jaspers' own words.

> Reason is attracted by what is most alien to it. It wants to illuminate and give being and language even to the passions of the night which threaten to destroy the laws that govern the day. It does not allow them to disappear into nothingness. Reason strives to avoid the sin of forgetfulness and self-deception, losing the One in a harmony that is only apparent. It presses on constantly to the place where unity is broken through in order that in this break-through it may grasp the truth that is in it. By breaking up every attractive semblance of unity (whose insufficiency is thereby proved) it attempts to ward off the metaphysical breach and rending of Being itself, the real Unity. Reason, itself the origin of order, attends even the powers which destroy order. It is always there listening to that which is most alien to it, to that which breaks in upon it, to that which fails it (p. 40-41).

In this sense, reason illuminates that which science cannot, although the two are inseparably bound. What then constitutes the enemy of reason, what Jaspers calls 'anti-reason'?

> This enemy is the unphilosophical spirit which knows nothing and wants to know nothing of truth. Under the name of truth it gives currency to everything that is inimical and alien to truth, to all the perversions of truth (p. 66).

It is in their desire for the 'more than science' that people turn to the irrational, the occult, and the fantasies of their own imaginations. The power of this desire is derived from the common human yearning 'not for reason but for mystery'. This resides in the irrational – 'not for science but wizardry disguised as science – not for rationally founded influence, but for magic'. Jaspers characterises this yearning for mystery as 'blind unrestraint and blind obedience' at one and the same time (p. 67-68).

The falling into this state occurs when reason becomes equated with mere intellect and not with the whole human personality. This is because humans want more than the objective knowledge science, apart from reason, produces. Without its partnership with reason, science creates a world without meaning full of 'pale abstractions' (p. 69).

Jaspers has thus told the mythical story of his faith in reason. It has been defined as the endless pursuit of real unity, following the methodological procedures of the scientific method. And it is engaged in a battle, a warfare against the powers of irrationality and pseudo-reason which, where it is victorious over these enemies of darkness, leads humanity ever onward toward freedom, meaning, and authentic existence.

The place where reason's struggle can be witnessed most clearly on the intellectual level for Jaspers is in the universities, 'where everything open to scientific research can become the object of enquiry'. The activity of reason, its ritual performances, can be seen 'through the mutual intercourse and discussion of scholars and scientists' (p. 84).

I want to suggest that the same struggle between reason and irrationality is increasingly being acted out ritually in Western society today through psychotherapy, particularly in its cognitive-behavioural forms. Based on scientific principles, the whole of psychotherapy (even in its Freudian configuration, which Jaspers condemned) aims at releasing individuals from the debilitating power of the irrational thereby freeing them for realistic choices in the world and positive, fulfilling lives. Psychotherapy, therefore, in my view, ritually exemplifies the telling of Jaspers' mythologumenon.

Psychotherapy as the Ritual of Reason

By selecting psychotherapy as a principal ritual activity of the faith in the autonomy of reason, I have put myself initially in the difficult task of defining what I mean by psychotherapy generally. Andrew Samuels, a depth psychologist, argues in a recent book on contemporary criticisms of psychotherapy that the field cannot be defined intellectually, functionally, socially or by means of cultural analysis precisely, because in it there are 'too many fragmenting tendencies' (1992, xi). This is why I shall concentrate on one type of psychotherapy which is easily amenable to the faith in reason, the cognitive-behavioural school. Nevertheless, I would contend that in the midst of the many theories and practices which make up this vast field, certain assumptions are made which allow me to pursue my argument that psychotherapy as a whole comprises one of the major ritual activities of the rational faith of Western culture.

Windy Dryden and Colin Feltham (1992) seem to support my view when they claim that 'psychotherapists are engaged with their clients in a search for truth, clarity and rationality' (p. 1). This involves an active pursuit against what they call 'the fearful, superstitious, addictive and avoiding parts of their clients' (p. 1) and it takes place in 'the post-theistic culture of the West' (p. 3).

This faith in reason, like faith in God, is acted out ritually to achieve, as Jaspers suggested, the triumph of reason over anti-reason. Its psychotherapeutic ritual forms, as Samuels notes, are diverse and, on the surface, sometimes contradictory. But I would contend with Dryden and Feltham that all of them encourage the 'truth-seeking, fear-confronting, cobweb-clearing parts of their clients' (p. 1). As such, psychotherapy includes the activities of professionals who engage, in the words of Dryden and Feltham, in the repeated activity of 'formal talking-centred treatments or attempted treatments of psychological difficulties' (p. 5). The noted British psychiatrist Anthony Storr supports this definition. 'Psychotherapy, as I define it,' he writes, 'is the art of alleviating personal difficulties through the agency of words and a personal, professional relationship' (1990, xii).

According to Dryden and Feltham, those belonging to the profession include psychoanalysts, psychotherapists, clinical psychologists, counsellors, psychiatrists, and social workers (1992, 5). The clergy, who are often listed among such practitioners, are not included by Dryden and Feltham, presumably because their ultimate recourse is not to reason but to God. In the light of the faith I am exploring in autonomous rationality, I would concur with this view.

I find further confirmation of this in a debate between Albert Ellis (1992), the American founder of Rational-Emotive Therapy, and Gill Edwards (1992), whom Ellis describes as a 'New Age, mystical and spiritual' psychotherapist (p. 218). In his rebuttal to Edwards' claim that traditional psychotherapy is lagging behind the physical sciences by its continued devotion to Cartesian-Newtonian concepts of causality (p. 199-200), Ellis discloses why in his view mystical approaches to human well-being are characterised by what Jaspers would call anti-reason, a pseudo-rationality.

Ellis argues that so-called spiritual or mystical techniques to attain psychological health are circumscribed by certain religious beliefs:

higher energies, higher consciousness; higher-order reality; a higher self; absolute truth; God-like intuition; creation of matter by mind; magical ways of communication, and survival after death; reaching beyond our human (to, presumably, super human) potential; *certain* knowledge of a true mystical world view; everyone's ability to completely cure himself or herself of physical and mental dis-ease; deification of "inner experience"; full acknowledgement of human power and divinity (p. 218).

Ellis, from the standpoint of scientific rationality, joins Jaspers in reason's battle against the yearning for mystery among those who want 'more than science'. Ellis claims that although 'most mystics are certain that they can achieve communion with God and are positive that they can attain knowledge of spiritual truths through intuition', this is what 'virtually no modern scientists ... believe' (p. 214). He takes up the subject-object dichotomy noting that although humans do not see objects in the world 'in themselves', this does not deny that objects exist nor that they comprise the content of consciousness. 'Try kicking a stone and see!' (p. 214)

Dryden, Feltham and Ellis thus confirm that psychotherapy falls within a faith in reason in a way which conforms to its mythical telling as related in Jaspers' mythologumenon. Storr, moreover, agrees with me that the school of psychotherapy to which a practitioner belongs, within the broad parameters of the definition provided above, is of minimal importance and sometimes irrelevant to the client's overcoming the psychological problems which induced treatment in the first place. This is because 'research discloses the common factors which lead to a successful outcome in psychotherapy … is largely independent of the school to which the psychotherapist belongs' (1990, xiii). According to Storr, modern psychotherapists generally share a common belief that their role is more concerned 'with understanding persons as wholes and with changing attitudes than with abolishing symptoms' (p. xiv).

By selecting cognitive-behavioural therapy as my example of a ritual of reason, therefore, I am not suggesting that the many other schools of psychotherapy could not also have been chosen for this purpose. I do believe, however, that cognitive-behavioural therapy, because of its emphasis on changing thoughts, attitudes and behaviours, provides an unambiguous example of the acting out of a faith in reason. This is particularly true when the therapist holds a differing view from the client concerning the causes of the client's problems. A cognitive-behavioural therapist frequently works at directly changing the client's understanding of the cause of the presenting difficulty by helping the client reconstruct thought patterns in conjunction with learning and practising different behaviours (Dryden, 1989, 7). Before moving to a case study of cognitive-behavioural therapy, therefore, I need to delineate the main features of its approach.

Basic Elements in the Cognitive-Behavioural School
Cognitive-behavioural therapy is a term which applies broadly to a psychological approach which takes into consideration a person's behavioural, cognitive and physiological responses to any situation. Psychological problems occur when the consequences of any of these responses produce disruptions in the capacity of a person to carry on in normal everyday living. Examples of such disruptions include phobias, depression, recurrent headaches, insomnia, sexual problems, seemingly uncontrollable impulsive behaviours, violence and obsessions.

Richard Stern and Lynn Drummond of St. George's Hospital in London define behavioural psychotherapy as 'a group of treatments with the central hypothesis that psychological distress results from learned behaviour, and can therefore be unlearned' (1991, xiv). They refer to cognitive therapy as an approach which is particularly useful in depression and non-phobic anxiety because it aims at changing negative thoughts and predictions into more reality based assessments. They argue that 'it makes sense to incorporate cognitive approaches into behavioural ones, especially where a pure behavioural treatment is not at first effective or where one is lacking' (p. 7).

The cognitive-behavioural assessment of a person's difficulties involves examining overt behaviours related to the problem, thoughts or cognitions which accompany it, and physiological reactions in association with it. Australian psychologists Wilson, Spence and Kavanagh (1989, 4) explain how these three modalities operate together.

A person with a public-speaking phobia may manifest avoidance of speaking situations, thoughts about appearing foolish prior to being in a speaking situation and an increase in heart rate when exposed to the speaking situation.

In this example, the overt behaviour consists of avoiding the situation; the cognitions relate to what others might think if the speech is poorly presented; the physiological factors refer to the increased heart rate. Each reaction can be traced to the initial cause, the task of presenting a speech, with consequences that are likely to affect the performance of the task negatively. By recognising the antecedents and the consequences, the cognitive-behavioural therapist can determine the factors which need treatment to bring about the capacity for the person to achieve the desired end, in this case, giving a speech.

One specific form of cognitive-behavioural treatment is called Rational-Emotive Therapy (RET) founded, as I noted above, by the American psychologist Albert Ellis and expounded widely in Britain by Windy Dryden of Goldsmiths' College, University of London. Ellis has written over 60 books on the approach and its application to specific problems people encounter in daily living.

The fundamental contention of Rational-Emotive Therapy is that the primary cause of dysfunctional feelings and actions is not the situation which seems to produce them, but the thoughts people hold about the situation. Ellis often presents this as the ABCs of Rational-Emotive Therapy.

A refers to the activating event which an individual perceives as the cause of upset feelings. B represents the beliefs or thoughts which the person maintains about A. C stands for the emotional and/or behavioural consequences resulting from the beliefs the person holds about the activating event.

Ellis argues that most people incorrectly believe that emotional and behavioural consequences (C) are caused directly by the activating event (A) rather than the beliefs (B) the person holds about A. Ellis explains,

At point A (an Activating Experience or Activating Event) something occurs. For example, you have a good job and get fired from it.

At point C, an emotional and/or behavioral Consequence, you react to the happenings at Point A, and feel quite depressed about your job loss and tend to stay at home much of the time and avoid going out to look for another equivalent, or perhaps even better, job.

Noting, now, that the emotional and behavioral Consequence (C) almost immediately and directly follows after the occurrence of the Activating Experience (A), you (and others) falsely tend to assume that A *causes* C. And you (and they) erroneously make conclusions like: "I lost this good job and *that*, my loss, has depressed me and made me avoid looking for another one"...

Actually ... what really happened included A (the job loss) and C, the consequence of loss or deprivation or frustration (no longer getting what we wanted); and even at that, C didn't *automatically* follow from A but from B, your Belief about A...

If you merely desire or wish or want the job, at point B, and tell yourself: "I definitely would like to have it, but if I don't ... I only find that unfortunate and undesirable", ... you then will tend only to feel disappointed, sorry, and regretful at C...

But if you *also* believe that you desperately *need* this job, by insisting to yourself, at point B, "I *must* have it! I can hardly exist without it and find it absolutely *awful* to lose it!" you will then experience something like a feeling of despair, depression, and complete inadequacy at point C, [and] probably will feel unable to go out and look for another job (1977, 6).

This example demonstrates that according to RET when emotional consequences result in disruptions to everyday life, they are inappropriate to the situation and almost invariably result from an array of irrational beliefs the person maintains resolutely about the situation. Appropriate emotional consequences, by contrast, follow from rational beliefs about situations and do not produce dysfunctional behaviours.

Rational-Emotive therapists, therefore, assume a directive and didactic role in the therapeutic process by actively disputing, and helping the client to actively dispute, irrational beliefs and change them to rational beliefs. In order to reenforce this, homework assignments, often requiring behaviours which the client would not or could not accomplish without changing irrational beliefs, are provided between therapy sessions. The objective of this approach is to help the person live rationally by responding appropriately to the manifold events which occur during a lifetime, very many of which are beyond the person's direct control.

For RET, irrational beliefs tend to form in clusters around main ideas. One chief cluster of irrational thoughts centres on the 'musts' people give themselves (Ellis, 1977, 8). They tell themselves things like, 'I **must** succeed in this project at work' or 'I **must** be liked by every significant person in my life' or 'The world **must** treat me in a completely fair way'. When such musts enter the thinking of a person, inappropriate emotional and behavioural consequences almost always result.

If an individual **must** succeed at a project at work, undue anxiety develops around the project, not only creating personal stress but also increasing the likelihood that the person will not succeed in the project. If the individual **must** be liked by virtually everyone, almost everything possible will be done to avoid any situation which might show the person in a bad light, thereby decreasing the chances of being genuinely liked for uniquely individual characteristics and lending support to the negative self-image the person already possesses. If a person **demands** that the world always be experienced as just and fair, feelings of intense anger will be ready to erupt even over the many minor injustices which confront each of us every day.

Another, and often related, cluster of feelings centres around what Ellis (1977, 10) calls 'awfulising' or making catastrophes out of events. People say things like, 'Wasn't that awful!' 'That was terrible!' or 'If this were to happen, I couldn't stand it!' The consequence of catastrophic thinking is almost always high levels of anxiety resulting in behaviours such as avoidance or trying to control others which will keep the perceived calamity from occurring. Related inappropriate feelings such as intense rage when the horrible event occurs or self-blaming and depression may also result.

Irrational beliefs often converge around extreme overgeneralisations (Ellis, 1977, 9) such as 'If this happens once, it will always happen every time in every similar situation'. Or, 'If such and such occurred, it would be 101% horrible'. Or, 'If I fail at this situation, such as keeping the one I love, I am a complete and total failure as a human being'. Such ways of thinking exaggerate the impact of specific situations on a person's life.

Rational-emotive therapists are taught to search for the 'musts', 'oughts' or 'shoulds' (forms of absolutistic cognitions) in a client's thinking and help the client replace such thoughts with preferences. 'I would rather succeed at the project at work and I will try my hardest to do so, but if I don't it's not the end of the world and it doesn't mean that I am a failure as a person'. This rational thought reduces anxiety, although not completely, and it helps the person approach the project at work in a more realistic and constructive way.

RET therapists are also instructed to look for and challenge evaluations either of oneself or others in order to help clients rate behaviours rather than people. This avoids the tendency to overgeneralise the impact of specific actions on personal characteristics. Irrational thoughts like, 'If my wife leaves me and runs off with another man, then I am a complete failure as a husband and a lover', more appropriately are replaced with rational thoughts such as, 'I am deeply disappointed and hurt that my wife left me for another man, but this does not mean that I am a failure as a human being nor that I will never be able to love or be loved again'. The person may also begin to identify behaviours which were harmful to his relationship with his wife and thereby learn to change them rather than condemning himself as a person for them. Or thoughts like, 'Because my wife left me she is a totally horrible person and needs to be condemned to hell' are better changed into 'My wife treated me unfairly and I wish that she had not, but I do not have control over her and I cannot demand that every person I care about will treat me in just the way I want them to.'

Inappropriate emotional consequences thus usually centre around undue anxiety (panic, phobias, irrational fears), depression (self-downing and total condemnation of one's value as a person), and rage (extreme anger at oneself, others or situations). Such inappropriate emotional consequences produce dysfunctional behaviours. RET contends that the dysfunctional behaviours will be changed by combining techniques to dispute the strongly held irrational beliefs with behavioural homework assignments in which the person encounters situations and learns to deal with them rationally. Ellis explains,

> RET utilizes a great deal of behavior therapy and does so as an integral part of the rational-emotive method. Its theory states that humans rarely change and keep believing a profound self-defeating belief until they *act* often against it. Consequently, RET therapists have pioneered in giving activity, in vivo homework assignments to their clients (1977, 211-212).

It should be noted at this point that not all cognitive-behavioural therapists emphasise the conceptual aspect in treatment to the degree that Rational-Emotive Therapy does. For example, Dave Richards and Bob McDonald (1990, 3), both nurse therapists, prefer the term 'learning theory' to behavioural or cognitive-behavioural psychotherapy. Although they opt for an 'integrated' approach including behavioural, cognitive and physiological assessments, they do not believe that research justifies the extent cognitions are emphasised in the treatment of psychological disturbances by those employing Rational-Emotive Therapy. This is a point emphatically disputed by Ellis who has provided exhaustive clinical evaluations supporting the success of his approach (1977, 35-71).

Richards and McDonald admit that theirs is a controversial point, but they prefer to stress behavioural techniques which they regard as more measurable scientifically than cognitive disputation. However, they acknowledge that 'many "cognitive" therapies include basic behavioural strategies.' They cite the work of cognitive-behavioural therapist Aaron Beck who 'encourages clients with phobias to undertake "behavioural experiments" to assist in challenging negative beliefs.' And they add that behavioural therapists 'encourage the client to use "coping statements" such as "it's only panic, it will not harm me" when facing up to feared situations.' Such coping statements are actually directed at the cognitive elements in a person's feelings of anxiety (1990, 111-12).

An example supporting the success of both the cognitive and behavioural treatments of anxiety is recorded in the research of the cognitive-behavioural psychotherapist, Donald Meichenbaum, who conducted experiments in which he introduced his subjects initially to coping verbalisations such as 'calm' or 'relax'. C. H. Patterson (1980, 261) explains Meichenbaum's method.

> Subjects said the name of the phobic object (e.g. "snake"), followed by fear engendering thought (e.g., "It's ugly; I won't look at it") that elicited the shock. Then the subjects said the coping self-statements (e.g. "Relax, I can touch it"), which led to cessation of the shock, and the clients then relaxed.

In order to test this approach, Meichenbaum established a control group of those using coping statements and a group which only experienced the termination of the shock when they employed fear engendering statements. Both groups felt relief, regardless of which statements they employed. Following interviews with both groups, Meichenbaum inferred that those who experienced relief after employing fear engendering statements actually had learned behaviourally that such statements in the experiments would cause the phobic object to disappear. Meichenbaum observed, 'What seemed to be happening was that the subjects were learning a set of coping skills that could be employed *across* situations, including confronting the phobic object' (Patterson, 1980, 261).

Richards and McDonald (1990, 112) conclude that although differences of theoretical emphases occur broadly within the cognitive-behavioural school, 'in view of the similarity of actual practice, it would seem to be better to drop all the different terms and use elements of cognitive and behavioural therapies to the best advantage of our clients'.

The Ritual: A Case Example in Cognitive-Behavioural Therapy

The following case study utilising cognitive-behavioural therapy is provided by John Watkins in his description of what he calls the 'Rational-Emotive dynamics of impulsive disorders'. Watkins defines a person with an impulsive disorder as one 'who acts without forethought, who acts on the spur of the moment, who expresses his urges upon experiencing them without reflection or prior deliberation' (1977, 135). Frequently these actions lead the person 'into social and legal difficulties'. The case chosen relates the behaviour of a young man who impulsively stole automobiles.

The Auto Thief

Although Tony was not old enough for a driver's license, he had stolen three automobiles. He got a thrill from driving cars and had taken several on the spur of the moment. The goal in therapy was to assist him in developing greater internal controls over his behavior. His cognitive dynamics seemed to be that he understandably enough enjoyed driving automobiles, but that he probably also was saying to himself something like: "I must have what I want when I want it. I can't stand waiting until I am of age. I've got to drive that car."

In the first few sessions, Tony worked on learning the distinction between his wants and needs. He learned to identify the statements he was making to himself between point A of seeing an automobile and point C of taking the car. He learned that he was telling himself both rational and irrational statements at point B: "I want to drive that car. I need to drive that car." After learning that there was no convincing evidence which could be given in support of his irrational claims, he came to the conclusion that while it would be a thrill to drive the car, he did not have to get into it or drive it. His homework assignment for the first few weeks was not to avoid situations in which there was an attractive automobile, but, rather, to approach the car, look it over carefully, and fully acknowledge how tempting the car was. He was then to discriminate between his wants and needs and to challenge the irrational claim that he needed to drive that car. After carrying out the homework assignment, we would discuss the results in his next session:

THERAPIST: Any temptations this week?

CLIENT: Well, I saw this new blue Malibu, a real slick car.

THERAPIST: What did you do?

CLIENT: I said to myself, "I sure would like to burn rubber with that. I've got to drive that."

THERAPIST: And then what?

CLIENT: I said, "Wait a minute. I don't have to drive that car."

THERAPIST: Why not?

CLIENT: It's not an absolute necessity. I am not going to drop dead if I don't get into that car.

THERAPIST: So, while you really would like to drive that car, you don't have to; the world isn't going to come to an end if you don't.

Tony was seen for a total of ten individual sessions. In the later sessions the therapist engaged in a technique called "counter-challenge", which involves testing the strength of the cognitive and behavioral effects produced by therapy. As Tony was relating how he had applied RET to himself in the face of his most recent temptation, the therapist would counter-challenge his rejection of his irrational demands by something like the following:

THERAPIST: What do you mean you don't have to burn rubber in that Charger with the overhead cam, 387 engine, and wide tires? Your eyes are the size of golf balls, bulging out of your head! Your tongue is hanging out all the way to the pavement; you're drooling all over yourself! Tell me you don't have to drive that car!

CLIENT: No, no I don't have to drive that car! I want to drive it, but I don't need to. It's not necessary that I drive it. I won't drop dead if I don't get into it.

There were no recurrences of auto theft during the four months Tony was in treatment. Follow-ups two, three and five months later found him to be free of any further difficulties in controlling his impulses (Watkins, 1977, 143-144).

Although the Watkins case study represents a summary of many therapeutic sessions with his client, I have chosen it as an example of a ritual of the Western faith in reason as expressed through cognitive-behavioural psychotherapy. The case study is based on a fundamental faith in the capacity of rational thought to transform life, overcome basic difficulties, and prepare the client to face any future problems through the replication of rational thoughts in new situations.

I call this a ritual because it reflects the *activity* of the faith in reason, just as Jaspers has told of that same faith in what I have called his mythologumenon. The ritual has a sacred practitioner (the therapist) and a sacred participant (the client). Although the session is conducted between the therapist and the client alone, a sacred community (those practising psychotherapy) surrounds the session, which is repeated in similar ways again and again between other therapists and their clients.

The ritual takes place in a designated area, the sacred space of the therapist's office and engages a sacred time, the moments set aside between the beginning and the end of the session. After the session, the client leaves the sacred space and time of therapy and moves out into the world to live in profane space and time where chaos, the falling back into psychological dysfunctioning, always threatens.

The client remembers the therapeutic ritual and tries to practise it in real life situations, but there will always remain a discrepancy between the ideal of the ritual itself and actual experience in the world. Just as we noted in J. Z. Smith's analysis of the bear hunting ritual, the time and space of the therapy session produce ideal responses from the client in a controlled environment. The client, however, notes and acknowledges this incongruity when faced with the possibility of recurrences of impulsive behaviour.

For both therapist and client, and for the many therapists and clients engaged in psychotherapy, the rituals conducted in therapy sessions are intended to produce transformative effects on believers by enabling them to act out repeatedly and reenforce persistently their common faith in the beneficent and salvific power of reason.

Eliciting the Mythemes from the Mythologumenon and Ritual of Reason

As I did with the mythologumenon and the ritual of the Karanga as related in the last chapter, I should be able to identify mythemes within the story and ritual activity of reason as related by Jaspers and by cognitive-behavioural psychotherapy. These mythemes will then elucidate the myth, the horizon of understanding for those who live within a faith in the autonomy of reason.

Mythemes from the Mythologumenon

1. The faith in reason holds that right thinking involves the application of the scientific method to an accurate apprehension of reality.
2. The scientific method assumes that effects can be understood causally, although not always in a predetermined way, by proper methods of experimentation and testing of hypotheses.
3. Reason always asks new questions and discovers new problems in the apprehension of reality.
4. Reason assumes that the final goal of the rational process is the uncovering of an ultimate unity in thought, but it acknowledges that this is an unachievable ideal.
5. Reason presumes that the mind plays a determinative role in structuring reality, but reality nevertheless is not the creation of the mind.
6. The faith in reason frees people from magical thinking, superstition, and the illogic of false causal connections to the liberty of the ongoing rational process of questioning, experimentation, conclusions and further questioning.
7. Reason does not conclude the stages in the rational process through abstractions but amplifies personal existence through the subject's apprehension of objective reality.

Mythemes in the Ritual

1. Faith in reason accentuates the positive capacity for humans to live to their fullest creative potential.
2. Faith in reason establishes realistic limits on people's expectations and helps them live within those limits.
3. Faith in reason enables people to perceive the true causes of events.
4. Having recognised the true causes of events, reason directs people toward an understanding of how they can most effectively respond to and affect events in life.
5. By the use of reason, people can resolve many of the daily difficulties which under the power of irrationality appeared insurmountable.

6. The use of reason requires persistent practice and reenforcement against the tendency of humans to think and act irrationally.

7. Reason lies within the power of humanity and represents its primary means for achieving individual and social well being.

Elucidating the Myth from the Mythemes

I began this chapter by stating that the faith in reason represents my own myth, my personal confession, and hence it defines my own horizon of understanding. Because of this, I encounter the same problems of any believer endeavouring to speak objectively about one's own faith. The 'inside' position often distorts the descriptions of the faith due to the prior commitment of the believer. I will return to this when I seek to step outside of my confession into a place between confessions by applying the principles of diatopical hermeneutics. Within my own limited perspectives, nevertheless, I will endeavour to express the meaning of the myth of those who believe in the autonomy of reason.

The fundamental assumption of the myth of reason is that the world makes sense, that it corresponds to principles which the rational mind can discover within it. That such principles may be overridden, changed, or proved false later does not disturb the myth, because the process of changing principles is still a rational one. If a hypothesis is proved wrong, it is done so according to the methods of reason. The world still makes perfect sense because it corresponds to the capacity of the rational mind to apprehend and understand it.

The faith of reason acknowledges and even affirms that rationality cannot comprehend everything about the world, or more humbly, that it actually understands very little about the whole of reality. Again, this does not shake the faith. The belief remains that what is known and continues to become known in an open and indeterminate universe still operates according to clearly defined scientific methods.

The correspondence between the rational mind and the objective world therefore is fully trustworthy, even if limited. If it is a mystery, it is not shrouded in mysticism. The mystery represents only the ever unfolding horizons of our application of reason to the critical and uncompromising challenge against our present conclusions. The faith that reason will break through to deeper knowledge thus is never enveloped by fear, but always in the confidence that knowledge thus obtained is liberating.

Any other type of world appears to reason either as silly, invented, illusory, or fundamentally unacceptable. I do not live in any other universe than the universe which is rational. This surrounds my life, gives it meaning, and makes this world, if not secure in its battle against irrationality, at least one in which I feel at home and one that is infused with hope. Reason is accessible to everyone.

Stepping Outside of My Confession into a Place between Confessions

I embrace the world according to reason confessionally. I believe it offers the best opportunity for humanity to achieve its collective goals and for individuals to attain satisfying and creative lives. I would therefore commend it to everyone.

If I am to achieve understanding of others who do not live by my myth, as we have seen in the analyses of Panikkar and Krieger, nevertheless, I must move out of my confessional stance and enter a territory where I can meet the other on a new and open ground. In this case, I am proposing to step outside the myth of reason and meet the myth of the indigenous Zimbabwean in order to illuminate a new horizon of understanding.

In the last chapter, I suggested that the Zimbabwean myth is bounded on all sides by the protective and guiding care of ancestors. The world only makes sense when events are interpreted either as the result of ancestral beneficence or in some sense a withholding of their protection. The cosmological scheme provides a paradigm for the traditional social structure making every aspect of life infused with order and meaning. Evil is also accounted for in this structure as a breakdown of order in the cosmological realm with immediate repercussions for social and/or individual well being.

The myth of reason fundamentally accomplishes the very same end. Reason enables individuals and societies to identify and achieve worthwhile objectives. The scientific method produces practical beneficent results in all areas of life from health care to social and economic planning. When warfare, injustice, totalitarian regimes and oppressive forces prevail in human affairs, it is explained as the victory of irrationality over reason. When individuals suffer from emotional and behavioural dysfunctioning, rational thinking can reconstruct how a person experiences and reacts to life events. When tragic incidents occur beyond either scientific explanation or control, such as natural disasters, individuals and societies react to them most constructively through rational thinking and logical responses.

Reason and the ancestors, therefore, adopt the same role for their respective believers. But does each always achieve the ends that it seeks? It is here, following Krieger's stages in methodological conversion as outlined in the last chapter, that I must undertake an evaluation of each myth as if I were exposing my own confession, in each case, to critical analysis.

The myth of reason can be subjected to the critique that it represents an intellectual, elitist perspective on the world. It is easy to talk of fulfilment, creativity, acceptance of limitations, and a commitment to an ever unfolding process of dialogue with the results of science if one is socially and economically secure. For the homeless, the unemployed, the hungry, the victims of warfare, and perhaps the great majority of humanity, the faith in reason is a luxury. David Pilgrim raises this point when he complains about the ritual of psychotherapy. 'In the case of humanistic therapies the problem mainly resides in overvaluing human agency and understating material constraints on our ability to choose our destiny' (1993, 225).

Another problem with the myth of reason precisely is its almost unquestioning faith in rationality itself. This is seen clearly throughout Jaspers' exposition and in practice in cognitive-behavioural therapies. C.H. Patterson (1982, 267) poses a series of important questions in this latter regard.

Is it necessary or more efficient to teach the client directly? Is didactic instruction necessary for or the most effective way to

130

achieve client learning? Is the client's failure to think logically or rationally always because of a lack of understanding of the nature of reasoning, logic, or problem solving? Is the most effective way to change client self-statements through teaching?

Patterson suggests that reason may not provide the most important dimension to achieving human well being. 'Self-exploration and self-discovery may be more effective and more lasting than learning as a result of being taught' (p. 267). This implies that reason emphasises cognitions at the expense of experiential learning, personal insight, and, as Gill Edwards would argue, by radically diminishing the human spiritual potential (1993, 197). One might ask why reason becomes the most important element in human development rather than other human capacities, for example, the instinctual, the aesthetic, the intuitive, or the mystical.

Many other questions and issues could be posed about the faith in reason. I have raised them here to show that part of the process of methodological conversion is to adopt a critical attitude toward one's own confession of faith.

Krieger calls for the scholar to do the same with the tradition the scholar wishes to understand, in my case, the Karanga indigenous religion of Zimbabwe. A critical examination of the Zimbabwean myth would show that undue suffering can be perpetuated by holding onto many traditional perspectives. A good example of this is the refusal of many traditional believers to accept scientific advice in rural Zimbabwe regarding lightning prevention methods. Tradition continues to maintain that lightning can be created by specialists and directed against various individuals. Proof of this is often cited when lightning strikes a hut full of people and only one person dies. The victim, according to this logic, was the predetermined target of the lightning which had been ordered to strike by one who possesses special powers.

Science understands the phenomenon of lightning and knows that it results from atmospheric conditions. It strikes in certain places according to well defined circumstances. Huts, especially kitchens, are rounded with metal wiring at the top, providing natural conductors. Often kitchens are situated at the highest place in the homestead with no trees surrounding them. The people gather in the kitchen during the storm, placing themselves in the most vulnerable position to the lightning.

Scientists can show people how to minimise their risks from lightning, how to install lightning rods to divert the charge away from the hut, what to do if one is in an open field during a storm, and where to build homesteads. The scientific method, therefore, could reduce the number of deaths in Zimbabwe from lightning, which a recent report listed at an average of about 250 each rainy season (Chivinge, 1995, 5).

Opposition to science, however, is met on the basis of the traditional horizon of understanding. The secretary of the Zimbabwe Traditional Healers Association (Zinatha), Dr Peter Mutandi, explained in an interview that the Shona believe that 'Mwari or the ancestral spirits are capable of sending lightning to people who fail to perform certain rites' (Chivinge, 1995, 5). Although this does not kill the people, it serves as a warning that members of the family need to determine what is grieving the ancestor. Mutandi added that 'wicked people are also capable of harnessing the powers of lightning and directing it at people they want to settle disputes with' (Chivinge, 1995, 5). This type of lightning results in death.

A commonly recounted story among the Shona is that lightning originates from a bird which takes the form of a dark cloud. When it strikes it lays eggs in the ground. A *n'anga* is consulted to remove the eggs. If this is not done, lightning will strike again in the same place. During an interview, Dr. Tony Schwarzmuller of the University of Zimbabwe showed me some protective devices worn by people to avoid being hit by the lightning, including an ostrich feather, because, he said, the people believe that ostriches are never struck by lightning (28 May 1995).

A scientific critique of this approach would call for a complete change of belief. However, to do so requires not just a change of belief but a surrender of the myth itself. The world is surrounded by ancestor spirits who can communicate with their children by various means, including lightning. In some instances, if they have been offended or neglected seriously, or if one of their family has actually committed an injustice against another, the ancestor may permit the lightning specialist to achieve the aim of killing as a recompense to the wronged party. One of these specialists, Mr. Josiah Toto-Tangwena, is reported to have said, 'It [the manufacture and sending of lightning] only works if there is a real grudge between the sender and the intended victim. If one tries it on an innocent person, then the bolt comes back to kill the offender' (Chivinge, 1995, 5).

Because their horizons of understanding make sense of the world for both the believers in reason and the indigenous Zimbabwean, neither can be surrendered nor converted confessionally to the other. But both can be criticised and, in the ground beyond the confessions, a new horizon can unfold. Where either myth actually causes physical, mental or spiritual suffering, induces fear, disease, and death, or in any sense diverts attention away from the social deprivations of people, the critique must accuse either myth of failing to achieve the role it holds for itself as the provider of well being. On humanitarian grounds, the critiques must be ruthless on these points and the believers, standing in a territory outside of confessional allegiances, incorporate the critiques without succumbing to the temptation to offer apologetic explanations. Apologetics, by definition, occur only within confessional boundaries.

The Personal Intra-Religious Dialogue

What horizon of understanding emerges when the Zimbabwean indigenous religion and the faith in reason meet in a place where both have stepped outside of their confessional boundaries? The process of answering this question defines the task of diatopical hermeneutics. Another way of understanding this method, as Krieger suggests (1991, 68-69), is to allow the meeting of the two faiths to occur as if one were a believer in both at the same time without being confessionally or apologetically bound by either.

In such a meeting, it becomes clear that the emerging myth would perceive the world in personal, even anthropomorphic, terms. The universe is a place where each individual is known intimately by the forces comprising reality. The objective world, therefore, is not comprised strictly or even primarily of matter, but is infused with life and personality. This makes the universe an open, responsive, and dynamic reality.

The subject, who perceives the objective world, therefore, is not observing static laws, fixed systems, predetermined effects, or lifeless matter. The objective world actually interacts with the subjective perceiver in ways which make the universe always full of new possibilities. This is because the interaction between subject and object is always personal.

Because the world is personal, however, does not make it capricious. It is dependable, trustworthy, capable of being understood according to levels of consistent principles which adhere within it. The interaction between the subject and the object, therefore, represents a rational process.

This means that the world, although dynamic and personal, cannot be invented by the subjective observer. It does not consist of thoughts in the mind of individuals, but possesses an objective reality external to the mind. It is what it is and not anything other than what it is. This does not confine the possible ways in which it may respond under a variety of circumstances, but the world does not conform to the way humans might wish it to appear.

Nevertheless, within this personal universe, a fundamentally beneficent potential exists to bring people to levels of personal satisfaction and communal well being. Because the mind of the perceiver corresponds to the reality of the objective world, there exists within every individual human and within humanity collectively the means to identify and achieve that which will maximise well being on every level: physical, psychological, and social in an overall harmony with the personal cosmos.

In addition to the capacity for beneficence within the universe, a corresponding sense of justice permeates all things. The justice perceived by the human mind, however, operates according to the rational principles which are inherent in the objective world. This means that justice is always subjected to rational discussion and is separated from concepts such as revenge, retribution, and irrational anger. Moreover, the justice which humans may wish applied to every aspect of the universe according to illusory expectations needs to be tempered by the observations of the way things really operate. Nevertheless, the new horizon holds a faith both in the inherent capacity for beneficence and the ultimate rule of justice within the personal universe.

This faith recognises, however, the very real possibility of failure when the principles inherent in the personal universe supporting beneficence and justice are overridden by thoughts and actions of humans which contradict individual or communal well being. There is, therefore, a sense of a struggle against evil in the world with no final guarantee of success.

The new horizon of understanding, the myth resulting from the meeting of the Zimbabwean indigenous and rational faiths, thus describes a world which fundamentally can be trusted, when understood and treated properly, to maximise the potential for human well being. Maximising this potential, as the word implies, involves a process, the end of which could be described as ultimate, but which is never achievable finally.

Methodological and Theoretical Conclusions

The method of diatopical hermeneutics is intended to achieve understanding of any tradition through the meeting of two divergent confessions in a place outside the confessional boundaries of either. Moreover, this meeting proposes to uncover a new myth emerging from this non-confessional, non-apologetic engagement. The next stage is to test my interpretation by determining first if it is confirmed in actual field data and second if it meets the phenomenological criterion of being capable of being affirmed by believers. In these regards, a number of questions are likely to emerge:

1. Could believers in indigenous Zimbabwean religions accept that ancestors symbolise a beneficent, personal universe?

2. Could those committed to the autonomy of reason acknowledge that the external world itself is dynamic and malleable to human will?

3. Would it be possible for indigenous Zimbabweans to accept that the objective world dictates its own conditions which potentially override their traditional understanding of causality?

4. Would those who hold a faith in reason accept that the personal character of the universe opens possibilities for explaining causal conditions which may contradict, seemingly in irrational ways, currently accepted theories?

5. Can adherents to Zimbabwean indigenous religions accept that justice, perceived anthropomorphically as a direct personal correspondence between right and wrong, finds no direct correlation in nature and can only can be approximated in society according to rational principles?

6. Can the faith in reason accommodate the natural desire of humans that they should experience the world to be just in daily experience?

7. Can the indigenous Zimbabwean accept that concepts of well being extend to deep levels of creativity and self-actualisation which are not limited to material and social stability?

8. Does a person who holds a faith in reason understand fully enough the significance of the material and social constraints on the human potential?

These questions point back toward an understanding of what is important for the adherents within either tradition, but they also expose that in the meeting of the two a new horizon has emerged. If the questions can be answered affirmatively, not only will a deeper understanding and appreciation of the traditions result from adherents and scholars alike, but some quite practical effects in the way believers in either tradition behave are likely to follow.

The model of diatopical hermeneutics employed here can be applied within any tradition in the way that I have outlined. Panikkar has done a similar thing in his discussions of Vedantic Hinduism and Christianity. Although in its present form in this book, my approach has been largely theoretical and thus in a sense removed from believers, the accuracy of my elucidation of the myths and the relevance of the new horizon depicted can only be judged in actual inter-religious encounters.

I conclude by suggesting that what I have attempted in this chapter is a methodological conversion, not an actual one. I am not now a partial believer in Zimbabwean indigenous religions. I am committed still to a faith in reason. However, I believe through the process outlined in this chapter that I have achieved a greater understanding of the indigenous myth and I have attempted through this method to convey that understanding to the reader.

This methodology affirms that the world remains religiously plural and it assumes that understanding traditions other than my own, without seeking coercively to impose my own faith on them, offers the best hope for a humane and peaceful world. Moreover, to acknowledge that new horizons appear when faith in reason meets other faiths in a non-apologetic environment, in my view, significantly advances the scholarly effort to decipher meanings embedded within living religious communities.

References

Chivinge, C. 1995. 'Scientists, *n'angas* come together to study lightning', *The Herald* (Harare), 6 June, p. 5.

Dryden, W. and Feltham, C. 1992. 'Psychotherapy and its discontents: An introduction' in W. Dryden and C. Feltham, (eds.), *Psychotherapy and its discontents*. Buckingham: Open University Press, 1-6.

Dryden, W. 1989. 'The therapeutic alliance as an integrating framework', in W. Dryden (ed.), *Key issues for counselling in action*. London: Sage Publications, 1-15.

Edwards, G. 1992. 'Does psychotherapy need a soul?', in W. Dryden and C. Feltham, (eds.), *Psychotherapy and its discontents*. Buckingham: Open University Press. 194-212.

Ellis, A. 1977. 'The basic clinical theory of Rational-Emotive Therapy', in A. Ellis and R. Grieger (eds.), *Handbook of Rational-Emotive Therapy*. New York: Springer Publishing Company, 3-34.

1977. 'Research data supporting the clinical and personality hypotheses of RET and other cognitive-behavior therapies', in A. Ellis and R. Grieger (eds.), *Handbook of Rational-Emotive Therapy*. New York: Springer Publishing Company, 35-71.

1977. 'The Rational-Emotive approach to sex therapy', in A. Ellis and R. Grieger (eds.), *Handbook of Rational-Emotive Therapy*. New York: Springer Publishing Company, 198-215.

1992. 'Response', in W. Dryden and C. Feltham, (eds.), *Psychotherapy and its discontents*. Buckingham: Open University Press, 212-20.

Jaspers, K. 1971. *Reason and anti-reason in our time*, Trans. Stanley Godman. Hamden, Connecticut: Archon Books.

Pilgrim, D. 1992. 'Psychotherapy and political evasions', in W. Dryden and C. Feltham (eds.), *Psychotherapy and its discontents*. Buckingham: Open University Press, 225-43.

Richards, D. and McDonald, B. 1990. *Behavioural psychotherapy: A handbook for nurses*. Oxford: Heinemann Nursing.

Samuels, A. 1992. 'Foreword' in W. Dryden and C. Feltham (eds.), *Psychotherapy and its discontents*. Buckingham: Open University Press, xi-xvi.

Schwarzmuller, T. 1995. Interview with J. L. Cox, 28 May.

Stern, R. and Drummond L. 1991. *The practice of behavioural and cognitive psychotherapy*. Cambridge: Cambridge University Press.

Storr, A. 1990, 2nd ed. *The art of psychotherapy*. Oxford: Butterworth-Heinemann.

Watkins, J. T. 1977. 'The Rational-Emotive dynamics of impulsive disorders', in A. Ellis and R. Grieger, *Handbook of Rational-Emotive Therapy*. New York: Springer Publishing Company, 135-52.

Wilson, P. H., Spence, S. H., and Kavanagh, D. J. 1989. *Cognitive behavioural interviewing for adult disorders: A practical handbook*. London: Routledge.

Chapter Eight

SOME CONCLUDING METHODOLOGICAL REFLECTIONS

In this book, I have sought to point a direction toward achieving an understanding of African indigenous religions first by discussing issues in classification and then by analysing the meaning of myths and rituals within them. This was undertaken primarily for methodological reasons aimed at achieving an understanding by engaging in diatopical hermeneutics. I sought to do this in the previous chapter by making my own confession of faith in the autonomy of reason as the basis for elucidating a new horizon of understanding in the dialogue between my myth and the myth of the indigenous Zimbabwean. In this concluding chapter of part one, I seek to address issues which emerge from the attempt I have made to apply diatopical hermeneutics practically.[1]

A Genuinely New Horizon or Academic Coercion?

It could be argued that since my methodology for uncovering meaning continued to employ rational discourse I have not actually stepped outside of my own confessional boundary, but instead I have imposed my own myth on the African believer. By identifying mythemes within African mythologumena, I could be accused of persisting in a devotion to rationality throughout my analysis. This could be regarded as maintaining a power relationship between reason and indigenous religions, bordering on coercion.

This critique of the method would contend that the endeavour generally to achieve an understanding of religions falls within the academic language game and thus must be played according to the rules established by principles of reason, argumentation, and scientific verification or falsification. Diatopical hermeneutics, as a method for academic understanding, therefore, possesses an inherent contradiction. Because methodological conversion remains methodological rather than confessional, it never really involves a conversion. It actually

---

1. A portion of chapter eight was presented originally at the Annual Congress of the Association for the Study of Religions in Southern Africa, 26-27 June 1995, held at the University of Durban-Westville. I am grateful for the many probing questions which I received in response to my presentation at that conference, a number of which I endeavour to address here.

exropriates the scholarly insight obtained through research and incorporates it within academic objectives delineated exclusively by the rational explication of meaning. As a result, the hermeneutic is not diatopical at all but takes place within the confessional boundaries of reason.

I think the argument that the primary aim of diatopical hermeneutics is to achieve an understanding of any religion which then can be rationally communicated to the academic community must be admitted. To say this, however, does not imply that a coercive power game is being perpetrated on unsuspecting 'objects' of research. If the method is followed in practice, such an outcome is impossible.

The confession which researchers make both to those they are seeking to understand and to those to whom they present their results embodies a self-disclosure based on a mutual contract between two faith communities. Researchers admit, in this process, that their own confession of faith in the scientific approach cohabits a world of multiple confessions comprised of competing truth claims.

Coercion only appears when any faith community seeks a power advantage to violently damage another faith community. Diatopical hermeneutics specifically seeks to avoid such a result. However, it will still speak within its own frame of reference, within its own myth. The other confession will do the same. The aim is not to destroy the faith of either party but to achieve a humane understanding based on the principles that truth is possessed exclusively by none and that understanding is gained best by human interaction based on respect and nonviolence.

If scientists of religion were to pretend that their aims were anything other than scientific, that their faith were in anything other than the autonomy of reason and that they could act 'as if' they were believers in the religion under study, their approach would border on hypocrisy and coercion. But because diatopical hermeneutics operates on the basis of disclosure, mutuality, respect and nonviolence, the charge of coercion appears misplaced.

Can One Step Outside of One's Myth and then Go Back into It?

If the exchange between the believer in reason and the religious adherent genuinely takes place outside of either confession, is it possible, as I suggested above, for each to return back into the original myth and speak its language? By exposing a new horizon of understanding, have not both partners in the dialogue been changed irrevocably?

If I answer these questions affirmatively, it may appear initially that I am involved in a fundamental contradiction. The original aim to achieve understanding may have been academically defined according to the principles of rationality, but the act of stepping outside of one's own confession seems to alter the original objectives. The new horizon of understanding is comprised neither of scientific principles nor of the faith of the religious community under study. The horizon has changed; the perceptual reality has been altered.

If, however, I step back into my own confession, the new horizon has not been elucidated at all. Indeed, to step back means that I have never really stepped out. To have experienced a new horizon based on mutual interaction inevitably transforms the old way of perceiving the world and opens up the possibility of even further horizons of understanding.

This critique correctly assumes that understanding alters the way we experience the world. This is true of any breakthrough in knowledge and might be described as the principal objective of any genuinely scientific method. The fact that diatopical hermeneutics consists of a way of achieving understanding does not mean, therefore, that the conclusions it produces are invalidated because it persists in a scientific methodology.

There can be little doubt that the way the world is perceived today following Einstein's relativity theory and the advances in quantum physics, for example, reveal an entirely new horizon of understanding. This new horizon does not revoke the old one based on Newtonion physics, which still operate effectively within the limitations of fixed space and time, but it does disclose something entirely new, that which could not be anticipated within the old way of viewing the world.

I am contending that faith in the autonomy of reason, when engaging in diatopical hermeneutics with another faith, produces something new and even unexpected. Although the new horizon which emerges does not entail a rejection of the old one, the understanding which emerges creates a reality which is objectively there, but which would never have appeared had the method not been employed. This implies that the understanding envisaged through the method does not preclude by any precommitment the results which may follow. In my view, this does not consist of an internal contradiction at all; rather, it maintains an unstructured and dynamic openness toward reality.

Does Diatopical Hermeneutics Produce a Fusion of Horizons?

In his important analysis of diachronic hermeneutics in *Truth and Method*, Hans-Georg Gadamer speaks of a 'fusion of horizons' between past and present historical perspectives. The historian, who views the world from within a horizon dictated by present circumstances, seeks to understand horizons of different eras. Understanding can be achieved only when interpreters acknowledge their own prejudices, 'the horizon of a particular present' as representing that 'beyond which it is impossible to see' (1980, 272).

The scientific enterprise thus initially involves distinguishing other horizons from one's own and one's own from others. This, Gadamer explains, 'is why it is part of the hermeneutic approach to project an historical horizon that is different from the horizon of the present' (p. 273). Our horizon of understanding, however, is never static but is 'constantly being formed' by testing our prejudices through an encounter with the past from which our present understanding has come. In addition to differentiation, therefore, scientific understanding always entails a fusion of our current with past horizons (p. 273).

Fusion begins by acknowledging that because horizons are always in the process of formation, they are not entirely distinct from one another. Historical consciousness, Gadamer explains, is

something laid over a continuing tradition, and hence it immediately recombines what it has distinguished in order, in the unity of the historical horizon that it thus acquires, to become again one with itself (p. 273).

Although hermeneutics involves a process of projecting a historical horizon different from our own, no alienation of horizons occurs. Nevertheless, what has once been projected is 'simultaneously removed' because it does not remain as it was originally; it is fused into the present (p. 273).

Fusion, therefore, is not to be regarded as a simple synthesis of horizons. It involves the achieving of understanding through interpretation. Interpreting a text from a different historical period other than our own, for example, involves an inevitable 'tension between the text and the present'. The hermeneutical task involves not a covering up of the tension 'by attempting a naive assimilation but consciously bringing it out' (p. 273).

In his discussion of Gadamer, Krieger argues that the meeting of the past and present horizons produces a 'crisis of meaning' precisely because 'the "foreign" horizon of the past confronts and challenges our present horizon making it "problematical" in its totality' (1991, 143). The crisis can be overcome only by fusion.

> "Fusion of horizons" (*Horizontverschmelzung*) occurs ... whenever meaning emerges and understanding takes place. The fusion of horizons is the way in which tradition itself through human understanding becomes "productive" of ever new and ever different ways of thinking (p. 144).

The process of fusing the past horizon into the present one occurs fundamentally through language. For Gadamer, all human experience is linguistic because, in Krieger's words, 'humans are the beings who speak' (p. 144). Understanding, therefore, rests in language itself. The fusion of horizons becomes in this sense a linguistic fusion between the interpreter and the historical object. Kurt Mueller-Vollmer explains,

> Understanding and interpretation for Gadamer constitute the mode of being of all our cultural traditions. These traditions are necessarily embedded in language (*die Sprache*). It follows, therefore, that understanding and interpretation are, above all, events in an historical process (1986, 40).

Krieger interprets Gadamer's position as constituting 'boundary discourse', the use of language at the point where two historical horizons of understanding interact (p. 48-50). This is not a theoretical kind of discourse, but involves commitment and participation in choices. Interpreters cannot separate themselves from their own historical horizon.

To speak boundary discourse means that one takes a stand on the issue that one is for oneself. There is no neutral ground upon which arguments about the appropriation of one's own existence in history could be coolly discussed. On this level of discourse, to speak is to decide (p. 144). The act of speaking at the point of the meeting of the horizons thus entails commitment from the interpreter. For this reason, Krieger ultimately rejects Gadamer's fusion of horizons calling it an act of violence: as it projects a horizon, it simultaneously destroys it.

As we have seen, diatopical hermeneutics as posited by Panikkar is intended to go beyond boundary discourse by stepping outside one's own confession into a place between the boundaries. According to Krieger, this is not what Gadamer means by the fusion of horizons. Rather, Gadamer is concerned with 'the hermeneutical retrieval of founding patterns of meaning and actions' and thus sees the fusion of horizons as 'communicative action which *produces socialization, integration into a community and personal as well as cultural identity*' (p. 146, emphasis his). As such, Gadamer's idea of fusion takes on an exclusive attitude toward the other horizon by reincorporating it into the present horizon. This defines precisely what is meant by apologetic universalism since, in Krieger's words, fusion entails 'narrative proclamation, mission, conversion and confession through ritual enactment' (p. 147).

Diatopical hermeneutics thus cannot be equated with Gadamer's fusion of horizons. It is not primarily concerned with diachronic boundary discourse taking place largely within one cultural frame of reference. It seeks rather to engage in what Panikkar calls a 'dialogical dialogue' with the other in order to disclose a new horizon of understanding. 'This new sort of dialogue can proceed only by mutually integrating our testimonies within a larger horizon, a new myth' (Panikkar, 1979, 244).

Gadamer's use of the analogy of the horizon as fluid, dynamic and progressive, however, does help to clarify what occurs in diatopical hermeneutics. Horizons do not come into one's perception as clearly distinguished from one another. They tend to flow into one another. What appears at one place is always related to a previous horizon, and even when the movement is far beyond one's original perspective, the chain of horizons can be traced and thus related to the observer's original horizon.

This can be applied to the understanding of different religious traditions. As one steps outside of the boundary of one's own horizon of understanding, by engaging with others of differing perspectives, new understandings emerge. Such understandings, however, do not appear solely through abstract discussion but occur in historical, social, economic, political, geographical, and psychological contexts which in themselves constitute not only the backdrop for a particular horizon but define the points at which the horizons merge and interact practically. Boundaries, in other words, are fluid and often are indecipherable.

This means that whereas for the purposes of achieving understanding, as, for example, in the case of the myths resulting from faith in reason and from faith in the indigenous religions of Zimbabwe, different traditions are treated as if they exist behind clearly demarcated boundaries. In reality, the horizons have already merged in many ways defined by political, historical, cultural, social and religious contexts. The exercise of diatopical hermeneutics presents a methodology for becoming self-reflective of this process by endeavouring to articulate the meaning contained within new and evolving horizons. On this point, Gadamer's analysis provides a helpful modification of Krieger's concept of boundary discourse.

Is Diatopical Hermeneutics another Term for Syncretism? The Case of Juliana

Syncretism is often associated with the process of assimilating two religious traditions into one thereby producing a new religion based on the prior ones, but distinguishable from either. The *Penguin Dictionary of Religions* edited by John Hinnells (1984) defines syncretism as 'the fusion of religious cults or movements' occurring 'in situations of intercultural contact ... either spontaneously or by intentional adaptation' (p. 317). Diatopical hermeneutics, as I have tried to exemplify it in the last chapter, could be construed in this way. I want to argue, however, that as a methodology for understanding, diatopical hermeneutics cannot be equated with syncretism because its aims and approaches are quite different. To exemplify this, I want to describe briefly what I consider to be a genuinely syncretistic new religious movement based on an assimilation of African cultural traditions and Christianity. This is the recent phenomenon begun under the direction of Ambuya Juliana[2] in the southcentral region of Zimbabwe.

From 28 to 30 July 1995, I conducted a series of interviews with people in the area of Chief Chingoma in the Mberengwa District, where I had undertaken research three years earlier. My intention in returning briefly to the area was to determine how the persistent droughts of the past few years were being interpreted by those I had interviewed in 1992. As I noted earlier, the chief and the spirit medium I interviewed then largely attributed the lack of rain to the failure of those in government to follow traditional rituals and to respect the authority of the chiefs.

On this visit, however, I encountered what to me was the unexpected influence of Juliana, who throughout the sixteen chieftaincies of the Mberengwa District had made a substantial change in the way rain rituals were being conducted. Although I was unable to reach Juliana personally during my brief visit, I interviewed five people who had attended one of her large gatherings held in November 1994 in Chief Chingoma's region and one person who had attended a meeting she conducted in June 1995 in the Garenyama Area of Mberengwa.[3]

The story of Juliana requires extensive research and may deserve a book in its own right. Two articles have been published recently on the Juliana phenomenon (Mawere and Wilson, 1995, 252-87; Mafu, 1995, 288-308) and an unpublished conference paper has been prepared by Gurli Hansson (1994) of the University of Uppsala. I refer to Juliana here merely to exemplify what I mean by a syncretistic movement and how that differs markedly from diatopical hermeneutics. According to those I interviewed, Juliana, who is Karanga having been brought up near Chivu,[4] reports that she was taken by an *njuzu* (sometimes translated as a mermaid or water spirit) at around the age of seven. She

---

2. The term 'ambuya' usually is translated as 'grandmother', but it implies a woman who has earned respect and thus can also be translated into English as 'excellent person' (Hansson, 1994, 3).

3. Fana Tazvi, Headman of Chief Chingoma and attendant to VaEmpty, the spirit medium for the Dunda territorial sprit; Christopher Hove, ex-teacher at Gwai School; Dhiriza Dziva, Headman of Chief Chingoma and one of the custodians of Juliana's rain-making village at the base of the Imbahura Mountain; Nelson Shumba, subsistence farmer in the Garenyama Area; Miclot Dziva, who is Chief Chingoma; and Douglas Dziva, a PhD student at the University of Natal, Pietermaritzburg and son of Chief Chingoma.

4. Mawere and Wilson (1995, 254) report that originally Juliana claimed to have come from Mt Darwin in the northeast region of Zimbabwe, but that later she admitted to Gurli Hansson that she originated near Chivu in central Zimbabwe (p. 286).

spent approximately ten years under the water where she was instructed by the water spirit in African customs and the Bible.[5] She also learned church songs there.

In an interview with Hansson, Juliana related her experiences with the *njuzu*:

> We lived like crocodiles, ate soil and mud. I was very skinny and pale when I returned from her. When you stay with the *Njuzu* you learn to be humble and well behaved. I was also taught about the Bible there. There is everything down there. When I left I had a *Shanga* – reed, growing on my head (Hansson, 1994, 5-6).

When she emerged from her instruction, she went to the Matopos Hills at Matonjeni and apparently became an *mbonga* or virgin attendant in the Mwari cult. This corresponds to what Mawere and Wilson (1995, 286) refer to as one who is 'based out of the shrines, who in the case of women must be virgins', and to what Leslie Nthoi (1998, 70) calls the 'wosana' whose main duty at the shrine 'is to dance and sing to the High-God during rain ceremonies'.

One of my informants told me that he understands that Juliana has now married the son of Chokoto, the late High Priest at the Dzilo shrine at the village of Machokoto in the Matopos Hills and thus is able to become the voice of Mwari at the shrine. This would be consistent with M. L. Daneel's accounting that later in life the *mbonga* may marry the high priest and become the 'Voice' of Mwari (Daneel, 1970, 49-50).

Sometime in 1992, after the failure of the rains to come, Juliana began a mission to the people of Zimbabwe by going out from the shrine at Matonjeni to various regions, largely across the southcentral areas. Subsequently, she has constructed a number of sacred enclosures, called *Majacha Emapa* or rainmaking villages, generally at the base of sacred mountains. I visited two of these, one at the foot of the Imbahura Mountain, under the care of the Chingoma spirit, and one in the Garenyama Area. At Imbahura, I interviewed Mr. Dhiriza Dziva, Headman of Chief Chingoma and one of the custodians of the *Jacha* which had been constructed at the base of the sacred mountain.[6]

The village at Imbahura Mountain, which was uninhabited at the time of my visit, consists of a rectangular enclosure bounded by pole fences, reportedly made of traditional wood which easily replenishes itself. I would estimate that the enclosure is approximately 125 metres in length and 75 metres wide. One enters by a small gate which opens onto a space extending from the entrance to the first buildings approximately 60 metres from the entryway. The buildings are constructed of the same poles as the fence which surrounds the village. The largest building, near the centre of the enclosure, holds the traditional beer calabashes and gourds used in rituals. Near this building on either side are two kraals for animals, a small one for goats and a larger one for cattle. The animals are slaughtered during rain rituals. Near the top of the enclosure are two huts, one intended for the use of

---

5. Hansson (1994, 5) relates that Juliana told her that she had spent four years with the *njuzu*. It is possible that as the story of Juliana spread among the people, her time spent with the *njuzu* increased.

6. On 29 July 1995.

Juliana and the other for the chief and his headmen. Toilets have also been constructed near the top of the grounds. The enclosure has been built on a relatively flat granite surface sloping upwards. Indigenous trees grow within it. A *mukamba* tree, often associated with the ancestors, grows just outside of the top part of the fence.

The interview I conducted with Mr. Dziva took place in the company of Chief Chingoma and the chief's son, Douglas Dziva (who interpreted for me). Before entering the enclosure, we were all required to remove our shoes and watches. As we entered the grounds, each one of us clapped our hands and uttered a praise word to Musikavanhu (the creator of people).[7] The interview was conducted on some raised boulders on the right side of the enclosure under some trees. Mr. Dziva told me that it was a traditional custom to sit in this place to discuss any matters of concern. He told me that just in front of this spot Juliana had conducted a *mutoro* (rain) ritual in November 1994 personally supervising the distribution of traditional beer and meat. He reported that over 2000 people attended, all fitting within the enclosure. He reported that, although Juliana used no microphones, she spoke in her normal voice during the ritual and could be heard clearly by everyone.

Adjacent to the entrance and attached to the fence was a small, square enclosure around 3 metres high with window-type openings around halfway up. I was told that those who did not participate in the ritual itself came to this structure from outside of the fence to obtain some of the meat and sadza which had been distributed to those within the compound. Mr. Dziva indicated that many of these were church members who did not feel comfortable participating in the ritual but still wanted to feel a part of the community. The primary teachings which Juliana conveyed to the people at the ritual, as reported to me by Mr. Dziva and confirmed by the others I interviewed, are as follows:

1) Mwari (God) is above all creation, including people and ancestor spirits.

2) Mwari is responsible for providing rain and will do so when the people return to their traditional practices and honour him.

3) The possession of spirit mediums by territorial ancestor spirits is strongly discouraged (if not forbidden) at *mutoro* rituals.[8]

4) The people should not work on Wednesday or on Sunday.

5) No wild animals should be killed, including snakes.

6) No sexual intercourse should take place on mountains or in forests.

7) When the people dip for water in wells, they should not use metal containers but rather should employ traditional gourds.

8) Promiscuity should be avoided; women especially should take care not to accept the casual advances of men.

I did not confirm directly from Juliana that these are her principal teachings, but of the six people I interviewed who had attended her meetings, a remarkable consistency appeared in their accounts. At the

---

7. At the Garenya *Jacha*, we offered praise to *Shoko* (monkey), the totem of the Mwari cult (Mawere and Wilson, 1995, 286).

8. Mr. Fano told me that if anyone started to become possessed during the ritual, Juliana would shout out commanding them to stop.

very least, one could conclude that these are the teachings attributed to Juliana which most impressed the people I interviewed.[9]

I would call Juliana's movement a syncretistic new religion. She knows the Bible by memory, since, as she claims, she was taught it by the *njuzu* spirit. The chief's wife, Mrs. Dziva (herself a schoolteacher), confirmed to me that Juliana is indeed illiterate since she is teaching her how to form English and Shona letters.

Juliana has integrated the teachings of the Bible, chiefly about the place of God the Creator as superior over any other created beings (including spiritual beings), into Shona customs. However, the practices she emphasises are not entirely traditional. She has reversed the normal order of approaching the high God through the territorial spirits who customarily send representatives of the chief to the Mwari shrines in the Matopos Hills. Instead, Juliana has come from Mwari to the people directly, virtually usurping the role maintained previously by the territorial ancestors. I regard this as a major change which, if if it were to be maintained, would diminish substantially the central importance of territorial ancestors within the chieftaincies in favour of the high God.[10] This appears to represent a Christian influence, evidenced through Juliana's use of church songs in her meetings and her frequent references to the Bible.

Nevertheless, her authority comes primarily from traditional sources; her calling is authenticated by the mystical force of the *njuzu* and reenforced by her central role in the Mwari cult at Matonjeni. Terence Ranger (1995, 239) observes that 'Juliana's mission is to make the land fit for the *njuzu*'. Her teachings are aimed at restoring the land through the repopulation of wild animals, respect for the environment, and the encouragement of sexual morality. She requires rest from work both on the traditional holy day (Wednesday) and that observed by Christians (Sunday). Juliana uses traditional symbols, such as the brewing of beer and the ritual slaughter of animals at a place beneath a sacred mountain, but she discourages communication from the spirits associated with the mountains. Instead, she substitutes God for the spirits.

In these ways, it seems to me, Juliana has assimilated aspects of traditional and Christian religious traditions by combining them for two clear purposes: the renewal of the land and its resources and the preservation of traditional culture. According to my informants, she does not claim to be a Christian, but sees herself involved in a mission to redeem the people from their persistent suffering due to repeated droughts.[11]

---

9. It may be significant that none of my informants referred to Mawere and Wilson's (1995, 257) reports of Juliana's ban on drilling bore holes and her insistence that commercial beer brewing should be halted. This may be because these instructions were largely ignored by the people due to the severe negative economic effects they would produce.

10. Precisely because of the political ramifications of such a change and the resentment felt by the people due to the competition between the traditional messengers to the Matopos Hills and Juliana's mission, Mawere and Wilson contend that the Juliana movement will not survive. Recent reports from Zimbabwe indicate that the Juliana Movement has, indeed, receded in importance.

11. Juliana is reported by Hansson (1994, 6) as having described her mission as follows: 'I have been sent by Tshokoto shrine to save the people of Zimbabwe. They have to listen to Musikavahnu, the Creator and also observe respect for the *Vadzimu*, our ancestral spirits'.

The Distinction between Diatopical Hermeneutics and Syncretism

The assimilation of traditions with a particular mission is what I mean by syncretism, as is clearly demonstrated in the case of Juliana. This, however, is not what I mean by diatopical hermeneutics. The points of difference need to be emphasised.

Diatopical hermeneutics provides a methodology for understanding which, as a method, maintains scientific objectives. It does not endeavour to prescribe the results of the method in advance and thus remains open to the phenomena which present themselves in the process. The objective of diatopical hermeneutics, however, is not religious. It does not endeavour to create a new movement by influencing beliefs and creating adherents. Although it admits a confessional starting point and seeks to avoid violence to traditions, it does not produce a new confession.

The horizon of understanding achieved cannot be understood confessionally without moving back into boundary discourse. In diatopical hermeneutics, one steps outside of boundaries in order to elucidate meaning. This differs radically from creating new boundaries based either on exclusive or inclusive claims to truth. As Krieger has shown, the question of exclusive or inclusive truths always represents boundary discourse (1991, 59-64).

I admit that the new horizon I have described in the last chapter as resulting from the meeting of reason and indigenous religions may seem syncretistic because aspects of both inform my conclusions. I would emphasise again, however, that the process is aimed at achieving new viewpoints for attaining understanding in a dynamic reality and cannot be reduced to religious motives. The distinction is a fine one, but critical to the method if the objective of a scientific elucidation of meaning is to result. The elucidation of meaning contributes to the academic study of religion; syncretism, as demonstrated in the case of Juliana, recreates religion itself.

The Next Phase: Diatopical Hermeneutics by African Scholars

The study of religion in Africa, as I have tried to demonstrate in this book, has a history of its own based on wide geographical, cultural, historical, and methodological considerations. In chapter two, I alluded to the largely theological motives employed in the study of African religions by many African scholars. My analysis of terminology, myths and rituals in the light of diatopical hermeneutics has been conducted from the perspective of my own faith in the autonomy of reason and not from 'within' an African perspective. This raises the question as to how an African scholar, who has been raised in both the indigenous and the rational traditions, might employ diatopical hermeneutics. The next phase in the academic study of African religions, therefore, might logically entail the application of diatopical hermeneutics by Africans.

Panikkar argued that he possessed insight into the meeting of the Hindu and Christian faiths because, as the son of a Hindu father and Roman Catholic mother, he held both confessions within himself at the same time. This may be regarded as the inspiration for the development of the method itself (Krieger, 1991, 45).

It seems to me that two issues stand out clearly if diatopical hermeneutics is to be applied by Africans to the study of African religions. The first focuses on the academic process itself with its basic commitment to the ability to generalise objectively on the basis of factual data. The need to acknowledge geographical, ethnic and linguistic culture areas, as I noted in chapter two, however, makes broad conclusions about religion in Africa difficult. Extreme caution, therefore, concerning general conclusions is required, perhaps so cautious as to submerge the search for a universal meaning beneath the fragmentation characterised by regional differences.

The second issue focuses on the personal experiences and confessions of African scholars themselves. Because an African may possess intimate knowledge of and even profess faith in two or perhaps even three confessions at the same time (indigenous, rational and Christian or Islam), the parameters for an African hermeneutical approach to the study of African religions will emerge not from a detached academic position, but as Gadamer has argued, from a standpoint of commitment. This poses enormous difficulties for religious studies which I believe the methodology outlined in this book helps to resolve.

These issues are not unique to the study of religion in Africa; the same principles and problems apply everywhere. Nevertheless, if the perspectives I have presented in this book accurately convey critical issues in the study of religion in Africa, an understanding of the dynamics involved in the movement from a so-called objectively detached approach to one of an African initiated use of diatopical hermeneutics may result in a new horizon of understanding extending far beyond what I have been able to elucidate.

Parts two and three of this book may provide a preliminary step in this direction since they are accounts of mythologumena and rituals obtained by Zimbabwean students. The major work of applying diatopical hermeneutics by African scholars, however, still remains. I have endeavoured in this book primarily to demonstrate how this can be done and, perhaps more importantly, *that* it can be done. New understandings of African religions, nevertheless, await a full application of the method by those whose horizons are transparently African.

References

Daneel, M. L. 1970. *The God of the Matopos Hills*. The Hague: Mouton.

Gadamer, H. G. 1980. *Truth and method*. London: Sheed and Ward.

Krieger, D. J. 1991. *The new universalism. Foundations for a global theology*. Maryknoll, New York: Orbis, 1991.

Hansson, G. 1994. 'Religious innovation in Zimbabwe: Mbuya Juliana Movement'. Unpublished paper presented at the Conference entitled Christians and Muslims in Contemporary Africa: Religious, Social and Political Perspectives, Uppsala, 25-28 August.

Hinnells, J. (ed.) 1984. *The Penguin Dictionary of Living Religions*. Harmondsworth: Penguin Books.

Mafu, H. 1995. 'The 1991-92 Zimbabwean drought and some religious reactions'. *Journal of Religion in Africa* 25 (3), 288-308.

Mawere, A. and Wilson, K. 1995. 'Socio-religious movements, the state and community change: Some reflections on the Ambuya Juliana Cult of southern Zimbabwe'. *Journal of Religion in Africa* 25 (3), 252-87.

Mueller-Vollmer, K. 1986. 'Introduction. Language, mind and artifact: An outline of hermeneutic theory since the enlightenment' in K. Mueller-Vollmer (ed.), *The hermeneutics reader*. Oxford: Basil Blackwell Ltd, 1-53.

Nthoi, L. 1998. 'Wosana rite of passage: Reflections on the initiation of wosana in the cult of Mwali in Zimbabwe', in J. L. Cox (ed.), *Rites of passage in contemporary Africa*. Cardiff: Cardiff Academic Press, 63-93.

Panikkar, R. 1979. *Myth, faith and hermeneutics*. New York: Paulist Press, 1979.

Ranger, T. 1995. 'Religious pluralism in Zimbabwe', *Journal of Religion in Africa* 25 (3), 226-51.

Part Two

THE MYTHOLOGUMENA

STORIES OF ORIGINS

1. MOUNTAINS, RAIN and the WORLD AS WE NOW KNOW IT

NEEDMORE THATI

RESEARCH AREA: Nhema Area, near Shurugwi

Fire on the Mountains

In the beginning a mountain located in the west erupted. This was later called the Shamba Mountain. It became the residence of the major spirit (*mhondoro*) of the whole area. When it was seen that this *mhondoro* needed a partner, a mountain to the east erupted, later called Bongwe Mountain. This became the residence of the *mhondoro's* wife.

When it was discovered that the mountains were only rocks and that it was necessary for them to have life in terms of vegetation, rain fell on the Shamba Mountain. Some of the water accumulated in a very deep pool at the base of the mountain. This pool never dried up.

Because Bongwe Mountain had not received any rains and the wife of the *mhondoro* still lived in a hot and dry area, a fire was lit on Shamba Mountain to signal to the wife that she should come to the side where the rain had fallen. The *mhondoro* and his wife would have a bath in the pool and drink some water to quench their thirst.

The wife responded by also lighting a fire on Bongwe Mountain to signal that she was feeling hot and was surely coming to have a bath and to drink from the pool. These same events occurred every year in the hot season. The *mhondoro* would light the fire first signalling his wife and then she would light her own fire. Then, the rains would fall to ensure that there was plenty of water for their bath and for drinking.

Because the rains had fallen first on Shamba Mountain causing vegetation to grow there, when the *mhondoro* lit his fire, it would spread quickly consuming the dry plants and trees. The rain would then fall instantly to avoid the fires causing wide destruction.

And thus the elders say today that when they see the fires burning on the Shamba and Bongwe Mountains they know the rains are about to begin. If in a certain year, the rains do not occur after the fires have been spotted, the elders consult the *mhondoro* to discover what has gone wrong. If someone has breached any of the traditions of the mountains, thunder can be heard expressing the *mhondoro's* anger. Then the elders knew that something had to be done. Usually, beer would be brewed for the ancestor spirits and would be drunk on one of the mountains. After doing this and even before the elders had descended the mountain, they would be soaked by the rain.

WILBERT MANHIMANZI

RESEARCH AREA: Nyanga District, Eastern Highlands

How the Mountains Were Formed

The story that Mr W. T. Manhenga told me when I interviewed him on September 24th 1992 is about the origins of the Nyangani Mountains in the Eastern Highlands.

Long ago, there lived in the plains now under Nyanga District, a certain woman called Nyanga. This woman inspired fear in anyone who set one's eyes upon her, especially strangers. Children dreaded seeing her since she was a giant with three horns protruding out of her head.

Nevertheless, she was a woman who commanded respect in her community. She could use her three horns to cure people ailing from any kind of illness and at times the three horns played a fundamental role in the event of a war breaking out with other groups of people. Consequently, Nyanga became a political, social and religious leader in her community.

Since the society in which she lived was patriarchal, Nyanga's influence was resented by certain power hungry men, who plotted to rid her from the community. One of the jealous men put a root which causes insanity (*chiwirowiro*) in her drink at a beer party, and gave it to her to drink. Not expecting any ill-will from her people, she accepted the drink.

No sooner had the beer party ended when the root began to show its effects. Nyanga began shouting, singing and crying. Some people thought she was joking; others thought she was deliberately doing it; still others thought it was the effect of too much beer. The majority of people, however, sympathised with her because they knew she was really going insane. Although the madness had proceeded a long way, Nyanga still had enough of her faculties to use her three horns to determine the cause of her behaviour. She discovered how and why the men had plotted against her. She exclaimed, 'I shall take revenge on the whole lot of you!'

She then ran out of the group and continued running for the whole day. By the time the sun was setting, she collapsed and her body was transfigured into a mountain, now called the Nyangani Mountain.

From that day, parts of the plain began to be covered by the mountains. The highest point of the mountain has sharp pointed ends believed to be the horns that Nyanga had. The rivers Nyangombe, Gairezi and Pungwe that have their sources in the Nyangani Mountains are thought to be her nose which never dried. Also the pool, Chirikuutsi, on the mountain, as well as the ever present mist and sometimes rain on the mountains, are linked to the tears that she shed that day.

Today the Nyangani Mountains in Nyanga are awe-inspiring in the same manner as was the person from whom they take their name. The mountains are holy and sacred. No person in his right mind can afford to go and hunt in its forests; neither can one fell trees on the mountain or even speak on the mountains. There are histories of people who disappeared on the mountains, some of whom have never been found. It is believed that people lost on the mountain can be recovered so long as customary ways are followed, such as kneeling down and pleading to the 'owners of that area' telling them that the lost people did not deliberately offend them but did it out of ignorance. It is believed that men are more difficult to recover than women because Nyanga is still wreaking vengeance on the male race.

The Nyangani Mountains also help the people living around the area in many ways. The rivers that flow from the mountains never run dry and hence most people never have a water crisis. When the rains fail to fall, respectable people go up the mountain to pray for rain. More often than not, even before they leave the mountains, the rains fall heavily. Only in some exceptional cases do the rains fail to come after a prayer has been given.

From the time of the formation of the mountains up to now, men and women who could not or cannot have children have been going up the mountain to seek for medicine to make it possible for them to conceive. It is believed that people only find the medicine they need with the assistance of Nyanga who sympathises with the women who always receive the blame should a couple fail to have children.

A.B. BONZO
RESEARCH AREA: Ngarura Village (Honde Valley)
Nyatene's Body and the Origins of the World
Cde. Chigaramazazu, who is 69, told me a story which he remembers being told to him as a child by his grandfather.

Before anything came into existence there was a person called Nyatene. Nyatene is believed to have been complex in nature. Everything that we now see around today was once fused together in the complex body of Nyatene. He had multiple breasts from which the various living objects on his body would feed. He also had various male and female sex organs through which he brought things into existence. Thus stones, rocks, trees, water, the sun, the moon, stars, animals, birds and all physical objects had their place on Nyatene's body. He continued to produce more and more objects on his body.

As time went by, Nyatene became so huge that he could hardly move, and, moreover, he could no longer endure the pain of the many births which kept occurring all over his body. Nothing ever died or degenerated so long as they were attached to Nyatene. They remained in intimate relationship with both Nyatene and other objects. It was therefore due to the predicament caused by accumulations of material on his body that Nyatene had to divide his body such that each organ would be responsible for its own reproduction and expansion. Nyatene would then remain the authoritative power over them.

Hence, he shook his body so strongly that all the heavy matter such as stones, rocks, soil, trees and various other objects fell to the ground.

Nyatene then assumed a raised position so that the fallen bodies combined to form the earth. Continuous shaking resulted in the formation of mountains, valleys and forests. Nyatene realised that there was no water for the living creatures on the earth and so he released part of his urine to form the rivers, seas and oceans in which other animals such as fish, frogs and various other water creatures would survive.

Man was not part of the objects shaken down to the earth but he and the sun, moon and the cloud remained attached on Nyatene. It was due to this attachment that man assumed a superior position over all the things which previously had been attached to Nyatene's body, much to their disapproval. Man began to boast that the things no longer attached to Nyatene's body were not really a part of creation, Nyatene's junior. In turn, the earthly materials were frustrated for they thought they were given an inferior position by being thrown down to the ground.

Nyatene tried in vain to reconcile man and the earthly materials. He tried to convince those that had fallen to the ground that they were still intimate despite the fact that they were now occupying different realms. The conflict was never resolved. At last, Nyatene reduced man to the status of other earthly objects by shaking him off to the ground. He also shook the sun, moon and clouds down to the ground so that none would complain of inferiority.

On earth, the sun, moon, clouds, mountains and animals, spearheaded by man, decided to join forces against Nyatene. They agreed that they should be re-united with Nyatene as before so as to be released from the many predicaments they were suffering on earth. The plan was that sun would ascend to the sky and burn Nyatene whilst the cloud and moon would entangle and blind him.

After launching this attack, man advised the other objects that had remained on earth to stop the revolt. The sun, moon and cloud were angered by this. They made a pact to inflict severe pain or suffering on the earthly creatures that had betrayed the revolt. Sun agreed to scorch all living creatures with intense heat; cloud would produce heavy rains accompanied by lightning and thunder to kill the living; moon would at times light the nights so that man would be influenced to move at night and hence become devoured by man-eaters such as lions.

Man, therefore, found himself at the mercy of forces of nature. In response, he built houses to keep out the heat of sun and the rain. This proved futile because lightning would burn and destroy the thatched houses. Man would run into mountain caves but thunder would shake the rocks to fall down. It was because of all these problems that man realised that he had offended Nyatene and that he had to be reconciled.

But first he had to placate the three objects that were threatening his life: sun, moon and cloud. Hence, man adopted respect for these objects by offering sacrifices on tops of mountains in order to be nearer the sun, moon and cloud. Man realised that continuous sacrifice and worship to the sun, moon and cloud would partially ease his problems.

However, Nyatene remained offended due to the fact that man had originally instigated the revolt. Hence Nyatene blew the wind with various diseases in it to the people so that the human race never lived a stable life. Humanity also tried to sacrifice and pray to Nyatene to relieve them from their predicaments, but Nyatene could not easily be placated.

154

Hence, from then on, living became something to be determined by chance or luck.

Due to the various diseases, man was now vulnerable to death. Men then began to venerate their dead ancestors so that they would act as their intermediaries, since prayer to Nyatene had proved futile. The ancestors would then act as protectors of their children against all evil forces. The living would brew beer and sacrifice to their ancestors so that they would remain pleased and avoid causing any more havoc amongst the people.

2. SETTLING OF A PEOPLE IN A LAND

ERESINA HWEDE

RESEARCH AREA: Gazaland (Chimanimani and Chipinge Districts)

The Founding of Gazaland

A man called Gaza travelled from South Africa with his family into Zimbabwe. He settled in Gazaland and he had one son called Chamusa. These became known as the Gaza people and their language was Tshangani, probably a Nguni dialect. They knew nothing about *midzimu* (ancestral spirits) and possession. They lived a simple life without religion or sacredness. When Chamusa's father (Gaza) died, his son called Nguvoyame became possessed by Gaza. By then Nguvoyame was seven years old. There was a severe drought in Gazaland and Chamusa and his family were starving.

One night, Nguvoyame's father had decided to move away with his family in search of water. When they woke their little son Nguvoyame to start their journey, he refused and he told his father to go and look for water at the pool which was near the hill where his grandfather Gaza was buried.

Chamusa argued with his son for a time refusing to go and later Nguvoyame started to speak in his grandfather's voice commanding Chamusa to go and fetch water at the pool. By then Nguvoyame was no longer calling Chamusa father but 'my son', implying that he was possessed by Gaza, Chamusa's late father.

When Chamusa went to the pool, he found it full of fresh water and he told his wife and children to fetch water. Nguvoyame told them to use the water for whatever purpose, even to water their gardens because the pool was never to dry up.

Nguvoyame built his fireplace near the pool. He became known as the *svikiro* (a possessed person), usually one who is possessed by the great ancestors or founder of a tribe or a family. They also named him *Goko rama Changani*, which means that he was the offspring of the founder of the nation or tribe. His existence resembled the existence of Gaza. Therefore, from the age of seven Nguvoyame acted as a *svikiro*. He intervened between Gaza and the people. He also became a king and, after his death, one member of the family became possessed by the same spirit and therefore became a king.

3. TOTEMS AND ANIMALS
JETHRO KUBARA
RESEARCH AREA: SaMushonga Village, Mutasa District

The Crocodile and the Monkey

This story comes from central Mutasa District in SaMushonga Village. It was told by an old man who says that he actually witnessed maDzviti (Ndebele raiders) when he was a young boy. The story seeks to explain the totemic behaviour of human beings and how it affects the whole realm of social life, especially among the Shona.

Once upon a time, there was a chief who stayed far away in a chaotic land where his people always fought each other. The chief devised a method and announced that nobody was allowed to stay with a species of his own so as to cut down the spirit of violence. The chief then invented totems to make sure that people were distinct.

One day a crocodile was sent away from his friends and declared unwelcome to return until a certain type of ritual was performed. The crocodile wandered in the forest and was lonely for a long time. When it was at the heart of the forest, it met a monkey which was also looking for a friend. The two introduced themselves to each other and comforted each other for some days.

One day, the crocodile persuaded the monkey to join him on a visit to his old friends whom he had long since forgiven for sending him away. The monkey made it quite clear that he could not swim. The crocodile said that he would carry his dear friend on his back and swim to his fellow friends. The two friends then departed on their long visit to the river where crocodile's relatives lived. They reached the river at midday and the monkey climbed on the back of the crocodile.

The two friends travelled happily and monkey was very excited to move in the water for the first time. When the two were at the middle of the river, crocodile stopped and said that he was too tired to continue and that he could not rest with monkey on his back. Monkey swore that he could do anything for crocodile provided he did not discharge him from his back into the water. Crocodile agreed and rested with monkey on his back. When he had enough rest, he started the journey. Crocodile stopped for the second time and told Monkey a fierce story, 'My friend, I was afraid to tell you in the early days of our friendship that I was sent away from my fellows. I could only be accommodated after some rituals. Our great family traditional healer said that this required me to use the heart of a monkey. My friend, you promised that you could do anything for me. I need your heart for a sacrifice when we reach home.'

The monkey was excessively sorrowful and thought of a plan out of the trap. The monkey acted as if he genuinely sympathised with his friend. He then instructed the crocodile to stop and said, 'My friend, I have pity on you, but I cannot give you my heart. I am also very sorry because our monkey forefathers taught us that we should not move about with our hearts for security reasons. I think you still remember those days before the declaration of the chief. From that day on, we leave our hearts on a certain type of tree close to that place we first met. So that means we have to go back. I will climb the tree and give you my heart. Without wasting time let us go back to get my heart'.

The two 'friends' returned with crocodile happy that his trick had worked whilst monkey was so happy that when they reached the banks, he refused to walk on the ground. He even promised crocodile a second heart which he was going to take from 'their tree'.

When they arrived at the tree, monkey climbed quickly, and when he had reached a safe distance, he threw a twig and hit Crocodile in the eye. Crocodile looked up in pain and monkey replied in mockery, 'My friend you are the worst fool in the whole chiefdom. How can any living animal move without a heart? I am sorry, I will never come down again because you are dangerous. But you can't think, my friend.' The crocodile went away sad and cheated.

From that day, the monkey stayed up on the trees out of fear of the crocodile, whilst the crocodile went and stayed for ever in the water out of shame, shy to meet the monkey.

A. MOYO
RESEARCH AREA: Mberengwa District
The Origin of Baboons

In my research, I interviewed an old man from our rural areas in Mberengwa and he related to me a story that concerns the origins of baboons. Although the old man is renowned for traditional stories, he made it clear that some of the details of the stories were fading out from his 'weary' brain.

Long ago, the earth was very productive. People cultivated it and produced bountiful harvests. There were no baboons then. The creator (*musiki*) had created people to till this earth and live by that.

Later, however, there arose a group of lazy people who found it very hard to till the land to earn a living. They resorted to stealing from the hard working people's fields and granaries. In a way these lazy people had declared a 'war' against the hard-working people who in turn sought to fight these new enemies and drive them from their community. They prepared spears, arrows and clubs with which to attack their new enemies. They usually ambushed the thieves in the fields and other strategic points ready to attack when they came.

On arrival in the fields, the thieves or lazy people had to bear the wrath of the ambushing farmers who attacked them by throwing spears, arrows and clubs at them and then chased them to far away places. Usually the spears, arrows and clubs hit at the backs of the fleeing thieves and sometimes got pinned there. These later became tails.

In some instances, earthen pots (*zvaenga* or *zvikari*), which those guarding the fields would be using while there, were thrown at the faces of those thieves who looked back whilst being chased. As the pottery broke, it produced grooves on their faces just like the pottery which struck their faces.

The relationship between the two groups became very strained, but life proved more difficult for the thieves because their lives were at stake every time they attempted to steal. In addition, the thieves were beginning to grow tails and grooved faces due to attacks on them. Thus the thieves also had to endure a lot of mockery from those who did not

157

steal. At first they vainly attempted to evade all this by arguing that what other people called tails were not actually tails, but their own clubs which they carried at their backs. They also argued that what others called grooved faces (*mahobi*) were actually a form of a cap. However, that did not alleviate their plight.

The thieves or lazy group finally decided to withdraw from the hostile community and form their own community in which they would continue to launch stealing expeditions. They withdrew to the mountains where they quickly developed extraordinary abilities to climb on mountains and trees. They also developed other qualities which people do not possess such as reddened buttocks which it is held resulted from rifles firing at the buttocks when the thieves were in flight. They also lost the ability to speak.

The mountains to which the thieves, now called baboons, had withdrawn had formed from a race that started among stones that rushed and clashed at certain favoured locations where mountains now stand. Trees had also experienced a similar race when they competed to occupy the best locations such as well watered valleys. This resulted in some areas being left devoid of trees. Thus the coming of the now called baboons almost coincided with the emergence of mountains and the organisation of vegetation into thickets and bushes.

Up to this day, baboons live in the mountains. They live on a variety of foods ranging from certain types of fruit to scorpions. They continue to raid people's fields and granaries in search of food. The baboons also developed strategies to counter the growing awareness of people guarding their fields and homes. One of these strategies was to establish a kind of watch baboon or sentinel (*nhariri* or *chenda*). One baboon remains on the mountain watching out for enemies who could attack the other baboons as they loot.

J. MUKOYI
RESEARCH AREA: Mutasa District, Manicaland
The Origin of Totems

In our culture, one has to possess an identity in the form of mutupo (totem). I interviewed an old man who lives near the Jenya Mountains in Mutasa District in Manicaland. He told me a myth about the origin of totems in our society.

There was once a man who was a habitual thief to the extent that he disturbed his neighbours very much. The man is said to have aimed at one item, that is chickens. Every night he made sure that he had stolen a chicken. His behaviour was very similar to that of a *bonga* (wild cat). A wild cat is an animal that kills chickens. The leader of the village was so disappointed with the man's behaviour that he decided to think of ways that would stop the man from stealing. The village leader took some villagers to a ritual which was attended by the thief. During the ritual, the leader announced that he was giving the man the totem *bonga*. Thereafter, his surname in the village became known as Bonga. It is said that the ancestor spirits were pleased.

One day, during a devastating drought, what they call *Gore remhare* (year of extreme hardships necessitated by the drought), the man had virtually nothing to eat. He then saw a *bonga* and killed it. It is said that while he was eating the *bonga*, he lost all his teeth.

Forty years after the incident, the same man decided to get married to a woman who was also named *bonga*. All of their children were born with a severe mental illness.

As time went by, another incident befell the man. The man went to Jenya mountain to a thick forest to do some hunting with his axe. Towards sunset the man decided to cut down a dried tree that was on a slope. Earlier in the day, he had killed a buck and he wanted firewood to cook the buck at home. His first attempt to cut the tree was a failure as he heard a mysterious shout from nowhere. However, he insisted on cutting the tree and it is said that instead of falling downwards on the slope it fell upwards much to the surprise of the man. Despite the fright he received, he took the tree home, but the small thin tree made him sweat as he never had done in his life. At his home, he made some firewood but, despite its dryness, the tree would not burn. Shortly afterward, the man died mysteriously.

To determine the cause of the man's death, his family consulted a *n'anga* who revealed that the tree had been a *mubonga*, meaning that it belonged to his totem and was not meant to be cut.

MBONGI KHUMALO
RESEARCH AREA: Khalanga Area of Southwest Zimbabwe
The Healing Snake

Most of the traditional stories are losing and even changing shape with time. People are now interested mainly in modern literature rather than traditional tales. Even Mrs Mbobozo, as she begins this story, is not sure if she will tell it to the end. She is doubting if she can still give it as was told in traditional circles. She is a Ndebele, and confesses that most of the stories she can tell seem to have emerged from the Khalanga circles, but had much the same message for the Ndebeles. Though told in Ndebele, most of such tales, including the present one, have songs or a song in the original Khalanga language. This essay records the traditional story told by Mrs Mbobozo Khumalo.

Long, long ago, before Unkulunkulu (the mighty one) had even created the moon, there was a polygamist who had many children. This old man was struck by a very serious illness, to the point of death. His sons went to consult a diviner (*isangoma*), to find the cause and cure. For cure, the diviner instructed them to go to a nearby river, where Nkabayile, the healing snake, resides. On arrival at the river, they were instructed to stand at the bank of the river and call the snake by its name, singing a song they were taught. In singing they were supposed to mention that their father is sick and they need Nkabayile's assistance.

These young men promised to follow the instructions, and were concerned very much about the health of their father. The eldest son was the first to go to the river to fetch Nkabayile, the healing snake, from the river. On arrival at the river, he stood by the river bank and began to sing the song they were taught. The snake sang in reply.

Son: *Nkabayile Kwayi ndomudanadana*
         Nkabayile Tate banogwala Nkabayile.

Snake: *Haye ndosunda ndola wenkabayile*
         Ndola musindile ho!
Son: *Nkabayile andi andinganhle Nkabayile*
         Tate Banogwala Nkabayile.
Snake: *Hayi ndisunda ndola weNkabayile*
         Ndone musindile Ho!

Translation into English:

Son: Nkabayile I've been sent to call you.
         My father is ill, Nkabayile.
Snake: I am coming I, Nkabayile,
         I am coming. Don't be scared of me.

As the snake heard the song, it came out of the pool singing in reply. When the big and terrible snake came out, the young man was terrified and he immediately ran away. He reported that the snake was so large and terrifying that he could not face it.

Their uncle and the four sons set out with weapons promising to bring the healing snake out alive. On arriving at the river, they stood by the river bank, and began to sing their song. The snake sang in reply as it came out of the waters. With fear, they all forgot their promise and concern about their sick father. The snake seemed too frightening for them to face. So, like the first son, they took to their heels, and went back home.

After all had failed to take the healing snake home, the youngest son offered to go out and bring it back alive. When he reached the river bank, he sang the song that they were taught. As it heard the song, the healing snake sang in reply as he coiled out of the waters. Nkabayile approached the young brave boy, and coiled around his waist.

The boy went home with the terrifying snake around his waist. When he got home, people ran away from him as they saw the snake around him. He then stood by the door of the hut where his sick father slept. The snake then uncoiled itself, and made its way to the already unconscious man. It licked him till he was healed. In appreciation, the father gave the snake a heard of black cows, and the youngest son took the snake and the cows back to the river.

When the son returned home, he found the father totally healed. The father made this son of his the heir over all that he had, and the son eventually inherited all that the father had. Up to this day, a number of snakes are held with traditional esteem, and are honoured as the dead ancestors of the family. On their visit to the home, the belief is that the home enjoys the blessings from the fathers.

M.A. CHINYOKA
RESEARCH AREA: Mberengwa District
The Plight of Kamba, the Tortoise

Once upon a time there was a mighty king who lived high up in the sky. The mighty king had his own counsellors and attendants who manned the palace and carried out the day to day activities of the palace. It so happened that on earth a severe drought occurred. There was not a single drop of water anywhere. Trees withered and creatures began to die.

160

Despite the drought, a certain old lady in the land had the sole fig tree which was leafy and had a number of fruits, fruits of all kinds. For the creatures, both animals and humans, to live, they needed to go to the fig tree that belonged to the old woman. But before anyone could pick the fruits from the tree, they had to pronounce the name of the tree – 'Munkangarakadyei'.

All animals went to the old lady in turns to enquire of the name of her tree, but by the time they got back to report to the others they forgot the name. Their dilemma was finally solved by Kamba (tortoise) who was seen as slow and useless. Kamba went and enquired of the name and came and reported it to the other animals who then flocked in a great stampede to the fig tree to help themselves. They devoured every fruit that existed, but Kamba got nothing since he could not climb up. He only helped himself with what dropped from the tree or from other animals' mouths. This angered the owner of the tree who, in order to punish the animals, uprooted her tree and disappeared into the sky with terrific speed.

The creatures on land became helpless again with no food, no water and nowhere to appeal for help. They started roaming about in desperation. The mighty king of heaven felt pity for the thirsty and hungry creatures and he ordered his servants to prepare a great feast. Much food and drink was gathered in the presence of the old lady who had fled from earth and who, as it turned out, happened to be the wife or spouse of the mighty king of heaven and obviously was the Queen of heaven herself.

When all was ready, the mighty king of heaven sent his messenger on earth to summon all the creatures to the great banquet. All the creatures rejoiced on hearing the invitation. In those days all humans, animals and birds had feathers except for one unfortunate creature who happened not to have wings to fly. The creature was Kamba. Because of this, Kamba was very unhappy and saw no chance for his survival.

The other creatures noticed Kamba's predicament and each donated a feather until finally Kamba had two excellent wings. The voyage began with every creature happy that their chances of survival had improved. On the other hand, Kamba thought here was his opportunity to seek revenge for the wrongs done to him by other creatures. He thought of a plan. On the way, he told the other creatures that they were to call him by a new name when they arrived at the King's feast. This new name was, 'All of you'.

When the creatures arrived at the dwelling place of the mighty King, plentiful food was put before them. The mighty king made a speech of welcome and finally announced that the food was 'for all of you'. He then withdrew into his palace. Kamba stood up and told the other creatures that the food had been openly declared his, for his name was 'All of you'. He ate all the food and gave the other creatures just the left overs.

Angered by this, the creatures took away their feathers that they had donated to Kamba. At the time of the start of the long journey home, therefore, Kamba had no wings. As the other creatures took off, Kamba became helpless. He finally decided to try to fly home without wings. His journey was very unpleasant.

After days of travel, Kamba finally landed with a thud, a crash so hard that his shell broke into pieces, since he had fallen on rock boulders. He later found a person who had the power to join his shell pieces together. At the spot where he dropped to earth, a spring formed gushing out water without ever going dry. This became the source of life for all creatures and plants.

SYDNEY JEJE
RESEARCH AREA: Mutare
How Animals, Birds and Babies Lost Their Speech

The story I am going to write is from an elderly woman called Mrs Chatimba whom I interviewed. The woman comes from Mutare and she claims that the story is well-known in her area. The story itself belongs to the primordial time when there was 'direct communication' between the people and God, the Creator.

Long, long ago when Mwari (God) had finished creating people and all the animals and other things, young babies were born speaking and all the animals and birds could speak. However, their minds were not so wise as to know what to speak in public and what not to speak. They could shout some vulgar words, speaking the unspeakables in front of many people. Animals could shout at each other and at people as well. Birds could take the information of what was happening here among the people and the animals and fly high to Mwari and report everything. The result was that Mwari had no rest since at all times there were birds reporting to him what was happening.

At the same time, the moral standards of the society declined. There was chaos everywhere. This did not please Mwari because no secrets could be kept. Ethics were forgotten; so it was a bad generation.

One day a woman caught a hare and roasted it very nicely. She left it in the kitchen where her baby was lying, sleeping. Her neighbour, a woman, came looking for her in the kitchen but she was not there. Her attention was caught by the mouth-salivating roasted hare. She looked around and saw nobody except the baby, so she decided to help herself to the meat. The taste was so welcome on her palate that she decided to carry the entire hare to her home.

When the owner of the meat came home, she was disgusted to find it gone. She was furious with everybody in the house, until the little baby told her that a woman had come and taken it away. In anger, she went straight to the woman and killed her with an axe.

This action was recounted to Mwari by the birds. This caused Mwari to be angry who decided to 'modify' his creation because the first attempt at creation was presenting too many problems.

Mwari then ordered that no bird or animal could speak like people because their minds are not wise and this has caused chaos and declining moral standards in the society. As for the little babies, he decided to put a little amount of powder in their throats so that they will not be able to speak. When they suck milk, they will be washing off the powder. By the time the powder is completely washed off, the baby would have been grown up and be able to know what is acceptable in the society and what is not acceptable. From that time up to now, little

162

babies cannot speak and animals and birds cannot speak the human language. By this action, Mwari restored order and moral standards which today still are maintained.

KUDAKWASHE MUCHINHAIRI

RESEARCH AREA: Unspecified

The Hare, the Hyena and the Snake

My old uncle was very pleased when he heard one evening last month that I was requesting him to narrate any of his customary ancient tales. Yes, he could be seen wearing a contented face, as he struggled to get into a sitting position. The story he told was purely in Shona, and I will try to translate it into English.

Long ago, God called Hare, Hyena and a snake called Spade to join him one bright afternoon and told them he intended to determine which of them was the most wise. In those days, the animal world was quite different from that of the present day, because animals could speak, and snakes could move about on two feet.

The chance to expose his wisdom was given first to the hare. It happened that the small animal was not eloquent, and this drew him back from winning the championship. His mistake was simply that he failed to overcome his weakness, which he could have done by dramatising whatever he had wanted to say.

Spade then leapt forward, first saluted God, and proceeded to kneel before him. In a humble tone, Spade explained to the creator that it was quite unfair for him to conduct the contest. His point was that the creator was so mighty that he should have sent one of his disciples to do the job while he did other things. Spade went on to tell the almighty that he had created everything, including the powerful Hyena and weak Hare.

On hearing that he was regarded as 'weak', Hare rose to challenge Hyena whom Spade had called powerful. Had it not been for God's intervention a fight would have broken out between Hare and Hyena. Thus, Hyena never got the chance to show his wisdom for Spade had been so crafty as to nearly cause a fight. Hyena and Hare were immediately relegated out of the competition, but, for reasons best known to himself, God did not bless Spade for his wit, and he even went on to punish him. Spade had his two legs taken away, and was also left almost blind. However, the creator was also quite fair in that, possibly due to Hyena and Hare's folly, he chastised the two first by making Hyena the most despised of animals and then by making Hare a chief prey of man.

MAXWELL MUKOVA

RESEARCH AREA: Gutu Rural Areas, Masvingo Province

Why Some People Behave Like Animals

In this story I am going to present a story which was told to a certain old woman when she was still young. The woman is now old and probably in her mid-seventies. The research for the story took place in Masvingo Province in the Gutu rural areas.

163

Long ago when Mwari created the universe, people, plants and animals were not different. All of them lacked hearts (*mwoyo*) and thus they did not know how to behave since the heart determines one's behaviour.

Mwari then sent a messenger with hearts to go and give them to people and animals. The hearts were put in one tray (*rusero*), although they were kept well separated from each other. People's hearts were placed at one corner of the tray with animals in a different corner. These hearts were not supposed to be mixed.

On the way, the messenger constantly recited what God had told him about the hearts. He kept a close eye on the tray to be sure that the hearts did not mix. Unfortunately, the messenger fell on the way dropping the tray and spilling the hearts out onto the ground where they became mixed. The messenger tried to sort the hearts out, grouping them into their original divisions, but he failed to organise some of them properly. In the group of those for people he put some baboon and lion hearts. Among the dogs, he put some people's hearts. Some, of course, he got right and stored them in their appropriate groups.

The messenger proceeded with the journey to meet Mwari's creatures and carried out the assignment of distributing the hearts. Some animals received their appropriate hearts, but some did not. Some people also were given their proper hearts but some received the hearts of various animals. These hearts, as was mentioned earlier, were to govern the reason and behaviour of Mwari's creatures, and were intended to distinguish human beings from animals.

Some people received the hearts of lions and became harsh, greedy and bullies. Others received the hearts of baboons and became dishonest thieves. People who received their appropriate hearts became reasonable, calm and of good behaviour. The animals which received human hearts became almost human, calm and principled. This explains why some people act like animals and why some are more rational than others.

RENNIAS NHAMO
RESEARCH AREA: Masvingo Province
How Animals and Humans Separated
The following story was related to me by my grandmother.

Originally, animals and humans lived together harmoniously. God used to stay with them as the ruler or landlord and source of everything. One day God had a meeting with the living creatures. At the meeting, there arose an uproar concerning the relative status and roles of animals and humans in the society. There was conflict over who had the greater status in society. God then waved for silence and indeed there was a dead silence. God announced in a loud voice that he was angered by their disagreement, but that both animals and humans were to make their final requests to him before he disappeared to a calm place.

Human beings demanded authority over animals, which God granted. Some animals said that they needed nothing from God, who announced in response that from that day onwards, the animals were to be servants of human beings. Hearing this, most of the animals ran away into forests, but some remained. God declared that those animals which ran away should be called wild animals, while those which remained should be called domestic animals.

Before God disappeared, he created the resources needed for the survival both of animals and humans.

4. DEATH
EMMANUEL MATIRONGO
RESEARCH AREA: Chipinge, Chimanimani Area

How Death Came to Be

Sekuru Gezana of Mutare, who was born in Chipinge, Chimanimani area, whom I interviewed, is probably one of the oldest men still living in Zimbabwe. His actual date of birth is unknown to him. He only remembers the end of the Ngungunyane war (about 1890 when the Gaza state of Ngungunyane provided one of the major obstacles to final colonial conquests of southern Mozambique.) At the time, he was a young boy. Sekuru Gezana tells a story of how death came to be. However, the story was told with difficulties and certain details seem to be lost or missing. The story was told in Ndau.

'Kare kare' (long, long ago in time immemorial) lived a certain *Maambo* (King). This king was a very great and powerful king. He ruled the whole earth (*pashipeshe*) with the help of his subordinates, *Madzishe* (Chiefs). One of the Chiefs called for a meeting in his territory, which was attended by every living thing.

What stimulated the meeting is not clear, but the issue at stake was death. It is also not clear whether death had occurred somewhere before or whether *Maambo* had given those attending the meeting a choice about death. Other things may have been addressed at the meeting, but the central issue certainly was death (*rufu*). At the meeting, possibly after a serious discussion, a resolution was made. 'Let not man die' (animals included). The Chief decided to send Chameleon (*Rwavi*) to *Maambo* with the resolution of the meeting. *Maambo* would then stamp out death and declare man and animals eternal. However, Chameleon lingered along the road so long that the Chief dispatched Lizard (*Gwenjere*) to *Maambo* carrying the second opinion of the meeting: 'Man must die'. Lizard was so fast that he overtook Chameleon and announced to *Maambo*, 'Let man die'. Maambo took the message and declared perpetual death for man and animals. This is how death came into the world.

Sekuru Gezana ended the story laughing saying, '*Rwavi* was very slow. If ever he was faster than *Gwenjere* and reached the place of Maambo first, I wouldn't be worrying about death!'

KULUBE KUDA
RESEARCH AREA: Dombodema

The Origin of Death

When I asked Dhlamini, an old man in the rural areas of Dombodema, to tell me a story, he related a story about the origins of death.

When Somandla (the all powerful one) created his people, he loved his creation so much that he did not want it to perish or die. Somandla decided to send chameleon with the message to his creation that there no one will die and that people will live for ever on the earth. Chameleon did not take the message very seriously, for, although during that time he could run fast, he moved very slowly. Along the way chameleon was attracted by *umpumpulwane* (some fruits) which were very ripe and good. Chameleon felt hungry when he saw the fruits and began to eat hungrily, thus forgetting the important message to the people.

Somandla was angry at this delay by chameleon because he expected chameleon to obey his orders and take the message urgently. In response, Somandla sent another creature, gecko, but with a different message. Gecko was told to run and tell the people that they will perish or die forever. Because gecko feared the creator, unlike chameleon, he took the message urgently and ran without stopping on the way. When gecko arrived where he was sent, chameleon had not yet appeared and so he delivered the bad news first to the people before they heard the good news which chameleon had.

Since the people knew nothing about death or dying, they accepted the message with happiness. Gecko then returned without delay and reported back to Somandla that his orders had been carried out. Chameleon, after finishing the fruits, continued with his slow journey to the people, but when he arrived to deliver the message the people did not believe him because his message was contrary to what they had heard first. They said to him, '*Sizwe elikanzulo elikanwabu asisalizwa*' (We have heard gecko's words first, so chameleon's words are not true).

When chameleon returned to report that his message had been ignored, Somandla punished him for delaying to deliver his message in time. Somandla reduced chameleon's speed, giving it to gecko. That is why today chameleon is very slow and gecko very fast.

When the people accepted death, they actually thought it was a good thing but by the time death attacked them, they began to fear it and decided to run away from it. However, death continued to exist among them. The people then decided to change their direction rather than run away from death. When a person dies, he is buried in a sitting position carrying his luggage and facing the west. It is believed that death was moving from the west to the east and so to counter it people had to change direction and move westwards so that they pass each other on the way.

RICARDO MLAMBO
RESEARCH AREA: Mwenibe Area, Mberengwa District
Why People Had to Die

The following story is a result of an interview I had with my maternal grandmother. She claims to have been born before the arrival of the whites saying that when the first whites came she was already a girl of about ten years. She says she was born in the Mwenibe area of Mberengwa and it is still in this area where she lives today. Mberengwa is in the Midlands Provinces of Zimbabwe and is roughly fifty kilometres from Zvishavane but the actual place I had this interview is approximately one hundred kilometres from Zvishavane. It was of interest to me to note that my maternal grandmother said this story was told to her by her grandmother who in turn claimed that the story had been told to her by her grandmother. Therefore, there are chances that

166

this story may have been altered in the process of being passed on from one generation to the other.

Long long ago, after Mwari had created this world, there were no animal or human beings in it except grass and trees. Since Mwari was the only thing in the world, he decided to make it more beautiful. He created large shade trees and populated them with lovely birds. But still he felt this was not enough. Therefore, he created people and animals.

The people in the world began to multiply and Mwari was pleased by it. When the people increased even more in number, Mwari withdrew to the skies so that he could monitor their activities. This was the time when animals, trees and stones could speak. Mwari took with him to the skies chameleon and lizard as his *vatumwa* (messengers).

As people continued to multiply, Mwari noticed that the world would become too small if humans continued to live without dying. But at first he did not regard this as a serious problem. Hence, he chose his messenger chameleon and sent him to the people to assure them that they were not going to die. However, as Mwari gave the case serious thought, he understood the implications of his decision that people were not to die.

He thus called lizard and told him to go down with the message that the people were to die. So off went lizard with the message. Because he is faster than the chameleon, he arrived in the world first before chameleon and passed his message to the people. When chameleon later arrived, he found that lizard had already delivered Mwari's message. That is why you see people dying and being born today.

SOCIO-MORAL STORIES

R. SHOKO
RESEARCH AREA: Mberengwa District
A Tree of Blessing and a Selfish Husband

I interviewed my grandmother in our home area, Mberengwa, asking her to relate a story told to her when she was young. The story as told by my grandmother follows.

Once upon a time, there was a severe drought on earth which brought much starvation and suffering to the people, such that survival seemed a dream if not a thing of the past. In the country of Chief Rutsambo, there lived a man named Mufere together with his wife and five children. Because of the ravaging drought, Rutendo, the wife of Mufere, had tried everything that she could come across in an attempt to feed her children. On the other hand, Mufere was a drunkard who cared very little about his children. He would spend all his days looking for beer leaving Rutendo with the dying children.

One day when Mufere was walking across the bush to the next village he saw a wonderful blessing from the spirits, a fruit tree which was full of fruits. The tree had survived the drought. He went under the tree and thanked his spirit for such a blessing and started singing under the tree.

Amai vaMufere kwaku-kwaku mvo-o
Amai vaMufere uku kudya kwabva nepiko?

Mother of Mufere, expressions of jumping and entering into
Mother of Mufere, where did this food come from?

By just singing and dancing the fruits started pouring down like big drops so that Mufere ate until his stomach could not take any more. He spent the whole day sleeping in the bush. When evening fell, he went home and found his wife and children still awake. When he was given the usual meal of bitter leaves, which had become their normal meal, he refused and told the wife to give the leaves to the children. 'My wife it's better you give them to the children because they are our important blessing. I am a grown man. I may sleep with no food'.

Rutendo was surprised by Mufere's behaviour because on one occasion he had almost killed her for not having left a similar meal for him. His refusal to eat food went on for five days until the wife became suspicious and wanted to know where her husband was getting his meals.

One afternoon when Mufere was going out for a beer drinking session, his wife followed behind from a distance. She saw Mufere come to a big tree, start singing the song and dancing. She listened carefully to what Mufere was singing and remembered everything. When Mufere was satisfied, he went away to drink beer. Meanwhile, his wife ran home to collect her children and big sacks. She and the children came and sang the song until there was not even a single fruit left in the tree. After collecting all the fruits, they tied sharp weapons like thorn sticks on the branches of the tree. They also tied stones and hard objects to the branches and then quickly left the place.

When Mufere was returning from the beer party he thought of passing through his wonder fruit tree. Drunk as he was, he went and sat under the tree and began to sing his usual song. To his utmost surprise not even a single fruit fell from the tree but instead spears, thorn sticks and stones pierced and hammered him. He was seriously hurt and went home bleeding. When he arrived home, his wife did not ask him anything about his injuries. Instead his wife offered him their usual meal. This time Mufere ate all the bitter leaves. His wife then teasingly asked, 'Today have you forgotten the special blessings (meaning children), since you have eaten and finished all the food?' It was at this moment that Mufere confessed that he had been unfaithful and thoughtless to the extent of being selfish to forget about his children.

He then told his wife about the fruit tree that used to feed him and how he had been hurt. Mufere asked for forgiveness from both the children and his wife. Rutendo then showed Mufere some sacks full of fruits and she also told him how she had acquired them. Subsequently, they reunited and started to live well as a united and happy family. They started to work hard for the next rainy season, and after a prolonged period of drought, the rains finally came.

MATTHIAS MAKURUMIDZE
RESEARCH AREA: Marange Communal Lands
The Man Who Instilled Fear

From an interview I carried out with a certain elderly man in my home area in Marange Communal Lands, I managed to record a quite interesting traditional story.

Once upon a time there was a powerful man who earned himself the name *Chazezesa* ('That which instils fear'). Once he had grown up in bodily stature, he married a woman, but he never respected her parents.

In the village where he lived Chazezesa feared no man as he always beat his breast assuring himself that he was the most powerful man in the region. He classed all other men under the title, 'woman'. News went round that as a youth Chazezesa had visited some far away place where a *n'anga* had given him some medicine (*mangoromera*) which would render him the most powerful man in his home area. The story also noted that whenever he experienced an itching-feeling that could come on at any time, he would feel like fighting. It is reported that one day the urge to fight came on while he was asleep. To release this urge, he woke up and beat hard against the walls of his sleeping hut. His wife thought he was mad when she saw her husband break down the walls of their hut.

This beating of the walls of the hut during the night began to occur frequently. As a result, Chazezesa's wife decided to go back to her parents' home in the vicinity. When Chazezesa tired of expecting her return of her own accord, he decided to visit the home of his father-in-law *Kwauyeyi* ('What has come'?) to seek his forgiveness. As they sat in Kwauyeyi's court discussing the matter, Chazezesa's urge to fight somebody made an unexpected, and an undesired, appearance. As his anger increased, he spat into the face of his father-in-law and scolded him for not properly looking after his daughter. In anger, the father-in-law, who was a weakly man, left the court and made for his bedroom with his wife following after him.

In his bedroom, Kwauyeyi ate the chaff from maize for almost three hours, but without getting his belly filled. Amazingly, and simultaneously, Chazezesa, who had returned to his home, experienced his stomach becoming inflated. This went on until such a time that, when Chazezesa's tight-fitting trousers and shirt could not resist anymore, they burst. And when there seemed no hope of arresting the situation, the father-in-law appeared, having been told of what had become of Chazezesa. In the face of all those who were wondering about what had caused this strange occurrence, Kwauyeyi attributed the suffering of his son-in-law to his lack of respect for his in-laws.

When this situation was revealed to Chazezesa, he vowed never to boast of his bodily strength again nor to show disrespect to his elders. His stomach then returned to normal.

J. CHIHLABA
RESEARCH AREA: Matenda in Zvishavane
The Three Jealous Girls

Sekuru Chigwengwe is one of the oldest surviving members of the Chigwengwe family in Matenda area, which is in Zvishavane district. I can suggest that he was born in the early 1900s because he always talks about the First World War (1914-1918). By virtue of his age, I considered him the most suitable person to interview on traditional issues. I then politely asked him to relate to me any one traditional story he still remembered telling or being told in the past. The story he related was the well-known folktale about Chipo and her cruel friends.

169

Long, long ago, when the Europeans had not set foot on this land, when the land was enjoying a period of peace, prosperity and plenty, there was in the land of Matenda a very beautiful, orphaned girl named Chipo. Chipo lived with her only surviving relative, Ambuya Mamoyo, her grandmother.

Chipo's striking beauty and her possession of the most coveted beads around, caused her friends, Nyadzai, Nyembezi and Maidei to become jealous of her. These three girls then devised a plan of killing Chipo. One day, on a Thursday, when all the village was at rest, being a day when no work was done in the fields, the three girls came to Chipo's place. As usual, Chipo accompanied the girls to a distant bush called Bera, where they used to fetch firewood. In the bush there was a river named Gonakudzingwa which was rumoured to be sacred because it was thought to be the abode of the sacred python called Machingura.

Nyadzai, Nyembezi and Maidei bound Chipo with ropes and then threw her into the Gonakudzingwa River. They hoped that the greedy crocodiles of the river would thank them for their generosity.

When they reached the village, the three girls said that Chipo had been taken away by the crocodile as they were bathing at the river's edge. Chipo's grandmother, Mbuya Mamoyo, wept bitterly when she heard this because Chipo had been her only comforter.

Chipo, however, was not eaten by crocodiles in the river, but was taken by a mermaid (*njuzu* spirit which is believed to live in sacred rivers). She lived with the mermaid at its home below the river for three solid months. When everybody in Matenda was now convinced of Chipo's death, Chipo unexpectedly appeared at her grandmother's hut in broad daylight. She was wearing a new and immaculate cloak decorated with the most beautiful beads ever seen before in the land. In addition, she was carrying a bag made of a lion's skin, which contained various kinds of herbs for curing even the most dreaded diseases. It was the mermaid that had equipped Chipo, not only with the bag of medicine (*nhava*), but also with the supernatural knowledge of divination and healing.

The whole village gathered at Mbuya Mamoyo's hut to hear Chipo's story. After she had narrated everything, the king ordered Nyadzai, Nyembezi and Maidei to be executed, and instantly they were stoned to death. After this, Chipo became a highly respected healer (*n'anga*) whose ability far surpassed all other *n'angas* hitherto known in the village. Eventually, Chipo was married to the king, Machinda, and she assumed the position of Queen of Matenda.

NICHOLAS MANGUDYA

RESEARCH AREA: Mutambara, Chimanimani

The Closed Cave

I interviewed Bennie Mangudya, an elderly man who resides in Mutambara village in Chimanimani. I asked the man if he could tell me a story of his interest that he remembers being told or telling in informal settings. He went on to tell me a story concerning three girls who had gone gathering some fruits from the forest.

A long time ago, in Mutambara area of Chimanimani, some girls asked their parents if they could go and collect some fruits from the forest. The girls were permitted and henceforth set out for the forest.

170

The girls gathered various fruits. However, in the process of gathering the fruits, the girls did not obey the general rules that were supposed to be observed. The girls went on to pass some rude remarks on the nature of some fruits, saying they were not delicious and that some were rotten to such an extent that had they known they would not have come at all. An aged woman, her skin shrunk and walking with the help of a stick, appeared on the scene and the girls froze in fear. The woman told the girls to carry the fruits they had collected and to leave the forest.

Without questioning, the girls accepted the advice of the woman. However, just as the girls had turned their backs on the forest, they started giggling. At that instant, the land roared with thunder and it started to rain. The girls decided to take refuge in a cave. After some time passed, one of the girls vowed to continue with the journey in spite of the heavy rain. The other two girls remained in the cave.

The two remaining girls inspected the inside of the cave and discovered some earthen pots, stones to sit on and some traditional weapons. The girls went on to break the pots, turned up the stones, giggled and passed some rude remarks. Having done this, the girls went to the mouth of the cave and gazed at the rain which by now was only but a drizzle. As they stood at the entrance to the cave, the aged woman whom they had seen in the forest came into view. Seeing her soaked clothes and the way she walked in slippery mud, the girls burst out laughing. The woman raised her walking stick and pointed in the direction of the cave. At that instant the mouth of the cave was closed, trapping the girls inside.

In the meantime, the girl who had refused to take refuge in the cave, reached the village and was asked where she had left the other girls. She told them that the other girls had taken refuge in a certain cave. When the girls did not show up, the whole village went to the cave and to their surprise, saw only a massive rock. When they surrounded the rock, they heard the girls singing, calling for help, but alas, no one could venture with any sort of help.

The rock came to be known as *Mutsiyabako*, (the closed cave) and the whole area in which that rock stands is known by that name unto this day.

R. MASVABO
RESEARCH AREA: Unspecified
Two Girls and a Stinking Old Lady

A number of girls from a certain village went to look for grass brooms. One of the girls sat on a stone to rest briefly before going back home and became stuck to it. The other girls had to leave her on the stone when they went back home. When it was becoming dark, wild animals of all kinds came the girl's way. As they passed her, she greeted them all politely regardless of their size or ugliness.

Among the animals was a very old woman who was in rags and who was so dirty and stinking that she was accompanied by a swarm of flies. The girl greeted her politely and assisted her as she had difficulty in walking. When the old woman asked the girl to help remove lice from her head (which seemed never to have been washed before), she did so willingly. When it was time to sleep, she was asked whether she wanted to go and sleep with the animals or the old woman. The girl chose the old woman.

During the night, the girl had to endure sharing a tattered, stinking blanket with the old lady. In the morning all the animals were pleased with her behaviour, so they took her back home with many beautiful gifts. They went straight into the girl's bedroom and left all the wealth and the girl there.

When the girl's parents came home, they called their neighbours and celebrated. However, one of the neighbours envied these riches. As a result, they told their daughter to sit on the same stone which the other girl had sat on the next time they went looking for brooms. She did so and got stuck. When the animals came, she started passing rude comments and, worse still, when the old lady came, she acted even more disrespectfully. The girl studied the old lady from head to toe and then asked the old lady when she had last bathed. The girl refused to remove lice from the old woman's head out of fear that she would end up having them herself. As the old lady was having difficulties walking, she tried to lean on the girl, who responded by giving the old woman a violent push and telling her it was not her fault that she was old. When she was told to choose where to sleep, she chose the animals saying she could not see how she could spend the night with a stinking old lady.

The next morning the same procession of animals was seen moving towards the girl's home. Her excited parents began to ululate. The procession went straight to the girl's bedroom and then left. When the animals had gone, the parents rushed to the bedroom only to find the girl's head waiting for them on a mat. The girl had been eaten up by the animals for her bad behaviour.

PATRICK MARIMAZHIRA
RESEARCH AREA: Mt Darwin
The Spoiled Young Girl

The story which I am going to relate was told by Mbuya Muchakara, who is now ninety-one and a widow. She said the story was told to her by her vamwene (mother-in-law) whose mother was the instructor of girls when the story happened.

There was once a woman called vaHazvirebwi (unsayable) who was married to Ndambakuudzwa (one who claims to be all knowing and does not accept correction). The couple had only one daughter called Ndakaisvei (what wrong did I commit). Ndakaisvei was protected from any conflict by her parents. Thus, she grew to be a mature girl without learning either cultural norms or respect for other people.

One day Ndakaisvei was at a village well with other girls. They were eating *Matamba* (wild fruits) and Ndakaisvei was sucking the juice and throwing the residue into the well water. The other girls politely told Ndakaisvei not to throw anything in the well, but she would not listen to them. The girls finally took away the *Matamba* from her and threw it away. Ndakaisvei screamed, left the well and went home crying.

When Ndakaisvei reported these events to her mother, the mother went to the girls who were still at the well and scolded them in front of their parents, who remained silent. They knew vaHazvirebwi's behaviour, especially in matters concerning her daughter. Afterwards they told their children never to correct Ndakaisvei.

On another day, women from the same village organised a trip into the nearby Muteo forest to gather some mushrooms. They arranged that all the girls who were to accompany their mothers into the forest were to be given instructions prior to setting off. Among the girls who were to receive instructions was Ndakaisvei. When the old 'ambuya' (grandmother), who was the instructor, started mentioning characters which were not expected in the forest, Ndakaisvei thought that she was ironically referring to her. So she marched off and went home.

The following day they set off into the forest. Since it was Ndakaisvei's first time in the forest, she was excited and surprised to see so many different fruits and mushrooms. While others picked what they liked, Ndakaisvei ran from one fruit tree to another, testing some and throwing others away. She shouted comments like, 'Oh, I have eaten some rotten fruit!' or 'Oh, this place stinks!' or 'I see many inedible mushrooms!' Her companions ignored her as she passed these negative comments.

Ndakaisvei then saw a very big locust. When she attempted to catch it, it hopped from one place to another as if it were unable to fly. As she chased the locust, she became separated from the others. Finally, in frustration, she took a dry branch to smash it, but it flew away before she could do so.

When others gathered to go back home, Ndakaisvei was not there. Her mother shouted for her, but Ndakaisvei was nowhere to be found. Her mother threw away all the fruits and mushrooms she had collected and went away empty handed. And that was the end.

At the conclusion of the story, Mbuya Muchakara said, *'Zvamunoona, kamoto kamberevere kanopisa matanda mberi'* (As you see, a small fire can burn logs ahead) , which means, 'A small habit left uncontrolled may develop into a serious defect which disqualifies a person and does harm to the whole community'.

L. TAMBAMA
RESEARCH AREA: Chiduku Communal Lands, Rusape Area
The Men Who Stole Beer

About 50 kilometres from Rusape in Chiduku communal lands, there is a pool very deep and full of water from the Macheke River despite the fact that the river is dried up in this drought season. So I went to an elder to find out what was special about the pool. Here are the stories he told me about the pool which is said to be sacred.

Long ago, people respected their ancestor spirits. In terms of customs of the Shona people, no rule was breached so everything went well with them. There were no droughts or even epidemics as we see today. The spirits were so pleased with the people that when someone got hungry while away from home he would kneel down and ask the spirits to provide food, which they did. Every year people would brew beer for the spirits at a mountain near by this sacred pool called *Chibhacha* (meaning a small dish). According to the customs of the people, no one was allowed near that place for it was the home of the spirits.

Now it happened that one day four men from the village went and stole the beer from the pot. When the spirits came to drink beer there was none, so they became angry with the whole village. Their cattle started dying and the elders went out and enquired about it. When they learned of the theft of beer, the four men were called to the chief's court. The *n'anga* who was there advised the king and his people to pay the spirits fifty cattle, goats, fowl and other things. A number of children taken from various families would be used also as payment. The spirits would then remove any trouble from the village.

Under the advice of the *n'anga*, the chief and his people brewed beer and a date was set for the required payment caused by the crime the four had committed. The whole village went to the pool during the night prior to the ceremony. Cattle were killed and people ate and recited a poem to please the spirits. There was a moment of silence when the chief started talking while possessed by the village spirits. The four thieves were called up front. They pleaded guilty before the crowd. The judgement that followed was that they should be thrown into the pool as demanded by spirits. After they and all of their possessions were thrown into the pool, the voice of the spirit was heard. 'This is what I have to tell you from now onwards. This pool is now sacred, for the spirits will no longer live in the mountain but in this pool.' There was clapping of hands from the crowd and shouting. The voice continued: 'Here are the rules that you must follow. When you are here at this pool, no washing of clothes using soap must be done; no fishing, swimming or fetching of water using black pots and other utensils.'

People dispersed to their homes happily that justice had been done and that life could become normal again. When people had problems, they would go to the pool, clap hands in a customary way, and their problems would be solved by the spirits.

NKULULEKO MALABA

RESEARCH AREA: Madlambuzi Village, Matebeleland South

The Two Boys and the Spirit of Rain

This story was narrated to me by my grandmother.

Once upon a time, there were two brothers, one named Nkosikhona and the other Nkosikayikho. These two lived at Mabonyane village, somewhere in the remote communal lands of Matebeleland South. They lived with their mother who was the spirit of rain. Everyday, these two boys used to go out to a distant communal area, called Madlambuzi, where they used to raid and hunt domestic animals belonging to the people of Madlambuzi area. Nwafo, their mother, used to help them in carrying out their missions.

Whenever the two brothers went out for hunting, they used to cross many rivers. On many occasions, as they were returning, they were pursued by the people of Madlambuzi who were very much opposed to the plundering of their animals by these two boys. Whenever the fleeing brothers came to cross any river, they sang a song to their mother appealing for help. The older one, Nkosikhona, would start the song by singing this verse:

Mother, Mother, we are about to die.
Help us before it is too late.
Use your heavenly powers to save us.

Nkosikayikho, the younger one would then join him by also singing this verse:

You are the goddess of rain.
Send heavy rains to fill the river
so that we may not be caught and killed.

Their mother would then respond to their plea by bringing heavy rains which, after the boys had crossed, would fill the river and prevent their pursuers from catching them.

Thus the two boys, with their mother's support, spent much of their time hunting and killing domestic animals belonging to the people of Madlambuzi area. The people of Madlambuzi were greatly worried by what these two boys were doing. What worried them most was the fact that they were failing to catch these two boys and punish them for their wrongdoing. Moreover, the two brothers were even killing sacred animals dedicated to the spirits. Therefore, the elders of the village were compelled to capture the boys.

So one day, the elders of the village convened a meeting during the night to discuss their programme of action to catch the boys. One wise elder suggested that it was quite apparent that some spirit was behind the two boys. Therefore, it was necessary to consult a *n'anga* who would be charged with the task of finding out which spirit was actually helping the two boys so that an offering could be made to that particular spirit. All the elders agreed with what the speaker had said. Therefore, a trusted and well respected *n'anga* was consulted who advised them that Nwafu, the spirit of rain, was the two boys' helper. The *n'anga* went on to point out that the spirit was not prepared to accept any sacrifice from the people, because she was acting in the interest of her two beloved sons.

When the elders heard the *n'anga*'s advice, they were shocked, confused and they had no idea about what to do. In the meantime, the two boys with their mother's support continued raiding their domestic animals and killing many in large numbers. At last the elders thought that it was better to seek help from the Chief God, i.e Nkulunkulu. So the elders assembled all the villagers at a sacred hill. The people then performed a ritual of purification, after which, the chief and other *n'angas* went inside the Chief God's shrine to present their problems to him. Upon hearing the plight of the people, the Chief God was very angry and he at once decided to strip Nwafo of her powers.

In the morning of the following day, as usual the two brothers went out to Madlambuzi's village to hunt. After they had plundered as many animals as possible, the local people began to chase them. After they crossed a river, they started to sing their song appealing for help from their mother spirit. When there was no reply in the form of rains, they were shocked and started to panic. In the end, they were eventually caught by their pursuers, and ruthlessly murdered on the river bed. Their corpses were ill treated by the local people; for instance, they were dragged about, thrown into a shallow river crevice and covered with stones.

When Nkulunkulu realised that the people of Madlambuzi had been very inconsiderate by failing to honour the dead bodies of the two boys, he was filled with compassion for the boys. He raised the two boys' spirits from death. They became avenging spirits and bothered the people so much that they decided to consult a *n'anga* who advised them to prepare a proper burial and funeral rites for the boys. Once this was done, they all lived happily once more.

MUNYARADZI CHATIKOBO
RESEARCH AREA: Masvingo
The Story of the Foolish Woman (Mukadzi Fuza)

Mukadzi Fuza (Foolish Woman) is a story about a young woman who was foolish and irresponsible. Her life was characterised by fatal mistakes which in the end earned her an axe on the shoulder and a divorce.

The woman was married to a young man and they had three children, all of them boys. These people lived in a certain far away place. The woman was so irresponsible that she did not even wash herself. Her children were always dirty. The mother and the children only used water for drinking and cooking. It was only during the rainy season that water got the chance to touch their backs.

One day, after another woman complained severely to her about her uncleanliness, the woman took her children to the river for bathing. The first two boys took a bath on their own and went back home. The woman remained washing the little boy. As she washed the child, a wild pig unexpectedly emerged from the bush and swam across the river. The woman was so frightened that she frantically dropped the little boy into the pool to save her skin. She ran a few metres and then realised that she had no child. She ran back to the pool but the boy was nowhere to be found; he had drowned.

The woman screamed for help after a quick fruitless search. She came back to the pool with the other villagers only to find the little boy floating on the water dead. When the father of the child heard it, he was so furious that he nearly sent his wife to her parents.

After a month had passed, while the memories of the lost child were fading, another fatal incident took place. The woman took her first born child fishing. While they were fishing, the woman's hook stuck on something in the pool, probably a log. The woman who knew very well that her son could not swim asked him to get in and take out the hook. She also knew that the river was infested with crocodiles. As the boy reached into the water for the hook, he fell straight into the mouth of a crocodile and was devoured. This time only the intervention of the village headman kept her husband from sending the woman back to her parents.

The boy was buried and soon after the burial several *n'angas* were consulted to find out what was wiping out the family. All the *n'angas* blamed the woman. They said that the ancestors were not happy with the woman.

Another incident followed which touched the whole village. The woman went to fetch some water from the well. In the well she saw a frog. Thinking that the frog was spoiling the water she took it out and crushed it. The well instantly ran dry. She went back to the village with an empty pot and related to the people what had happened at the well. This time the kraalhead did not support her; he was angry with the woman. The well ran dry because the ancestor spirits were angered by the woman who killed an innocent creature.

The kraalhead later on asked the husband of the woman to go and tell the *Mhondoro* (territorial spirit) what had befallen the community. The spirit said to the man, 'You are a very lucky man. I could have done away with your wife long back. I have, however, forgiven her, but I want a black bull.' The man quickly arranged this and gave the bull to the spirit, after which everything came back to normal.

The woman was set before the village court where she was counselled. The other women of the village also helped her thinking that she should rectify her mistakes, but she did not reform. One day, she went into the bush with other women to search for mushrooms (*howa*). According to the customs, no one was allowed to speak ill of anything in the forest. Although she was aware of this regulation, she went on to say, 'This jungle is full of wild mushrooms'. The other women cautioned her and went on with their searching. The woman became confused; she could not tell where she came from nor where she was going. While searching for the others, she entered into a cave where she met three ghostly figures (*madzimudzangara*): a husband, wife and child. The child had a 'runny nose'. The foolish woman told the mother of this child that her child was dirty. The mother reacted angrily and gave the child to the foolish woman. 'Do you think I cannot see it? There he is. Take him for yourself!' The husband was also angry and he slapped the woman in the face.

Those who went back home reported the woman's disappearance to the kraalhead and to her husband. The following day the husband tried to search for the wife but all was in vain. After a lapse of a week, she came back home and told the people what had happened to her. The elders of the community further counselled her.

For some time, she appeared to have reformed. One day, she broke another custom. She made a collection of firewood which was not to be used for firewood. Instead of producing the fire, the wood simply smoked. This surprised the woman who called her next door neighbour who told her to take away the firewood because it was against the customs to use them.

Days passed, weeks, months and years. The family was slowly forgetting about the two lost children. Only one child was left. Since the boy was alone, he performed almost all the duties. One day, the woman asked the boy to go and look for vegetables in a certain area outside the village. The boy refused saying that there was a lion which was seen in that area. The mother said to him, 'Come on, it's only a *Mhondoro*'. The boy finally went and that was the end of his life. The lion devoured the boy only leaving his head and other small pieces of his body.

When the husband came back from the bush, he found people gathering at his place wailing in grief. The events of his last son's death were related to him. He became boiling with rage. He nearly killed his wife with an axe, but she was quickly saved by the crowd who restrained her husband. The kraalhead suggested that he quickly prepare some beer for the ancestors.

The burial of the child was completed. After a week, the wife, with the help of other elderly women, started preparing the beer. One day her husband went out hunting as usual. In the bush he started thinking deeply about his children. 'For whom am I hunting? All my boys are gone'. In anger the man went back to the village with the intention of killing his wife. At home he found the women busy on the fire. He headed straight for his wife. The other women seeing his intention started screaming, but that was of no use. He threw an axe at her with the intention of cutting off her head, but the axe missed her neck catching the woman on the shoulder.

The man realised that he had acted out of uncontrollable emotions. He ran away, but later returned and took the woman to her parents. This is the end of the story.

LAWRENCE MUSARIRI

RESEARCH AREA: Chivhu Communal areas (Daramombe)

The Selfish Father

The following tale was told to me by Mrs Juliet Sibanda, aged 60. She says it is one of the tales she enjoyed listening to from her own grandmother.

Once upon a time, there lived in a certain village a man, his wife and four children, all of whom were girls. It was during one of the worst drought affected years. The sun was hot and the land was so dry that it brought forth no food for the people to sustain themselves. The ancestors were angry.

One day the husband said to his wife, 'Mother of the children, today I am going out to hunt. I am going into a forest full of thorns and wild beasts and I pray that the spirits of my ancestors protect me.' She then clapped her hands and threw down some snuff on the floor saying: 'It is well, Father of the family, that you go out to hunt. May the ancestors protect you and give you something to feed the family.' The husband collected his small axe, his bow and arrow, and his bag made from sisal. He filled the bag with roasted maize grains (*maputi*), called his dogs and left.

In the forest, the husband wandered for most of the day without coming across even a solitary mouse. He was getting very tired and very thirsty. He then bumped into a *mukuyu* tree (baobab) with very strange leaves and only one *uyu* (baobab fruit) on it. When he tried to pluck the fruit, he could not pull it off the tree. Then a voice summoned him to sing a song whose words were:

Vadzimu vangu kuturura uyu
Masango ndeenyu kuturura uyu
Mwana ndiriwenyu kuturura uyu
Nzara mumusha kuturura uyu

(Literal translation)
My ancestors, I am to pluck off baobab
Forests are yours to pluck off baobab

I am your child to pluck off baobab
Hunger at home incites to pluck off baobab.

The song can be interpreted to mean, 'My ancestors, the forests are yours and I am your child and there is hunger in the family, which sends me to pluck off baobab.' At the end of the song, many fruits would fall to the ground and a gourd of water would be provided. But seeing the food the man forgot his family; he never even thought of bringing home a single baobab fruit. He decided to have the fruits entirely to himself.

Whilst the wife and children survived on wild roots and the little that they could beg from their neighbours, the husband claimed that he went out to hunt. Everyday he would take his weapons and go into the bush, but he never brought home any animal – not even a mouse. The most puzzling factor was that he was always satisfied. He would refuse the food his wife prepared for him and claim he was satisfied. This puzzled the wife and children until one day the wife decided to follow the husband to the forest and discover what kept him satisfied when the rest of them were dying. The wife saw and heard all her husband did to get himself food from the baobab tree. When the man had finished eating and was on his way back home, the wife got out from her hiding place and did as she had seen and heard her husband do. She brought the food home and gave it to the children to eat. On seeing this, the husband knew his secret source of food had been discovered. In anger he took his wife outside and chopped her to pieces with an axe.

The children began to sing a song:

Mai Vakafa Chamupirin'ini hungwe
VAKAFANEI? Chamupirin'ini hungwe
Guyu rababa Chamupirin'ini hungwe
(Literal translation)
Mother died.
What was the cause?
Father's baobab.

The entire song means, 'Mother died. She died for father's baobab fruits'. On hearing this song, the father became even more furious and killed all his daughters. He buried the whole family single handed.

The next morning he went into the bush to his tree and sang as usual but nothing fell from the tree. He sang the song over and over again but nothing fell. When he was about to leave for his home, a loud buzzing was heard and suddenly a swarm of bees attacked the man and killed him. His body was food for the vultures.

DAVID KUNYONGANA
RESEARCH AREA: Nyazura, Mutare
The Ugly Old Woman and Two Girls

In this essay I am recording a story that my grandmother told me. Traditionally, such stories were related in informal settings. The following story was narrated to me in Nyazura near Mutare.

A long time ago, girls used to go to bath together at the river. Girls in one particular village would gather at set times to go and bath as did the girls of the next village. Each girl had to wear beads (*zvuma*) around her neck. For girls at that time these were of great significance.

On a particular visit to the river, a girl named Chipo (gift) forgot her beads at the river. She only discovered this after the girls had almost arrived back in the village. Chipo then asked the other girls if they could accompany her back to the river to retrieve her beads. Each girl refused. Since the beads were so important, Chipo decided to return to the river alone. When she arrived back at the river, she saw an old woman on the very spot where she had placed the beads. Chipo looked around, but could not find the beads. The old woman was poorly dressed, dirty and miserable. Politely and respectfully, Chipo asked the old woman whether by any chance she had seen her beads. 'Yes, my child,' the old woman replied, 'but before I give them to you, could you first of all wash my body?' Chipo agreed. She scrubbed her back and removed all the layers of dirt that had accumulated on the old woman.

By the time she had finished bathing the woman, it was getting dark so that it was dangerous for Chipo to walk home. The old woman invited her to spend the night at her home. Chipo thus accompanied the old woman to her home which was right in the middle of a thick forest.

Early in the morning, the old woman asked Chipo to go to the river to fetch water. Chipo was surprised that the pot the woman gave her in which to collect the water was the skull of a person. Chipo was a courageous girl and thus went to the river to fetch water with the skull pot.

The old woman then asked her to crush groundnuts so as to make peanut butter. Politely, she obeyed and carried out the order. To check whether she had eaten any of the groundnuts, the old woman took the bark of a tree and placed it on Chipo's tongue. Nothing like groundnuts was stuck on her tongue. The old lady was convinced that Chipo had not stolen any groundnuts.

The old woman then gave Chipo back her beads saying that she was an honest and well behaved girl. As a reward for her honesty, the old woman gave her many presents to take home. These included goats, cows and beads. Two lions were summoned to accompany her home and were instructed not to eat her up. The lions were to leave her and the presents at the door of her mother's hut. When she reached home, her parents were very happy to see her and thanked her for the things she had brought. From that time onward, Chipo's family lived happily and they became very rich.

When the other girls heard of these events, they were surprised. One of the girls planned to leave her beads at the river so that she could come back with wealth just as Chipo had done. When the girls went to the river to bath, Tarisai (look) deliberately left her beads at the river. After they had walked a rather long distance, Tarisai told the other girls that she was returning to retrieve the beads she had forgotten at the river.

On arrival at the river, she saw the old, dirty, smelly, poorly dressed woman at the place she had left the beads. Tarisai asked whether she had seen her beads. The old woman said, 'Yes, but could you first of all wash me?' The girl refused and harshly shouted that it was not her business to wash a filthy old woman. She simply wanted her beads. The old woman then invited Tarisai to her hut for the night. Seeing it was now dark, she decided to go with her. Early in the morning the woman asked Tarisai to go and fetch water in the skull pot. Tarisai refused and accused the old woman of killing a person. The old woman then asked her to crush groundnuts. Tarisai did this work so roughly that most of the groundnuts fell on the ground. Tarisai was asked to put the bark of a tree on her tongue to test whether she was eating some of the groundnuts. The old woman discovered that she had enjoyed some of the groundnuts.

Lions were summoned to eat Tarisai. The old woman then sent the two lions to Tarisai's home with her bones, skull and bloody clothes in a basket. The lions left the basket on the door of her parent's hut. When Tarisai's mother saw the basket, she thought her daughter had returned and that she was somewhere around. So she was happy since she was the one who encouraged Tarisai to leave her beads in order to obtain wealth just like Chipo's family. When Tarisai's mother decided to open the basket, she realised that her daughter had died. Her happiness suddenly changed to sorrow.

MARION MASEVA
RESEARCH AREA: Chief Chitsa's Village, Gutu District
The Story of Matirasha: A Foolish Woman

Many years ago in Chief Chitsa's village, which is found in Gutu District, there was a woman named Matirasha (one abandoned). This woman was so ill-mannered that her in-laws hated her even on the first day of her married life. Unfortunately, she was one of the chief's wives and the chief was always disgraced because of how his wife behaved. She was a woman who virtually could not live according to custom.

One day Matirasha and the other village women went into the forest to collect *mazhanje* (loquats). The other women were tasting the fruits but remaining silent. However, when Matirasha came to a tree whose fruits were sour she exclaimed, 'Ah, does this forest have no other type of *mazhanje* except bitter ones?' The other women were surprised that she could not just keep silent as demanded by custom. That very day Matirasha just disappeared and, although the other women called her many times, she did not come. Early in the next morning, however, Matirasha arrived back in the village. The chief reprimanded her and she promised to behave in the future.

Scarcely before a week had passed, Matirasha got into more mischief. She had gone to fetch water from the well, but noticed some frogs lying on top of the water. She used her clay water pot to remove the frogs from the well saying, 'These frogs are the ones who make our water not very tasteful'. She then killed the frogs and immediately the well dried up. This caused her to cry. Some of the villagers noticed this and asked what had happened. After she had explained, the chief rebuked her for doing such things. She was made to pay a goat for the village to regain its water. The chief threatened to divorce her saying she was disgracing him before his subjects but Matirasha begged forgiveness and vowed that she could behave well.

However, not long afterwards Matirasha committed another serious offence. She and the other women were coming home from the forest where they had gone to collect firewood. It was quite a long way and between the village and the forest there was a big mountain called

181

Marimuka which was so high and long that it prevented the women from going home by the shortest route. They had to walk along the mountain till they came to its end where they could then find their way home. When they had walked a few metres along the mountain, Matirasha exclaimed, 'To think that I could have been already at home had it not been for this ugly mountain which blocks my way!' After she said this, Matirisha disappeared without the other women even noticing.

That night the spirits of the mountain severely haunted Matirasha. She could hear the voice of a lion roaring just behind her and then she would run away trying to escape, thinking that she was on her way to the village. It was only after she had run for a long time that she discovered that the huge, magnificent and mysterious object before her was Marimuka, the mountain. And the voice of the roaring lion had drawn even nearer.

Two weeks after Matirasha's disappearance, the chief decided to consult a *n'anga*. He was told about the plight of Matirasha and was advised that if he wanted her back, he should take a black cow to the mountain and leave it there. The chief did as he was counselled and Matirasha returned.

After this frightening experience at the mountain, Matirasha appeared to have gained more moral stature. A whole year passed without her doing anything against custom and the traditional ways of living. One day, Matirasha and another village woman went to a river to bath. Suddenly, there was a slight wind and the woman whom Matirasha was with gradually sank into the water till she disappeared. Matirasha just laughed at the woman and later told the other villagers that the woman was careless and had made herself slip into the deep river after a slight wind had occurred. But the villagers knew from the description that the woman had been taken by a *njuzu*.

When the woman arrived in the underwater world, the *njuzu* gave her dried houseflies and worms as food and she accepted them. She was also fed with mud. The *njuzu* was pleased with the way she behaved and she was given a lot of beads with which to adorn herself and also colourful cloths to wrap around her body together with every type of medicine.

Meanwhile, the relatives of the woman were advised not to weep because if they did so their relative would not be released by the *njuzu*. They consulted a *n'anga* and were told that they should take a black, spotless cow to the river and leave it there. They did so and the cow also sank into the river.

After a few days the woman came back as a powerful *n'anga*. She was honoured in the village because of her new position. She received many gifts from the people she treated who came from all the surrounding villages and even from other countries.

Meanwhile, Matirasha became intensely jealous of the woman. She decided to go to Mutizamombe (the name of the river) alone but she told nobody about her intentions.

In the same way the woman had been taken, Matirasha was also taken by the *njuzu*. However, Matirasha was without dignity and was ill-mannered. When she was given the same food as the other woman, she exclaimed, 'How can I eat worms, and houseflies and mud?' She also pestered the *njuzu* to provide her quickly with medicines because she had other important business at home.

Matirasha's relatives did all that the other woman's relatives had done. But unfortunately the *n'anga* told them that Matirasha had been killed by the *njuzu*. The *njuzu* could not make her into a *n'anga* nor convert her into another *njuzu* because of her offensive and rude behaviour. That was the end of the story.

MARTIN GAMBIZA
RESEARCH AREA: Chirumanzu, Masvingo Province
The Mysterious Bird

In my attempt to do this work I did not have to look far for an elder. What I did was to go home (Chirumanzu-Masvingo) and meet my grandfather - Mr Jonny Mudzingwa Gambiza - aged about 88. He is still energetic though his eyes are giving him problems. When I got to him he was doing some manual work with his axe. After I explained to him my mission, we went home and sat outside where he narrated to me the stories he said were told to him by his grandfather years ago. Of these I now record the one I found most interesting and educative.

Mr Bhogodo was married to Tombi and they had six children, all of them girls. They both longed to have a son, since having a boy is important for the continuation of the family name and also for inheritance purposes.

For their fifth (Chipo) and sixth (Kudakwashe) daughters, they had consulted *n'angas* who had assured them of a baby boy on both occasions. Since they expected a boy, they were perplexed and disappointed when the girls were born. After the birth of Kudakwashe, they did not bother to consult a *n'anga* because they considered them ineffective.

Pressure was coming from most of Bhogodo's family members, who insisted that he marry another wife so as to beget a son. Bhogodo discussed this with Tombi. Though they both were of a negative attitude towards the whole issue, Tombi was more against it than Bhogodo. However, they agreed that they would not listen to what people were saying. When Kudakwashe was six years old, Tombi became pregnant. Four months into the pregnancy, Bhogodo promised his wife that if she gave birth to a baby boy he would give her something she would never forget.

When Tombi was eight months pregnant, she was taken to a midwife who lived one day's walk away. Before Bhogodo returned home the next day, he reminded Tombi of his promise. He also told her that he would return to collect her and the child in six weeks.

When her time was due, Tombi gave birth to a handsome baby boy. On hearing that the baby was male, she cried tears of joy. She had never been so happy in her life. She named the baby Farai, which means 'rejoice'. All the fears that Bhogodo might marry a second wife disappeared. She could not wait to show her husband their son and also to be given her gift. Thus, she packed her *tswanda* (basket) and *nhava* (bag) and made off two days before the day she had agreed to meet Bhogodo.

Tombi had the *tswanda* on her head, the *nhava* on her shoulder and Farai on her back. On her way she was all smiles. At that moment she really thought she was the happiest mother alive. All she was thinking of was the joy her husband would have at seeing that the baby was male.

About an hour's walk from her home where she planned to surprise her husband with their new baby boy, Tombi saw a beautiful bird. The bird was injured on its left wing and hence could not fly. It was so beautiful that she was decided to catch it.

Tombi diverted from the road and went into the bush in her attempt to catch the bird. After travelling a short distance into the bush in pursuit, she realised that the *tswanda* was a burden to her efforts, hence, she threw it down with the hope of picking it up later. As she drew closer to the bird, it increased its speed. She then dropped the *nhava* to improve her chances of catching the bird. At one moment she almost caught it and this in turn increased her determination.

She then untied Farai from her back and placed him next to a tree and continued with her pursuit. Her mind at that moment was pre-occupied by the bird and no longer by the joy her husband would have when he saw Farai. Tombi pursued the bird but her effort was futile. She was tired and exhausted and thus she gave up and sat down. She then realised that she had spent the whole afternoon chasing the bird. After resting for awhile, Farai came into her mind and suddenly she jumped up and back-tracked in the hope of finding him. Unfortunately, she went in the wrong direction. As darkness fell, she realised that she had lost almost everything: the baby boy, her luggage, the promised gift and, worse still, she had been unable to catch the beautiful bird. The question which rang in her mind was, 'What explanation am I going to give to my husband?' This question haunted her for a long time, but still she could not come up with a plausible answer.

TIMOTHY SANGO

RESEARCH AREA: Honde Valley, Eastern Zimbabwe

The Story of the Foolish Wife

In the village of Mr. Sadunhu, lived Mr. Rema with his wife Revesai and their three sons. Mr. Rema's wife was the most foolish woman ever found in the village and even beyond. She neither respected any man nor the spirits. It happened one year that there was a terrible drought that had threatened both human and animal lives. One day, Mr. Rema's wife went to a nearby river and began plucking a certain plant that was growing by the river banks. Among the villagers, such a plant was known to be inedible. Anyone who eats of that plant will die or have a terrible illness and only survive by the grace of the ancestors. After filling her basket, Revesai went home. Early in the evening, she began preparing the supper. After the food was ready, she called her family and they began eating.

As they were eating, one of the sons choked on the plant. Mr. Rema and his wife tried all means to help the child but to no avail and eventually he passed away. The next day, Mr. Rema, his wife and their remaining two sons began suffering from a terrible illness from which it took them three weeks to recover with the help of a *n'anga* (traditional healer) named Godobare. They were told by the *n'anga* that tradition forbade eating of that particular plant.

Some months passed and Revesai brought home a bunch of firewood. Among the firewood was some of the wood that is not supposed to be used as firewood. She placed the forbidden wood in the hearth to make some fire, but it would not light. She applied all different methods but it did not materialise. She even went to fetch some burning charcoal from a nearby woman, but the charcoal was extinguished when it came into contact with the wood. She later called her neighbour and explained to her what was happening. Her neighbour discovered that at the fire hearth there was some of the firewood that was not supposed to be used. She pulled the wood out and the fire started. When Mr. Rema heard this, he was almost boiling with rage. He almost divorced his wife, but the village elders told him not to do so.

Then one day during the summer season in the afternoon Revesai went to the village well to fetch water. When she arrived at the well, she saw a big frog in the well busy swimming. This frustrated her. She pulled the frog out of the well and in a rage crushed it with a big stone. As soon as the frog died, the water in the well disappeared and the well was left dry. The woman was not worried and she took her empty bucket and headed homeward. On the way home, Revesai met the chief's wife and explained to her what had happened at the well. The chief's wife told her that she had committed a great offence to the ancestor spirits who would need to be reconciled to the community for the water to come back. When Mr. Rema heard about this issue, he almost axed Revesai but once again the village elders comforted him. Mr. Rema was then told by the spirit medium that he should pay a black bull and a black cock to the ancestors, otherwise the spirits would destroy the whole family. Fortunately, Mr. Rema had the required things and he paid causing the water to return and fill the well as before. The chief told Revesai not to repeat the same mistake, otherwise she would be victimised by being a prey to the *Mhondoro* (lion, representing the senior ancestor spirits). On top of that, she was ordered to brew beer to the spirits in order to cool down their anger and ask for forgiveness.

Days, months and years passed without anything happening to the wife of Mr. Rema so that everybody in the village thought she had reformed. Even her husband was pleased with her and promised her a present for the good way in which she was controlling herself. However, it happened one day in the summer season that the women in the village, including Revesai, went to a nearby forest to fetch some mushrooms. As the women were scattered in the forest, Revesai came across some mushrooms which were inedible and she began to despise them and shouted out that they were poisonous. Suddenly, she began wandering about in the forest aimlessly and became lost. When the other women realised that she was missing, they were shocked. They began calling her name and looking for her, but they could not find her. They went home and told her husband and the chief. The next day the villagers searched for her, but they never found her. After a week, they went to consult the *n'anga* Godobare who instructed them to brew beer for the ancestors in order that Revesai might return home. When the beer was brewed and appeals were made to the ancestors, she returned home and immediately was divorced by her husband who was given her young sister for a replacement.

BESSIE GAUCHI
RESEARCH AREA: Chiendambuya in Rusape

Four Jealous Girls and a Baby

I interviewed an elder whose name is Sekuru Chieza. His original home area is found in Rusape in Chiendambuya but he is now living in the western part of Mutare. Indeed, he was very happy to be interviewed and told the story enthusiastically.

Once upon a time, there lived five girls in a certain village. These girls were very close associates and they had grown together since childhood. There was no secret between them, each one was free and happy to tell the other about their experience. So one day Chioneso broke the news to her friends that she was pregnant and she was to be married very soon. Chioneso expected her friends to be happy and join her in her joy but she was surprised. Her friends were not pleased; she discovered that they were jealous.

After Chioneso gave birth, the four other girls would inflict pain on the baby by pinching it. Musekiwa, who was the most jealous of all, even went so far as to give the baby some poisonous water. She put some herbs in the water, which she had obtained from a local *n'anga*. This did not hurt the baby because soon after drinking it, the baby spit out the water. The baby had been clothed with what they call in Shona *'dumwa'* to protect it from any dangers. When this failed, Fumiso, one of the jealous girls, suggested that she take the child to the river and throw it into the water. But they did not know how to get hold of the baby long enough to take it to the river. So one day, when they had finished bathing, they had a swimming race. At first Chioneso refused since she wanted to take care of her child. Musekiwa, however, persuaded her that no harm would come to the baby. Chioneso thus left her child on top of the water while they went swimming. Soon the baby sank beneath the water and began to drown. Chioneso looked back to see her baby, but she was no where in sight. She screamed for Musekiwa to find the child and began to cry.

Chioneso went home in a frantic state. When her parents asked her where the child was, she began crying and told them the whole story. Her parents were angry and told Chioneso's husband, who was equally angry. He said he wanted his child. The next morning Chioneso could not be found. The husband went to consult the local *n'anga* who told him that Chioneso had gone to search for the child in the river. He took his *gona* (horn) and went to the pool and looked for his family. He met his wife who was still worried since she had not found the child.

They went under the water, right to the bottom, and there they met a water spirit (*njuzu*) and asked if it had found a child. The water spirit said it had seen the child and beckoned the parents to follow it. They went deep down and reached a place which was just like it is on the surface. The spirit said the child was in one of the caves. The husband asked the horn and it directed him to the correct cave and they were given their child.

The *njuzu* asked the family if they would stay till the child had grown older. The parents did not want to do this. So when the *njuzu* had gone to catch fish and water creatures, the family climbed into the horn.

186

When it had returned from catching fish, it was furious thinking that the family was not still there. The *njuzu* searched the whole pool but could not find them. When it was tired of searching, it came back angry and furious. It then noticed the horn and thought that the family had gone but had forgotten their horn. It thus picked up the horn and threw it out of the water. On landing on the surface, the family got out of the horn and went home happily

The people at home suggested that they should go and consult a *n'anga* to determine if there was any need for a purification ritual. The *n'anga* advised and instructed them to have a cleansing ritual and to honour the ancestor spirits who had brought them back home safely.

KUDAKWASHE MAVENEKE
RESEARCH AREA: Buhera
Two Mischievous Boys

It is widely accepted that the views held by the Shona on the creation of the world are very closely linked with their belief in a High God who is called Mwari or Nyadenga or Musiki. The idea of God as the creator both of the world and of man finds numerous expressions in stereotyped prayers and sayings. The Shona believe that some outstanding objects, such as mountains, are associated with God. The tribe of Dzoto in Buhera views or speaks of the Gwetembo Mountain with almost poetic enthusiasm. According to Sekuru Zvirokwazvo, the Dzoto people maintain that people should not misuse anything in the Gwetembo Mountain since it is a dwelling place of God and ancestor spirits. Sekuru Zvirokwazvo's story is related below.

Once upon a time, when the world had come to life, when our tribe and the tribe of Mugomba lived together around the Gwetembo Mountain, the God of the living and the ancestor spirits were angry at the people of the land. The people were becoming rich and were not practising the traditions of the elders. People were drinking too much, children did not respect their parents and the cattle were not well kept. The elders warned that punishment from the Most High was imminent, and the people were to be ready to take the punishment.

It had been raining heavily at the night of the full moon, with furious thunder and lightning. The birds were silent, not even the brave lion roared, let alone the silly hyena who feels he must cry every night. There was a feeling that the world was coming to an end. Suddenly the rain stopped and the clouds were no longer seen and the moon was bright. It was a strange coincidence that these two events happened at the same time.

There were various sacred animals living in Gwetembo Mountain, such as buffaloes, elephants, lions, rhinos and hippos. The Shona people regard these animals as symbolising the ancestors. They should not be hunted and anyone who violates this, might encounter misfortunes, experience bad dreams or get lost in the forest.

In this mountain there are some sacred trees such as the fig-tree, sycamore and baobab and they are used for religious purposes. The trees are not supposed to be chopped down. The tribes of Dzoto and

Mugomba believe that while on the mountain the people should not make noise, since their noise would disturb the sleeping spirits. If you happen to walk through the Gwetembo at sunset, you might see some fires of the spirits all over the mountain. In seeing this, your hair will stiffen, your body pours with cold sweat, your heart beats madly. You may hear various sounds like voices and drums beating but you will not see the origin of voice and sounds.

On the morning following the night they had received strange rainfall almost simultaneously with the moonlight, two mischievous sons of the Dzoto tribe, Tapiwa and Tongesai, drove cattle into the mountain. As they were in the mountain they started to misuse some pots which contained grains of rapoko and they were using disrespectful words. Just adjacent to the grave of the eldest Dzoto there were pots, some with groundnuts, roundnuts, rapoko and one with beer. Tongesai and Tapiwa helped themselves, since they were hungry.

At the same time as Tongesai and Tapiwa were misusing the pots, another elder member of Dzoto family named Muchaererwa was busy chopping the fig tree which was near a pool in the Gwetembo Mountain. After cutting down the tree, he carried the logs away. At sunset Tongesai and Tapiwa tried to drive the cattle down the mountain so that they could go home, but they failed to do so. As they were trying to drive the cattle, goats and sheep down the mountain, the animals started to run into the caves.

Tongesai and Tapiwa followed the animals into the caves, where they stayed for about four days. The elders of both tribes of Dzoto and Mugomba climbed the mountain to look for the boys. They found the animals and tried to drive them out of the caves but they failed. As they passed by the pool Gandanzara, Muchaererwa, who had cut down the fig tree, saw it as it was before chopping. He was so shocked that he fell down and died on the spot. The Dzoto and Mugomba people fell to their knees. One of the elders shouted, 'This is a serious warning to us. To be forewarned is to be forearmed.'

The elders rushed down the mountain and consulted a *n'anga* called Sibira for the programme of action to be taken. Sibira said, 'Your children and animals will be safe if you perform the prescribed rituals. Muchaererwa died because he had disobeyed the ancestor spirits and the High God by cutting down the sacred tree.' On hearing this, the people performed the rituals and carried away the dead body of Muchaererwa. On the same day Tongesai and Tapiwa came home safely with the cattle, sheep and goats.

STORIES OF MYSTERIOUS OCCURRENCES

SHEPHERD NYAMUNOKORA
RESEARCH AREA: Honde Valley, Eastern Highlands
A Girl and the Njuzu

The following story is said to refer to events which occurred long ago before the advent of the first white men. I was told the story by a certain very old man who is living in Hama, Honde Valley.

A long time ago, there were four girls from a small village who went out on a fruit gathering spree in the Mutarazi Falls area which is part of Mahwemasimike and Nyangani mountains. On top of the Mutarazi River was a very sacred pool called *Chirikuutsi* (the pool that smokes), which was surrounded by a thick forest containing all kinds of wild fruit trees.

During those days, forests and mountains and rivers were thought to be controlled by natural forces; therefore, there were laws of nature in operation which had to be observed. As these girls were picking up fruits of all kinds, they came across the *mishuku* (loquat) trees. They were very surprised that some of these trees had human-like breasts. One of the girls could not keep the amazement to herself. She told the other girls about such an extraordinary sight, but the other girls just kept quiet.

Suddenly, the area was transformed into a very dark forest at midday. This was followed by a very strong whirlwind which was so powerful that it uprooted shrubs and small trees. In the midst of this whirlwind was heard a beating-drum and a whistle. The girls were shocked and frightened. The tried to run but could not manage because their legs became very heavy. They were swallowed by the mysterious whirlwind for about twenty minutes. When the whirlwind ceased, the three girls found that their friend, who had commented on breastlike trees, had disappeared. They then ran away with the thought that their friend had also run away.

When they reached home and discovered that their friend was nowhere to be found, they were very frightened. They were so afraid that they did not even report the incident to the parents of their friend. But as night came and as the girls were asleep in their huts, a daylight bird of a rare species came to them. It whistled all night long until dawn when it finally disappeared. This prompted the girls to report the fate of their friend to her parents. They related the incident of the day before to the parents and grandparents of the girl. As old people, they did not show any expression of fear but just said that the girl had gone to a relative somewhere.

When the girls had left, the parents of the girl agreed to consult a *n'anga* about the mystery. They visited a *n'anga* who lived some distance away from their village. There they were told that their child (the girl) was taken by a *njuzu* (a water spirit) because she had failed to recognise the laws of nature. She had been taken to the sacred pool of Chirikuutsi. The *n'anga* affirmed that the girl was still alive. The parents were strictly commanded not to shed any tears for their child in case she might be killed. In addition, they were told to brew beer to appease the angry spirits of the pool and forest or else they would be required to pay with the blood of the girl.

The parents kept what the *n'anga* told them to themselves and they performed the prescribed rituals. Despite having done all these things the girl did not return. Stories were told of people observing the girl sitting every morning on a reed mat (*rukukwe*) on top of the deep sacred pool of Chirikuutsi with beads of all metals around her. If a person approached her, she would disappear, or the person would also mysteriously disappear.

It then happened that after about five years had elapsed, the girl was finally brought back by the *njuzu*. Her mother saw her sitting on the

189

cross-path (*mharadzano*) with beads of all kinds around her neck and waist. She carried with her all kinds of objects used by a *n'anga* such as gourds of oil, roots, lots (*hakata*), a tail of a lion, a *ngundu* (hat) and many other objects. By custom such a person was not supposed to be greeted. The mother just told the most senior elders of the family. A *n'anga* was consulted to carry out the rituals of bringing this girl into the fold of the family after so many years of absence.

When the girl was finally brought into the family, she related what had happened to her while she was away. She said she had been made into a very skilful *n'anga* by the water spirits and that she had been released in order to help the people with their spiritual and physical ailments. She was to return occasionally to the *njuzu* to collect medicinal herbs which could not be found in the visible world.

After this, traditional beer was brewed to welcome the new *n'anga* home and to thank the family ancestors and the spirits of the invisible world for their care and protection.

CHARLES KATANDIKA

RESEARCH AREA: Nyangani Mountains

The Mystery on Nyangani Mountain

In 1961 my father-in-law Stephen Mutetwa, Phenias Mandipaza, Nhamo Nyagato and Peter Nyagadza were coming home in Nyamaropa from Honde Valley where they worked in the tea plantations. The path they took passed through the famous, feared, sacred and holy Nyangani Mountain. On their way they experienced many mysterious things, like noises which they did not know where they were coming from. The trees were densely populated in most parts of the mountain so that it nearly prevented them from seeing the sky.

As they were passing through the mountain, they saw many traditional utensils like wooden plates and cups, cooking sticks and clay pots. Some of the clay pots were about one and a half metres tall and were closed by heavy lids. It was from these pots that noises of people talking and children crying could be heard. Some of the clay pots were shaking as if there were things inside struggling to free themselves.

Birds and wild animals appeared as if they were domestic ones: eagles, Zimbabwe birds, crows and doves came and landed on their shoulders and heads as they were moving past. The four men held themselves together and never irritated these birds by pushing them off or passing insulting remarks because they had all heard of a story of a man who was attacked to death by a Zimbabwe Bird.

The animals too were quite funny and provocative. Their fearlessness is quite uncommon among wild animals. Monkeys and baboons made funny noises in the tree branches above their head. Some descended from the trees and walked on their twos in front of the four men as if they were leading the way. As they proceeded, they came across heaps of small stones and leaves to which each of them added his own stone and leaf.

Along the path as they were walking, a small greyish animal fell from the trees ahead of them and remained static as if it were dead, but after a few seconds it woke up, shook itself and moved in the path ahead lispingly. My father-in-law Stephen Mutetwa and Phenias Mandipaza, who had thought it to be a rotten branch of a tree, laughed but the other two remained silent. As they were laughing, the animal seemed violated, stood still and looked them straight into the eyes and made a loud shriek before disappearing into the bush.

Before long, a dark cloud gathered above them and heavy rain began to fall. To their surprise the areas around them were in sunshine and dust could be seen as animals jumped around. The heavy rain was soon accompanied by mist which was so dense that the four no longer knew where they were going. Stephen remembered an earlier incident when he accompanied a delegation to look for a white family which had not returned from a tour of the mountain. Before the delegation embarked on their search they placed tobacco on a leaf under a tree at the foot of the mountain and asked the ancestors to free the family. They apologised that the family might have violated the customs and traditions of the mountain because they were foreigners who were ignorant and unfamiliar with local customs. The search ended up in vain because the delegation never saw any sign or footprints which might have led to the rescue of the family.

The family returned after a week and testified, to the surprise of everyone, that they had seen the search party but failed to call them for rescue because their throats seemed blocked and they were speechless. They were wandering in the mountain without any sense of having been lost and they were surviving on wild fruits. When they were asked why they stayed there for so long, they answered that a voice was always telling them that it was not yet time for them to return. They wandered aimlessly around the mountain not knowing where they were going because they had not the slightest suspicion that they were lost.

Stephen was quick to link the mysterious story of the white family and the situation they were now in and saw that they had done something wrong. He asked his companions to sit down under a tree, unrolled a Madison cigarette and placed the tobacco on a leaf. They all squatted down and observed a few seconds of dead silence after which they appealed to the ancestors for forgiveness, for the wrong they had done, out of ignorance as young men. After confession they resumed their journey, the heavy rain subsided and it became blazingly hot, but they were still shivering of cold.

When they reached the village on the other side of the mountain, they were still feeling very cold despite the hot sun and they were frightened to the extent of being speechless. The elder at the homestead straight away read from their faces and concluded that something unpleasant had happened to the young men. He made them a fire to warm themselves up whilst the women prepared food. When they had finished eating, the elder asked them what had happened for them to wear such sad faces. After their narrative, the elder thanked them for realising their mistake early and for asking for forgiveness in the right manner, but warned them to avoid such risky paths which were full of temptations in future.

MARTIN MUKOSERA
RESEARCH AREA: Marange North
Strange Events on Makomwe Mountain
In a place called Nyagundi there is a mountain called Makomwe which, according to Sekuru Kufakwatenzi, and all the inhabitants of this area,

is sacred (rinoyera). Looking at the mountain from the western end, it resembles a crocodile basking in the sunshine. There is a very big pool on the mountain which does not dry up even in times of worst drought. Because of its height, it is very difficult to reach the summit of this mountain. According to Sekuru Kufakwatenzi, many cattle and other domestic animals have gone on the mountain for its green pastures and water, but they never came back. By now they have multiplied to big numbers and some have been eaten by wild animals. It is said when the rains are about to come, a fire starts on its own from the highest peak of the mountain. Sekuru Kufakwatenzi related a story about the mountain which was told to him by his grandfather.

Long back, before the arrival of the whites, a group of men went up this mountain. On their way up, they met certain things which they had never seen in their lives. They even heard voices talking and laughing, but they never saw anyone. As they continued to climb, they met a lion (*mhondoro*) but still they continued with their journey. As they moved further, they met a troop of baboons, which started fighting among themselves before disappearing into the forest. All of these occurrences were signs warning the men that they had entered a prohibited place without permission of the elders of the place. According to traditional custom they should have gone back immediately, but they were determined to go to the top of the mountain.

Suddenly, the men were enveloped by complete darkness, even though it was in the middle of the day. Eventually, they lost track of where they had come from and where they were going.

After the great darkness, there came an immense mist which covered the whole mountain. In this confusion, the men decided to return. But instead of getting down the mountain, they spent seven days just going around it, all the while thinking they were descending. Despite their lack of progress, the men felt fit and strong. They never felt hungry or thirsty, even though they had not eaten or drunk anything for days.

Eventually, the men began to disappear one by one into the unknown. Only two, who suddenly came to their senses, found their way home. But something mysterious had happened to each of them. One of them realised that his hair, which was black during the journey, had turned grey like that of a very old man. The other one, who began the journey with a full head of hair, had gone bald.

Only one of the five who disappeared ever returned. This one was taken by a *njuzu* (water spirit) which dwelt in a pool on the mountain. He returned after many years in the pool as a *n'anga* and became an important diviner and healer in the region.

J. MUTSHE
RESEARCH AREA: Khalanga regions of southwestern Zimbabwe
The Poor Herd-Boy

Long long ago among the Khalanga community there lived a boy who lost his parents and had no relatives. During this time there was a serious famine which claimed countless human lives and there was a massive death of cattle and livestock in general. The poor, unfortunate boy had nowhere to live and nothing to eat. As a result he took his two herding sticks (*svimbo*) which his late father had left behind and set off to find a job as a herd boy.

Wherever he went, people did not like him; he was chased away and ridiculed at the same time. At last, the boy came across the home of a childless couple. Since the man had no children, he herded his own cattle. When the boy told the couple that he needed a job and would herd their cattle, the couple refused explaining that there was no need to have a herd-boy as there was no rainfall and no grass for the cattle to feed on. When the poor boy patiently revealed his situation to the couple, they felt very sympathetic to him and agreed to offer him the job.

The following day, the man went with the boy to the forest to show him where the animals were supposed to feed and drink. The place had become a desert; there was not even a blade of grass and what the cattle drank was pure mud. The boy realised how pathetic the situation was. The following day, after the boy was shown the place, he was told to join his age-mates and go to the bush to herd cattle. The boy decided not to join the other boys; he wanted to take his herd to the mountains, although the water problem there was also severe. No one wanted to take his animals to that place and this man was no exception. But after an argument with the boy, the man conceded. The boy humbly took his herd and two knobkerries (*svimbo*) to the far mountains.

When the boy reached this lonely mountainous area, he left the cattle at the bottom of the mountain and climbed the mountain. At the peak of the mountain the boy lay on his back and faced the sky. He took his two sticks (*svimbo*), beat them together loudly and started singing. The *svimbo* produced a uniform, systematic and continuous sound. The song he sang goes like this:

Heliya gole, ngalihe pana
Liya heliya, ngalihe pano

(There is a cloud, let it come here!
There it is, there it is, let it come here!)

Suddenly, while the boy was still singing and beating his *svimbo*, roaring thunder was heard and blinding lightning was seen. Rain poured heavily and there was enough water to sustain the herd. The rain was confined to a small area around the mountain where the boy's herd could feed and drink. The boy's cattle became more healthy and fat than any other in the community. People were dazzled with this and began to ask the owner of the herd various dubious questions.

The man then asked the boy what had happened, but the boy would not tell him. One day the man decided to follow the boy without his knowledge. He trailed the boy till he reached the mountains. He then hid himself somewhere behind the rocks. The boy, as usual, sang his song, beat together his herding *svimbo* and the rain fell heavily drenching the man who had been hiding. The man slipped off without the boy's notice and rushed home to break the news to the traditional Chief and other common men.

The boy was called to the Chief's court (*idale*) where he was persuaded to perform his miracle for the benefit of the entire community. At first, the boy refused but later he agreed. He performed the same action there in the Chief's homestead as he had done at the mountain. The rain poured day and night for a period of seven days. Everything came back to life.

During the days when the boy was herding cattle for his master, he secretly wove a very long rope whose beginning and end no one knew or could know. The rope was so long that it could overlap to other neighbouring tribes. When the rain had stopped, the boy threw his rope up into the air and climbed up it into the sky. When he was up in the sky, he shouted orders, commanding the earth to form rivers and it did. Such big rivers as Limpopo, Zambezi, Gwayi and Mzingwane were formed and supplied people perennially with adequate water.

The whole community met and expressed awe and amazement at the boy's action. The community agreed that each family would give the boy a black bull or an ox. The Chief gave him a wife and built him a home of his own. From that time onward, the boy was given the honour of a rain maker by the community within which he lived. He was given great respect and honoured. In times of need and when drought seemed imminent, the boy was consulted by the community and asked to assist. He always did this on the mountains with complete success. The mountain became a central place for worship and rain making ceremonies.

CLEMENCE M. MAGAISAH
RESEARCH AREA: Silobela Rural Area
The Fisherman Mugandani

The following is a research report conducted among Silobela rural folk. It is concerned with a mythical story told about a fisherman – Mugandani. Mugandani is said to have been drowned in a river while fishing. The place of the incident is now known as Nyamidzi and has become a ritual centre for the local people.

In the 1950s, a fisherman – Mugandani – was drowned in a river. Mugandani survived on fishing as his source of income. One day he went fishing with his nephew, who was his apprentice. When the sun was going down, they heard a loud cry of a baby just below where they were. They ran to the place to save the baby which had fallen into the water.

When Mugandani tried to rescue the baby, he also fell into the water and both Mugandani and the baby disappeared. The nephew went back home and recounted the incident to the elders of the village and to Mugandani's relatives. The elders told the family members not to mourn because they suspected that this was an act of the *njuzu* water spirit. The village elders went to the place of the incident to check whether they could find Mugandani's and the baby's bodies floating on the water, but they found nothing. After searching for days along the river bank, their efforts had proved fruitless.

Then, a group of elders spotted a child of about four years of age sitting on the opposite shore. The child waved his hand and said,

> The person you are looking for is among us. He is alive and will come to you equipped with the skills to guide your people towards the spirits. From now on search no more. This place is to be further known as *Nyamidzi* (roots). Ask for anything at this place and you shall receive.

Immediately the child disappeared into the water. The elders looked at each other with alarm and fear. They went back home and reported

194

the news to the community as a whole. From then on, the place became a ritual centre for the local people. If you go there today, just at the shore, there is a fence inside of which are clay wooden pots and special clothing made of animal skins and cotton material with multi-colours. The only people allowed to visit the place, apart from the community at times of rituals, are elderly women who maintain the shrine. Mugandani never came back among his community, but some people say he has already come in disguise as a newly born baby.

Part Three

THE RITUALS

RITUALS HONOURING ANCESTORS

SIMBARASHE KAZIMBI
RESEARCH AREA: Zhombe District, Midlands Province
Offering to the Spirits

I heard there had been a spate of deaths and unprecedented misfortunes within a certain family. Then, within the same family, a young boy aged around fifteen was critically ill and as yet the illness had proved to be incurable. I was told by the neighbours that the family had consulted many *n'angas* to seek cures for the young boy and equally to know the possible causes of the misfortunes which had befallen them. It was only later when they had travelled deep to the Dande area that a prominent *n'anga* revealed to them that they would continue to suffer if they did not make some offerings to their spirits. The boy would certainly die if they did not follow formal procedures. He also told them that the late grandfather of the sick boy wanted his name revived through the young boy. It was then that they were told to observe the following procedures: they had to brew beer, offer it to the spirit, slaughter a beast (part of which was to be eaten unsalted during the ceremony), and revive the name.

This happened in Zhombe, a district in the Midlands Province. The ritual was performed a kilometre from my home area so I had the opportunity to witness the ritual. Beer had already been brewed when I arrived but had not yet been offered. A black bull was slaughtered with the help of the bond friend (*sahwira*).

Friends and relatives had gathered to witness the offering. Before anyone had tasted the beer, an elder of the family in question, whom I saw to be the eldest among them, emerged from a hut followed by a woman carrying a clay pot. Many of the family members emerged as well and headed towards the family field which was within the vicinity. I later saw they were heading towards a grave and when they approached it, the woman carrying the clay pot was in front and she stopped suddenly and the rest followed suit. She knelt down and delicately offloaded the clay pot which was filled with beer and withdrew to the rest of the family.

The elderly man mentioned above walked forward and uttered some words and knelt behind the pot. He poured most of the beer on top of the grave and drank the little remaining. The clay pot was left on the grave while they retreated home after a lengthy speech to the spirit.

It was only after this offering that beer was given to the attendants while the meat was shared among the people. The meat was not salted according to the norms and I was told this was because salting an offered meat means you are blinding your spirit.

The ceremony took as much as twenty-four hours because from the evening until the following morning there was beating of drums in a systematic manner and singing of traditional songs.

To my surprise, the following morning the sick boy seemed to recover and was no longer called by his former name but was now *VaMushayabasa*, which was the name of the late grandfather. When people dispersed, I could still hear for many days the beating of drums and singing.

MABHENA MAKHOSANA
RESEARCH AREA: Matebeleland North
Ndebele Thanksgiving Ceremony

The form of a ritual which I observed is a traditional ritual which is a feast held annually by most of the Ndebele families as a thanksgiving ceremony to their ancestors. The feast is held during the winter season when the Nkayi in Matebeland North region have finished harvesting.

The preparations for the feast involve the summoning of the family members, relatives and other members of the community who are known to be possessed of the ancestral spirits (*amadlozi*). These need not be related to the family.

Traditional (opaque) beer is brewed using maize meal and ground rapoko meal. A beast is also slaughtered, usually a white goat. The preparations had been completed when I arrived at the particular Ndebele family holding the feast.

The feast began on a Friday during sunset or approximately at 6:00 p.m. The slaughtered beast and the beer which had not yet been consumed were moved into the room where the feast was to be held. The beer was in three containers: two clay calabashes and another general clay container. One of the calabashes is considered to belong to the ancestral grandfather and the other to the ancestral grandmothers. The clay container is for the use of the guests.

The head of the family in this case was the father of the home. He led the family members and the close or blood relatives whose surname is the same as his into the hut where there was beer and meat. This individual was not possessed by the spirits. He is known as *udondolo* which simply means walking stick or snuff. He then began to address the ancestors. He scooped beer from the two special calabashes and let it drip to the ground addressing the ancestors saying, 'Here is your food which we have prepared for you'. A special bowl-shaped container (*inkezo*), with an elongated handle and made from cultivated pods, was used for scooping beer. The speaker then thanked the ancestors for

200

guiding the family and asked for more favours especially in the agricultural sphere that there might be more bumper harvests.

The speaker, or head of the family, officially opened the ceremony by perfoming a traditional dance known as *sitshikitsha*. He performed it alone with the family members helping with the singing. After the solo dance by the head of the family, the possessed member of the family and invited guests who were possessed as well, clad in black apron-like clothes with black beads strung over their shoulders and carrying sticks or rods, performed the grandmothers' dance known as *umgido wabogogo*. The majority of the dancers were women. The dance had two beats or songs, one called *uyelele*, when the drums were beaten at different intervals, and the *vuma* beat, when drums were beaten together. The songs for this particular dance were concerned with *idlozi*, addressing it and asking it whether it does hear their pleas.

A dancer in this group then ventured into the ancestor spiritual world, changing her voice. The person was now regarded as the representative of the long dead grandmother. The person's voice changed to a deep growl as her body tensed. The possessed dancer was then given a low wooden stool to sit on and people began asking questions about their problems. The possessed one in turn answered back pointing out problems in the family. The possessed one was given beer to drink. After she drank, she bid the family good-bye and assumed her original personality, usual voice, and manner of speech.

After this dance, there was the 'hunters' dance known as *abajumbi*'s dance. This consisted entirely of young men clad in red clothes and beads. They were carrying spears or knobkerries. They danced in a more active way than the dancers of the first group. During the dance, they were looking upwards. Eventually, the dancers were visited by the spirits in the same way as the first dancers. One young man was taken to the place where the meat and beer were placed. The family members then asked him questions pertaining to their lives. After pointing out the family member's problems and answering their questions, he then changed back into his usual status. He no longer was a manifestation of the ancestral hunters. The people then told him that they have been talking to their grandfather, the old hunter.

The last dance was the *sitshikitsha* dance. The majority of the performers were males but a few women participated. These were clad in animal skins, for example, hyena, cheetah, and a jackal. They also wore hats made out of feathers. These dancers were referred to as the *izangoma*. They carried knobkerries, spears, and skin hides used as shields in battles. They had snake bones around their necks. The dancers in this category, just like the two earlier ones, ventured into the spiritual world and were treated in the same manner as in the above two cases.

The majority of the dancers I observed in the three dances actually ventured into the spiritual world. Each dance represented the type of spirit which possessed them: the 'grandmother', the 'hunter', or the 'izangoma'. However, two dancers were visited by three kinds of ancestor spirits.

After the dances were over, around early dawn, the family members and relatives assembled before the meat and the beer. The head of the family took a sip from both the grandfather's and grandmother's calabashes, one at a time. He spat the first sip he took on the ground and swallowed the second one. The other members of the family did the same in order of their ages, ranging from the older to the younger.

After this, the ceremony was declared over by the head of the family and the beer drinking and meat roasting began continuing until sunrise when the guests departed.

DAVID MAHACHI
RESEARCH AREA: Buhera North
Doro Remvura Yenyota
Ceremony for Senior Ancestor Spirits

It is among the Zezuru-speaking people of Buhera North that I undertook my ritual observation. The ritual was *Doro Remvura Yenyota*. This ritual underscores the belief that a person, especially one who has been married, becomes thirsty after death. This thirst can be quenched only with beer.

The ceremony was held by a family for their senior ancestor spirit, Sekuru VaBhunu. VaBhunu had communicated his need for a drink by causing an illness to a young girl. This was learned from a *n'anga* who advised that as VaBhunu felt neglected, he should be satisfied by a beer ceremony.

A few pots of beer were set aside for a special purpose of ritual presentation (*zvirango*). A number of these were real beer and one was a product of beer known as *mhanga* made especially for women.

In the evening when every family member was present, a gourd full of rapoko was brought forward. The senior family member gave the gourd to the youngest member to pass it on to his immediate elder with the words, 'Tell your brother that this is what we have gathered here for. We have a beer pot (*kachikari*) especially prepared for our grandfather VaBhunu to quench his thirst'.

The words would be repeated as the gourd was passed in hierarchical order according to seniority until it reached the original senior who replied, 'We have heard the word and we are grateful'.

During this time, the women were seated on mats looking unconcerned at what was occurring. The senior then addressed them saying, 'Eh! you women as well! You have heard our cause of gathering. We have this rapoko for our Grandfather Bhunu'. The women replied by ululating and the men clapped their hands and nodded systematically.

While everyone in the house was barefooted, the senior proceeded to the platform (*kuchikuva*). In a high pitched voice he said,

Eh! Imi tateguru Bhunu! Mashoko ndi wayo, chikari chenyu icho, munyautsire pahuro. Mochidirawo kumhepo dzose dzingawire isu mapudzi enyu. Nyoka huru haizvirumi Mbuya Chikonamombe. Tiri ura hwenyu musatiise patsiga kuti makunguo agononga. Mhandu kana youya itandirei kure. Munzira mutibisirewo minzwa nemafeso zvose. Saka tati chikari chenyu ich o – o! Motisvitsirawo zvose kuna VaMaranda, VaMaheu, VaZinyemba nevamwe vose vatisingazivi pashaye

*anozoti hatina kunge taudzwa. Nemiwo, vanambuya musati
svava dzenyu dzakukanganwai. Heyo mhanga yenyu
yamachembere. Mutitaririrewo!*

English Translation:

Eh! You greatgrandfather Bhunu! This is what we say: Here is your
pot of beer to quench your thirst. Pour over (neutralise) all evil
spirits which may affect us, your offspring. A big snake does not
bite itself, Chikonamombe. We are your children. Do not expose us
to dangers. When the enemy comes, chase him away. Clear our
paths of all thorns and creepers. Thus, we say, here is your pot of
beer. Forward everything to Mr. Maranda, Mr. Maheu, Mr.
Zinyemba and all the others we do not know about, so that no one
will complain that he was not informed. And you too,
grandmothers, do not think your children have forgotten about
you. Here is your unprocessed beer for old women. Look after us.

These words were a mere presentation of the beer to the invisible
guest of honour, the departed VaBhunu, who should pass on the word
to the other spirits including the 'unknowns'. The senior asked for
protection from life dangers. To the departed women, he presented
mhanga and made pleas for protection.

While he said these words, he was squatting and clapping lowly.
Others were silent and were seated close by in a half circle facing the
platform. After he finished these words, some beer was poured onto the
platform floor. Women began ululating and men clapped their hands.
Amidst this applause, the senior sniffed a bit of snuff, threw some to the
ground, put the remaining in his nose, and sneezed. He then left the
room. After a walk outside, he came back and everyone in the room
began to chat and drink freely.

PATIENCE SAMANGO
RESEARCH AREA: Marange Rural Area
Maganzvo

I observed a ritual called *maganzvo* in Marange rural area. The sub-chief
of this area is named Nyiko. This ritual is carried out yearly at the
beginning of July. The elders of the area say the main purpose of this
festival is to 'worship' the spirits of the area as well as to thank them for
the harvests they would have gathered.

Before the observation of the ritual, I asked one of the old women of
the area the stages which are taken before the actual ritual commences.
She said that the kraalhead announces to the people as soon as the
people engage themselves in the final touches of harvesting that
'*tinotsingana njere*' (we plan together). The families would then
contribute some rapoko for beer to the chief's place. The beer is brewed
by those ladies past child bearing age. When the beer is ready, then
comes the day of the ritual I am going to describe as I observed it.

The beer was taken from the sub-chief's home in average sized
calabashes and clay pots. These calabashes and clay pots were carried by
the middle aged women to a forest called *mapirwe*. These were in
dressings made of a cloth called *maretso*. They had ring-beads around
their feet, hands and necks. These were the people who led the rest of

the crowd into the forest. As they got into the forest, one of the elders, also in *maretso* clothing, stopped the crowd by kneeling down. Everyone then imitated him. But the women with beer headed towards a big tree called *mukamba*.

They went straight under the *mukamba* tree in a single file and knelt one by one placing down the pots of beer right round the tree. The women then went back to where the other members of the crowd had settled down a distance from the *mukamba* tree, with their heads bowed down.

The crowd sat in two parts, men of all ages with quite a good number of young men aged about 18 years among them. Seated on the other side were women of all ages again with a mixture of girls around 18 years old.

In their hands, old women and men had knobkerries, *Zvitsvimbo* and rattles (*hosho*), but all were in *maretso* clothing as well as in red clothes with white and black designs on them.

When the women had sat down with the crowd, ten elders led by the sub-chief walked quietly down from a nearby mountain bare-footed in a single file. All of them were clothed in different animal skins from head to toe. As they walked down, big drums were hit by men and women ululated. The elders headed for the *mukamba* tree where the beer had been placed. All knelt around the tree each with a calabash in front of him.

The sub-chief then took one calabash and held it in the air beginning with these words, '*Vari pasi Tinzweiwo...*' (Those who are below, hear us). He went on mentioning dead elders starting with 'Sumwa', a recent dead chief whom the chief asked to pass the dedication to the other ancestors according to the hierarchy.

After dedication of the beer, the sub-chief assumed a crouching position and engaged himself once again in the clapping of hands. He spoke in an unusual voice and said that they have prepared beer for the ancestors to thank them for the harvest. His fellow elders remained in the kneeling position clapping hands. When he had finished speaking these words, each elder took a gourd (*mukombe*) and then fetched beer from the respective clay pots. Both of them poured the beer on the ground saying '*Tati mutapudze nyota*' (We are saying, quench your thirst). When the beer had all sunk into the ground, they then did the fetching of beer for the second time and each elder drank the beer from the calabashes without stopping. After that, the elders once again fetched the beer for the third time and they gave the beer to the crowd to take a sip sharing the same beer from the same calabashes. As all finished, women ululated and men clapped their hands in approval.

The elders then went back under the tree and carried the beer to the crowd for them to share amongst themselves. But the sub-chief's clay pot of beer was left under the tree with the gourd in it.

When the beer was finished, the crowd rose and began to sing traditional songs and to dance. Men and women would dance confronting each other as if they were going to fight using their *tsvimbo*. Big drums were hit in a stylistic manner and everyone would sing while women ran around ululating and waving their *maretso* cloth in the air. Vulgar language was spoken by anyone without shame. The dancing was done for the rest of the day in the forest and continued until late at the sub-chief's home.

RESEARCH AREA: 57 kilometres from Mutare
near the Mutare-Nyanga road.

Mukwerere

During the vacation, I happened to witness an African ritual called
Mukwerere. This ritual is done especially when the land has been struck
by severe drought or it is done regularly on an annual basis. It is an
appeal to the ancestors for rain. The ritual took place in the land of Chief
Nyamandwe which is situated about 57 kilometres from Mutare along
the Mutare-Nyanga road.

It was on a Saturday morning when I saw people from all over the
village bringing clay pots and rapoko mealie meal to my grandfather's
home, who was their kraal head. When I asked my grandfather what it
was all about, he told me that the material was for the brewing of beer
which was going to be offered to the ancestors. He said that every head
of kraal and his people were supposed to brew the beer and then they
would bring the beer to the chief on the day of the ritual. On a Monday,
I saw women coming to my grandfather's home. I was told that all the
women who had come were beyond child bearing age and they were the
ones responsible for the preparation of the beer. Women of child bearing
age were not allowed. Unfortunately, I was not allowed to enter the hut
where the beer was being prepared.

On the day of the ritual, all the villagers except children assembled at
my grandfather's home whom in Shona they called *Sabhuku*. Young
women then carried beer pots and all the adults were on their way to the
chief's place. It was early in the morning and I could hear a drum which
was being beaten loudly at the chief's place. I was surprised to notice
that no work was being done. As the procession was on its way, the
people were singing obscene songs. I even noticed a woman who
intentionally lifted her dress aware that she was exposing her buttocks.

The people headed towards a very big fig tree. When I asked, I was
told that the fig tree was linked with ancestors and unusual things were
said to happen there. Even lions were reported to have been seen there.
The tree was of great importance to the people. It was of spiritual value
to them. The chief and his followers were already sitting on stones that
were under the tree. All of them were dressed traditionally in animal
skins. People began coming from other villages. Each village came with
its own beer pots. Everyone was in a serious mood and no one was
joking or laughed.

The chief then took a beer pot and went very close to the tree trunk
and kneeled there looking up. Suddenly, he began speaking in a loud and
terrifying voice. He began by announcing names of people. An old man
who was sitting beside me told me that they were names of the ancestors.
He was reminding the ancestors that when the rainy season arrives, they
were not supposed to forget their people. I was surprised to hear him
saying that they would only want a drop of water. The old man told me
that it was a way of reducing oneself before the ancestors. After the long
speech, he poured the beer that was in the pot on the ground saying,
'*Mukombe wenyuwo uyu*' which translated means, 'Here is your beer'.
The old man beside me told me that the beer that was poured on the

ground was for the ancestors to drink. He said that the ancestors are greatly honoured to the extent that they must be the first beings to drink the beer. After this, there was the beating of drums, drinking of beer, eating of meat, and singing of traditional songs by the rest of the people. By sunset, the people were on their way home with their beer pots now empty.

CHARLES NYAMUDEZA
RESEARCH AREA: Nyanga, Manicaland
Kupira Midzimu

I observed an ancestral ritual in the communal areas. The whole ritual is called *kupira midzimu* in Shona. Under normal circumstances, the ritual is done once a year but when a need appears, the ritual *kupira* or *kuteterera kuvadzimu* can always be repeated. What the ritual is all about is quenching the thirst of an ancestor by brewing beer and doing all the procedures which I will explain below.

This ritual took place at our home; thus I saw how people started preparing for the ritual until it ended. First and foremost, before the ritual the person responsible must brew beer and prepare food in advance for the big day.

Two days before the ritual, neighbours and relatives are invited. On the day of the ritual, people are welcomed by the inviter. Later, the inviter makes a special announcement as to why he has summoned them. After this announcement, people clap hands (*kukwidza maoko*).

After this stage, the inviter then sends his nephew (son of his sister) with a clay pot full of beer to the people. The nephew on behalf of the uncle then tells the people as follows: 'This is what I was given by uncle to give you (people) so that you will drink before the actual drinking of the beer.' This first pot of beer is called *mataibaya* or *mataitumbura.*

As people will be drinking beer at an open area outside, close relatives of the inviter are called into the kitchen. Most of the beer will be in the kitchen. The inviter then goes to the *chikuwa* where he talks to the ancestor spirits.

Ndisu vana wenyu weshumba gwara tati
timbokubikirai kahari kokubvisa nyota.
Mutichengeterewo wana nawamai nemishayo
zvose. Imi sekuru Bande mutisvitsirewo kune wari kumushayo

English translation:

It is us your children, Mr Shumba Gwara.
We have thought of brewing beer to quench your thirst.
Please look after our children, wives and homes.
You, grandfather Banda, pass over our word to those whom you stay with.

Many more things will be said.

Soon after this stage people in the kitchen clap their hands. All the people then assemble outside the kitchen and the inviter announces that the full time for the drinking of beer has arrived. People usually drink beer until their throats seem full. Drums are sounded and people dance their traditional dancing styles. At the end of the day, the inviter gives the people a big pot of beer called *mataipedza* signifying that by the end of this pot people must go to their respective homes.

TAFADZWA CHIKOMBERO
RESEARCH AREA: Njerama, Manicaland
Kupira Midzimu

The Manyika people who belong to the Shona tribes of Zimbabwe carry out a ritual which they call *kupira mudzimu* (offering to the ancestors). I happened to observe one of the rituals that was held at a homestead in Manicaland in a village called Njerama in Chief Mutasa's area.

Before carrying out the ritual, the elders of the family went to inform Chief Mutasa and the village head (*ishe*) that they were going to carry out a ritual of *kupira midzimu wemusha*. This act is called *kusuma mambo naishe wedunhu* (presenting to the king and chief of the area) and is done to make the authorities aware of what was going to take place in their area.

After receiving the approval of both authorities, beer was brewed from millet. This process was done by very old females of the family who could no longer bear children. Middle aged women were not allowed anywhere near the place where the beer was being brewed. However, young girls below the age of fifteen were allowed at the place of the beer brewing. These carried out duties like fetching firewood and water, and they also washed some clay pots as needed. This whole process was started early in the morning before sunrise.

When the brewing of the millet beer was over and the beer was ready for human consumption, some members of the family took a small amount of the beer in a clay pot to the chief's homestead. Also, another clay pot full of the brewed millet beer was taken to the village head's home. Relatives and neighbours of the family were invited to take part in the ritual.

At dawn on the day the main part of the ritual was to be conducted, a very old man who was probably the oldest member of the family took a boy with him into the forest. They took a black hen with them and some beer in a clay pot. They got to a certain thorny tree known as *mupangara*. The old man took off his sandals made of a worn out vehicle tyre. He asked the lad to follow suit. They started to clap rhythmically and at this time they were kneeling under the tree.

After clapping, the old man began to utter the totem praise names. When he had finished, he took an axe that was being carried by the lad. He used this axe to chop an opening into a branch of the *mupangara* tree. He then tapped some liquid that came out of the branch into a small clay pot. When he had collected a few millilitres of the liquid, he picked up the bark that had fallen off from where he had chopped the branch. He replaced the bark on its original place on the branch. After doing this, the old man took a feather of the hen and placed it on the part of the tree where he had tapped the liquid.

The old man and the boy then squatted down and started to clap rhythmically with the old man uttering praise names in the process. The black hen was left at this place together with the millet beer. The two then departed for the homestead where relatives and neighbours of the family had started to converge. At the homestead, the old man took the liquid he had tapped from the tree and mixed it with some boiling water. He left the mixture until evening.

Towards evening, all the people got into a big hut. The people took off their shoes and hats as they entered the door of the hut. However, women entered with their heads covered with veils. The eldest man in the family went to a place in the hut resembling an altar. In Shona this is called *chikuva*. This man had a black and white cloth wrapped around his body.

When everybody got into the hut, men started to clap rhythmically and in an orderly way and the women followed suit. After this, the oldest man, who conducted the ceremony, took a small clay pot of millet beer and put it on the *chikuva*. He also took some snuff in a wooden plate and put it beside the millet beer. At this moment, there was dead silence in the hut. The silence was broken by the man's uttering totem praise names. When he had finished, a black male goat was brought into the hut and it was also offered to the family ancestors as had been done to the millet beer and the snuff.

As a part of offering praises to the ancestors, the conductor of the ritual told the ancestors that the family was giving them the meat, millet beer, and snuff as token signs of appreciation for the ancestors providing the family with well-being and fertility. The conductor of the ceremony used a soft low voice when talking to the ancestors. This process of offering and talking to the ancestors was punctuated by the rhythmic clapping of hands by the men who were joined by the women. Later, the women ululated and the men whistled.

After this, the leader of the ritual took a snuff box and put a little of the snuff into his palm and inhaled some of it through his nose. He gave the snuff box to the other people in the hut to do the same thing. Millet beer was also passed among the people. Every person in the hut was expected to take a sip of the beer from the clay pot as it circulated among them. The clapping of the hands, ululating and whistling was done after the pot of millet beer had circulated and had been put back on the *chikuva*. After this, the conductor of the ritual went outside and faced first to the east and then to the west before returning back into the hut.

The other phase of the ritual was characterised by the beating of drums, singing traditional songs, ululating, whistling, and dancing throughout the night. The black goat was slaughtered for the people to eat. The blood that came out of the goat was mixed with the liquid of the *mupangara* tree and the mixture was burnt until it evaporated. This was done by the man who had gone into the forest to collect the liquid. The merrymaking lasted until the following morning with the youths playing the largest role, especially when it came to the beating of the drums, singing and dancing. Those who had been invited started to depart on the following day. Some carried meat from the slaughtered goat with them to their homesteads but the left front thigh of the goat (*bandauko*) was left in the *chikuva*.

MATHIAS SIBANDA

RESEARCH AREA: Hwange

Sharing Good Fortune

I observed this ritual on 29 June, 1991 when I was at home in Hwange. My elder brother had come home from Bulawayo after having been

208

given a two week leave from his job. It was his first time to come home since he started working and it was also his first time to give Father some money ($100) as a gift. After being given this money, my father thanked him, but he did not use the money without performing a ritual.

On the following day in the afternoon, Daddy came into our room where we used to sleep. He had the money in his hands and he also had a cup full to its brim with water. He told both of us to sit on the floor facing each other. Daddy later sat down facing both my elder brother and myself. He then spread the money on the floor. Following this, he sipped half of the water from the cup and rinsed it in his mouth before spitting it on the money. After this, he said out the names of our elder brothers who had jobs and thus were employed. He said out their names in a low tone which could be heard only by us who were in the room. His eyes were closed and his head was facing downwards. He also clapped his hands while saying their names.

After saying their names, he also asked my ancestors to guide my elder brother just as they had done to these who were working. His plea was accompanied by the clapping of his hands with his head bowed down. He also asked God to protect my brother. Lastly, he picked up the money from the floor and thanked my brother for the gift. The water which he had spit was left to dry on its own.

RICHARD MAPOSA
RESEARCH AREA: Chipinge District
Kupa zita

This paper is an attempt to describe graphically a ritual, *kupa zita*, which was performed on 1 January 1991. It was to give a name to a bull for the family when the former bull bearing the name had died. It must be noted that cattle have a special value for the Ndau people of Chipinge District.

The officient was my father. He was on the forefront of a fairly long procession of family members going out of the homestead yard toward the cattle kraal which was about a stone's throw away. My father was holding a short spear in his right hand with a leopard's skin wound around his neck. He was barefooted. My *tete* (aunt) Tendai carried a fairly large pot full of beer right to the brim. The pot was decorated with hunting scenes. Aunt Tendai was hugging the pot very tightly against her breasts. My mother followed and then myself. I was trudging well behind my mother. I had my young sister at my back.

As my father was just about three metres from the entrance to the cattle kraal, he suddenly stood and looked back. He waved the spear up into the air and then touched it. He unwound the leopard's skin off his neck and gave it to Aunt Tendai. He moved a step further. He stopped again and everybody else did the same. He stood still right at the entrance. He picked up some cow dung and tossed it into the air. My mother laughed at that. Suddenly I heard my father utter the words,

Zvino yasvika nguva. Mose muchapinda kuno muchibaya chemombe musina kana kutaura kana kutarisazve shure. Uyu ndiwo mutemo wedu...

These words can be translated as,

The time has come. All shall step into the cattle kraal in silence and without looking back. This is the ancient law.

209

My father made a hand gesture and *Tete* Tendai stepped into the kraal first. She went to stand at the corner and there put down the beer pot. The pot was balanced by using three small mounds of cow dung with the assistance of my mother. The entrance was closed by father using our long Mopani poles. He walked rather stealthfully to the beer pot and asked for *tsani* (long gourd to draw beer from the pot). He then stirred the beer with a gourd and the beer foamed. With an audible but shaking voice, he began to invocate,

> *Baba! Hezvo tauya kuzokupai. Gono renyu zita. Ndimi makataura kuti hakuna zita rinofa rega. Zvino tinokumbira kuti mutaurire vose vose ikoko kuti Gono renyu tinaro, uye tichakurangarirai nokusingaperi.*

These lines can be translated as,

> Father! We are here to officially bestow your great name to your bull. This is the ancient custom we are following. We plead with you to intercede for us before all, so that we continually remember you all...

As he stopped invocating, he drew a gourdful of beer and made a mouthful. He then spat the beer from his mouth. The second time, he drank a mouthful. He then poured a few drops of beer on the cow dung. He drew yet another gourdful of beer and handed it to *Tete* Tendai. She drank. Third, the gourd of beer was handed to myself. I drank the beer. As I did so, she remarked softly, '*Ndiwe uchasara nebasa rino. Nyatsa kuona.*' ('You are to inherit your father's role. Observe with care'.)

For a moment, my father kept quiet. But he intently looked to a big black bull (*mukono*). The bull was lying peacefully at the corner amongst other cattle. Nearly all the cattle were chewing the cud. My father's eyes twinkled here and there. He was holding a gourd full of beer. He took hold of the spear and stood up. For a moment, he sighed and then coughed quite heavily. He began to walk steadily. With each step he took, he looked backward, then forward and then sneezed. He then hesitated. He was holding the spear firmly in his left hand and in his right hand he was clutching the gourd of beer. The leopard's skin had been wound around his neck again. He walked towards the bull he had identified as the one selected by the ancestors.

Just a step away from the bull, which was still lying down, my father sipped a mouthful of beer and spat it towards the bull. The bull stopped chewing the cud. Some cows became awakened and stood up, but the bull remained lying down. My father waved a red cloth which he untied from his waist. Suddenly, he sprinkled the beer over the body of the bull. He took the spear and threw it across the bull's neck. He then sprinkled beer for the second time.

Just then, the bull bellowed so loudly that it sounded as if it were dying. There was a sudden cheering from Aunt Tendai and my mother who shouted, '*Baba iwe, Zvaitika!* ('It has been done!') My aunt danced around but my mother clapped and ululated. The bull bellowed for the second time. It rose up and moved. Immediately, my father uttered the following words,

> *Ndiro Gono renyu iri. Musazokangamwa kwete. Tanzwa tese kukuma kwenyu.*
>
> *Doro renyu tamupa. Chengetai Gono renyu kuti muzochengetazve isu ...*

These lines can be translated as,

This is your bull. Do not forget it anymore. We have heard your acceptance.

Your beer too has been prepared. Keep your bull and, through it, keep your family.

My father commanded that the bull, alongside other cattle, had to be driven to the homestead. I drove the rest of the cows, but my father and *Tete* Tendai were on the spot checking the bull all the way. My mother carried back the beer pot. At the homestead, the bull was driven first to stop at his hut. For about five minutes, the bull stood in the front of the hut. My father said, 'This is your hut, your family. Bless it'.

Next the bull was driven to the grain barn in front of which were green cobs in a traditional basket. The bull mauled one cob and ate it. My young sister, Chipo, wanted to chase the bull, but this was forbidden her by my father who said, 'Don't chase the bull away. These are not our cobs. The bull will leave some for us to eat'. (Evidently, some green cobs were left behind in the basket.) My father remarked, 'This is your storage and granary. Keep it from disaster so that we survive from hunger here on earth'.

While this was being said, Father made some gestures that all should sit down. But he commanded me to kneel down. He also kneeled down and started to clap his hands. My aunt and mother also clapped their hands in unison. The clapping had some rhythmic pattern, hence, *kuombera mudzimu*. My father stood up. The rest remained standing. The bull moved and rejoined other cattle that were eating grass east of the homestead. My father then said, 'It is over. Thanks for a ceremony well done'. By the time this last step was observed, many neighbours who had been invited previously were beginning to arrive at our home to drink the beer.

LUKE MANYENGAWANA

RESEARCH AREA: near Nyanga, Manicaland

Mukwerere

The ritual I observed was taking place among the people of a clan in Manicaland near Nyanga. The totem of the people is *Shumba* (Lion). The wave of modernity has not yet overwhelmed the tradition of the people for their homes are in a rugged place between mountains. There are no roads except paths that lead into this village. I visited them at the time they were observing a ritual they call *mukwerere*. The term seems to have stemmed from the verb *kweva* which literally means 'drawing to' or 'attract'.

Before I arrived, a lot had happened as one of the old men told me. It helped me to understand what I then observed and so I think I might as well outline what I was told by the old man. Each family at that time of year (the time of shedding leaves on the trees) donates the ingredients needed for the brewing of beer. The young men, who are the sons, gather firewood while the daughters-in-law fill the drums with water. Elderly women are responsible for the actual brewing of the beer which takes six days. I arrived on the seventh day when the beer was ready.

The old men were directing how things were to be done. The young women were busy cooking. An ox had already been killed and it looked

211

as if they were going to have a feast. I was at once struck by the division of labour amongst them. I observed one group that consisted of old men who, from the manner they were addressing each other, were brothers. Each of them was assigned to supervise a certain area, such as cooking, while another saw to it that everybody received beer and food while still another (who looked to be the eldest) was seated and seemed to be engaged in a serious discussion with another elder who looked like an invited guest.

The other group was made up of strong young men who, from the look of things, were the sons of the old men. These were engaged in various tasks like chopping firewood and many other tough jobs. The third group consisted of elderly women who were the wives of the old men. As I mentioned above, they were the ones who had brewed the beer. The daughters-in-law were the fourth group.

When the food was ready, they brought it to the elderly man. Pots of beer were also brought there. Everybody else sat around the old man. They all bowed down as the old man stood up and began to call upon the ancestors. He speech went as follows:

> Greetings to you all, you who lie in the peace of the holy caves: Mudziwepasi, Sandukwa, Mugojori, Zambuko, Shangunda, Tondo, and all you who went before them.

> Attend, you court of our ancestors, to the voice of your family gathered. Hear, you, Mudziwepasi, the one who began it all.

> You led our ancestors from Binga and gave them this land. During their journey, you assisted them in their wars. You gave them meat from the forests to sustain them.

> Look now. Here we are many. We thank you for the riches of this land we enjoy. We implore you to continue to bless us here. Bind us together as one family. Protect us from the evils that threaten us.

A dish of porridge was brought to the 'stranger' whom I had observed discussing with the old man. He poured some herbs into it and mixed it as he said, 'May all who partake of this porridge be protected from all evil and remain as one. May a curse fall upon all who try to harm any of them.' They all, in turns, went down on their knees with clenched fists and licked the porridge. When everybody had done this, the old man took the dish, washed it, and poured the dirty water into a hole in the ground made by termites.

He came back and dug a hole in the ground and spat into it saying, 'I have nothing against anyone'. Everyone else did the same. After this, the food was dished and beer was given to all to drink. There was a family atmosphere in all this. Later, some began singing and drumming. Finally, almost everybody seemed to be enjoying the activities.

Around evening, small pots of beer were taken up into the mountain nearby where they put them at the entrance of the caves. They said their ancestors are buried there. The ancestor spirit was invited to join the celebrations by the old man who did the placing of the pots. He also swept the cave, removing the dead leaves and weeds. I was not able to find out what became of the beer because it was left there. This was the end of the ritual although the people spent the whole night drinking and dancing. I left the place the following morning.

RITUALS OF COMMUNICATION WITH THE ANCESTORS

CLEOPHAS GWAKWARA
RESEARCH AREA: Gonamombe, near Daramombe

Bira Ritual

The *bira* ritual was carried out at a family homestead of the headman. It was carried out for fathers, the elders, the great grandfathers and the mothers of the family who have died. Relatives of the family had already been told long before that the ritual would take place and thus had sent their contributions in the form of rapoko which was used in brewing the beer.

Seven days before the actual day of the ritual, the headman stood in the middle of his homestead, sprinkled some snuff on the ground and said,

To all those who are down, the fathers, the mother and those beyond our reach, your children have thought of giving you a brew ... that you may not turn against us saying that we did not inform you.

He then took a cupful of water and poured in a big basket of rapoko. This was when brewing started and those who took part were elderly women, those inactive in sex and no longer bearing children.

Nobody tasted the beer until the day of the ritual. Nobody slept during the night before the ritual since the people were singing and dancing the whole time. The song which was sung repeatedly can be translated thus:

The elders need those who are gathered,
The elders need those of Gonamombe,
The elders love us of one country,
The elders do not live where they are not gathered,
They do not like those who kill each other.

There was one woman who danced all night long and you could hear people say, 'Do not play with Bazvi...'

Early in the morning, people gathered at the cattle kraal. The headman pointed with his walking stick at a big black bull and said,

All those gathered here, this is our uncle, Bazvi, our elder, our leader, for whom we all have gathered here. What is left is for the brothers-in-law to do their duty.

All the people clapped their hands as women danced around the kraal.

Singing continued as people returned to the yard. The headman again stood before the people and sprinkled some snuff on the ground and said, 'To those who are below, your children are gathered here. Lead us as we enter into praising you for keeping us in one good piece'. A clay pot was taken out of the hut. The first calabash of beer was splashed on the ground around the pot. 'This is your beer. No one has ever tasted it before you. Drink this and your children will be happy'. He went on as the people clapped hands.

As this was going on, the bull was being killed by the sons-in-law. They used a knife to strike it because an axe was against their customs.

213

Blood was collected in a clay plate. A woman just dashed from the house and ran to the kraal. One could not help following anxiously the woman's actions. She collected the clay plate full of blood and gulped the whole contents to the point of licking. People clapped their hands as she did so. Some meat was cooked while the sons-in-law were given a portion of meat and a clay pot of beer to enjoy themselves. The sons-in-law sat together. Fathers-in-law sat in the shade of a mango tree forming their own distinct group. The 'owners of the home' sat in a hut.

Soon after midday, singing resumed, this time tinted with shades of alcohol as we joined in the chorus:

> The bees sting.
> Take my arrow; I want to go.
> They sting. Oh, chief! Oh, chief!
> Gwindingi has a lion that kills.
> I want to go.
> Beware! Gwindingi has a strong lion.

As people sang this song, an old woman pointed to the mountainside that stretched westward. Inquiring later, I was shown where Gwindingi (the popular old hill) was situated. Another song was:

> You are poor, Oh King.
> Let them build if they so wish.
> Let them build on those who are living.
> One day it shall come back to them.

Pent up emotions began to be aroused by the tune: 'Poverty, oh, mother'.

> We now sacrifice with a goat,
> Poverty, oh, mother.
> The sun is almost setting before we sacrifice,
> The sun comes down before you come.

Singing reached a peak with the song,

> Spirits come back, oh, spirits, come back.
> Greetings to you *sekuru*
> We receive you happily, old man.

The old woman who had pointed at the Gwindingi Mountain had now become possessed of the family ancestor named Bazvi. She could jump sky-high as if the ground were hot. She would rush as if she wanted to go out or charge backwards before she fell into a squatting position. What did not change was the pointing of her walking stick, three times downwards, once towards Gwindingi Mountain and once upwards. Her walking stick was black with a carved face of an old man on it.

The woman then fell violently and started weeping and speaking in certain voices which I do not want to believe that I was the only one who could not comprehend. She then began to sing in a very manly voice:

> The English took my wife,
> Everything is bad.
> You are not a relative; why do you fight?
> The English took my wife.
> Things are bad.

She asked for her clothes and was given a piece of joined black and white cloth which she hung around her shoulders. A baboon skin was placed on her head and she was given a smoking pipe which she put in her mouth. She then requested some water. She gulped a big calabash down without even breathing and asked for more. One old man then said, 'You have come old man. We see you. We are also very happy, but do you not realise that if you drink more, she who is near you will have nowhere to put her beer'?

Bazvi responded: 'You, you, you want to be too clever. I will cut off your testes!' People gasped in surprise. Bazvi continued, 'Why are you surprised? This is nothing. Anyway, your plea has been heard. Where is my wife?' An old woman came and sat there as they exchanged snuff in a wifely and husbandly manner. 'This is my wife and I love her. Today we are going to sleep together. You understand!' She continued looking at the woman addressed as VaDihori.

During my time, I was very stubborn. I used to have a brown woman and I would beat her at the buttocks. If the woman reported to the fathers-in-law that she was beaten, I would ask, "Where?" Can't you see her face is fine? At that time, I would know that I had finished off with the buttocks and she will never show them.

All the people laughed.

Anyway, my children, I am happy with your gathering and that is why I joke with you. So far no evil has transpired. I will tell Nyakuvamba (the initiator) that your children still remember you. I am not here for long and am already about to leave.

A claypot was placed in front of him and one elder said, 'As you said, you are about to leave. Our contribution to you, Bazvi, is this: take this pot and drink with your children'.

Bazvi began sharing the beer with the people, and after a few rounds, gave the responsibility to the old woman VaDihori and just said, 'I am leaving my children. Thank you'. Bazvi made a violent sneeze, convulsed and then fell down. People clapped hands as this occurred. A little later the old woman, who had been in possession of Bazvi, was asking what was happening, but no one dared to tell her. They only gave her some beer. Singing continued late into the night. The old woman drank, danced and joked with others as if nothing had happened. She danced late into the night.

The following morning, a beer pot *chiparadza* (the last pot) was brought out and rapoko sadza was eaten with intestines without salt. A claypot of beer and meat was put on the outskirts of the homestead for those who are not related to the family to eat and drink. No salt was provided. It was also directed to the spirits that move around the air. It was only after this that people began to disperse. Nobody was allowed to take any meat or beer home. If one did that, one would meet a lion or some misfortune, they said.

NDUMISO SITHOLE

RESEARCH AREA: Matopo, Matebeleland South

Ukuthethela: Talking with the Dead

On the first day of July, 1991, I observed a traditional ritual called *ukuthethela* amongst the Ndebele people in my home area called

Matopo in Matebeleland South, a few kilometres south of Bulawayo. The ritual involves talking with the dead of one's own family. It was conducted because some members of my uncle's family had become ill and five head of his cattle had died in two successive days.

The ritual began at dusk. By this time, the next of kin had arrived from their homes. We were all gathered in a small hut where brewed beer had been placed in two large clay pots and into five smaller ones. Fresh goat meat had also been stored in the hut. The beer and the meat were prepared for the ritual.

Grandmother, the responsible figure in leading all our families in rituals, showed us the beer and the goat meat and told us that it was food for our ancestors and that it had been prepared for them. After showing us the food, she led us all, except for the daughters-in-law, to a grave in which lay my grandmother's dead father.

She ordered us to sit down and face the grave. She introduced us to her dead father with the words:

Honourable Father, we have come to honour you as our father... Gathered here are your children. They have come before you to appeal and ask for protection and defence against bad luck, misfortunes, ill-omens, and generally all forms of evil.

As she said the above words, she was taking sips of beer from a gourd. She took two sips, spitting the first one out and swallowing the second. She concluded her speech by telling the dead father that Uncle is experiencing terrible misfortunes which worry all the kin. She mentioned that if the misfortune came as a result of our wrongdoing which have angered the dead, may they be pardoned because it had been done unintentionally and ignorantly. She also mentioned that if the misfortune was caused or sent by some evil person, that misfortune should rebound doubly to its owner/initiator.

Finally, she asked her dead father to convey our appeals and petitions to his seniors who would in turn pass it to Unkulunkulu (God). She was talking in a low solemn voice so much that one standing just a few metres away could hardly understand what she was saying. She then turned to her snuff contained in a small wooden container and sniffed a little into her nose whispering a few words as she did so. She poured the rest of the snuff onto her hand and carefully poured it on the ground at the same time whispering some words none of us could hear. Then we left.

As we left, we were made to take a sip of beer from the gourd and spit it out on the ground and then take a second sip and swallow it. As the grave is within the homestead, we soon gathered in a large round hut where we were to celebrate. When we returned, we were surprised to find the hut full of neighbours having come to celebrate with us according to custom and tradition. Without wasting time, the beer and cooked goat meat were dished out to the gathering by grandmother assisted by her two elder sons. After eating and drinking, traditional songs were sung accompanied by the beating of drums. People danced ecstatically until morning when they went to their homes. Beer and meat were continuously given to the people each time they needed it during the night.

FLORENCE SHOKO
RESEARCH AREA: Mberengwa District
The Ancestor Chooses a Medium

I observed a traditional ritual in the Mberenwga District amongst the Karanga. One of the family members became seriously ill all of a sudden. Since this particular family is strongly anchored in traditional customs, it had to consult a *n'anga*. The *n'anga* advised them to go and brew some beer. He outlined to them the procedures which they were to follow for this beer was to be brewed in a different style to other types of beer. When the whole process of beer brewing was over, the family had to go back to the *n'anga* for 'general cleansing' before they met the father (ancestor). The *n'anga* told them that the sick man was to become the 'home' of the ancestor.

On the day of the ritual, the whole family including grandmothers, grandfathers, great grandchildren, aunts, uncles and sons, and daughters assembled. Before the actual ceremony started, the *n'anga* circled the home five times where the ritual was to be held. When he was through, first he called elders of the family concerned. Before entering the room in which the ritual was to take place, each had to kneel on the door, clap hands, remove any jewellery and remove shoes. After these, came the women and the children belonging in the family. Everybody entered the room in the same way the elders had done. We all sat in a circle. The one who was to be in ecstasy sat on a mat in the middle of the circle. He was clothed in white and black pieces of cloth.

The eldest man of this family stood up to welcome everybody. After a word of welcome, he told the group the purpose of the gathering and said that everyone was to work jointly with this family for the success of the ritual. After these words, the whole house clapped hands while some whistled. The elder man then announced that the ritual was to start right away.

The ritual started with the low beating of drums. Gradually, the drums became louder and louder and people began to be moved by the beat so that everyone started to sing with all of his/her might. Traditional songs were sung for almost two hours. There was then a time of silence when drum beaters and those operating some *mbira* were given a chance to show their skill in operating these instruments. This continued for almost half an hour. The singing and dancing then started all over again. (One thing which surprised me was that the man who was to be the 'home' of the ancestor and the *n'anga* were just seated all the time when other members in the room were busy singing and dancing.)

After some time, the *n'anga* suddenly stood up and began to sing and whistle and to wave a knobkerry in the air. Gradually, the beat of the drums died out. We got scared and there was silence in the room. After some minutes of utter silence, we started clapping hands. The *n'anga* motioned for silence. First, the *n'anga* took some snuff. After a frightening sneeze, which continued for almost five minutes, he suddenly faced the big crowd. We all held our breath as we waited for the message from him. (I realised that I was shivering due to fear because I had never seen such a ritual before.) The *n'anga* began to talk in a very coarse and strange voice. He appeared different from what he was before the ritual began.

The *n'anga* ordered all the family members concerned to sit in a circle in the middle of the room where the other man was seated. When they were all seated, he took a wooden plate filled with snuff mixed with water. Every member drank from the plate. Anyone who drank from the plate coughed and sneezed. When the whole group had drunk the contents of the wooden plate, the *n'anga* then took a hairy tail which he used to hit each family member on the back. The man in white and black cloths suddenly fell. (I almost ran out of the room due to fear.) The *n'anga* sat on top of the man and uttered some indistinguishable words. He repeated the same words for a long time. When he at last stood up, the man appeared as if he were dead. (I could not help screaming before someone seated next to me put his hand on my mouth.)

The *n'anga* later ordered one of us to start a song. The beating of drums started again. When the man who appeared to be in a coma heard the beating of drums, he woke up all of a sudden and shook his head vigorously. He then sat down and the whole room stopped singing and we all sat down. The *n'anga* ordered us to clap our hands to encourage the man to speak. After a long clapping, the man motioned for silence and he began to speak in a strange voice. His speech was directed to the family members who were in the centre of the room. First, he thanked them for having paid heed to his request for recognition as a father of the family. To the eldest man in the group, he said that the family had done a good job and hence he appreciated the leadership of the old man in making the ritual a success.

When the man finished his speech, he sat down. He then asked for beer which was brought to him in that wooden plate once used for the snuff. He first poured some little beer on the floor saying, 'Drink this, those who went before me'. After he had also drunk, he then ordered that the beer was to be distributed to all those who wanted to drink. After saying this, the ecstatic man just fell on the floor and lay straight. When he woke up, he was back to his old self again. The ritual was then over.

JESTINA MADYA
RESEARCH AREA: Garise Village, Makoni District
Spirit Possession

As is customary among the Mashona people, when an ancestor spirit wants to manifest itself in a living person, the relatives gather and perform a ritual to welcome the spirit. This was done at Garise Village in the Makoni District on 2 July 1991. Though I was not a member of the village, I was given the chance to observe the ritual.

Starting at sunrise, there was beating of drums and singing of traditional songs. The singers were dressed in traditional attire. At about 10:30 a.m., a man aged about 35 addressed the people. He told them the purpose of their gathering and warned everyone to behave so that the ritual would be welcomed by the great ancestors. People were then told to sit in groups each according to his or her age or position in society. I moved to a group of young girls. I was happy to meet my cousin, for she could help me in understanding the ritual since it was my first time to attend one.

I noticed immediately that no one was wearing shoes. Even the watches and necklaces had been removed. All of us were warned to remove our shoes and jewellry.

As I watched at the place where the old men and women were seated, I observed that they were drinking something from the same gourd. I did not know what they were drinking since I was so far away. As they exchanged the gourd, they said some words. I could not hear the words clearly, but they had something to do with the ancestor spirits.

The dancers who had been performing dances all day stopped around midday and were replaced by the dance of the elders. The rest of the other groups only had to sing, clap, whistle, and ululate. During their dancing, each of the elders was pointing to the other elders with a knobkerrie or a small sharp axe.

When the elders were still dancing, an ill person near to death was brought into the middle of the circle. He lay there weakly. If it were not for his big eyes which shone like lightning, one would think he was a corpse. An hour passed, but the dying person was still motionless on the mat. His eyes were now half closed. During the singing and dancing, however, the ancestor spirit came out in the dying man. He shook himself heavily and stood up.

The singing, beating of drums and jingles was lowered. Two old women ran to the man and knelt down. They clapped their hands in honour of the spirit. It came out and made itself known through the sick man. The spirit identified itself and asked to be permitted to live in the sick man and to express himself through him occasionally.

The words as they came from the possessed man were said loud and clear. The spirit said,

It is I, Garise, who died five years ago. I have noticed the afflictions of my people. They have suffered a lot from the spirits of the Inyangombe. And as a father I have come home to protect my children. I love them and I cannot leave them anymore.

The spirit paused and asked for water. But instead it was given blood and drank it all. The last words of the spirit were,

Children, I depart to an unknown world, but I will always be there to fight for you and protect you. All of this will be on the condition that you follow my wish. And surely I will not turn against you, neither will I punish you with illness or death.

Thus, the spirit departed.

Following this, the sick man laid down again. He was fed with some thickish red porridge. He was given water to drink. After that, he was able to stand up and he moved around the place.

Then a black and white cloth was tied around his waist. A knobkerry, a big knife and snuff were handed to the man. After a big smile, he sneezed, rubbed his nose, and went back to his home.

At sunset, we were given a lot of sadza, meat, sweet beer and cooked pumpkins. We left the area with the family members cheering and ululating for the success of the ritual.

RITES OF PASSAGE

NOMUSA NCUBE

RESEARCH AREA: Matebeleland South

Childbirth

Childbirth is a very important ceremony amongst the Ndebeles. Lots of preparations are done a few weeks before the birth and, even after the birth, many things are done to welcome the new baby into the society. It is customary for a pregnant woman to leave her husband on the ninth month of pregnancy to go and await a new baby at her parent's place.

As I was at my uncle's home in Felabusi, his daughter came home to await the birth of her baby. The day she came, she started preparing for this baby. The room she used was polished with cowdung and no other people were allowed to enter that room for it was said that the baby must find it clean. Even the food given to the expecting mother was the best food in the house.

So when the moment arrived that everyone had been waiting for, the pregnant woman was taken to her room and the only people allowed in that room were her mother, her granny and one or two other ladies. It is forbidden for any man to be found in the room when a woman is giving birth (even if it is the husband of the woman).

The other three ladies in the house did not play any major part in helping the pregnant woman but the primary role was played by the grandmother. The pregnant woman was asked to lie on her back with her thighs apart. Before touching the woman, the grandmother first washed her hands in medicated water and then helped the pregnant woman. When the baby came out, the grandmother was the first person to touch the baby. She cleaned the blood off the baby with the medicated water.

At this stage, the baby was still attached to its mother by the umbilical cord. The grandmother cut the umbilical cord leaving some of it hanging to the navel of the baby. A string was then used to tie the end of the hanging umbilical cord so as not to allow any air to enter into the body of the baby. The grandmother then took the baby and washed it again with medicated water. It was then wrapped in a cloth and left to sleep.

When the baby was sleeping, the grandmother prepared fire in the room, and then after some time, burning coals were collected from the fire and put in a different place. Another type of medicine, different from the one used to bath the baby, was put into the burning coals. The grandmother then awakened the baby and held it in a way that its head was in the direction of the smoke from the medicated coals.

The baby cried for more than an hour and in the end it fell asleep. The sleeping of the baby did not change the position of the old lady. She still held it to the smoke for another thirty minutes. Since its birth, the baby had not been given any food except for the smoke.

The baby slept until the next morning when it awakened with a cry. After sucking from its mother, it was again held to the smoke. This procedure of holding the baby in the smoke after sucking from its mother continued for one week until the piece of the umbilical cord fell from its navel. The baby was then recognised as a person and given a name. The mother of the baby was allowed to go out of the room and start her work again. The people were then called in to celebrate the birth of the baby, and it was at this time that people came with different gifts for the baby.

After the celebration, the father of the baby was called in to see his child. He was given the piece of the umbilical cord and told what to do with it. The father then called the mother of the child and together they went to the kraal and dug a hole into which they placed the piece of the umbilical cord. But before they covered it, the father said something to the ancestor spirits asking them to look after the newly born child and at the same time thanking them for the child. After this, the father took the mother and the child with him back home.

ALSEN MOYO

RESEARCH AREA: Matebeleland South

Ndebele Death Ritual

The ritual I observed takes place after one year of mourning for the dead person. As a ritual is a function of the society, many people are called when there is a death ritual to be performed. All family members gathered at the hut of the dead person and through the use of snuff the elderly member of the family made known to the dead person that they were going to bring him home. Other dead family members were also told for their spirits to gather together to make the ritual a success.

After announcing the ritual to the dead, female family members, especially elderly ones, carried brewed beer in calabashes to the hut of the dead person while elderly male family members were slaughtering a bull. The dead person was a man. All meat was put in the hut of the dead person with some of it being eaten.

All family members went to the grave of the deceased and encircled it. The elderly family member cut a branch from a tree called *umlahlabantu* and he called the name of the dead person telling him to come home and stay with his family. He also told him that all family members are glad to have him come home to guard them from any kind of danger. He pulled the branch going home with the rest of the family members behind him who were singing traditional songs. One song was, *Mgedluka woz ekhaya* which means, 'Mgedluka, come home'.

Most people were crying and speaking about what he did when he was still alive. The elder family member took the branch to his hut and it was put on top of the meat, that is, the slaughtered bull for the deceased to eat, drink beer, and be merry.

Fire was made and all family members removed the black material which they pinned at his death on their sleeves. The wife of the dead person, who had been wearing a black mourning suit, removed it. All the black mourning symbols were burnt using fire which was prepared next to his hut. All this described above took place in the late afternoon towards sunset.

In the morning of the next day, the tree branch was taken out and put on the roof of the hut. One of the calabashes of beer was poured into a dish made of straw for all family members to drink while kneeling down. After everyone had drunk, the son-in-law took the dish and calabash and went back to the hut of the dead person.

After that, people were free to take meat to cook and to drink beer. People sang traditional songs and drums were beaten. People joined in dances which were different as people gathered from different communities. People enjoyed having their family members gathered together.

GAMUCHIRAYI CHIMBERA
RESEARCH AREA: Mutoko Region
Burial Ceremony

Over the vacation, I attended a ritual in a village some kilometres away from Mutoko. It was really a burial ceremony whereby a young man of that particular family had passed away.

As we got there, there were, as expected, many people gathered outside singing, clapping and doing all sorts of things. As we tried to greet or rather shake hands, the people who were there looked at us and continued with whatever they were doing and never bothered about the handshake. We sat down and became part of the gathering although we could not understand the kind of language that they were using. We were there from morning till about noon. It was then that I discovered that the body of the deceased was laid in a hut and it was on straw, wrapped in a black and white cloth. There were four old ladies sitting round and these were dropping some form of medicine (*mushonga*) on the corpse. Nobody else was allowed in the hut.

Later, an old man came holding something like a horn. He blew this several times and whilst he was doing this, another old man came and began to say something which was or seemed to be going hand in hand with the blowing of the horn. Most of us did not understand what the old man was saying.

The daughters-in-law then stood up in a line. There were about eight of them. They started dancing by moving front and back, back and front and continued doing so for about five minutes. The man with the horn did not stop blowing, but was now rhyming with the dance of the ladies. They stopped dancing, but when they resumed, they moved forward as if they were sweeping that place. When they got to the hut where the corpse was, they stopped, got in, and continued with their sweeping. They were not actually using brooms, but were using their hands. They moved round the body and then got out. Money was given to them. They then moved back to their places.

When the time came to go to the graveyard, an old man who had a round horn filled with medicine was in the lead. The medicine was sprinkled all over the body and it was then laid on the straw and put in a scotch cart. As we were leaving, they carried the body round. We all followed and as we proceeded to the graveyard, the daughters-in-law would run to the front of the cart forcing it to stop. This then gave them the opportunity to start dancing in front of the cart with their sweeping motions. They would not stop this until they were given some money.

At times, the funeral procession stopped. The old man blew his horn while others said a number of things. The others kept quiet with their heads lowered down. From there, we continued for quite some distance without stopping. When we thought we were almost there, there was again an interruption by the daughters-in-law performing their dances. This time they danced with vigour. People started singing and clapping. As soon as money was thrown to them, they moved on now in the lead acting as if they were sweeping with their hands but without using brooms.

We then moved on but a few metres before we arrived at the grave. All the people stopped. Two men from the crowd stepped forward and went to the grave. One of them, who seemed to be older than the other, somehow sat down with one of his legs down in the grave and the other one protruding across the grave. The people threw in various medicines. After this, several things were said and the body was laid down. The rest of us were not allowed to go near the grave. When all was over, we went back and people left with their belongings.

DAVID BISHAU
RESEARCH AREA: Zimunya Area, Eastern Zimbabwe
Saimba: Death Ritual of a Married Man

When the death occurred, a senior member of the extended family ordered the members of the immediate family of the deceased to vacate the hut of the deceased. It must be noted that the death occurred when members of the extended family were already gathered. (When the illness became serious, the relatives were informed and they took turns to serve the ill person.)

The chief was informed immediately after the death of the man. I noted that it was not the ordinary members of the family who went to inform the chief but elders of the extended family. When the chief came, he assumed a central role of advising the relatives of the deceased as to the correct procedures to be taken during the ritual.

Before this, but immediately after the death and immediately after the members of the immediate family vacated the hut of the deceased, certain rites were performed in the death hut. (I had the opportunity to observe these because I was a member of the extended family.) Selected members of the extended family got busy on the body. The deceased's eldest brother closed the eyes and mouth of the deceased and folded the hands to give the body the correct posture for the grave. In the process, he was mumbling some sort of sounds which were stifled. With the help of the other selected members of the extended family, the eldest brother of the deceased placed the body centrally just close to a raised platform at the rear side in the hut. After this, the men vacated the room and went to light fire outside the hut where they sat for most of the time during the ritual. Meanwhile, the bereaved wife of the deceased, his mother, and his aunt came to sit immediately around the body (now placed in a coffin).

A goat was slaughtered for supper. During supper, the chief sat down with the senior members of the deceased's extended family. The plans for the burial the following day were drawn. The chief wanted to know the person who would start the digging of the grave and whether there were any customary issues which would cause delays in burying the dead. The deceased was left overnight in the death hut.

I discovered that it was very important that the deceased had to leave the death-hut for the grave at or after twelve noon. In my observation, time has a special place. Certain rites were performed when the corpse was about to and was leaving the death-hut. The heir or the senior member of the family informed his junior (the one immediately below him in the family rank) who informed his own junior who informed his junior and so on until all members of the family were informed until the message was taken up to the chief that they were now taking the deceased from his hut to the grave. The senior member then released some stifled sound, a form of a gibberish, to the corpse. The cousins of the deceased then carried the coffin, led by the chief and the elder or senior members of the family, out through the door, around the death hut once and on towards the grave.

The journey to the grave was slow and was punctuated by several stops with the coffin being laid down to rest on the ground. Meanwhile, the people going to the grave picked two stones each. I also picked mine and finally we reached the grave.

Several speeches were made before the coffin was laid down. Then, a sleeping mat was laid in the grave and the strings binding the reeds of the mat removed. The coffin was then laid down in a specific way by the sons-in-law who had proceeded earlier to dig the grave. The head of the body was tilted towards the hut, hand-side, with the head facing the west. After this, there was silence.

The face of the deceased was uncovered and the relatives, led in a procession by the senior member of the family, peeped through into the grave saying certain words quietly. The senior member then posed in a crouching position and clapped his hands reciting the names of the forefathers and persuading them to receive the dead man. He then spat saliva on a handful of soil, prepared some mud and threw it onto the coffin which by this time had been closed. Once again, he led the procession with relatives each throwing a handful of earth onto the coffin and bidding the deceased farewell.

After this, the coffin was covered with soil but a certain hole was left and people each placed the two stones they had picked on the way into it. Women still capable of bearing children were asked to leave the grave and stand at a distance while the hole was closed. After this, the senior member or heir of the deceased swept the grave using a specific branch of a tree. Then we left the grave.

JUSTUS MAPFUCHI

RESEARCH AREA: Masvingo Province (Zezai of the Karanga)

Christian and Traditional Funeral of a Family Father

This piece of work is a descriptive account of an observed funeral of an old man in a Karanga family, of the Zezai tribe in the Masvingo Province southeast of the Great Zimbabwe. The funeral took place with two traditions, the tribal tradition and the Roman Catholic Christian tradition intermingled. A Roman Catholic priest and the eldest cousin of the family (*muzukuru mukuru*) conducted the ritual together. The funeral took place on 27-28 June 1991.

Soon after the old man died, the women and men who were present removed the corpse from the sickroom. They carried it to the big family kitchen where a mat had been spread behind the door along the wall. They wrapped the corpse in blankets and covered it with a bed sheet fixed to two poles leaning on the wall covering as a canopy. When they had finished laying the corpse, the women then started wailing at the top of their voices and the message was quickly spread to all relatives and neighbours who began to come to the home.

Among others, the *muzukuru* (one of the eldest cousins) came running, panting and wailing like the women. The women ran for him and threw themselves on him. Later, they led him to where they had laid his uncle (*sekuru*). He reached and bent over the corpse. He lifted the bed sheet and shook the shoulder of the dead man and called the name of the dead man three times. He called for him to wake up. He then covered the corpse and sobbed. He was joined by those in the hut and by those who were arriving.

The *muzukuru* later asked people to leave the hut except for a few close relatives who remained and washed the corpse, clothed him with fresh clothes, and placed him back on the mat. Later, the priest was called in and he said some prayers for the dead man. He pointed in his prayers and ordered the people to stop crying and to start singing songs of victory and congratulations over the achieved goal and the success of the man in his lifetime as a journey to the spiritual world which he had achieved by death. Suddenly, people changed the whole situation into a time of joy with lighter faces.

They sang songs of the spiritual world where the dead man was said to have joined his ancestors. The songs indicated that in fact the spirits had taken their member to them. He was said to have joined the ancestors in protecting the remaining members of the family. Less crying was heard and joyous songs continued with drumming and dancing.

Meanwhile, the close relatives were in one of the huts discussing the funeral arrangements and procedures. Later, the priest left since the burial was for the following morning. The wife of the dead man told the group of relatives where the husband had said he would be laid. This was to be in the family burial area on the nearby mountain in line with his ancestors and elders.

The grave was thus prepared underneath a big stone in a small cave in line with the other family elders' graves. They dug the cave deeper and developed its shape and then prepared a laying floor of flat stones fixed with mortar. That night, all the elders of the family spent the night by the fire guarding the grave.

At home, that day the sons-in-law killed an ox. They gave the meat for relish and they took the hide and treated it perfectly. They removed the fat off the hide, salted the hide and pegged it in the sun to dry. The sons-in-law were seen helping almost in every way possible. They made a wind break shelter (*musasa*) and made a fire in front of the hut with the corpse and spent the night there. The women were in the hut with the bereaved widow. They sang and danced Christian religious songs the whole night.

At dawn, the *muzukuru* collected all the belongings of the deceased man from his bedroom. He then called all members of the family and relatives and showed them the property left. They also discussed the life of the wife and the children and how life was to be organised after the funeral was over.

The eldest in the family called all to kneel and he poured snuff and water on the fireplace and spoke words of presentation of the member of the family to the ancestors. He asked for the reception of the new spirit who was joining the spiritual world. That new member was then to help with the continuous protection of the family. They then clothed the corpse with the best which the man liked when still alive. They wrapped him back in the blankets and rolled a white linen on him. All members were called to review the body for the second time before taking the corpse out of the hut.

When the elders were preparing to bring out the corpse for the funeral service, the daughters-in-law came and sat on the doorway preventing the corpse from being brought out. They had covered their heads completely like new brides. The sons-in-law came and gave some money to each and they jumped with joy uncovering themselves. One brought a mat and put it approximately a metre from the doorway.

Four men then came out with the corpse from the hut and placed it silently on the prepared mat. There was a loud sound of ululation from the daughters-in-law as they danced and ran around shouting the totem of the deceased. Another team of four came and lifted up the corpse and made three round turnings and then put it back into its original position. They then lifted the corpse to the mat in front of the table which was prepared for the priest to use. The priest had come that morning and then it was his turn to conduct most of the remaining procedures and rites.

The priest stood up with the book in his hand (prayer book). His assistant stood near him with the charcoal burning in a container and incense in another hand. Beside him was a big cup of water with a little branch in it. The priest bowed to the dead man and started to read from his book introducing people to the ritual of praying for the deceased.

The priest read some prayers for the dead in which he asked for forgiveness for the deceased's iniquities. He poured a spoonful of the seed used to make the incense onto the charcoal and scattered the incense around the dead body speaking words intended to cast away the evil spirits from the dead man. He took the water and said some words of blessing over it and sprinkled the water on the corpse with words of cleansing and calming the wandering spirit of the deceased.

After the incensing and sprinkling of the water, the priest sat down. One of the relatives of the deceased rose up with a book (Bible) and read from it words of consolation and encouragement. He read a passage from the 'Chronicles' on the signs of the time. He then explained the passage with reference to the good done by the deceased who was pictured as a successful hero of the family worthy of imitation.

The priest rose too and read a reading from the Bible. He consoled the family and spoke much on the benefits of death as a process of development and achievement of new life. He hailed the deceased as a hero who had run his race and won. After the talk, the priest went on with the sacrifice of the Eucharist with all prayers directed for the dead man to be accepted into the spiritual world.

After the service, the *muzukuru* organised the teams for carrying the corpse to its burial place. The procession started with one daughter-in-law carrying a full pot of water. She crawled on her knees all the way to the place of burial. The corpse on a stretcher was behind her being carried alternatively by the teams of four. On the way, they stopped and rested so another team could take over. Each team was comprised of relatives such as in-laws, cousins and nephews.

Songs were sung the whole way but they were more solemn than the earlier ones. There were also short petitions and the saying of common prayers until they reached the gravesite.

When they arrived at the gravesite, they placed the corpse on a mat near the grave. The priest came in front and said some prayers over the grave. He addressed the grave as if it were a home: 'You, James, this is your home now which we, your family and friends, have made for you'. He put incense on the grave to chase away the evil spirits from the new home and sprinkled water on it as a sign of purifying it. He then called the name of the deceased three times and ceremoniously gave him his home as his new place to dwell. He said, 'James, get into your new house until the day of the resurrection for all'. He said this three times and then made a sign of the cross on the grave and on the corpse. He then asked the *muzukuru* to put the deceased into the tomb.

The *muzukuru* then called four relatives to get into the grave to prepare the burial. They were given some thorny small shrubs and then spread them on the place where the corpse was to be laid. They took the mat and broke it and then spread it on the prepared place. They then took the beast skin and spread it over all. The corpse was then handed in and laid on the place and then rolled in the beast skin. A bag of clothes was also handed in and was put together with many other items which the man was using when he was alive. After all was packed, stones were given to those in the grave by the people. No one was allowed to hold two stones at one time. They then brought in mortar to seal the holes. After sealing the holes, the team climbed out of the tomb.

The priest went again in front and got a handful of soil from the heap in front of the grave. He then threw the soil in the grave with these words, 'Man, remember you are dust, to dust you shall return'. The people present did the same thing starting with the next of kin, then friends, and then any others present. The tomb was then filled with soil and the grave was finished. The burial was over. The priest came in front and gave a concluding prayer.

TAWANDA F. MAKUVISE

RESEARCH AREA: Mupandawana Area near Gutu

Christian and Traditional Funeral

On the 8th of July 1991, the young brother of my father passed away. On the following day, he was buried. I happened to be there and I observed the ritual of burying him. I was a participant observer.

Early in the morning of the 9th of July, the wife of the dead man washed the corpse and applied oil on it. The corpse was placed in a coffin and was put in the kitchen house where close relatives were gathered. People who came to pay the dead person respects went into the house. Women moaned as they went in and men shook their heads. In the house, they shook hands with everyone who was there. Following the shaking of hands, they would ask the question, 'What happened?' The story of the man's death would then be re-told. I observed that when people were approaching the hut, as soon as they could be seen, they started to moan.

The eldest son of the deceased drew the plan of the grave on the place where the grave was to be dug. As soon as he was finished, digging started. Whilst the strong men were digging, some women tied people they met to a tree and smeared them with ashes or residue of the traditional beer. They were ululating and were talking ill of the deceased. I was also tied and was smeared with ashes.

The women I am talking about prepared the way to the grave. The way was thoroughly swept removing all grass. Everything which they had removed from the way was put into paper bags. They decorated the way with stones which were painted white and placed along both sides of the path on the way to the grave.

In the house, some were singing church songs while others were moaning. Prayers were made. Scripture was read and a long sermon was given by the catechist who was leading the prayers. During the sermon, people laughed. Some who laughed had tears on their cheeks. I also laughed.

When those who were digging the grave indicated that they had finished, the coffin was placed at the door of the house and was opened, revealing the face of the deceased man. Relatives and friends of the man were asked to come and view him. Some people refused. Two daughters of the dead man fainted.

Following the viewing of the body, the auntie of the deceased inquired who had made the fire which was outside the house. She was directed to me since I was that very person. She gave me some salt and ordered me to throw the salt in the fire.

The coffin was carried to the grave. The catechist, who was in a black cassock, led the procession. The coffin was carried by the members of an Association in the Roman Catholic Church (*Nzanga YaJoseph*). The coffin had a cross made of pieces of white and black cloth; the two pieces crossed each other. Songs of the Catholic Church were being sung on the way.

Half way to the grave, the bearers stopped. A mat was brought and the coffin was placed on it. The catechist said some prayers. The women who had tied people with strings demanded the strings back. For the string to be removed, one had to pay some money. If one could not pay, something was taken from him. That is what happened to me. They took my watch. To get my watch back, I had to pay money. On the way, each person in the procession was asked to take a grain of maize and put it in a plate.

When the group arrived at the grave, those who had prepared the grave were ordered to get into it. They were given the coffin and they placed it down. As the coffin was being placed in the grave, some prayers were made. The dead man's spirit was commended into the hands of those who had died before him. The names of these persons were mentioned. The grave was sprinkled with water from a pot made of clay using a small branch from a tree. Incense was also swung over the grave.

When the coffin was covered, each person present was ordered to take some soil and to throw it into the grave. The strings, which were used to tie people, were placed in the grave when it was half filled. The contents of the paper bags were also thrown into the grave. Also, a cup and a plate were destroyed and placed in the grave along with a bow and an arrow. At times, stones were used. After the grave had been filled, a pot with water was placed at the grave and everyone present came and dipped a small branch in the pot and sprinkled water right round the grave. A stone was placed on the side where the head of the deceased was.

Following this, people were ordered to sit down. The eldest in the family of the deceased told again the story of the death of the father. In the process of retelling, he broke into tears and almost every woman and many men joined him in crying. Next, the head of the kraal spoke and ordered the people not to work for the next three days. Lastly, the catechist said some words.

After these speeches, anyone who had lent the dead man something or anyone who had borrowed something from him were asked to identify themselves. After this, people gathered into small groups to have some food and beer.

WESLEY MUTOWO

RESEARCH AREA: Chief Nyadewa's Region, Northeast Zimbabwe

Death by Suicide

I observed a burial ritual of a girl who had committed suicide in the region of Chief Nyadewa of Korekore in the tribe of Chera.

Before the girl was cut down from the beam she was hanging from, she was whipped very hard by the oldest man there who was chosen because he was the oldest of the paternal kins. She was cut down and fell directly onto the ground. The old man made sure that he did not come into contact with the corpse.

Persons called *vabanze* (strangers) were hired to carry the corpse home. On arrival, they created an entrance in the back of the hut in which the body was prepared for burial. This enabled the corpse to gain entrance into the hut but not through the normal door.

Before being dressed, a *n'anga* was consulted to look into the cause of the death of the suicide. After casting pieces of wood, *hakata*, the *n'anga* pointed to a man among the mourners as the cause of the action. The man admitted to this accusation. I heard some of the gathering shouting, '*Anofanira kuroora guva*' (He should marry the grave), and he readily agreed to do so.

The *vabanze* afterward dressed the body, making it ready for burial. The body was first rubbed with certain oils called *mupfuta* and then a certain liquidish chemical was sprayed over it. Lacerations of varying depths were then made in the skin of the body by the mourners. It appeared as though those closest to the deceased made deeper lacerations while those not so close just made scratches.

After being dressed in a *fuko* (white burial cloth), the body was laid on a *rukukwe* (reed mat). The gathering assembled in the hut and the man who had whipped the body of this girl made certain intonations and incantations to the world of the unknown.

After these incantations and intonations, the *vakwasha* (sons-in-law, the ones who did the heaviest chores) were called upon to go and dig the grave. The strangers carried the body in its mat round the *ruvanze* (yard) and slowly and carefully headed towards the grave. Together with the body was the deceased's clothes, shoes, and other items. The body left through the place of its entrance and as soon as it was out, some men immediately began to seal this temporary entrance. As the body left, four women swept the path before it and four other women swept the path after it carefully erasing the traces of those who were carrying the body and their footprints. Those doing the sweeping were referred to as *varoora* (daughters-in-law).

A scotch cart containing soil stood by the gravesite with soil which was very different from that of the local area. On arrival, the eight *varoora*'s faces were tied and covered. They were instructed to look away. The body was then dumped unceremoniously into the grave with its clothes and items the girl had worn while alive. Since this girl had not given birth to any children, the same old man who whipped her produced a live rat from a heap of items he had which he handed over to the strangers to tie to the corpse.

This was followed by more incantations accompanied by ululations from women and clapping from men. The *vakwasha* then took over the duties concerning the dead from the *vabanze* and first used the soil in the scoth chart to cover the grave. Soil placed on the top of the grave, however, was soil which had been dug out of the grave itself. Stones were neatly arranged to mark the boundaries of the grave and it was sealed by mud. After this, the people started to disperse as they sang low and sombre songs, most probably lamentations or dirge songs. This singing was accompanied by the beating of a drum. The drum was made especially for that purpose and was destroyed by burning that very day.

At home, beer was bought and some was brewed as people drank, talking lowly and sorrowfully. A black cow was slaughtered and the meat was eaten without salt and no other flavouring was allowed. The hide was nailed on top of the fowl-run and spread out to be exposed to the sun.

The people hardly slept that night. They tried to console the relatives of the deceased. At dawn, during the early streaks of sunrise, the people went to the grave. This was an exercise where everyone fell on his/her knees and the elders clapped their hands while the women ululated. This they called *kumutsa mudzimu*.

On arrival at home, a white goat was slaughtered and was eaten without salt and other flavouring spices. The blood was sprinkled onto the ground and covered with the earth under the tree on which the deceased passed away. This was followed by a dispersing of people except for one or two who remained behind for further comforting.

FELIX SHOKO
RESEARCH AREA: Gokwe District
Re-burial of a Man Killed in the Liberation Struggle

The re-burial rite was for a man killed during the war of liberation for Zimbabwe in 1979. On the day he had been killed, several other people had also been killed and had been burnt before being buried in a mass grave. The man to be reburied had a family, so his spirit had to be rested formally near his family's home. What follows is my description of what I observed.

It was dawn. All the women of the family were dressed in black and were seated around a newly dug pit. A *n'anga* lead the ceremony. He wore a crown made of ostrich feathers and an apron comprised of shreds of leopard skin around his waist. Three men from the family were

230

standing at the edge of the grave following the directions of the *n'anga*, who also had an attendant who carried a bag which contained materials to be used in the ritual.

The attendant produced dried roots from his bag and gave them to everyone present to chew, starting with the men and then going to the women. Some special water was sprinkled onto the back of the mother of the deceased. Everyone was barefooted. They marched in a procession to the mass grave which was some distance from the village. The *n'anga* led the way, followed by the men and then the women. As they marched, no one spoke or looked backward or sideward.

When they arrived at the mass grave, they all stopped and were sprinkled with water. The group was instructed to sit down around the grave. The *n'anga* then threw a heap of leaves from his bag onto the grave. He said the following words: 'To all of you who are in this house, we have come only to take our grandson, Tendai. So, you who are not of our blood, do not follow us.' The attendant then produced some powdered tobacco snuff which he gave to the father of the deceased who in turn knelt in a stooped position, clapped his hands, and said something very quietly. As he was doing this, he shred tobacco snuff on the edge of the grave. While he was still kneeling, the father raised his head and put the tobacco into his nose. At this stage, the father addressed the grave as follows:

Tendai, you died of war and you were buried in war. I, Farai, your father and the rest of the family have come to take you home where a real house has been prepared for you. Come, my son, and let us go now. May all the spirits [the father looked into the sky] of our family come and escort their grandson home. You, the grandspirits, must send away any alien spirits trying to follow us hereafter.

The *n'anga* then told the father to dig a volume of soil about ten kilogrammes from the face of the grave. The soil was put onto a black piece of cloth. The cloth was wrapped, tied and in a ball form placed a few metres away from the grave. All then stood around the soil parcel and the deceased's mother came forward. She knelt and said the following words in a solemn voice, 'Tendai, my son, now get on to my back as you did long ago when you were still an infant. Do not curse my back, I implore you.' She then placed the wrapped soil on her back and fastened it there using a new big bath towel. When she arose, she briefly observed a moment of silence.

Starting with the men, then the women, followed by the mother and the *n'anga*, they then silently marched home ceremoniously. Just as before, they did not talk or look around, but looked straight ahead. On arriving at the newly dug pit, the women sat grouped together, not more than three metres from the pit soil. On arriving, the mother waited for the *n'anga* to go to the opposite side of the pit. She was then instructed to go round the pit three times before the soil parcel was put gently beside the pit.

The *n'anga* then sprinkled the pit with some special water. The deceased's father got up, looked at the wrapped soil, and said, 'Tendai, this is your real house. Remain in it. Stop wandering about the bush.

Now, start looking after your family.' A man then jumped into the pit, received the soil parcel from the deceased's father and gently put it down into the pit. The deceased's mother, after the father, took soil dug from the pit and threw it in. All the other women came forward and repeated the same action. Some poles were placed over the parcel before the whole pit was covered with soil. Everyone then sat down except the *n'anga* who went away into the bush alone without any formality. The deceased's father then thanked all those who helped in the whole business involving the ritual. After this, all the people went home. The women, however, remained dressed in black for the rest of the day.

EVANS SANGANZA

RESEARCH AREA: Honde Valley, Eastern Zimbabwe

Kurova Gata (Divining Ceremony after Death)

I will explain the events that took place during the ritual of divining after death. In Shona, this is known as *kurova gata* which means that relatives of the deceased visit a *n'anga* (traditional diviner and healer) in order to seek information on what killed the deceased. I witnessed this ritual after the death of a relative.

After the deceased had been buried, only a day passed before the close relatives of the deceased had to seek information on what had caused his death. The mother, father, wife and a few close relatives were chosen to go to the *gata* where the divination would take place. The family members who had been chosen to go to the *n'anga* assembled in the hut where the deceased last lay. The parents of the deceased informed the ancestors about the journey they were about to undertake to the *n'anga*. They asked for assistance and protection from the ancestors. They uttered their ritual prayers from a bench which had been rubbed in earthen dung and which was located at a place in the hut where pots and water cans are kept. In their prayers, they would continually clap their hands.

When they had finished their prayers to the ancestors, the whole group rose into a single file and started on their journey to the *n'anga*. On reaching the *n'anga*'s place, the group did not go into the yard. They sat on the edges of the yard where they removed their shoes, watches, and money. The eldest of the company then went into the *n'anga*'s yard and shouted out that they had rebuked the *n'anga*. The *n'anga*'s messenger then invited the supplicants in.

On entering the *n'anga*'s hut, I was struck by the kind of dressing she wore. She had a feathery hat on her head. The feathers were black. The diviner bound her breasts with a black cloth. Her skirt was made of skin but had also some black feathers on it. On her neck were beads which were red and black in colour. When we had all sat down barefooted in the hut, the *n'anga* fetched from her side a stick that had black feathers on the other end and started fanning herself with it. After fanning herself, she started fanning the whole company one after the other. She said she was cleansing herself and the whole group from evil spirits. After some silence, the *n'anga* began.

I am here for insults. I had seen you before you set off. I see you have serious problems. My payment is a goat that has been

232

castrated. We always start the business when everything is clarified. Now present your case so that we tell grandfather (*sekuru*).

The father of the deceased told the *n'anga* their problem. He explained that his son died after a short illness and now they were seeking the cause of death. After the brief explanation, the *n'anga* took some snuff and started grunting before she sneezed violently. She was shivering like a reed in a flooding river. She took her divining sticks (*hakata*) and smashed them and called each lot by name. After this, she started addressing invisible beings which she called 'the ones in the air'. She even pointed into the air and talked as if someone were answering her.

After casting the lots twice, she sat passively like all was finished. Within a short time, however, she was at the lots again with a jerk like someone frightened. This final cast seemed to bring out the answer. She said she had identified the culprit. The *n'anga* then mentioned past incidences which had taken place between the deceased's family and the culprit. During the retelling of these past events, the deceased's parents at once knew the culprit, although he was not mentioned by name. The deceased's father then asked why the culprit had been given access to his family and who had granted this access.

In response to the question, the lots were consulted again. The *n'anga* grunted, shook her head, and withdrew from the lots to view them from a little distance. The *n'anga* then said that an angry ancestor had granted access to the culprit. This ancestor had not been granted his proper burial rites. This ancestor had been buried by the deceased's father's father but he was bringing punishment on the living generation.

The *n'anga* instructed the deceased's relatives to pay for their mistakes to the ancestor by brewing some beer and offering a bull as the ancestor's property. The diviner said that if this was not done, then more would fall by the ancestor's anger. The *n'anga* was then given a black hen and was promised that her goat was coming soon.

The whole company then sang out their thanks to the *n'anga* and the eldest said, '*matirutsa chiremba*' (we have been vomited). The whole company again returned to the hut where the deceased last lay. Here they offered some prayers again to the ancestors in gratitude that they had been led well in their journey. The ancestors were promised some beer after all was rectified.

FORTUNE SIBANDA
RESEARCH AREA: Chipinge District
Kurova Guva (Beating the Grave)

The ritual took place from dusk to dawn. The preparations had been conducted: kinsmen had been called, beer had been brewed and put on the kitchen platform, snuff was also there for use in the ritual. When all were seated on mats, the eldest man among the kinsmen led in the systematic clapping of hands in which he humbly begged to their dead ancestors for guidance in the ritual, pin-pointing the names of outstanding ancestors.

He went on appealing to them for guidance so they could perform the ritual correctly in order to bring the spirit of the dead person into the family. He also talked of the sharing among relatives of the dead man's clothes and how, possibly, it was still to be judged by conditions whether the wife and children will be under one of the younger brothers of the family. He then poured a little beer on the floor and drank some. He also did this with the snuff, spreading some of it on the floor and sniffing the other portion. They all clapped their hands whilst the women added a wave of ululation. Clothes were then shared amongst kinsmen. The initial crucial stage had been conducted.

This stage was followed by dancing, eating, and the drinking of beer. Drums were beaten whilst flutes were played. Those from the neighbourhood could now join in the entertainment. People drank beer to their full and were rejoicing. Two goats were then slaughtered.

At midnight, order and silence was once more maintained. The dead man's wife and young men of the deceased's family were instructed to sit on the mat in the middle of the crowd. From among the young men, the widow could choose a husband to take care of her and to bear children with him on behalf of the dead husband. If she wanted one of the men, she was to take a jug of water and indicate that by giving it to the man of her choice. If she did not want that, she would take the jug of water and give it to his eldest son, indicating that she now only desired care without further child-bearing. The wife took the jug of water and gave it to the new 'husband' whom she liked. The husband accepted. Ululation by women and clapping of hands by men followed this act.

As dawn approached, they took with them a small pot of beer to the grave of the dead person. The dead was told of all that had taken place. A little beer was poured on top of the grave and they drank the remaining one. They then returned home to the kitchen in the homestead indicating that they had brought the spirit of the dead person home to join the other ancestors. Everyone then left to return to their homes.

EZRA NYAMUJARA
RESEARCH AREA: Manyika territory
Kurova Guva (Beating the Grave)

I managed to attend a ritual ceremony, a *kurova guva* (beating the grave), and made my observation of what was going on. This is a ritual ceremony of bringing the soul of the deceased back into the family line of ancestor spirits. The property of the deceased and all that he has owned is shared among the members of the immediate family including the wife and children. This might be different from how the Zezuru or the Ndau or Tonga do it. I am going to describe how the Manyika do it because I understand some tribal clans do it in a different way. Some immediately share the *nhaka* (the property of the deceased) with the inheritors immediately after his death and later on 'beat the grave'.

The ritual I attended was that which was conducted by a family in the Manyika territory for a man who died in 1990 and is survived by his wife and three children, a son and two daughters. It was now about five to six months following the death of this man who lived in our village.

About a week before the ritual was due to be celebrated, the elders of the family went and consulted a distant *n'anga* who lives in the Honde Valley, but I was not allowed to accompany them because the elders said

I was not a member of the immediate family and also the proceedings there are kept in the strictest secrecy. Only elders are allowed. I asked one elder what the purpose of consulting the *n'anga* was and he said they wanted to enquire what had caused the man's death. They would also be given directions on conducting the ceremony and would be told whether they would face any problems with the ritual or succeed.

During the preparation week, members of the immediate family who lived far away were contacted and invited. Two goats, a male and a female, were bought and also a few chickens to serve as food on the ceremony day. A white cloth, about 1 metre by 1.5 metres, was bought. Besides this, rapoko was also prepared for making beer. The beer was made and well prepared and all of these preparations took about six days. On the seventh day, everything was ready and the people had gathered for the ceremony. Beer was now ready and the goats and chicken were slaughtered and prepared.

The ritual ceremony started around 5:30 p.m. People were called into a small hut where the beer was kept. As they entered, they left their shoes outside the door. The eldest person in the family took some snuff from a small *nhekwe* (a snuff container) and put it in a wooden plate which he took to the *chikuva* (a small stage in front of the kitchen where water containers are put). He knelt down and started saying,

To you who have already departed to the unknown, starting with ...(name of the deceased) who is the youngest, tell Mhotseka to tell those above you whom we no longer remember that this is the beer of "beating the grave" for ...(name of the deceased) to come back to the family and keep it from misfortunes.

Several other things were said but I failed to account for them all. All along, the person who was saying this was clapping hands and also fetching some of the beer from a gourd and putting it into another gourd and also drinking a sip in the process. Those in the hut were clapping hands too and women were ululating and jumping up. It was just a spectacular sight. The person who was saying this to the *chikuva* had his shoulders covered with a plain white sheet of cloth which draped to his legs.

When he had finished this, food and beer were served. They also sang traditional songs and danced to the beat of the drums. This continued to around midnight when the singing and drinking were stopped by the master of ceremonies.

It was now time for sharing property of the deceased to the inheritors. A bundle of clothes tied together was brought out. These were the clothes which used to be worn by the deceased. These were distributed by the eldest son-in-law of the family to members of the immediate family. When this was finished, there came the most exciting stage of inheriting the deceased's wife and children.

The wife was asked to sit down on a mat together with the would-be inheritors. These were about three younger brothers of the deceased. The wife was asked to fetch some water in a small dish which she did while walking on her knees. When she had done this, she was then asked to give the dish with water to the man whom she wished to be inherited. Instead of giving one of the seated men on the mat the water, she went and gave it to her aunt amid ululation and clapping hands and beating of drums. The aunt accepted and washed her hands. I asked what this meant and was told the woman no longer wanted to be married but will just keep her children. The aunt will take care of her. The bow and arrows were given to her eldest son and also the sword was given to him.

When this was over, the drinking and celebration continued until the next morning. At around 5:30 a.m., a small pot of beer was taken by the elders of the family who went with it to the grave of the deceased which was just nearby. I also accompanied them. When they reached the graveside, the eldest member of the family, who had initially conducted most of the offerings or *kupira* in the first stage, knelt down and started clapping hands saying they had brought back the soul of the deceased to the family so it was now his duty to keep the family from misfortunes. He poured a little of the beer on the grave and the rest they shared among themselves. After this was done, they went back home and before they could do anything, they said something to the *chikuva*. People also clapped hands and ululated and the ritual ceremony was over.

DUDZIRO NHENGU
RESEARCH AREA: Chivi District, Masvingo Province
Kurova Guva

I observed a ritual of '*kurova guva*' – bringing back the spirit of the dead. The ceremony began at six o clock in the morning. All the relatives of the deceased gathered near the deceased's grave. A tin full of water and a gourd were brought. A black goat was tied on a stump to make it stand in front of the people. In turns, the deceased's relatives began to take some water from the tin using the gourd, pouring the water on the goat's head. After the tenth person had poured water on the goat's head, the goat began to shake its head violently. The women ululated and all the men clapped their hands saying, 'He has agreed to be brought back home'. All the relatives were told to go and gather inside a mud hut while all invited guests and friends remained seated outside.

In the hut there were varying sizes of clay containers full of home brewed beer. One of the old men stood up and the whole hut was suddenly filled with silence. He took one of the smallest containers of beer and went in front of all the people where he knelt down and took out a snuff container from his pockets. He began to speak in low but powerful tones, sprinkling the snuff into the beer and on the ground. After calling all the names of the family ancestors, he said, 'We invite your presence. Come and bring back your child to us.' He began to clap his hands and all the other men clapped in unison. The women began to ululate. After that, the old man carried the small container of beer to the grave. At the grave, he knelt down and said,

> Taruvinga (name of the deceased), we are calling you back to your home today. Come and take care of your family. Here is some "water" to quench your thirst.

After that, he poured the beer on top of the grave. The men and women who were watching from afar clapped and ululated respectfully.

The same black goat on which some water was poured at the beginning was untied from the tree stump and handled by two men. A

236

pit was dug near the grave and it was filled with water. The two men immersed the goat's head in that pit full of water until the goat died of suffocation. The goat was then skinned and its dung was spread on top of the grave. All the relatives of the deceased knelt around the grave and said, 'We have finished your work'. The women ululated and the men clapped their hands.

All the people rose and went to the homestead where they sat under a tree. The goat's meat was cooked and served with sadza cooked from rapoko mealie-meal. This food was eaten only by the deceased's relatives. The goat's head was rolled in the goat skin and given to a certain old woman who was amongst the invited guests. Some bit of the rapoko sadza and the goat meat was put into a clay plate. That same old man took the sadza to the grave where he knelt and said, 'Here is your food'. Later, the old man ate that food.

After that, an ox was slaughtered. A lot of meat and maize meal sadza was cooked and distributed to everyone including all the invited guests. Beer was also given to the people to drink. Later on, the people were silenced by the old man as he shouted, 'Bring us the deceased's knobkerrie'. People sat down in a circle leaving some space inside the circle. The knobkerrie was laid down on the space inside the circle and the deceased's wife was told to walk across it. When she did, there was a lot of ululating and clapping of hands. The relatives of the deceased's wife shouted, 'Surely our daughter did not put us to shame'.

After this, a mat was spread under the tree shed. The deceased's eldest son was made to sit on the mat. A piece of the slaughtered ox hide was cut and made into a bangle which was tied on the hand of the deceased's son. The old man addressed the deceased's son saying, 'You have taken your father's position and you are going to look after your father's home'. The men clapped and the women ululated. After that, more beer was given to the people. One of the old men announced that the deceased's clothes were going to be distributed the following day.

CLEVER MUCHENGI

RESEARCH AREA: Binga

Kurova Guva (Beating the Grave)

I am going to describe a *kurova guva* ritual which was performed by the Tonga people in Binga on 28th June 1991. After hearing that such a ritual was to be performed, I woke up very early in the morning and made for the village in which the ritual was to occur. On my way, I saw five women going into the cemetery. These women started removing grass and sticks on and around one grave. When they finished, they knelt surrounding the grave. Two more women arrived and offered them something. After this, they all left the cemetery and I followed them into the village.

On arrival at the home of the deceased, I went into the kitchen and sat down. Almost everyone looked at me; possibly I was not meant to be present. This petrified me. A man stood up and called *muzukuru*, the sister's oldest son of the family, to come forward. The *muzukuru* was asked to be in charge of the ritual. From that moment, I knew who this *muzukuru* was.

The *muzukuru* knelt before the *chikuva*, an elevated platform where clay pots are placed in a traditional kitchen, and addressed the spirits informing them of the ceremony which was to take place. In fact, he started clapping his hands and invoked ancestors beginning with the spirit of the deceased and going on to mention many other ancestor spirits. He concluded the ancestral invocations by saying, *'Kune vari kumhepo'* (those in the air).

When the *muzukuru* paused, some women ululated and he went outside. We all followed him. The *muzukuru* tied an ox, moving his lips, but saying nothing audible. He ordered the ox to be slaughtered. When this had been done, some of the meat was roasted and eaten without salt. The rest of the meat was taken home and cooked.

People spent the whole day drinking millet beer and in the afternon sadza and meat were dished to the people. In the evening, some few elders gathered. From there, these elders formed a procession and made for the cemetery. They were joined by several others and so I also accompanied them. On the way, they were singing *ngondo*, traditional funeral songs and were drumming. When we arrived at the cemetery, the *muzukuru* went closer and stood beside the grave I mentioned earlier. We all sat down a bit further away from the grave, except the *muzukuru* who remained standing. I could not see him properly and since I wanted to observe all his actions, I went in front.

There was some silence and when I looked around, I saw a woman, who was carrying a clay pot, moving on her knees towards the grave. The *muzukuru* received the clay pot and placed it on the grave. He cut a small branch of a tree, plunged it into the clay pot and sprinkled the contents of the clay pot on the grave. I could not tell whether it was water or beer which was being sprinkled on the grave.

As the *muzukuru* was doing this, we were all quiet. Each time the *muzukuru* paused, some women ululated. The *muzukuru* asked for a clay pot of beer and a woman brought it to him, again, on her knees. He fetched some beer from the clay pot with a ladle made from a gourd, drank some of the beer and poured the remaining on the grave. He called on the spirit of the deceased to quench his thirst with the beer. He also informed the deceased spirit that he was to be taken back home in order to look after his family and to guard it against evil spirits. This was followed by ululating by some women.

Once more, there was some silence and this terrified me. I also looked around and saw some men approaching with a black goat. The *muzukuru* received the goat and cut its throat. The goat was held in such a way that the blood spilled on the grave. The *muzukuru* took the dung from the goat's stomach, mixed it with beer and smeared it on the grave. One woman started shrilling and was joined by several others. A man from the crowd jumped, danced for a while, seized the goat, and rushed away shouting and jumping around.

The *muzukuru* then cut a big branch from a nearby tree and placed it on the grave. He poured some beer on the branch and asked the people to stand and sing a traditonal joyous song. The people sang and danced for a while. During this time, the *muzukuru* went around the grave but I did not see what he was doing.

When the people sat down, the *muzukuru* told them that the climax of the ceremony had come. He said that the spirit of the deceased had been purified and he was now taking it back home. He started to pull the branch. The people stood up and began singing joyous traditional songs. The *muzukuru* got in front of everyone and led the procession slowly towards home. He neither sang nor danced.

When we approached the home of the deceased, the people who had remained behind came running and joined the procession. The noise from singing and drumming was louder than that of the previous procession. There was a joyous atmosphere which almost made me dance.

The *muzukuru* pulled the branch into the kitchen. Some people also went into the kitchen. Most of the people remained outside since they could not all fit into the kitchen. I also did not have the chance to go into the kitchen so I did not observe what took place there. Since it was dark, I went back home.

GONORESHUMBA NDAKARUZA
RESEARCH AREA: Gutu South, Masvingo Province
Kurova Guva

The ritual I observed was *kurova guva*, to beat the grave, held in Masvingo Province, Gutu South. A lot of millet beer was brewed before the ceremony. On the evening before the ritual began, relatives of the deceased arrived at the deceased's home. Each brought a pot of beer and some food to be eaten during the ceremony. Some relatives brought small pots of beer and yet others very large ones and many of them. I interviewed one of the relatives of the deceased concerning this and she told me that each is expected to contribute depending on his relationship to the deceased. Close relatives usually contribute a lot as compared with distant ones.

When most of the people had gathered, a large pot of beer was placed on a platform in the hut of the deceased's wife. This was followed by a formal address from one of the relatives. He was the deceased's sister's son, *muzukuru*, so I was told. I was informed that he was telling the spirits of the forthcoming ceremony. He was saying names of quite a number of people and in the end, he said, 'Here is your beer. It is the beer of the deceased. Come and drink with him.' After this, there followed singing and the beating of drums. Some people were crying. I asked why and was told that the people were singing funeral songs for the deceased. I was also told that weeping showed honour to the spirit. Both men and women danced to the drum beating and singing. Then boys and girls took over with the dance until early in the morning of the next day.

The next day was the real day of the ceremony. Early in the morning, an aunt (*tete*) of the deceased carried a pot of beer on her head and started moving to the grave and a procession followed her in silence.

The *muzukuru* underook the duties of leading the ritual at the grave. He took the pot of beer off the head of the *tete* and placed it at the centre of the grave. He took a calabash of beer, poured a little on top of the grave and drank the rest. He started talking, looking right into the pot.

239

I did not hear the words because I was too far away. I was told later that he was addressing the deceased and was asking for his protection and that he had to come to guide the family as well as to join the other spirits of the family. After this, the *muzukuru* filled the calabash with beer and gave it to the women who ululated and clapped their hands. Each woman came forward and said some words to the grave. After this, men were given their own calabash. They also clapped and went forward uttering something I could not hear. Then the rest of the people joined the drinking until the beer was finished. Non-relatives never said any words at the graveside. When the pot of beer was empty, the people made their way home leaving the pot behind.

When we reached the home, much music and dancing took place. At the same time, some specially chosen people killed a bull. Only those who actually did the slaughtering were allowed to be present when the bull was killed. One of the people I talked to told me they took the blood from the bull and smeared it on the grave. This was done only by relatives.

I was told that while the blood was being smeared on the grave, the relatives of the deceased pleaded with the spirit to guide them. Each person announced himself and made some plea for guidance and protection.

Then followed much feasting and dancing. People were singing a song called *Kwaziwai Tovera* (Greetings to Tovera). The song goes like this:

Mudzimu dzoka (Spirit, come back).
Ahuwe-e- kwaziwai Tovera (Hello, greeting to Tovera).
Vana Vanachema ahuwee kwaziwai Tovera (Children are crying, hello, Tovera).
Vana-chema kumba- a huwee kwaziwa Tovera (Children are crying at home, greetings to Tovera).

This went on for quite a long time.

After the music and dancing had finished, the *muzukuru* took the walking sticks, axes and some garments of the deceased and smeared them with some liquid after having washed them in water. The wife of the deceased was escorted to her hut by some women. Later I was told these were her sisters. The walking sticks, axes, and garments were placed outside the wife's hut. She then came out and jumped over the things. This was followed by joyful noises, clapping of hands, and ululating. The wife's sisters grabbed her with joy. I was told later by an old man that this meant that the widow had proved that she had not had sexual relations since her husband's death.

Next a ritual involving a goat occurred. A male goat was placed at the centre of the compound and people gathered around it. Relatives of the deceased walked in a single file toward the goat. There was a pot of water by the goat and a calabash. Each relative in turn took a calabash of water and poured it over the goat. When the *muzukuru* poured the water, the goat shook its body vigorously for about two minutes. This was immediately followed by joyful noises. The goat was taken away immediately to be slaughtered.

In order to understand this, I made an effort to interview the *muzukuru* himself. I asked him what the ceremony of the goat meant, but to my astonishment, he broke into a cry. I was forced to look for another person to ask. She told me that the rite was intended to see who among the kin of the deceased was his beloved one, his most favoured one. The fact that the goat shook its body vigourously when the *muzukuru* poured water on it symbolised that he is the one most favoured by the deceased.

The meat of the goat was roasted. Its skin was burnt with all of its bones. It was eaten without any salt. Only a small part of the skin was left from a part of the body.

Then came the inheritance ceremony. The *tete* divided the clothes of the deceased among his relations. Some were given more and better clothes than others. Then the widow was given a dish of water by the *tete* which she gave to her husband's young brother (*babamunini*) who washed his hands from the dish. Again, this was followed by noises of joy. Later, I was told that the whole process was to discover whether or not the widow wanted to be a wife of one of the relatives. The fact that she gave the dish to *babamunini* showed that she was for the idea and had in fact chosen *babamunini* to be her husband. The fact that *babamunini* washed in the dish showed approval. If he was against it, he could have refused to wash his hands. Also, if the widow did not want any of the relatives, she could have emptied the dish. After this, both the widow and *babamunini* sat on a mat. Each person now addressed him by the name of the deceased exhorting him to perform properly the duties he had received.

After this, the eldest son of the deceased tied the small piece of the skin of the goat around his wrist. Dancing and music followed. The *muzukuru* thanked everyone and declared that the ritual had come to an end.

PHILLIP MARUFU

RESEARCH AREA: Lower Gweru, Midlands Province

Kurova Guva

In this essay I will describe a ritual which I observed in Lower Gweru in the Midlands Province. The ritual is called *Kurova Guva* (beating the grave). The language used for the ritual was Shona. The ritual was performed in order to bring back home the spirit of a man named Kufarira who had died eleven months earlier.

The ritual started around 7:30 a.m. Around that time, people gathered at the centre of the homestead clearing and the brother of the deceased announced that the day had been set aside for bringing Kufarira back home and giving him his duty of looking after his family and friends. The elderly man said anyone who had tobacco was to leave it outside the homestead clearing. We were all told to follow *muzukuru* (nephew) who was the son of the eldest daughter of the family. The nephew led the way followed by daughters-in-law of the family. Behind them were the sons-in-law of that family. (I was one of the sons-in-law.) Behind the sons-in-law were the children of the deceased's family. The children (all were married) were followed by the brothers and sisters and friends of the deceased. Altogether, the people who left the homestead were twenty-eight.

When we reached a *muchakata* tree, which was about 450 metres from the homestead clearing, I saw a black goat which was tied under the tree. It had a black cloth around its left front leg and a white cloth around its neck. The daughters-in-law and the sons-in-law knelt down and started to clap their hands. All the other people sat down beside the eldest brother of the deceased who addressed the goat by name. He said, 'Kufarira, young brother, we have come to take you home as we promised yesterday'. As he addressed the goat, the daughters-in-law and sons-in-law continued to clap their hands. The elderly man knelt and put some brown tobacco on the ground.

Three sons-in-law, led by the eldest nephew, went and untied the goat from the tree. The goat cried and the sisters of the deceased began to ululate. Silence was maintained once more as the goat was pulled towards the people. The daughters-in-law moved on their knees toward the goat and touched it on the neck using a white cloth. After the daughters-in-law, all the people present placed the small piece of cloth on the goat. After that, the eldest brother of the deceased told the spirit that some people had failed to come due to money problems and he then called out the names of the people who had failed to come.

The wife of the deceased then gave the goat some water which was in a big pot. The goat drank the water and the people clapped their hands and the sister of the deceased man ululated. The eldest daughter-in-law moved on her knees and poured more water into the pot. The three sons-in-law who were holding the goat all sat down as more water was added to the pot. The eldest nephew put some black substances into the pot. Two other daughters-in-law moved on their knees to the pot and poured some millet beer into the pot. The eldest brother of the deceased then told the sons-in-law who were holding the goat to do their job ('*Chiitai basa renyu Vakuwasha*').

The three sons-in-law all knelt and from that position they lifted the goat and pressed its head into the pot. The brothers and sisters of the deceased rubbed their hands as the goat was dipped into the pot. After about five minutes, the goat was put down and it was already dead. The other sons-in-law (including this writer) were told to go and find some firewood.

When we came back, the nephews lit the fire. The goat by then had been skinned and nearly half the goat was roasted by the nephews. The roasted meat was cut into small pieces and everyone present was given a small piece. We were told to rub our lips with the small pieces of meat. No salt was put on the meat. After that, we were told to follow the brother of the deceased who led us to a small hole which was to his right side. He then put the small piece of meat in the hole which had been dug. (I was later told that the hole had been dug when I had gone for firewood and that the contents of the pot in which the head of the goat had been dipped was poured into that hole.) We all followed the elderly man in placing the pieces of meat into the hole.

When we had all finished this, a small branch of the *muchakata* tree was cut by the eldest nephew. A black cloth was thrown on top of the branch by the wife of the deceased. Some water and millet beer was poured at the cut end of the branch. The daughters-in-law then led us on our way back home and people were singing and dancing. Just behind the daughters-in-law were the sons-in-law dragging the branch of the tree. On arrival at the homestead clearing, water and beer were poured on the branch by the eldest daughter-in-law of the family.

On entering the homestead clearing, the daughters-in-law knelt and began to move on their knees. People began to sing and dance and others were drumming. The daughters-in-law led the way to the main bedroom. The daughters-in-law and the sons-in-law did not enter into the bedroom. The branch was given to the nephews who entered with it into the house. The brothers, sisters, nephews and children of the deceased man went straight into the house and all the other people remained outside singing and dancing. One song had words which said, 'Today, we have got a guardian'.

After about ten minutes, those who had gone into the house came out. The eldest brother went straight in front of the kitchen door and dug a small hole in which he put some brown tobacco, amidst dances of great joy. After that, the daughters-in-law were told by the oldest brother of the deceased to start giving people some beer.

From every pot of beer, some amount was poured on the ground before people began to drink from it. It was then that the eldest brother of the deceased announced that the ritual was over and that 'Kufarira adzoka pamusha kuzochengeta vana, hama neshamwari dzake dzose' ('Kufarira is now back home in order to look after his children, relatives, and friends').

The ritual ended at 10:50 a.m. However, people continued to drink beer and sing up to about 11:00 p.m.

BRIGHTON NCUBE
RESEARCH AREA: Kezi Area, Matebeleland South
Bringing Home Ceremony (umbuyiso)

The ritual observed was a bringing home ceremony, that is, the ritual of bringing the spirit of a dead person home. The deceased was the father in the home. The ritual was performed in the rural areas. Neighbours and relatives from town were invited and there were approximately five hundred people present.

Early in the morning, fifteen men went to the kraal to slaughter a bull. The *n'anga* first talked to the ancestors appealing to them to accept the sacrifice. The other men were clapping hands and nodding their heads expressing their appreciation. These were the elders of the village. The *n'anga* gestured as if he were fighting an enemy using a spear and a shield. The *n'anga* was wearing strips of skin around his waist, bones hanging on his neck, white, red, and black long cloths crossing on his chest and an animal skin hat. He told the elders that the ancestors had agreed that they should slaughter the bull. The other men were wearing ordinary clothes but watches, hats and shoes were removed.

The men pierced the bull with a spear, the traditional way of hunting, and the *n'anga* took its blood and poured it in the centre of the kraal. As he did this, he asked the ancestors to provide the family with more cattle and thanked them for the food. He cut a piece of meat and roasted it as he was supposed to be the first one to taste the meat. He ate it without putting salt on it. He was humming a song. Women came with baskets to get the meat. Gall was given to the boys to smear on their bodies. They were told to whistle loudly and to imitate the bull as a way of appreciation for what the ancestors had done for them. Everyone then went home and no one was allowed to look back as the ancestors were performing certain duties in the kraal even though they were invisible. Everyone sang the song that encouraged the ancestors to keep the family and to keep the cattle during drought periods.

Sadza was cooked and it was mixed with meat without tomatoes, soup or any modern additive. A drum half full of the food was carried to the hut where the deceased had been staying. The *n'anga*'s helper known as *Isangoma* thanked the spirits for the food. He asked for a multiplication of the daily food and that the food should give good health to the people. Tobacco was poured right around the drums as a way of discouraging those among the crowd who might have come with poison to kill their enemies. The *n'anga* was the first one to taste the food. After the above procedure, the food was ready for distribution.

The grandmothers of the village had brewed the traditional beer the previous day. It was put in the same hut where the sadza was. The *n'anga* thanked the spirits for the beer and all blood relatives were called inside the hut. They removed their shoes and each was given a sip of beer after having thanked the ancestors. They said, 'My beloved ancestor, … (name of the ancestor), I thank you for all your blessings'. After all had thanked, the *n'anga* reiterated the thanks of the relatives making gestures like someone praying and he ended up speaking in a language that was not understandable. He took a dirty tin that contained water and some herbs. He drank and then forcefully spat on the face of each blood relative.

After lunch, the *n'anga* came in his traditional attire with the elder son of the deceased, the mother and the sons and brothers. They went to the grave site and a branch that covered the grave was removed. The *n'anga* talked to the deceased pleading with him to come home and protect the family. He put a clay mug of beer on top of the grave and they returned home. The elder son and the *n'anga* began dancing. Some of the people were beating drums, playing *mbira*, or shaking *'hosho'* (a round container that has small stones inside it). Other people clapped their hands and whistled as they danced.

The elder son fell to the ground in a trance. He was rigid so that no one could fold any joint in his body. He sneezed loudly and everyone said, *'Woza huhle'*, meaning 'Come peacefully, our beloved spirit'. This was referring to the spirit of the late father of the family. He sat down and groaned like a bull. He was given traditional beer and a twist of mbanje to smoke. He became ecstatic and he ran to the grave and drank the beer that was left secretly and took a piece of soil from the grave. He scattered the soil around the home showing that the spirit of the deceased was amongst the people. He started talking in a language that was unknown and the *n'anga* interpreted.

The blood relatives were asked to come one by one expressing their problems to the spirit. They knelt down, dropped some fine tobacco around a clay mug of traditional beer, and sniffed some tobacco. This sniffing was followed by a violent sneeze. They clapped hands and told their problems to the spirit. Many asked for employment, success at school, or promotion at work. Some wanted to be cured of diseases and some wanted cows and a greater harvest in the fields.

The spirit then told the people what it wanted. It wanted a black and red long cloth, a spear and shield, an animal skin hat, a drum, *mbira*, bones of a puff adder, elephant, lion, and leopard. He wanted to dwell in a black bull that was supposed to be called grandfather and never be beaten up or used for ploughing. The spirit said that it had come to protect the family and this ritual was supposed to be repeated annually.

As the elder son was possessed, he looked fierce and his eyes were squinting. He was taking deep breaths quickly. He then slept for about a minute and when he awakened, he had returned to his normal state.

The family members then went to the grave and they were very happy because the beer that was left on the grave was no longer there signifying acceptance of their offering. The dancing resumed at home welcoming the spirit of the deceased. A new branch was put on top of the grave and beer was poured around the grave by each member of the family.

As they departed from the grave, they took a sample of soil and mixed it with beer and other herbs. This was put in every corner of the home. The hair of the family members was cut and the *n'anga* took it to bury in the grave. This was the end of the ritual but the people continued dancing and singing.

WHENCELOUSY DZENGA
RESEARCH AREA: Budya Area, Mutoko District
The Death of Chief Nyamhunga[1]

The story is based on the death of Chief Nyamhunga of the Budya area in Mutoko District. The story was told to me by Mr Choto, a man with first hand information about it. The death of a Chief among the Budya tribe is very important and involves a great deal of secrecy. The burial of Chief Nyamhunga was extraordinary.

The Chief of the Budya people, Chief Nyamhunga, had suffered an illness for a very long time, but none of his tribe knew of it apart from his immediate family. One Saturday morning, clouds padded the sky and lightning formed. Suddenly, a heavy rain flooded the ground. At the very moment that it began to rain heavily, Chief Nyamhunga died.

The news of his death spread quickly among the family members. The Chief's advisor, named Tsoko, assembled the family and told them not to leak the information that the Chief had died to non-family members. He told the in-laws to fetch water from a sacred well in Chiera mountain.

The wives of the deceased were given water in a clay pot to wash the corpse and to dress it in chiefly attire. They then went out of the hut and formed into a single file line from the door, in order of seniority. Each in turn entered the hut and talked with the corpse as if it were alive. They kissed their husband for the last time.

There was division of labour among the in-laws. Some were responsible for mending fibre for transporting the corpse and others

---

1. This was presented originally by the student as part of the mythologumena, but its content fits more appropriately as a rite of passage. The reader should note, however, that this description was not observed directly by the student.

245

carried and rolled the stones to seal the cave entrance. When these preparations were completed, the sons and wives made a procession to the cave.

When the corpse was ready to be carried, the in-laws closed the door to the hut tightly. They then systematically de-thatched the hut without dropping any piece of mud on those inside. Instead of using the doorway as a passage, they raised the corpse and lowered it over the pole walls. They then left for the burial. Nobody was allowed to mourn or lament. The in-laws carried the corpse on a fibre mat. They did not stop along the way.

The Chief's sons and the widows had already arrived at the cave. They entered one by one into the cave laying down their gifts without making any noise.

When the corpse arrived, the in-laws put the corpse at the entrance to the cave. It was then uncovered and the sons and wives looked at their 'father' and 'husband' for the last time. At that juncture, they made a procession home before the burial took place.

The elders and the in-laws rested the corpse in the cave and put a clay pot full of water and a gourd beside it. In addition to the clay pot, they put a he-goat in the cave and closed the entrance with the stones. They left a hole small enough for the goat to struggle out.

After that, they went home singing and dancing, while other immediate family members started lamenting. The in-laws started beating drums so that all the Budya tribes flocked to the homestead of Chief Nyamhunga. His dearest friends mourned. A few cracked jokes to relieve sorrows engendered by the death of the Chief. In an incredibly short space of time, the homestead was flooded with people of various ages.

The in-laws slaughtered five black bulls and the meat was roasted. The daughters-in-law were given the task of cutting and distributing the meat to the mourners. There was a lot of singing and dancing while the drums were beaten.

The aged women brewed *Mahewu* (a non-alcoholic millet drink) and served it to the children and women. As the day advanced, the number of mourners reduced gradually till only immediate members and elderly people were left.

The next morning, a friend named Chitoto took over and assembled the family. He ordered the wives to have their heads dressed with black cloths. The children, numbering to about twenty, had their heads shaved and groundnut oil was rubbed into their scalps. No sexual contact was allowed for a period of 30 days. The immediate family members were not allowed to take part in any parties or celebrations for the stipulated 30 days.

A SPECIAL RITUAL OF PROTECTION

NICHOLAS MUKARAKATE
RESEARCH AREA: Murewa Communal Areas

Protecting Clan Members from an Avenging Spirit (ngozi)

Sunday, 7th July, I observed the traditional African ritual of protecting clan members from the wrath of an avenging spirit of an unrelated person who had been killed by a late member of that clan. The ritual took place in the early hours of the morning, immediately after sunrise on a private place by a riverside in the Murewa communal areas.

The first part of the ritual required ten selected male members of the clan to go to an agreed place by the riverside. This occurred long before the sun rose. They made there a very big fire on which a big drum half filled with water was placed. While the water was being boiled, the men slaughtered a huge black he-goat and skinned it. The liver and the lungs of the goat were taken and thrown into the drum of hot water and left to boil. No salt or cooking oil or any other ingredients were added to the drum. The men were chatting and talking as if nothing serious was happening. A *n'anga*, dressed in a black cloth wound around his waist down to just below the knees and wearing a necklace of black and white beads, watched the whole procedure carefully. His face was expressionless. He held a black tail of a beast in his right hand.

Just as the sun began to rise, the rest of the members of the clan started arriving at the place where the men and the *n'anga* were boiling the meat of the slaughtered goat. They did not all arrive at the same time but in groups of five or six and not more than ten people at a time. They all grouped together in the bushes along the river talking in low and subdued voices, but they were not solemn.

When it seemed that everybody was present, the *n'anga* instructed an elderly member of the clan to tell the people to go and wash in the river in two groups. The males went a little distance down the river while the females went somewhere up the river. Only unperfumed washing soap was used. No lotions were to be applied after washing. The men bathed first and the boys last according to seniority, but all bathed at the same spot. I assume the same thing happened to the women and girls. All the washing was done in silence.

From the point of bathing, the eldest member of the clan led us all in a single file back to the drum of boiled meat where the *n'anga* had remained. The women also came in a single file from the other direction to meet the men at the drum. At the drum, the *n'anga* with the help of two aides gave everybody a very small piece of the liver plus some soup (the water which was tasteless from the drum) using a small cooking lid. It was compulsory to finish all that was in the lid. After everybody had his share, the fathers returned to get some meat and drink for their sons and daughters who were absent. Nobody seemed to be in any mood for conversation at this stage in the ritual. (It should be noted that the fathers went to collect the food for their absent children since the mothers had remained behind because of the fact that they do not have the same totemic symbol with their husbands. Only the people of the heart totem were present at this ritual.)

After this, the *n'anga*'s aides called us all together again and then divided us as in the first time when we went to wash. The males were told to follow the *n'anga*'s male aide to another spot in the river. The aide went into the water and walked to a point where the water level comes just below the waist. Whilst there, the aide waited with a small dishful of reddish water (as if some blood had been added to it), and there was an African body oil container, *chini*, in the dish. Again, from the most senior man of the clan to the youngest boy, everybody took turns getting into the water where the *n'anga*'s aide stood waiting. An expression of seriousness and businessmindedness constituted the features of the aide's face. In the water, everybody was instructed to dip his hands in the dish and rub them on his face and body and to utter the following words:

Please, you vengeant soul of the murder victim, leave us alone. We are mere kids. The evil was done by long-gone elders and we do not know anything about it. Leave us alone. We are innocent.

These words were said after the aide, i.e. we were merely repeating what the aide said.

After this, each participant got out of the water and put on his clothes without drying his body first. But before putting on the clothes, the *n'anga* stamped the person on the chest with a black piece of cooked meat. The women later came to the same place after the men had finished and underwent the same process.

After this procedure, we all grouped together as in the beginning to have some razor blade cuts made twice on the neck, twice on both hands, and twice on both feet. These are called *nyora* in Shona. Then the *n'anga* and his aides rubbed some black powdery medicine on the bleeding places where they had cut us with the razor blades. Then the ritual was over but no one was allowed to go and bathe again that day, to use perfumed soaps, or to apply any lotion.

BIBLIOGRAPHY

Abimbola, W. 1994. 'Ifa: A West African cosmological system' in T.D. Blakely, W. E. A. van Beek and D. L. Thompson (eds.), *Religion in Africa*. London: James Currey and Portsmouth, New Hampshire: Heinemann, 101-31.

Aschwanden, H. 1989. *Karanga mythology: An analysis of the consciousness of the Karanga in Zimbabwe*. Gweru: Mambo Press.

Banana, C. S. 1991. *Come and share: An introduction to Christian theology*. Gweru: Mambo Press.

Bascom, W. 1984. 'The forms of folklore: Prose narratives', in A. Dundes (ed.), *Sacred narrative. Readings in the theory of Myth*. Berkeley: University of California Press, 5-29.

Baylis, P. 1988. *An introduction to Primal Religions*. Edinburgh: Traditional Cosmology Society.

Bediako, K. 1995. 'The significance of modern African Christianity - a manifesto', *Studies in world Christianity* 1 (1), 51-67.

Beach, D. N. 1980. *The Shona and Zimbabwe 900-1850*. London: Heinemann.

1984. *Zimbabwe before 1900*. Gweru: Mambo Press.

Beek, W. E. A. van 1994. 'The innocent sorcerer: Coping with evil in two African societies (Kapsiki and Dogon),' in T.D. Blakely, W.E.A. van Beek and D. L. Thomson (eds.), *Religion in Africa*. London: James Currey and Portsmouth, New Hampshire: Heinemann, 196-228.

Beek, W. E. A. van and Blakely, T. D. 1994. 'Introduction', in T. D. Blakely, W. E. A. van Beek and D. L. Thomson (eds.), *Religion in Africa*. London: James Currey and Portsmouth, New Hampshire: Heinemann, 3-20.

Beier, U. 1980. *Yoruba myths*. Cambridge: Cambridge University Press.

Blakely P. A. R. and Blakely, T. D. 1994. 'Ancestors, "witchcraft", and foregrounding the poetic: Men's oratory and women's song-dance in Hemba funerary performance,' in T. D. Blakely, W. E. A. van Beek, and D. L. Thomson (eds.), *Religion in Africa*. London: James Currey and Portsmouth, New Hampshire: Heinemann, 399-442.

249

Bleeker, C. J. 1963. *The sacred bridge. Researches into the nature and structure of religion.* Leiden: Brill.

Bolle, K. W. 1990. 'Review of *To Take Place*', *History of Religions* 30 (2), 204-12.

Bourdillon, M. F. C. 1976. *The Shona peoples.* Gweru: Mambo Press.

1990. *Religion and society: A text for Africa.* Gweru: Mambo Press.

1993. *Where are the ancestors? Changing culture in Zimbabwe.* Harare: University of Zimbabwe Publications.

Brown, J. E. 1984. 'Religion in primal societies; North American Indian Religions', in J. Hinnells (ed.), *A handbook of living religions.* Harmondsworth: Penguin Books, 392-412.

Burnett, D. 1988. *Unearthly powers. A Christian perspective on Primal and Folk Religions.* Eastbourne: MARC.

Campbell, J. 1970. *The masks of God: primitive mythology.* New York: The Viking Press.

Cave, D. 1993. *Mircea Eliade's vision for a new humanism.* New York and Oxford: Oxford University Press.

Chigwedere, A. S. 1980. *From Mutapa to Rhodes 1000-1890 A.D.* London: Macmillan.

Chiura, T. 1991. *Mutiusinazita religious cult in Marondera District, Zimbabwe.* Unpublished MA Thesis, University of Zimbabwe.

Chivinge, C. 1995. 'Scientists, *n'angas* come together to study lightning', *The Herald* (Harare), 6 June, p. 5.

Clothey, F. W. 1981. 'Ritual', in K. Crim (General Editor), *Abingdon Dictionary of Living Religions.* Nashville: Abingdon Press, 624-8.

Coward, H. 1988. *Sacred word and sacred text.* Maryknoll: Orbis.

Cox, J. L. 1996 2nd ed. *Expressing the sacred: An introduction to the phenomenology of religion.* Harare: University of Zimbabwe Publications.

1993. 'Not a new Bible but a new hermeneutics: an approach from within the science of religion', in I. Mukonyora, J. L. Cox, and F. J. Verstraelen (eds.), *'Re-writing' the Bible: the real issues.* Gweru: Mambo Press, 103-123.

1994. 'Religious studies by the religious: a discussion of the relationship between theology and the science of religion', *Journal for the Study of Religion* 7(2), 3-31.

1995. 'Ancestors, the sacred and God: Reflections on the meaning of the sacred in Zimbabwean death rituals'. *Religion* 25 (4), 339-55.

Daneel, M. L. 1970. *The God of the Matopos Hills.* The Hague: Mouton.

1998. 'Mwari the liberator: Oracular intervention in Zimbabwe's quest for the "Lost Lands"', in J. L. Cox (ed.), *Rites of passage in contemporary Africa.* Cardiff: Cardiff Academic Press, 94-125.

Dinoia, J. A. 1992. *The diversity of religions. A Christian perspective.* Washington, D. C: The Catholic University of America Press.

Dorson, R. D. 1973 2nd ed. 'Africa and the folklorist', in R.D. Dorson (ed.), *African folklore.* Bloomington: Indiana University Press, 3-67.

Dryden, W. and Feltham, C. 1992. 'Psychotherapy and its discontents: An introduction' in W. Dryden and C. Feltham, (eds.), *Psychotherapy and its discontents*. Buckingham: Open University Press, 1-6.

Dryden, W. 1989. 'The therapeutic alliance as an integrating framework', in W. Dryden (ed.), *Key issues for counselling in action*. London: Sage Publications, 1-15.

Dundes, A. 1984. 'Introduction', in A. Dundes (ed.), *Sacred narrative. Readings in the theory of myth*. Berkeley: University of California Press.

Edwards, G. 1992. 'Does psychotherapy need a soul?', in W. Dryden and C. Feltham, C. (eds.), *Psychotherapy and its discontents*. Buckingham: Open University Press. 194-212.

Eliade, M. 1958. *Patterns in comparative religion*. London: Sheed and Ward.

1959. *The Sacred and the profane*, Trans. W. Trask. New York: Harcourt, Brace.

1969. *The Quest: History and meaning in religion*. Chicago: University of Chicago Press.

1978. *A history of religious ideas. Volume I. From the Stone Age to the Eleusinian mysteries*. Translated by Willard Trask. Chicago: University of Chicago Press.

Ellis, A. 1977. 'The basic clinical theory of Rational-Emotive Therapy', in A. Ellis and R. Grieger (eds.), *Handbook of Rational-Emotive Therapy*. New York: Springer Publishing Company, 3-34.

1977. 'Research data supporting the clinical and personality hypotheses of RET and other cognitive-behavior therapies', in A. Ellis and R. Grieger (eds.), *Handbook of Rational-Emotive Therapy*. New York. Springer Publishing Company, 35-71.

1977. 'The Rational-Emotive approach to sex therapy', in A. Ellis and R. Grieger (eds.), *Handbook of Rational-Emotive Therapy*. New York: Springer Publishing Company, 198-215.

1992. 'Response', in W. Dryden and C. Feltham, (eds.), *Psychotherapy and its discontents*. Buckingham: Open University Press, 212-20.

Ferguson, J. 1982. *Gods many and lords many. A study in Primal Religions*. Guildford: Lutterworth Educational.

Finnegan, R. 1969. 'How to do things with words: Performative utterances among the Limba of Sierra Leone', *Man* NS 4 (4), 537-52.

1970. *Oral literature in Africa*. Oxford: The Clarendon Press.

Freud, S. 1961. 'The future of an illusion', in *The Standard Edition of the Complete Psychological Works of Sigmund Freud: Volume XXI*, Trans. J. Strachey. London: Hogarth, 5-56.

Gadamer, H. G. 1980. *Truth and method*. London: Sheed and Ward.

Gard, R. (ed.) 1962. *Buddhism*. New York: George Braziller.

Gelfand, M. 1968. *African crucible. An ethico-religious study with special reference to the Shona-speaking people*. Cape Town: Juta.

Gennep A. van [1908] 1960. *The rites of passage*. London: Routledge and Kegan Paul.

Graham, W. A. 1981. 'Qur'an', in K. Crim (General Editor), *Abingdon Dictionary of Living Religions*. Nashville: Abingdon, 592-94.

Hall, T., Pilgrim, R. B. and Cavanagh, R. R. 1986. *Religion: An introduction*. San Francisco: Harper and Row.

Hansson, G. 1994. 'Religious innovation in Zimbabwe: Mbuya Juliana Movement'. Unpublished paper presented at the Conference entitled Christians and Muslims in Contemporary Africa: Religious, Social and Political Perspectives, Uppsala, 25-28 August.

Heusch, L. de 1994. 'Myth and epic in Central Africa', in W. E. A. van Beek, T. D. Blakely and D. L. Thomson (eds.), *Religion in Africa*. London: James Currey and Portsmouth, New Hampshire: Heinemann, 229-38.

Hinnells, J. (ed.) 1984. *The Penguin Dictionary of Living Religions*. Harmondsworth: Penguin Books.

Hinnells, J. and Sharpe, E. (eds.) 1972. *Hinduism*. Newcastle upon Tyne: Oriel Press.

Hopfe, L. 1983. *Religions of the world*. New York: Macmillan.

Honko, L. 1984. 'The problem of defining myth', in A Dundes (ed.), *Sacred narrative: Readings in the theory of myth*. Berkeley: University of California Press, 41-52.

Hooke, S. H. 1966. *Middle Eastern mythology*. Harmondsworth: Penguin Books.

Husserl, E. 1931. *Ideas: General introduction to pure phenomenology*, Trans. W. R. Boyce Gibson. London: Allen and Unwin.

Inwood, M. J. 1995. 'Husserl, Edmund', in T. Honderich (ed.), *The Oxford companion to philosophy*. Oxford: Oxford University Press, 382-4.

Janzen, J. 1994. 'Drums of affliction: Real phenomenon or scholarly chimera?', in T. D. Blakely, Walter E. A. van Beek, and Dennis L Thomson (eds.), *Religion in Africa*. London: James Currey and Portsmouth, NH: Heinemann, 160-81.

Jaspers, K. 1971. *Reason and anti-reason in our time*, Trans. Stanley Godman. Hamden, Connecticut: Archon Books.

Kahari, G. 1992 2nd ed. *Aspects of the Shona novel*. Gweru: Mambo Press.

Kirk, G. S. 1970. *Myth: Its meaning and functions in ancient and other cultures*. Cambridge: Cambridge University Press.

King, N. G. 1986. *African cosmos: An introduction to religion in Africa*. Belmont, California: Wadsworth Publishing Company.

Krieger, D. 1991. *The new universalism: Foundations for a global theology*. Maryknoll, New York: Orbis Books.

Kristensen, W. B. 1960. *The meaning of religion*. Translated by J. B. Carman. The Hague: Martinus Nijhoff.

Kunene, D. P. 1971. *The heroic poetry of the Basotho*. Oxford: The Clarendon Press.

Kup, A. P. 1961. *A history of Sierra Leone: 1400-1787* Cambridge, Cambridge University Press.

Lanternari, V. 1988. 'Melanesian religions', in S. Sutherland, L. Houlden, P. Clarke and F. Hardy (eds.), *The world's religions*. London: Routledge, 843-53.

Leach, E. 1970. *Levi-Strauss*. Glasgow: Fontana Collins.

Legesse, A. 1994. 'Prophetism, democharisma and social change', in T. D. Blakely, W. E. A. van Beek, and D. Thomson (eds.), *Religion in Africa*. London: James Currey and Portsmouth, NH: Heinemann, 314-41.

Lott, E. 1988. *Vision, tradition, interpretation: Theology, religion and the study of religion*. Berlin: Mouton de Gruyter.

Lyotard, J. F. 1991. *Phenomenology*, Trans. B. Beakley. Albany: State University of New York Press.

Mack, B. 1991. 'Staal's gauntlet and the queen', *Religion* 21, 213-8.

Mackey, J. 1992. 'Magic and Celtic Primal Religions', *Zeitschrift fur Celtische Philology* 45, 66-84.

Malinowski, B. 1948. *Magic, science and religion and other essays*. Boston: Beacon Press.

Mafu, H. 1995. 'The 1991-92 Zimbabwean drought and some religious reactions'. *Journal of Religion in Africa* 25 (3), 288-308.

Mawere A. and Wilson, K. 1995. 'Socio-religious movements, the state and community change: Some reflections on the Ambuya Juliana Cult of southern Zimbabwe'. *Journal of Religion in Africa* 25 (3), 252-87.

Mitchell, R. C. 1977. *African Primal Religions*. Niles, Illinois: Argus Communications.

Mueller-Vollmer, K. 1986. 'Introduction. Language, mind and artifact: An outline of hermeneutic theory since the enlightenment' in K. Mueller-Vollmer (ed.), *The hermeneutics reader*. Oxford: Basil Blackwell Ltd, 1-53.

Nthoi, L. 1998. 'Wosana rite of passage: Reflections on the initiation of Wosana in the cult of Mwali in Zimbabwe', in J. L. Cox (ed.), *Rites of passage in contemporary Africa*. Cardiff: Cardiff Academic Press, 63-93.

Pals, D. 1986. 'Reductionism and belief: An appraisal of recent attacks on the doctrine of irreducible religion.' *The Journal of Religion* 66(1), 18-36.

Panikkar, R. 1979. *Myth, faith and hermeneutics*. New York: Paulist Press.

1984. 'The dialogical dialogue,' in F. Whaling (ed.), *The world's religious traditions*. Edinburgh: T. and T. Clark, 201-21.

Parrinder, E. G. 1981, 3rd ed. *African Traditional Religion*. London: Sheldon Press.

Partin, H. B. 1981. 'Hajj', in K. Crim (General Editor), *Abingdon Dictionary of Living Religions*. Nashville: Abingdon Press, 290-92.

Percheron, M. 1982. *Buddha and Buddhism*. Woodstock, New York: Overlook Press.

Pilgrim, D. 1992. 'Psychotherapy and political evasions', in W. Dryden and C. Feltham (eds.), *Psychotherapy and its discontents*. Buckingham: Open University Press, 225-43.

Platvoet J. and van der Toorn K. 1995. 'Ritual responses to plurality and pluralism', in J Platvoet and K. Van der Toorn (eds.), *Pluralism and identity: Studies in ritual behaviour*. Leiden: E.J. Brill, 1-21.

Prozesky, M. 1985. *Religion and ultimate well being*. London: Macmillan.

Ranger, T. 1995. 'Religious pluralism in Zimbabwe', *Journal of Religion in Africa* 25 (3), 226-51.

Ray, B. 1973. '"Performative utterances" in African rituals', *History of Religions* 13 (1), 16-35.

Richards, D. and McDonald, B. 1990. *Behavioural psychotherapy: A handbook for nurses*. Oxford: Heinemann Nursing.

Rowe, D. 1988. *Choosing not losing. The experience of depression*. London: Fontana Paperbacks.

Ruthven, K. K. 1976. *Myth*. London: Methuen and Company.

Saliba, J. A. 1976. *Homo religiosus in Mircea Eliade*. Leiden: EJ Brill.

Samkange, S. 1968. *Origins of Rhodesia*. London: Heinemann.

Samuels, A. 1992. 'Foreword' in W. Dryden and C. Feltham (eds.), *Psychotherapy and its discontents*. Buckingham: Open University Press, xi-xvi.

Schmidt, R. 1988, (2nd ed.) *Exploring religion*. Belmont: California, Wadsworth Publishing Company, 2nd ed.

Schneiderman, L. 1981. *The psychology of myth, folklore, and religion*. Chicago: Nelson-Hall.

Schwarzmuller, T. 1995. Interview with J. L. Cox, 28 May.

Segal R. 1983. 'In defense of reductionism', *Journal of the American Academy of Religion* 51 (1), 97-124.

Sharpe, E. 1986. *Comparative religion: a history*. London: Duckworth.

Shaw, R. 1990. 'The invention of African Traditional Religion', *Religion* 20, 339-53.

Shinn, L. D. 1981. 'Myth', in K. Crim (General Editor), *Abingdon Dictionary of Living Religions*. Nashville: Abingdon, 514-517.

Smart, N. 1973. *The phenomenon of religion*. New York: The Seabury Press.

1984a (14th Impression). *The religious experience of mankind*. Glasgow: Collins Fount Paperbacks.

1984b. 'Scientific phenomenology and Wilfred Cantwell Smith's misgivings', in F. Whaling (ed.), *The world's religious traditions*. Edinburgh: T. and T. Clark, 257-69.

1989. *The world's religions. Old traditions and modern transformations*. Cambridge: Cambridge University Press.

Smart, N. and Hecht, R. 1982. *Sacred texts of the world: A universal anthology*. London: Macmillan Reference Books.

Smith, J. Z. 1980. 'The bare facts of ritual', *History of Religions* 20 (1 and 2), 112-27

1987. *To take place: Toward a theory in ritual*. Chicago and London: University of Chicago Press.

Smith, W. C. 1964 and 1978. *The meaning and end of religion*. New York: New American Library (1st ed.). San Francisco: Harper and Row (Torchback ed.).

1972. *The faith of other men*. New York: Harper and Row.

Staal, F. 1979. 'The meaninglessness of ritual', *Numen* 26 (1), 2-22.

1989. *Rules without meaning: ritual, mantras and the human sciences*. New York: Peter Lang.

1991. 'Within ritual, about ritual, and beyond', *Religion* 21, 227-234.

Stern, R. and Drummond L. 1991. *The practice of behavioural and cognitive psychotherapy*. Cambridge: Cambridge University Press.

Storr, A. 1990, (2nd ed.) *The art of psychotherapy*. Oxford: Butterworth-Heinemann.

Strenski, I. 1991. 'What's rite? Evolution, exchange and the big picture', *Religion* 21, 219-25.

1993. *Religion in relation: Method, application and moral location*. London: Macmillan.

Taber, C. R. 1981. 'Life Cycle Rites', in K. Crim (General Editor), *Abingdon Dictionary of Living Religions*. Nashville: Abingdon Press, 426-8.

Taylor, J. B. (ed.) 1976. *Primal world views: Christian dialogue with traditional thought forms*. Ibadan, Nigeria: Daystar Press.

Taylor, J. V. 1963. *The primal vision: Christian presence amid African religion*. London: SCM Press.

Turner, H. W. 1971. *Living tribal religions*. London: Ward Lock Educational.

Turner, V. W. 1969. *The ritual process: structure and anti-structure*. Harmondsworth: Penguin Books.

1985. 'Liminality, kabbalah, and the media', *Religion* 15, 205-17.

Walls, A. F. 1980. 'Ruminations on rainmaking: the transmission and receipt of religious expertise in Africa', in J.C. Stone (ed.), *Experts in Africa*. Aberdeen: University of Aberdeen African Studies Group, 146-51.

1987. 'Primal religious traditions in today's world', in F. Whaling (ed.), *Religion in today's world*. Edinburgh: T. and T. Clark, 250-78.

1990. 'The translation principle in Christian history', in P. Stint (ed.), *Bible translation and the spread of the church*. Leiden: E J Brill, 24-39.

Watkins, J. T. 1977. 'The Rational-Emotive dynamics of impulsive disorders', in A. Ellis and R. Grieger, *Handbook of Rational-Emotive Therapy*. New York: Springer Publishing Company, 135-52.

Weir, R. (ed.) 1982. *The religious world: communities of faith*. New York: Macmillan.

Werbner, R. 1989. *Ritual passage. Sacred journey*. Washington: Smithsonian Institution Press and Manchester: Manchester University Press.

Whaling, F. 1986. *Christian theology and world religions: a global perspective*. Basingstoke: Marshall Pickering.

Wiebe, D. 1985. 'A positive episteme for the study of religion', *Scottish Journal of Religious Studies* 6 (1), 78-95.

Wilson, P. H., Spence, S. H., and Kavanagh, D. J. 1989. *Cognitive behavioural interviewing for adult disorders: A practical handbook.* London: Routledge.

Wittgenstein, L. 1953. *Philosophical investigations.* Translated by G.E.M. Anscombe. Oxford: Basil Blackwell.

Younger P. and Younger, S.O. 1978. *Hinduism.* Niles, Illinois: Argus Communications.

INDEX